EYE to EYE

EYE to EYE

YOUR RELATIONSHIPS

AND HOW THEY WORK

EDITED BY

PETER MARSH

SIDGWICK & JACKSON

LONDON

CONTRIBUTORS

AC
Dr Alan I Cooklin
Consultant in Family Psychiatry
Marlborough Family Service, London, UK

AFF
Dr Adrian F Furnham
Lecturer in Psychology
University College, London, UK

BAM
Dr Beverly Alban Metcalfe
Lecturer in Organizational Psychology
University of Leeds, UK

BE
Dr Brian M Earn
Associate Professor of Psychology
University of Guelph, Canada

BF
Dr Bruce Fogle
Portman Veterinary Clinic, London, UK

BM
Dr Barry McCarthy
Lecturer in Psychology
Lancashire Polytechnic, Preston, UK

BMM
Dr Barbara M Montgomery
Associate Professor of Communication Studies
University of New Hampshire, USA

CAC
Dr Catherine A Colby
Adjunct Assistant Professor of Psychology
University of Western Ontario, Canada

CC
Professor Cary L Cooper
Professor of Organizational Psychology
University of Manchester Institute of Science
and Technology, UK

DM
Dr Dorothy E Miell
Lecturer in Psychology, The Open University, UK

DP
Professor Daniel Perlman
Professor of Family Science
University of British Columbia, Canada

GB
Dr Geoffrey W Beattie
Lecturer in Psychology, University of Sheffield, UK

GGB
Gill Gorell Barnes
Consultant, Institute of Family Therapy, London, UK

IHG
Dr Ian H Gotlib
Associate Professor of Psychology
University of Western Ontario, Canada

JCB
Dr Julia C Berryman
Lecturer in Psychology, University of Leicester, UK

JTP
Dr Jane Traupmann Pillemer
Wellesley, Massachusetts, USA

MC
Dr Mark Cook
Lecturer in Psychology
University College of Swansea, UK

MP
Professor Miles L Patterson
Professor of Psychology, University of Missouri, USA

PB
Dr Peter E Bull
Lecturer in Psychology, University of York, UK

PM
Dr Peter Marsh
Lecturer in Psychology, Oxford Polytechnic, UK

PR
Dr Peter Rivière
Lecturer in Social Anthropology
University of Oxford, UK

PT
Dr Peter Trower
Head of Psychology (Rehabilitation)
Solihull Health Authority, UK

RG
Robin Gilmour
Lecturer in Psychology, University of Lancaster, UK

RL
Dr Roger Lamb
Lecturer in Psychology, University of Oxford, UK

SD
Professor Steven W Duck
Daniel and Amy Starch Research Professor in
Communication Studies, University of Iowa, USA

ST
Professor Stephen Thayer
Professor of Psychology, City College of the
City University of New York, USA

VEW
Dr Valerie E Whiffen
Research Associate in Psychology
University of Western Ontario, Canada

4

First published
in Great Britain in 1988 by
Sidgwick & Jackson Limited

Devised and produced by
Andromeda Oxford Ltd
Dorchester-on-Thames
Oxford OX9 8JU

ISBN 0–283–99691–9

Typeset by Opus, Oxford

Origination: Scantrans, Singapore

Printed in Italy by Sagdos, Milan

for Sidgwick and Jackson Limited
1 Tavistock Chambers, Bloomsbury Way
London WC1A 2SG

EYE TO EYE VOLUME EDITOR
AND COMMISSIONING EDITOR
FOR PART ONE
HOW PEOPLE INTERACT
Dr Peter Marsh
Lecturer in Psychology
Oxford Polytechnic

COMMISSIONING EDITOR
FOR PART TWO
HOW RELATIONSHIPS WORK
Robin Gilmour
Lecturer in Psychology
University of Lancaster

CONTENTS

PROJECT EDITOR
Stuart McCready

TEXT

Copy editors
Nancy Duin
Ruth Holmes
Casey Horton
Avril Price-Budgen

Research consultant
Richard Newnham

Indexers
Sonia Argyle
Margaret Hammond

Word-processing
Reina Foster-de Wit
Susan Flanders
Julie Smith

PICTURES

Research coordination
Thérèse Maitland

Research consultant
Linda Proud

Researchers
Colin Jacobson
Lynda Marshall
Susanne Williams
Charlotte Ward-Perkins

ART

Art Editor
Chris Munday

Layout design
Michael Grendon

Layout mark-up
Ann Trew

Art assistant
Martin Anderson

Artists
Simon Driver
John Erwood

PRODUCTION

Assistant
Roberta Dyde

ADMINISTRATION

Assistant
Michele Roslyn-Smith

PROJECT DIRECTOR
Michael Desebrock

MOST PEOPLE are unaware that they possess a quite remarkable skill. Because this skill is exercised daily, and in the most ordinary of contexts, it is usually overlooked. But without it, our lives would be unfulfilled and empty. It is the ability to relate to others, to engage them in conversation, to operate as social and sociable individuals and to develop both short-term and long-lasting relationships which lies at the heart of our very existence as human beings.

We are not born with this ability. There is nothing wired into the human brain that provides us with set responses to social situations. Natural sex drives doubtless underlie much of our courtship behavior. There may also be genetically based forces that make us aggressive in certain circumstances. It is even possible that the drive to become involved with friends and accepted by them is part of our evolutionary heritage. But to perform effectively in a world that relies so heavily on social interaction, encounters and relationships, we have to learn what to do.

Small babies, as any parent will remember, are among the least sociable beings that you could imagine. They are totally demanding, utterly selfish and scream with rage if their every whim is not immediately satisfied. Somehow, this unlikely raw material is transformed over the years into a being which relies for survival on being able to form reciprocal bonds with others and to follow complex rules that govern every aspect of its social life. The monstrous infant becomes the caring, responsible adult whose life experiences revolve around both the joys and pains, and the giving and receiving, of friendships and other relationships. It is this remarkable transformation which is the central characteristic of being human.

Eye to Eye attempts to identify precisely what it means to be a social animal – to uncover the central features of our uniquely human skills and abilities. Drawing extensively on recent research concerned with the practical aspects of social life, it seeks to provide fresh insights into how we interact with others and to provide ideas for improving social skills.

Part One of the volume is concerned primarily with the often overlooked features of everyday encounters. When you are having a casual conversation with a friend, or a discussion with someone in the office, have you ever paused to consider how such interactions are possible? We might think that conversations are so common that

6

DISTINGUISHED CONSULTANTS

FOR PART ONE

Dr Michael Argyle
Reader in Social Psychology
University of Oxford, UK

Professor Ralph Exline
Professor of Psychology
University of Delaware, USA

FOR PART TWO

Professor Steven Duck
Daniel and Amy Starch Research
Professor in Communication Studies
University of Iowa, USA

Dr Margaret S Clark
Associate Professor of Psychology
Carnegie-Mellon University
Pittsburgh, Pennsylvania, USA

they cannot have much complexity. But this apparently simple behavior requires considerable skill and subtle understanding. By appreciating what is really involved, we become able to see ways of improving our conversational effectiveness.

Similarly, do we ever stop to think about the messages we communicate just by looking the way we do? What signals do our clothes give off? What is make-up really for? What do our color preferences say about us? The way we appear to others in initial encounters can radically alter the ways in which they perceive us and behave toward us. We also make judgments about others solely on the basis of their appearance, even though we might not want to admit it.

Body language, as well, profoundly influences social encounters. Nonverbal messages are very often more powerful than those communicated by the spoken word. When we talk with others, how do we stand? What posture do we adopt, and what facial expressions do we make? How far away do we like to be from another person and what role does our tone of voice play in the communication process?

All of these features have a profound influence on conversations, meetings and encounters. With appropriate patterns of communication we can be socially effective, have influence over others, win their confidence and friendship and find social fulfillment. Inappropriate or unskilled use of nonverbal signals can lead to communication failure, misunderstanding, rejection and isolation.

Considerable emphasis is placed in Part One of *Eye to Eye* on applied social skills, bringing together many strands of research in a way that makes them relevant and useful in real-life social contexts. The same is true in Part Two, which focuses on relationships. Here we examine the ways in which attachments, friendships, love affairs, marriages and relationships of all kinds are established, developed and maintained.

Without relationships of one kind or another, the world would be a frightening and alienating place. Fortunately, most of us are able to develop enduring bonds with others.

Understanding what goes on in the formation of a relationship improves our potential to develop this skill. By becoming more sensitive to the underlying principles that determine satisfactory outcomes in relationships, we broaden our potential for deeper satisfaction in this most significant area of human existence.

It must be stressed, however, that *Eye to Eye* is not a "cookbook." There are no simple recipes for a complete and fulfilled social existence. There are, however, certain principles that social scientists have uncovered and which have been shown to be effective in a range of settings and contexts. The authors who have contributed to this volume are recognized as leading experts in their fields and the material they present has been based on years of painstaking scientific research. It is a privilege, as Editor, to feel that the fruits of such endeavors can lead directly to an enrichment of the everyday social lives which we all lead. **PM**

A special word of thanks is due to the Distinguished Consultants for all their advice and encouragement, to Stuart McCready for his tireless work in preparing the text for publication, and to the entire Andromeda team.

7

USE this alphabetical guide to find the main subjects in Part Two of *Eye to Eye*: How Relationships Work. A single reference is given for each, indicating the page or beginning page of its fullest treatment. For a guide to Part One see page 8. For a wider reference to a subject and for a more extensive list of subjects, see the index at the end of the book.

PREVIEW GUIDE TO PART 1
How People Interact

In successful encounters with others we adapt our behavior to the rules and circumstances of the **occasion**. This means adopting a role and acting it out. How effectively we do this may depend on how we react to our surroundings.

TURN TO PAGE 18

Before we speak, our **gestures**, postures and expressions are already broadcasting messages to those around us. And while we are speaking, they continue to do so, usefully clarifying what we say – or contradicting us in telltale ways.

TURN TO PAGE 46

Highly ritualized **interviews** that do not put interviewees at their ease often fail to achieve their purpose. To adapt to such situations, interviewees – and negotiators – must know their best points and how to present them most effectively.

TURN TO PAGE 28

Your **posture** can reveal whether you are interested in what is going on and how much you like the people involved. It can show whether you are in or out of sympathy with an idea, and it can help you to influence the course of events.

TURN TO PAGE 56

Personalizing your home or the space assigned to you at work expresses an emotional attachment to a place, or "**territory**." It announces that you are in control there, and that your relationship to the place is a committed and enduring one.

TURN TO PAGE 30

Most of us pay attention to our **appearance**, rightly suspecting that attractive looks and appropriate dress can often bias others in our favor. The confidence with which we perform our social roles also depends on the image we project.

TURN TO PAGE 60

By adjusting the **distance** at which you interact with others you can express a wish for intimacy or for noninvolvement, or you can increase or reduce your influence. Mingling in a crowd can make you tense and defensive, or it can remove inhibitions.

TURN TO PAGE 38

Scent signals that we register unconsciously can have a significant effect on our response to other people. We are fully aware of body odors that we find repellent but not of the natural scent signals that attract us most strongly.

TURN TO PAGE 68

How we use our *eyes* when speaking to others not only determines whether we hold their interest but also signals information about our sexual identity and social status. And where we look when listening can be just as significant.

TURN TO PAGE 72

The art of **conversation** involves intricate skills of social coordination. Showing interest and being interesting, starting conversations and ending them, taking your turn in interrupting bring all our communication resources into play.

TURN TO PAGE 104

How you get along with others can depend on how well you interpret their **facial expressions**. Spontaneous smiles and frowns are especially informative – but only if you can distinguish them from their voluntary counterparts.

TURN TO PAGE 78

An element of **humor** in your social style can increase your influence and make you feel more assertive. At the same time, the lighter mood that humor brings to social encounters relaxes people, and relationships develop more easily.

TURN TO PAGE 112

How, where and when we **touch** others can make or break our relationships. If the message conveyed is appropriate, most people, most of the time, will respond positively to being touched. On some occasions it is inappropriate not to touch them.

TURN TO PAGE 88

Research has revealed principles for detecting lies and deceptions. Although facial expression is least revealing, the rest of the body may leak signs of **insincerity**, as can our speech pattern, tone of voice and style of blinking.

TURN TO PAGE 116

Our **greetings** and farewells not only reflect the state of our relationships as we see them but are also powerful social tools: their style heavily influences people's impressions of us, and their neglect can cause deep offense.

TURN TO PAGE 98

Like riding a bicycle, **skillful interaction** is automatic when we know how, but all of us have times when we are not quite sure how to behave. Managing these situations means learning – from observation, from friends, even from specialists.

TURN TO PAGE 120

13

LIFESPAN GUIDE TO PART 2
How Relationships Work

Birth   10 years   20

| Infancy | Childhood | Adolescence |

Finding a Partner: p196

Brothers, Sisters and Only Children: p150

Keeping in Touch with Kin: p158

Child and Adolescent Friendships: p176

Family Pets: p154

Coping with Shyness: p182

Overcoming Loneliness: p188

▲ **The chart on these pages** *shows phases of the human lifespan and the chapters of Eye to Eye Part Two that touch on them. Topics are related in particular to infancy, childhood, adolescence, young adulthood and mature adulthood, including old age.*

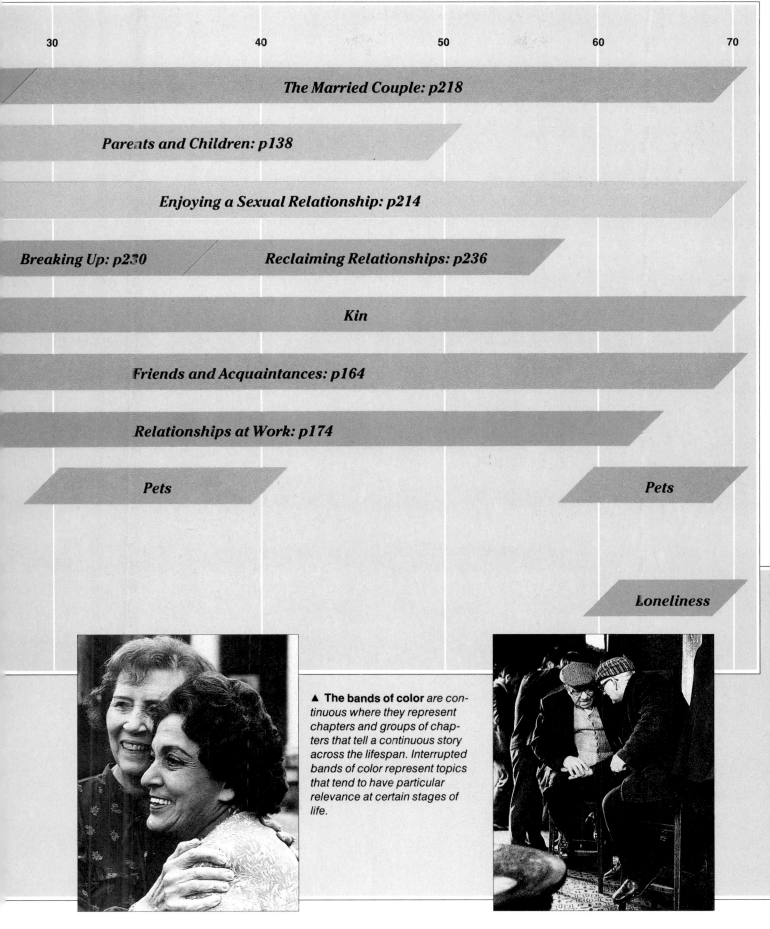

30	40	50	60	70

The Married Couple: p218

Parents and Children: p138

Enjoying a Sexual Relationship: p214

Breaking Up: p230   *Reclaiming Relationships: p236*

Kin

Friends and Acquaintances: p164

Relationships at Work: p174

Pets   *Pets*

15

Loneliness

▲ **The bands of color** *are continuous where they represent chapters and groups of chapters that tell a continuous story across the lifespan. Interrupted bands of color represent topics that tend to have particular relevance at certain stages of life.*

1

HOW
PEOPLE
INTERACT

EYE TO EYE PART ONE

Adapting to the Occasion

WHEN we can, and when we think it worthwhile, we get *ready* for social encounters, trying to set the scene in ways that will create the right mood, help us to make the right impression, and make planned activities successful – for example, we tidy the house for visitors, prepare a meal, change our clothes, set the table and open the wine to let it breath to adjust its flavor.

Sometimes, though, social encounters seem to *happen* to us. You are invited to a formal dinner, for example, where you feel unable to be yourself, and all of your preparations – dressing in a formal way, reading up on rules of etiquette – are for the sake of fitting in with what seems like somebody else's idea of how people should behave. Or you might meet someone you have been longing to meet, but unexpectedly, and in circumstances that you would never choose.

The difference in the control we exert over different social situations, however, is a matter of degree. Even in the most difficult setting, the fact that *you* are a participant is one of the circumstances that sets the scene. Social encounters are profoundly cooperative – in a sense "staged" jointly by everyone present.

The host at a party may control the physical surroundings and the timing of the event more than the guests, but countless details about the guests themselves also help to deter-mine what the party will be like – the moods and attitudes that show in their faces and the way they are holding their bodies, for example; the way they are dressed and groomed; the relationships they have previously established with each other and the roles they are playing; the different personal aims they are pursuing at the party.

Each guest also helps to set the scene by bringing to it a set of social skills. Successful encounters are those in which people interpret the behavior of others and adapt their own in the light of circumstances and the aims they and others are pursuing. This allows us to coordinate our behavior to maximize satisfactions.

Largely, we achieve this coordination by following social rules, including rules for the specific type of occasion. Many of these are informal rules that we follow unconsciously. The rules of the society in which the encounter takes place are themselves perhaps the most important element of the setting. We exert control by mastering them.

Rules are pervasive

We are conscious of many of the rules that govern the way we act with other people, but these are usually only the tip of an iceberg. People grow up acquiring the rules for social encounters in much the same unconscious way that they

SEVEN FACTORS THAT MAKE UP THE SOCIAL SETTING

■ *Every social occasion has a setting – much like a scene from a play. Physical factors of the setting are like a stage with props and backdrop. Social factors are like the complex of roles, problems and expectations that the story so far has created. Unlike actors, the participants in a genuine social encounter are the joint authors of their own script – they create the story as they go along. But, like a good playwright, they produce action and dialogue that fit the situation that has already developed. The most important factors that set the scene for social interaction are highlighted here.*

1 YOUR GOALS

■ *What you hope to achieve by participating in a given social encounter depends on your needs, your personality and the roles you are playing.*

2 YOUR ROLES

■ *Some of your roles affect most encounters – you are a man or a woman, a child or an adult. Others are specific to the occasion – you are the host or a guest.*

3 YOUR MOOD

■ *Your mood is affected by your personality, past events, the behavior of others, physical factors of the setting and the social significance of the place where the encounter occurs.*

In successful encounters, we adapt our behavior to the rules and circumstances of the occasion. This means accepting a role and pursuing the aims that go with it. How well we achieve this may depend on our adjustment to the physical setting.

learn the rules of their mother tongue. Few of us can state many rules of grammar, or even many of the different nuances that ordinary words have in different contexts, but we all *speak* more or less correctly. Similarly, people who interact effectively in a wide range of social situations usually cannot describe what you have to do to achieve this.

The more formal the setting, the more explicit are the rules. Some social events are so formalized that the rules are actually written in books. You follow a church service as it is laid down, for example. People look up the rules of unfamiliar formal occasions, in something of the same way you might look up words in a foreign-language phrase book. The social performance that results can often feel, too, like an attempt to speak someone else's native tongue.

In less formal settings, rules *seem* less important. We are less conscious of following them, feel more relaxed, feel more like we are being ourselves. Although they are more difficult to state precisely, however, we take trouble not to break the rules of informal occasions, and make excuses and apologies when we do.

We know, for example, that we should be on time and know what being on time means in a wide range of situations – as much as an hour or more after the start of a drinks party, but not more than 30 minutes after the time mentioned in an invitation to dinner, and not more than five or ten minutes after the time agreed for a business appointment.

We become especially conscious of such rules when people of different cultures mix. In some cultures being on time can mean turning up several hours after the appointed hour, even for business meetings. The problem is particularly apparent at the United Nations. Anglo Saxons and western Europeans are used to three mealtimes a day and organize their timetable around them. East Europeans often do not have strict rules like this – people eat when they feel inclined and every family follows its own idiosyncratic timetable. Far Easterners are used to meetings going on for hours and hours without any official break – people come and go and may even leave to be replaced by others. Every group has its own rules about time, and when they see others breaking them they may feel they are being unreasonable, insincere or even trying to sabotage joint endeavors.

Think of how detailed the rules about eating are and how much they vary with the kind of meal and from country to country, from culture to culture within a country and even from family to family. Which kinds of food are people

◄ ► **A social encounter becomes an "occasion"** *when we make it special – for example, seeing people we do not see every day, dressing up for them, gathering in a special place or bringing out special china, silver and tablecloths. Part of our motive for introducing these formalities is to make a good impression, but also we enjoy the stimulation of doing things in a less familiar way.*

19

4 THE PLACE

■ *Physical factors such as color, noise-level and lighting affect mood. And there may be rules for how to behave in the place. Is it someone's home? Is it a church, a library?*

5 THE OCCASION

■ *The occasion – for example, a party, a wedding or a funeral – may have a set agenda that limits the goals participants can pursue. It may require a special physical setting.*

6 THE RULES

■ *More general social rules will be supplemented by rules of the occasion. These may affect the goals you can adopt, the location, the way people play their roles, even dress.*

7 FEEDBACK

■ *We constantly adjust our goals, reinterpret our roles and refine our understanding of rules in light of the reactions people have to what we say and do in the situation.*

Because they know them so well, people follow the "display" rules of their culture automatically and unconsciously. In large part, these rules – rather than nature – tell us what attitudes and emotions it is 'natural' to show in each situation.

allowed to pick up with their hands in your family? Are they the same kinds on informal family-only occasions as when company comes to dinner? Do the rules vary between breakfast and dinner? How far away does the salt have to be before you must say "Please pass the salt" instead of reaching for it? We will not usually be able to answer all of these kinds of questions with airtight statements of rules, but we know the answers in a sense, because we recognize when someone is *breaking* the rules.

Responding to social initiatives

An understanding of a wide variety of rules is required simply to understand the meanings of the different kinds of social act that make up encounters. We understand what is happening when someone says "I promise" and "Have this for yourself" because we intuitively understand the complex balance of rights, duties and obligations that is altered every time we utter a promise, issue an invitation, offer a gift or agree to an exchange.

A set of rules that particularly affects communication are the ones that regulate the display of emotions and tell us what attitudes people are supposed to show in a given situation. It may seem odd to speak of rules for communicating emotions and attitudes – when we feel happy we *spontaneously* smile; when we feel attracted to someone we spontaneously move closer.

Others can observe these natural displays of feeling and draw their conclusions. However, cultural variability in the meanings of facial expression (see *Ch 9*) and interpersonal

distance (see *Ch 3*) shows how much these are ruled by social convention.

The same point applies to all other body-language channels as well. Communication of emotions is natural in the sense that any human anywhere will let feelings show in much the same way (so long as there is no rule *against* letting feelings show) just because of the way the human nervous system connects the brain to muscles in the face and the rest of the body. But, however automatically and unconsciously we follow them once learned, we all learn different rules for just how much feeling it is appropriate to show, and in what circumstances.

And we often unthinkingly follow learned rules for communicating the *attitudes* that it is appropriate to show in different settings. We learn the importance of looking solemn as a sign of respect during a funeral and learn how to do this. We make a friendly face at utter strangers when we are being introduced.

At some time most of us learn that *being* interested in a conversation is not helpful enough to a speaker. You must show the interest as well, and there are intricate conventions for doing this (see *Chs 5, 8, 9, 12, 15*).

A very central part of social skill is knowing how to respond to each of the great variety of social moves that can be communicated, and how to adapt your response to the situation. A basic rule of most situations is that we *must* respond. An encounter or a relationship cannot develop if there is no interaction.

Also, people will be offended, reading a personal rejection into your unresponsiveness unless they understand and sympathize with some genuine excuse. For example, you may be uncontrollably shy, or come from another culture

UNWRITTEN RULES

◀ **Rules for a day at the pool** do not end with the sign that tells you where to use dinghies or the book that says how to play chess. The Japanese at leisure know the rules for claiming a sunbather's territory, a wader's space or a café table. At the Szecheny Bath House in Budapest, Hungarians know the rules for polite spectating and the ones that tell you how to display a knowledgeable doubt.

▶ **A Japanese wedding picture** calls for a relatively solemn facial display. Apparently not all Japanese are aware of this.

known to expect less demonstrative behavior. In few cases, however, could such tolerance overcome resentment at a greeting not returned, an invitation not answered or conversation met with a blank stare.

Your manner of responding helps to set the scene for the next step in the encounter, and helps to define your relationship, thus helping to set the scene for future social encounters. You may respond to a greeting with polite interest or instead with warmth, and this will help to determine the emotional distance between you and the other (see *Ch 11*). Similarly, in conversation you may respond to the self-disclosures of another by saying things about yourself or not (see *Ch 12*). If you do, the way is open to further self-disclosure on both sides, creating obligations of trust and rights of confidentiality under the unspoken rules of a gradually developing friendship.

The effect of roles

A social encounter usually requires us to play different roles – for example, salesman and customer, doctor and patient. In almost any encounter we have to take turns at the roles of speaker and listener. The success of the encounter is affected by how well the participants understand the rules for playing their roles.

A particularly important scene-setting difference in role is that between visitor and host – the person who has claim to the territory where the encounter occurs. We always need a special reason to be on someone else's territory, such as being invited, and when we are there we respect the owner's power to create local rules. For example, you would not begin moving furniture – which regulates where people will sit and how far apart (see *Ch 2*) – without permission.

There are also roles that correspond to the personal relationships between participants, and these too help to set the scene. For example, all present are strangers and they cannot be too familiar with each other. Or one is the employer – who can adopt a freer manner – the other the employee, who has to be careful not to challenge the employer's superior social status. Or the participants are established friends who encounter each other with ease, but each nevertheless takes note of whether the others are being friendly *enough*. The rules of friendship and the rules for showing friendship influence any encounter between them.

Our roles "in life" help to determine what kinds of encounter we will have, a richness of roles leading to a richness of experience. In a typical day we each play many different roles, and our behavior changes as we move from one to the other. A woman might start the day playing the role of mother as she dresses the children for school and then that of wife as she eats breakfast with her husband. At work, her role might be that of a middle manager. Most

ONE PERSON CAN PLAY MANY PARTS

Marriage partner
Parent
Son or daughter
Friend
Brother or sister
Graduate
Jogger
Committee member
Employee
Swimmer
Delegate
Neighbor
Regular customer
Amateur actor
Political supporter

▲ **Role versatility** *contributes to the variety of the situations that make you feel at home. This in turn enriches and strengthens the social support that you can draw on (see Ch 16) by making a wider range of relationships possible. It also protects you against the stress of role loss – the greater the number of roles from which you derive your self-esteem, the less empty it will make you feel when you end your career or your children grow up and leave home.*

▶ **Dressing for the part.** *Official regulations decide the question of how to appear the graduate on graduation day or the young naval officer at an Army-Navy football game. Conforming to the regulations helps you to feel at home in your role. Unwritten rules of how to dress for your role can be almost as rigid (see Ch 6).*

Playing a role with which you easily identify makes the situation seem like one in which you can be yourself. Many situations and many roles probably make you feel like this – several natural "selves" enrich our everyday social experience.

people can slip from playing one role to another with unconscious ease, but only because they understand the rules and expectations that accompany each of them.

In all the roles in which you easily identify yourself, you will feel that you are *being* yourself. And yet, because there are several of these roles, there seem to be several selves that you naturally are. We more readily recognize this about ourselves than about others. Several studies have revealed the prevalence of "actor-observer differences" in our assessments of personality.

When we see someone else being extroverted, we tend to conclude that this is an extroverted type of person. When you are extroverted yourself, you are less likely to notice the fact – since you are focusing your attention on the people you are with and what *they* are doing. If you do notice, you are more likely to account for it as the way that it is natural to act in the given situation. You are likely to be more conscious than an observer is that when you are not happily entertaining friends in your own home – when you are at the office, for example – you are more retiring. **AFF PM**

Socially stereotyped roles

Roles can be restrictive, because of social stereotyping. To play a masculine role, you are supposed to be, for example, independent, unemotional, assertive and logical. To play a feminine role you are supposed to be, among other things, dependent, talkative, emotional and home-oriented. Not every man and woman feels right about every aspect of the assigned role, and many resent the social expectation that they should conform to it. Surveys and observations reveal that most men and women, however, accept these stereotypes.

This acceptance markedly affects their social behavior. Men invade the personal space of women more than women do the space of men, and men tend to take up more personal space. Women, in contrast, adopt postures that take up a minimum of space, and when walking along the street, tend to avert their gaze, move out of the way sooner and more frequently than men. Field studies have also shown that men touch women more often than women touch men – a gesture thought to show status rather than affection (see *Ch10*). Men talk more often and for longer periods of time, especially in male-female conversations. Males interrupt females more often, talk over top of women's speech, change the topics of conversation, and prevent women from changing the topic. Men take the lead in self-disclosure.

Women tend to express more warmth. They smile more than men, look more both when listening and speaking and ask more questions. They tend to support men's statements and opinions. These differences are also reflected in forms of speech. Women use tentative and "powerless" forms. They more often use hesitant features of speech as modifiers ("sort of," "I think"), so-called empty adjectives ("divine," "fabulous"), tag questions ("...don't you agree?"), statement-endings that turn into questions ("Dinner is ready?"), intensifiers ("I'm so happy") and overly polite

▲ **Role distancing**. *People who find that their role creates a psychological distance between themselves and others often look for opportunities to distance themselves from the role. A common strategy is to make gentle fun of it, like these British police on crowd-control duty at a fair.*

speech ("Would you be so kind..."). Research shows women to be generally more socially skilled than men in the expression of warmth and friendship, and to be better at reading the social cues that others send. But they do not have as much skill at self-assertion.

In fact, there is little evidence to suggest that men and women are very different in their underlying abilities and desires. Women have just as much innate drive as men but learn to suppress it in order to conform to their sex role. Breaking out of the least attractive aspects of their stereotypes – rejecting them as a scene-setting given – means, for women, learning to be more assertive, and, for men, learning to be more responsive (see p126). **PT**

Setting the agenda

People create a social situation because they have activities and goals that they want to pursue. The better we understand what these are, the better we understand precisely what situation we are dealing with. Formal meetings are provided with a written agenda for this purpose. Informal ones usually have a verbal one. You are invited to someone's house "for drinks" or "for a meal." In

both cases, however, participants can take the opportunity to pursue objectives of their own within the situation that is created. Since this is likely to affect their behavior, their personal agendas also contribute, sometimes even secretly, toward giving the encounter its setting.

Encounters break down when people realize that they have misunderstood what others were trying to achieve. This often happens in interactions between members of the opposite sex. One person might interpret certain behavior as sexual attraction while the other might have a lower level of involvement in mind. To avoid misunderstandings, we often make our aims clear at the beginning of an encounter if we can. But in many situations – bargaining, for example – we may have to disguise our interests to effectively pursue them. And in almost any interaction with other people we modify our goals as we go. When we are getting to know people, for example, we frequently adjust our notions of the kind of relationship we want to have with them, and this can lead to changes of manner in mid-conversation.

Knowing the agenda is like knowing what game people are playing. Different people with their different roles and aims, play different "positions," all governed by rules. This

IS THERE A SHARED AGENDA?

■ No voluntary encounter will last for long if participants do not see a reason for interacting. The striker who seeks your support in a San Francisco street, like the salesman at your door, has only a crucial few moments to make you think there is something worth stopping to talk about. Opportunities to negotiate our goals present themselves more readily when you already have an established – perhaps less challenging – agenda to build from. For example, the setting is a quiet park, and someone is willing to chat with you simply for the stimulation of

it, or you are an old friend and the readily agreed agenda is to renew a contact. Set occasions like parties and weddings also present opportunities, because invariably one of the expectations is that people will make conversation and learn about each other's interests. Among the rules of these occasions, however, are prohibitions against burdening people with personal obsessions or private business. It is advisable to probe carefully for signs of genuine mutual consent before asking people to consider important commitments.

▲ ► **Sitting down to share a meal.** Stockmarket pressures do not respect mealtimes, but when we can we make a social occasion of eating. Food-sharing is a fundamental adaptation of our species. Like the conversation we exchange as we eat, this joint activity binds us emotionally, and table-

manner rules help diners achieve the purpose. These rules are usually intended to give everyone a fair share of what is on the table and easy access to it, a fair share of attention in the conversation and a mealtime atmosphere that is relaxed, pleasant and unifying.

People create a social situation because they have goals to achieve through interacting. The better we understand what the goals are – both stated and unstated – the better we understand precisely what situation we are dealing with.

person is the host, who has a special responsibility to make everyone feel comfortable, welcome and entertained. This other is a guest, who needs to show appreciation to the host and provide good companionship to the others. This person is the customer, who needs to communicate that he wants a cup of coffee and a doughnut. This other is the waiter who has to understand the order and fill it.

The rules for pursuing the special aims of the game may require a special physical setting – a board meeting requires a board room, and a tennis match requires a tennis court. Special equipment may be required – a church service may need at least an altar, and families sometimes make it a rule that everyone will be seated around a table for at least some meals, not always in front of television, in order that they can be occasions for family interaction.

Social rules tell us some of the goals we *should* pursue – alleviating the distress of others, for example. An appeal for help from someone in distress may simply make you *feel* like getting involved with them. However, if the emotional response by itself is not sufficiently motivating, society stands ready to criticize us for not living up to its standards, which specify long lists of the ways that we should help others, the circumstances in which we should do this, and

the excuses and mitigating circumstances that relieve us of the responsibility to help others.

Established roles and the rules of relationships especially influence the aims that we will adopt, the activities we will take on, and the encounters we will experience as a consequence. Your employer has a right to summon you to meetings and to set the agenda. Neighbors have the right to expect that you will exchange a few words and help with small problems. The entitlements of friendship and kinship are greater (see *Chs 16, 20, 21*). Mothers may be expected to give more help and comfort to children, fathers to have more fun with them (see *Ch 17*).

Social rules also govern where and how a goal or activity can be pursued. The most intimate encounters have to occur in private. Noisy encounters should not inconvenience others. Personal objectives should not be pursued at the expense of the activity the encounter is mainly focused on – hosts and circles of friends often lay down rules restricting people from "talking shop" at dinner parties and other small gatherings. At a large drinks party, pairs and small groups can form to focus on topics that interest them especially, but at a funeral the business of showing respect for the deceased will rule out many other activities.

The physical setting itself may be a *place* that is governed by rules that restrict activity. Unexpectedly meeting an old and much loved friend during a tourist visit to a hushed

cathedral, your greeting will be much more restrained and may seem less warm than if the encounter had taken place outside in the café across the street.

Physical surroundings affect mood

Physical settings affect us, of course, even without having special rules. To have a quiet relaxing visit with a friend you look for a quiet relaxing spot. When you are in a mood for romance, you are drawn to dimly lit cafés – because the lighting creates a sense of intimacy – decorated in warm, rich colors – because they are arousing.

The ordinary comforts of home are especially appreciated when we are forced to carry out ordinary interactions in unfavorable surroundings that we do not control. Airports, for example, are notoriously impersonal places. In the typical arrangement of seats in waiting areas, the chairs are placed in line, back to back. In these circumstances, two people can talk to each other, but a group of three or more is split up. People sitting on their own are likely to find themselves uncomfortably sandwiched among groups that have been unwillingly spread out.

As an experiment, alternative arrangements using the same amount of space and the same number of chairs were provided in a major European airport. Video cameras concealed in the ceiling monitored the behavior of waiting passengers, and the videotapes were studied for behavioral cues of tension and relaxation. A cross-shaped arrangement was found to be significantly more conducive to social encounters. Singles could sit at the ends of the cross and face away from their neighbors. Groups of up to eight people could occupy the internal angles and interact happily with all of the other members. The management of the airport did not act on these findings, possibly because it is more profitable to keep an airport's bars and restaurants as the only inviting places to sit.

Excessive heat can produce aggression. Temperature can also affect attraction. In one study, subjects were placed in a room with a temperature of 40°C (100°F) and a humidity of 60 percent. They were given simple tasks to perform for 45 minutes. Other subjects were given the same tasks but in more comfortable conditions. At the end of the session, both groups were invited to rate how much they liked a fictitious stranger, about whom they had been given bogus information. Those who had experienced the hot conditions tended to view the stranger less favorably. Other studies have shown that the discomfort produced by heat can actually improve relations within a group because people are drawn together in their joint suffering.

Excessive noise can make us less willing to help people.

◀ **Romantic café lighting** makes us draw closer and use softer voices than we would in bright light. People at other tables seem more distant. All of this increases the sense of relaxation and the level of intimacy. The warm, rich colors typically used to decorate intimate restaurants further stimulate the emotional arousal that closeness creates.

DECORATING FOR SOCIAL ACTIVITY

■ Color can have a direct effect on our moods, and this in turn will strongly influence the way in which we interact with other people. Having a conversation with someone in a deep red room will be less relaxing than if it takes place in a green one. In television studios, the area where artists and guests relax before a show is known as the "green room." Even though it is not always decorated in that color, the furnishings and wall colors are carefully chosen to create a calm atmosphere.

People typically chose muted browns, beiges and creams for their living rooms, but chose stronger colors for the kitchen, with its higher activity level. Deep burgundy and brown colors have been found to be related to the levels of violence and disturbance in bars.

The colors we use in decorating change according to fashions. In the 1960s, strong colors were very much in vogue and even quite conventional homes featured splashes of orange, red and purple in the age of "psychedelia." In the 1980s such colors seemed inappropriate in most social settings, and particularly in the peace and quiet of home.

Color influences the mood of an encounter and it also reflects the mood of the times. When the economy is booming, unemployment is low and there is a general feeling of optimism, bright and cheerful colors are more common. When the economy becomes depressed, people are forced to be much more businesslike in order to get ahead in an increasingly competitive world. Colors become more serious too, providing settings for less frivolous patterns of social interaction. **PM**

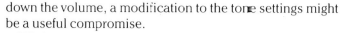

The right physical setting for the occasion is the one that helps to create the right level of intimacy and the right emotions. When we are forced to adapt to too much stimulation and too much intimacy, our social sensitivity declines.

In one field experiment, the researcher dropped packages near a very loud road drill. The number of people who helped in picking them up was much smaller than when the accident was staged in quieter surroundings. This could simply be a matter of discomfort. The noise hurts our ears, so we walk on past the person who needs help in order to reduce the discomfort. Unhelpfulness may also be due to "overload" – the level of noise becomes the primary focus of attention, and other signals, such as implicit requests for help, are simply not received.

When children are screaming around the house, or the neighbor is mowing grass, we find it more difficult to concentrate on complex tasks, and a number of experiments have shown that noise interferes with the ability to learn. There are also links between noise and feelings of anger and irritability. Laboratory experiments have also shown that noise can add to the effects of other aggressive stimuli – watching a violent film, for example.

These findings clearly have direct implications for the management of leisure settings. Barroom brawls and violence in discos might be reduced if sufficient attention were given to the effects of noise. But how can you have a quiet disco? Preliminary research suggests that it might not be just a matter of sheer volume. Cutting down on the amount of bass in the music, without altering the overall level of noise, seems to have a beneficial effect in some cases. If teenagers at home cannot be persuaded to turn down the volume, a modification to the tone settings might be a useful compromise.

While heat and noise can have negative effects on our social behavior, it is clear that many people appear to cope with quite extreme levels of both. People who move to a house near an airport, for example, might find the area very noisy at first. After a while, however, the noise of jets taking off and landing will often not be noticed. This process is known as adaptation and each of us has an adaptation level, depending on previous experience. If you have lived all of your life in a city, then you will probably not view the streets as particularly busy and disturbing. Your friend from the country, however, may take a very different view.

There is evidence, however, that we can pay a price for adapting to negative aspects of the physical setting. In an experiment, subjects placed in a laboratory environment with loud, uncontrollable noises eventually adapted to the conditions and performed clerical tasks without any noticeable impairment of speed and accuracy. However, when they were later placed in quiet surroundings, they performed less well on other tasks than did people who had not worked in the noisy setting.

The after-effects of stressful settings in normal life may be less obvious. It does seem, however, that one product is a general decreased sensitivity to social cues. Having spent so much time shutting out unwanted stimuli or unwelcome interactions, it becomes habitual. We should, perhaps, occasionally take stock and consider to what extent our sensitivity to others has been blunted by our everyday experiences. **AFF PM**

27

▲ **A mood of aggression** *is what contact sport thrives on. Fields are laid out with identified territories that players must rouse themselves to invade and symbolically seize in encounters that ritualize hostility. Conventions for channeling this hostility* *in acceptable ways are all-important, and in the charged atmosphere that results when rules break down, the guardians of the rules themselves may be in physical danger.*

▲ **A mugging in the New York subway.** *The notorious tendency of big-city inhabitants to ignore the plight of someone in trouble has been blamed in part on the "stimulus overload" that makes them unresponsive to social cues that signal distress.* *Passive crowds embolden aggressors, as do the numerous enclosed physical settings in cities, such as subways trains, underground passages and stairwells, where inhibiting thoughts of outside interference are few.*

PREPARING FOR AN INTERVIEW

■ On average, job interviews last less than an hour. Most are highly structured, formal, ritualized affairs with clear-cut goals, rules and roles. This influences most people to behave in more or less the same manner. They have little opportunity to show what they are really like.

Research findings show that interviews can provide useful information, but often they do not identify the right person for the job – the one who not only has appropriate skills and credentials, but has the sort of personality that people working with them will like.

The way the interviewing organization sets the scene for the event can do a great deal to overcome its inbuilt handicaps, but the candidate too helps to create this distinctive social situation and should not lose opportunities to influence it.

ANTICIPATION

The preparations of both the intelligent interviewer and the intelligent interviewee have the same starting point – an examination of what the job requires for successful performance. To find out how well the candidate fulfills these requirements will be the main goal of the interview. Thinking this goal out is a stage that is frequently neglected by organizations.

Candidates are all the more advised, therefore, to accumulate as much information as possible about the job.

It can be useful to call the company and mention your interest in the job and your name as you probe for further details. Job descriptions in advertisements rarely provide anything more than an attractive introduction. Better still, arrange a visit, if the company agrees, so that you can gather the information you want and make an early impression.

Prepare a case in advance, not when you are under pressure of time and circumstance on the day. By arriving with a strong, prepared case, you tilt the circumstances to an important degree in your favor.

The application form offers an opportunity to inform the interviewer in advance of skills and personal qualities. Under "interests" you can establish a link between your nonwork experience and important aspects of the job. There is no reason why you should not submit a short letter in support of your application. You certainly cannot be penalized for it and you can make this an opportunity to provide the selectors with well-prepared reasons for accepting you.

It is crucial to be positive-minded during preparations.

Do not deprive yourself and the organization of your skills and talents by talking yourself out of the job in advance on the grounds that someone else might be better suited. If you feel uncertain of yourself, it can be useful to brainstorm with a friend for ways of applying your skills, qualities and experience to the job. Remember that you have a wealth of information about yourself and are uniquely placed to bring it out.

SELF-PRESENTATION

Practice helps as well. Ask a friend to interview you, so that you can think more sharply on your feet when the real event arrives. Thinking about questions and answers in advance may also make you more conscious of the underlying reasons for what the real interviewer asks. Something that every candidate must be prepared to do is to provide the relevant information that unskilled interviewers have not tapped. Develop ways of introducing important information about yourself, using, for example, phrases such as "I was very interested to note that..."

Do not be afraid to make an impression. One of the benefits of your first telephone call is that it singles you out at an early stage in the selection process. It reflects your unusual interest

DRESSING FOR AN INTERVIEW

■ Going to a job interview, you choose your clothes carefully. This is easy for men, who know they cannot go wrong with a suit and a tie. Women have greater freedom in office dress, but this means they might wear clothes for an interview that create a wrong impression – too severe, on the one hand, or too flighty on the other.

In a study of hiring tendencies, personnel managers who were not aware that the study was concerned with dress

watched videorecorded interviews of women wearing four different styles. The managers were asked to make hiring recommendations.

The four styles ranged from "least masculine" – a light beige dress in a soft fabric, with a small round collar, gathered skirt and long sleeves – to "most masculine" – a dark navy tailored suit and a white blouse with an angular collar.

Women wearing the most feminine dress were chosen

least often. But women wearing the most masculine dress were not chosen quite as often as women wearing the next-to-most masculine dress – a tailored beige suit with blazer-style jacket and a rust-colored blouse with a bow at the neck.

Choosing the right clothes for an interview clearly is difficult for women. Something masculine, but not too masculine seems to be the happy medium most likely to create the right impression. **MC**

Interviews that are highly ritualized and do not put candidates at ease often fail to identify the best person for the job. To adapt to this situation interviewees must know their good points and take opportunities to talk about them.

and, presumably, motivation and suggests initiative. It also offers the person to whom you talk a sample of your behavior, even if only on the end of a telephone. As in any form of interaction, the first encounter significantly affects the other person's perception of you thereafter. So prepare yourself to be scrutinized to some extent, probably unconsciously, when you call or visit.

When it comes to the interview, confidence in a hand-shake, eye contact and general demeanor are very quickly assessed. There is no doubt at all that nonverbal communication affects the outcome of many interviews. A study that observed over 100 candidates found that three particular body-language patterns were significantly correlated with success. These were more smiling, more eye-contact and more nodding than other candidates. Obviously, however, these can be overdone.

SKILLS

Observation of interviewers suggests that they rarely pre-pared themselves well for the interview in terms of knowing what to focus on. Also, they fail to probe deeply enough to make an informed decision, and they tend to adopt a direct questioning approach – asking, for example, "Do you get on well with people?" rather than asking candidates to describe how they would handle a situation that would, as it happens, reflect this skill.

In one study, it was observed that interviewers tend to draw out from candidates information and behavior that helps to make a self-fulfilling prophesy out of an opening impression. Observers who were not informed of the purpose of the study watched videorecordings of interviews. In some of them, the researchers had given the interviewer an unfavorable impression of the candidate in

advance. In others it was a favorable impression. When asked to rate the candidate's suitability for selection on the basis of interview performance, the impartial observers rated the negatively viewed candidates less suitable. The lesson for candidates is to be on their guard against being led away from talking about their positive points and from presenting themselves favorably.

Behavior is often strongly determined by the setting we find ourselves in. Thus, to change the behavior we must change the setting. We know that people tend to be more relaxed and behavior more in character in informal settings than in formal ones, and that the more informal the setting, the more we may actually get to know people. Yet, when organizing job interviews, people often ignore this piece of common sense.

Interviewers who want to learn as much as they can about candidates are advised to practice skills of objectivity and skills of putting people at their ease. The way the candidate is greeted will affect the mood of the encounter (see Ch11). Candidates speak more easily and remember more useful information when the interviewer emphasizes questions that allow them to put forward positive points. Searching for reasons not to select a candidate creates a defensive and unforthcoming mood.

The interviewer's body language can also help the candidate to be informative. A friendly facial expression and an open, relaxed posture will produce longer, more revealing answers than a frown and tightly crossed arms. The physical setting is important too. If the interviewer and candidate are seated too far away, or across an imposing desk, there will be a less relaxed atmosphere. **BAM**

■ It is very important to remember that the first few minutes of an interview are crucial, for there is considerable evidence from research that interviewers tend to decide within the first five minutes whether to accept or reject a candidate. The rest of the interview is a search for evidence to support their decision. That means that the behavior of the candidate when greeted, introduced and given the first few questions is vitally important in stabilizing first impressions.

Marking Territory

IN EVERYDAY language we talk of "my place," "our home" and "her neighborhood." Walking through any urban area we see signs like "Private," "Members Only" and "No Trespassers." Phrases such as "A man's home is his castle," "home territories" and a person's "turf" or "patch" are commonplace. Usually, however, we are not very conscious of our territories until one of them is violated, for instance when someone else sits in our favorite chair. There are many other types of territory, and they directly influence the ways in which encounters start and how they proceed.

Why are we territorial?

Being territorial involves owning particular areas or objects. In some cases ownership might be a legal right, as with a house or apartment, but it could be purely symbolic. When you reserve a table in a restaurant there is no suggestion that the table will literally belong to you. Your "ownership" of that territory will last only for as long as the meal. Less formally, people "mark" temporary claims to,

say, a seat in the library by placing an object on it while they browse through the shelves.

The origins of human territorial behavior, some scientists believe, lie deep in our evolutionary past. Most species of animal lay claim to geographical areas for obtaining food and breeding partners. These spaces are often marked out using scent signals. For example, dogs cock their legs against trees and fences. Birds sing not only to attract mates but also to inform other birds of their territorial claims, and fish attempt to repel invaders from their feeding areas on the river bed.

Animal territorial behavior makes sure that individuals are dispersed over the areas where food is available. When the population is small and food is plentiful there is little need for territorial defense. As the population grows and food becomes scarce, stricter territories are established in order to force some animals to fend for themselves elsewhere.

With present-day humans, however, the situation is much more complex. Our own animal ancestors, and our early tribal hunting forefathers, doubtless established territories for similar reasons of physical survival, but we now use control over space in a much more complex way. It helps to set the scene for social interaction.

Belonging to a certain place

Primary territories are distinct places that are clearly owned exclusively by a person or group. A family's house or a person's office are spaces which nonowners do not enter unless specifically invited. These territories are stable and lasting and their individuality is usually enhanced by the owners. Homes, for example, are decorated to suit the lifestyles and personalities of the occupants. Offices are personalized with family photos, framed diplomas and ornaments. These express our emotional attachments and

◄ A place of your own. *Everyone needs to get away from other people and to feel a sense of being in charge of a place. Even within families we attach ourselves to personal territories. The kitchen tends to "belong" to the one who prepares the meals. We like to have our own workrooms and our own bedrooms, or at least our own side of the bed. Children in their playtime dens and tree-houses create special spaces all of their own where they practice the territorial claims they will later exercise as adults.*

► By personalizing our territories *we emphasize where one begins and the other ends. We also show how much attachment we feel to them and how involved we are prepared to be with the surrounding community.* TOP *A cottage in the Irish countryside signals with its lupins and its ivy that we should knock at the door for a friendly encounter. Across the fence there is much less invitation.* BOTTOM *Housepaint helps residents claim their individual identities in the Chelsea district of London, England.*

Personalizing your home or the space assigned to you at work expresses an emotional attachment to a place, a commitment to stay and be part of the community or workplace. It also announces that you are in control of territory.

serve as markers that discourage unwelcome intrusions.

A study of American university dormitories showed how personalization of students' spaces was related to their sense of belonging to the university as a whole. The investigators counted the number of personal items in the students' rooms, such as posters, hi-fis and rugs, and found that students who dropped out were the ones with the least number of personal items on display. The few that they did display announced loyalties to other places or groups. Personal marking is related to the desire to keep a space as a home territory.

You could make the same observation in your own neighborhood. Look at the houses or apartments that show personalization. New fences and boundary markers, door colors that stand out from the rest, or freshly painted window frames. Noting how territories are marked should allow you to predict who is most likely to leave the neighborhood and who is most likely to stay and become involved in membership of the community.

Getting away from other people

Within the home there are more territorial demarcations that depend on the level of intimacy of different rooms and spaces. On the doorstep and in the front hallway we meet relative strangers and people making deliveries. Friends and relatives are invited into the living room or kitchen, but rarely are people from outside the immediate family admitted to an adult's bedroom. This is not a place for casual encounters – it is a place for sleeping and intimate activities like love-making.

Another function of demarcations within primary territor-

▲ **Being part of a community.** A resident of Shipka, Bulgaria, contemplates the comfortable sight of rooftops he has known all his life. Our feeling for territory reflects our sense of familiarity and involvement with the people who use it – our family and neighbors. Establishing themselves in a new town or country, uprooted people are likely to put up pictures of home. The greater the number of local objects they feel inclined to put on display, however, the more likely they are to stay and form relationships.

ies is to allow the people who share them to escape from each other. We need to be able to relax and be ourselves, and for most of us there is a part of the home, perhaps a bedroom, a den or a study, where we can find solitude. These private territories allow us to avoid overloading ourselves with stimulation.

People differ in the amount of activity they need to avoid either boredom or exhaustion. Some like to be with friends and acquaintances most of the time while others prefer a quieter pattern of life. Everybody, however, needs to be able to regulate their contacts with other people. When the surrounding environment makes this difficult, we can easily become stressed.

Overcrowding is one major cause of such stress. In poor housing conditions, where a large family or even several family groups share one dwelling, physical privacy may be difficult to find. Under such pressures, however, a number of remedies emerge. Members of the group come to respect each other's rights to particular areas at certain times of the day. Territorial rituals concerning limited furniture or access to basic amenities become established and allow a sense of independence or seclusion.

These special social rules are familiar to anyone who has been camping or cooped up with a group in a confined space. Those who work in open-plan offices also know how important it is to establish rules about intrusion. Filing cabinets double up as territorial markers, desks are positioned so that eye contact with other workers is avoided and personal mementos are used to mark the area as personal. Where physical boundaries are lacking we either create them with available materials or erect symbolic substitutes and establish tacit agreements so we can regulate our contact with others. Social rules and conventions can act in the same way as doors, providing essential control over encounters.

The "home-field" advantage

In our homes we can control what happens. When we encounter someone there who is not a member of the immediate family, they are there because *we* issue the invitation and set the tone of the meeting by selecting which room is to be used and how the guests are to be accommodated. We are the hosts, and certain rights and obligations stem from this. There are also distinct rules about how your guests should behave. Some of these are obvious, but others are more subtle. Compare the ways you and a friend behave together when you meet in your own home and when you meet at the friend's.

On your own territory you are more likely to lead and sustain the conversation. Any pauses and silences are filled

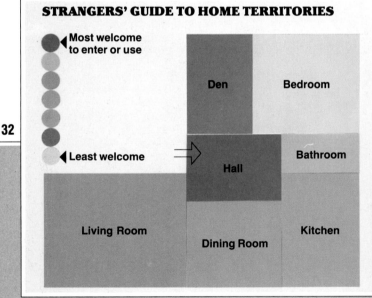

STRANGERS' GUIDE TO HOME TERRITORIES

◀ Most welcome to enter or use

◀ Least welcome

Den

Bedroom

Hall

Bathroom

Living Room

Dining Room

Kitchen

▲ **Access to someone else's home** *is by invitation only, and at each stage of penetrating to more and more private areas of the house, a fresh invitation is required.*

▶ **Indoor territory** *offers the greatest scope for personalization. Here, where only those whom we invite will see it, we display detailed information about ourselves. Each item in the decor reflects a different aspect of our individual outlook or personal history.*

In primary territory you can control what happens. You are likely to sustain the conversation, and when a visitor disagrees with you, you are more likely to maintain your position, even when it is someone of slightly higher status.

by you rather than the other person. Here you are the master of ceremonies. You will tend to sit with a more open and relaxed posture and in the least formal chair. This sense of relaxation increases your dominance and control. When discussing a topic with someone who disagrees with you, you are much more likely to maintain your position when you are the host and to give way when you are the guest. When, however, attitudes are fairly similar, the host is the one who will usually give way on minor points in order to be hospitable.

The same kind of differences in behavior are seen in *formal* primary territories such as offices. The office owner is more dominant even with someone of slightly higher status. If you want a raise or promotion you are most likely to achieve your aim if you can get your boss to discuss the matter in your own office – otherwise you will be at a double disadvantage.

Similarly, you are in a better position to settle a contract or win an order if your negotiating partner visits you. If this is not possible, then it is best to meet on neutral ground rather than be dominated by the other's territorial advantage. This is one reason why so many high-level discussions take

place over lunch in exclusive restaurants or hotel suites. The cost of such arrangements is usually small in comparison with the need to equalize the territorial effect.

The tendency to be more dominant at home lies at the root of the "home-field" advantage in many sports. A football team may have more knowledge about its own ground and its idiosyncrasies, thus providing a small technical advantage. But it is more likely that visiting players are intimidated by entering a foreign territory and therefore do not play their best. Host teams win, on average, 64 percent of the basketball games played in the United States.

One other home territory is the car, that special kind of home on wheels over which we have elaborate rights. Others are allowed in it only when invited, and we also lay claim to the space immediately around it. When another driver gets very close to our rear bumper, we become agitated. Our anger, however, is not generated primarily by fears of a collision but by the fact that a piece of our territory has been violated. The same is true when other drivers cut in front of us. In many cases our reaction to these territorial invasions is far more dangerous than the maneuver that prompted it.

The territorial nature of the automobile explains why there is so much aggression on the highways. If the car were simply a functional object which allowed us to travel from

■ **Open-plan offices**. *Favored for economic use of space, ease of communication and a more "open" feeling, these offices nevertheless make concentration more difficult. LEFT A management concern for efficiency leaves the seated worker with no relief from her view of the workspace. For the standing worker there is an unbroken and uninteresting vista of ceiling and identical cubicles. A different approach* involves larger subspaces shared by several workers separated from others by high shelving. TOP Workers in an open-plan office like barriers, such as desks and filing systems, to strengthen their sense of personal space and their ability to concentrate, but they may prefer low ones – looking away from work toward other people reduces the sense of isolation.

one place to another in relative comfort, we would be quite calm about minor collisions or small scratches in the paintwork, but most of us do react strongly. Simply *touching* a person's car without permission can be a very dangerous exploit, provoking hostility and even violence.

Territory and status

There is a natural relationship between status and the size of primary territories. If you have an office at work, consider how it compares in size with that of your boss and your subordinates. Very rarely does a senior manager have a territory smaller than a junior.

In many cases this ranking of the enviroment is set out when the building is designed. Like company cars, offices are carefully graded in size, appointment and location. The most prestigious offices are usually on higher floors, sometimes served only by an executive elevator. Vice-presidents or managing directors of large companies will usually have a suite instead of a single area, and reception-ists' offices and waiting rooms insulate them even further. While some of this space may be functional, it is essentially for show. In advance of a meeting, it reminds visitors of the dominant position of the inhabitant.

More subtle signs of dominance may be seen in shared spaces in quite different settings. In a study set in a psychiatric ward, it was found that high-ranking patients ranged beyond the areas around their own beds to claim free access to all parts of the ward. Those of lesser status tended to stick to particular areas. In American prisons, too, studies showed that the most dominant inmates were the most mobile within places of free access. They also, of

Extra office space for higher-ranking members of an organization may give them a few functional advantages, but mostly it is for show, signaling dominant status. Status also demonstrates itself in the number of other spaces freely entered.

course, claimed the best bunks, not only the most comfort-able but also the most private.

Shared territories

Some spaces are *secondary* territories, less central in people's lives than their homes, but used regularly – a neighborhood bar or café, perhaps. A core of regulars may feel that they have some influence and control over what goes on within the building.

In British pubs, particularly those in rural areas, it is not uncommon to find certain seats or stools unofficially reserved for well-known customers. Innocent strangers occupying one of these seats are likely to be given stern glances or simply told to move by other customers.

Private clubs are even more restrictive – admittance is strictly limited. There may be rules relating to dress, behavior or the way you speak. Being a guest of a member of such a club involves accepting the jurisdiction of the territorial owners and adapting to their expectations.

A rather different kind of secondary territory consists of the entrance areas, hallways and corridors of apartment buildings. The urban planner Oscar Newman, in his influential book *Defensible Space*, stresses the importance of these areas because they link the primary territory of the home to that of the public world. Where buildings are designed in a way that leaves the occupants without a sense of jurisdiction over secondary areas, problems of vandalism and crime are commonplace. Entrances are often occupied

34

TERRITORIAL COMBAT

◄ **Arm wrestling,** *like so many competitive sports, involves pushing opponents back into their own territory and symboli-cally taking it over. In football, you possess as much of the football field as you can keep behind the ball, and when that is the whole field, you have scored. In the 1987 Finnish Women's Arm Wrestling Championship seen here, the contested space lies between the green blocks.*

OFFICE LAYOUT — EQUIPPING A PRIMARY TERRITORY FOR INTERACTION

■ The ways that people furnish their primary territories to influence encounters with visitors have been studied especially in the case of office layouts. Studies of single-person offices show that they convey two important messages to other people. First, they show the occupant's status and probable role within the organization. Second, the arrangement of furniture reflects the occupant's expectations about how visitors should behave.

The most important signal is the positioning of the desk. This piece of furniture divides the room into two major zones – a private zone where the occupant of the office sits to work and a public zone, the area where visitors are greeted and asked to sit.

The seating arrangement for visitors controls the distance at which visitor and occupant will interact. In interviews in particular this will affect the level of intimacy and the impression of dominance that the interviewer creates. A common ploy to reduce the interviewee's status is to place visitors' chairs well into the public zone at an uncomfortable distance from the occupant's desk.

A desk position that allows the occupant to face outward from a wall has a number of advantages. You can see everything that goes on in the room and can also face people directly as they enter the office. This allows you to be ready for interaction even when occupied with other tasks.

University teachers tend to sit sideways to their office doors, adopting more open and less well-defined zone patterns in their offices than commercial and government employees. Since teachers need to make students feel welcome and at ease, they tend to express their leadership role in a less dominating style, and they try to minimize social distance. In contrast, occupants of commercial and government offices tend to arrange their rooms to give them a psychological advantage during negotiations with customers or rivals.

Social status does not influence the arrangement of furniture in academic offices, but it is an important factor in commercial settings. Managerial and higher status staff are likely to position their desks to face the door directly.

In contrast, clerical and administrative staff more often sit side-on to the door. Academic staff gain prestige through academic achievements, and do not need surroundings that convey information about status.

Deep-pile carpeting and pictures on the wall help to personalize offices and express personal attitudes. Chair size conveys status. The higher the back of a chair the greater the status. Swivel chairs convey more power because the occupant is more able to change orientation. They also allow for freer movement in times of stress, which can prove useful for covering up some of the signs of anxiety.

Particularly in offices where there are no walls to mark out territories, these symbols are important. So is positioning, distance and zoning. Different measures of importance are attached to certain parts of the room. The corner positions, for example, tend to have a high status value, because they are more secluded, and so are predictably taken over by the more senior members of staff.

▲ **Barriers and distance** help to control what happens in an office. From his distant position on the sidelines, the man on the left is less likely to take initiatives than the one who has been seated in the blue chair. The occupant, sitting in a position of power behind his desk, will take the lion's share of initiatives.

▲ **Moving behind the boss's desk** is an aggressive act of territorial invasion, especially when accompanied by signals of hostility. It can produce a startled response.

▲ **Three ways of arranging your desk.** (1) "The throne" – a desk between occupant and visitors – reinforces the occupant's sense of control. (2) A desk touching a wall allows for more informal and more personal encounters. (3) Sitting side-on to the door allows for even more informality and ease of approach.

by vagrants and alcoholics and amenities such as elevators are the constant target of criminal damage. Interactions within these spaces are mostly impersonal and even close neighbors fail to greet each other.

Newman proposes simple remedies that can be achieved through design modifications. He suggests that proper control can be established only when about four or five families share a single entrance. People then get to know each other, and they take a strong interest in potential threats to their shared area.

Subdividing large buildings into small units radically alters the way people living there behave. Symbolic territorial markers can be used to show the boundaries of these units, such as low walls, hedges, separate stairways and windows that open directly onto shared areas. Surveillance is increased and the occupants come to feel that they have an obligation to notice what goes on around them.

Holding temporary territories

Territory in public places is held on only a very temporary basis. Picnic tables in a park are available to anyone, but when occupied by a group or family they are effectively out of bounds to anyone else. Similarly, by placing mats on a beach, erecting an umbrella and spreading a few bodies on the sand, the space becomes occupied. Not only will other people avoid using it but, depending on how busy the beach is, they will also keep several meters away.

The way you hold onto a piece of public territory varies, of course, with local customs and cultural rules. But there are certain techniques you can use almost anywhere. Two of the most obvious can be seen in any crowded bus, train or airplane, where most people not only want a seat but also prefer a vacant seat next to them as well – a sort of territorial buffer. When others get on there is a danger of being asked to give up this valuable extra space, and one trick for

PORTABLE TERRITORY

■ Cars are "mobile territory" (see p33), and the things we use to carry our possessions when we are away from home are "portable territory." Like our homes, they have interiors whose privacy we expect other people to respect. The interior of a lady's purse is a classic example of a place that others should leave alone. We feel upset about having our houses, cars or suitcases searched by police or by other officials, such as the airport security officer below, at work in Montreal, Canada. Our tension does not necessarily reflect a fear that authorities will find something we should not have. It reflects our having to put aside a natural urge to assert control over the spaces that are most personal to us.

Our territorial instinct extends to spaces that we do not have exclusive claim to – the street parking in front of the house, or the table you always sit at in your favorite restaurant – even the seat you temporarily occupy on a bus.

escaping requests is to avoid any eye contact, for example by looking out of the window. The slightest meeting of the eyes establishes a basic contact that can lead to the newcomers asking if the seat is taken. Another strategy, of course, is to place objects on the spare seat that will require some time and trouble to remove. Several small items are more effective than one large bag.

The use of different objects as territorial markers has been studied. In one experiment, chairs in a campus hall were marked with textbooks, neatly arranged journals, coats or combinations of objects. Unmarked chairs were taken within 20 minutes, but the most effectively marked were left completely alone. A combination of a personal item (coat) and signs of work in progress (textbook and notebook) proved to be the best markers. Scattered journals were the least effective, but simply putting the same journals in a neat pile on the chair almost doubled their marking power.

It is interesting to note what happens when territorial marking is ignored. In only about one quarter of cases is the "offender" actually challenged by the person who attempted to save the space. So, though you may not be popular if you take what is obviously a reserved seat, the chances of a hostile encounter are quite small.

Instead of marking a particular space, we can keep people away by particular activities. For example, if two people are having an intense conversation then few will wish to intrude into the area immediately around them. A couple holding hands and staring romantically at each other in a bar will effectively reserve their whole table. Having a row would produce the same effect.

A degree of privacy in public places can, therefore, be achieved by behaving as if you *were* in private. Strangers feel uncomfortable intruding and, although there are no physically defined borders, your actions form their own symbolic frontiers. **P M**

▲ **"Seat occupied"** *is the unmistakable message of the coats, bags, papers and books left at empty places in this study room in the University of Gothenburg, Sweden. The more personal the items used to mark a temporary territory, the more effective they are. Library copies of a journal are twice as effective if left in a neat pile.*

▶ **A dispute over water rights** *takes representatives of two Chinese communes back to territorial basics – who is to have access to the resources of a place? Assertive postures announce that the issue has not been decided.*

Keeping a Distance

THE DISTANCE we keep in social interactions is important because it affects the impressions that others develop about us and because it affects our ease of interacting with them. Changing your distance can express a desire for intimacy or a desire for noninvolvement, or it can heighten or reduce your influence over another person. Distance is also important because it affects how we use eye contact, touch, orientation and other elements of body language.

In crowded or confined spaces where we cannot control physical distance, we may react defensively, maintaining an emotional distance by limiting interaction. Sometimes, however, we welcome the emotional excitement and the obscuring of individual identity that results from participation in crowd activity.

What distance tells us about people

The distance at which a person stands provides information when we are forming impressions. It gives different information according to the social setting and the relationships between people, but in general if people stay too far away, they seem unfriendly, cold or perhaps anxious. If

they come too close and make us uncomfortable, they appear pushy or insensitive. A good friend who stays farther away than usual may be saying there is something wrong. Of course, as a single cue, distance may give a false impression unless eye contact, facial expression and body language are also noticed.

When we discern other people's relationships, distance again is part of the information we use, and again we always take the context into consideration. The meaning of a given distance, and its related body-language signals, depends on the social situation and its rules, the relationship between people and their thoughts and feelings. Two people sitting quite close, next to each other, could be friends, lovers or family members sharing some time with one another. Seeing them close to each other, we are still likely to assume some such relationship.

However, if they are sitting next to each other in a large room, and most of the other people in the room are sitting at similar distances from their neighbors, we are much less likely to infer a particularly close relationship. They might, for example, be two students in a large, well-filled

◄ **Relationships stand out in silhouette** *in an office-building stairwell. On the upper level a man and a woman signal an emotional closeness that a second man respects by standing slightly apart from them. On the lower level a man and a woman pass a few moments together as mere acquaintances.*

▲ **Using your possessions** *as territorial buffers guarantees that you can keep yourself at a comfortable distance from strangers while you temporarily occupy a piece of public space.*

By adjusting your distance you can express a desire for intimacy or for noninvolvement, or you can heighten or reduce your influence. Mingling in a crowd can make you tense and defensive, or it can bring you an enjoyable release from inhibitions.

classroom who, like their fellow students, have to sit close to their neighbors. The close arrangement may not be what these students themselves prefer, but it is also not particularly stressful or significant. In a full classroom, students expect to have someone sitting immediately next to them. If only 10 percent of the seats were occupied and he chose to sit next to her, that would be quite different. She would undoubtedly notice the close approach and draw some conclusion – perhaps that he is attempting to make her acquaintance in too forward a way.

Distance signals intimacy. Being very near, gazing into each other's eyes and touching, shows the obvious emotional closeness between lovers. Contrast with this the increased distance from a stranger or someone not liked: a signal of low or "negative" intimacy. Such spacing patterns occur spontaneously in our interactions as a result of people's feelings for each other.

Close approaches when intimacy is not desired can cause resentment. Being close to another person can also increase the likelihood of a territorial intrusion. For example, approaching colleagues in the office by sitting on the edge of their desk brings you physically close and may also represent a challenge to territorial control (see *Ch 2*). A negative reaction is probably the result both of being too close and of intruding. Although you may not be able to

know which factor is more important, the high involvement signaled by close approaches is a separate issue.

How we use the space between us

Distance helps to regulate interactions, especially when individuals face one another. If they are quite close and in easy view, interaction will be smoother and more predictable than when they are *too* close or too far away, which can be distracting and disrupt the give-and-take of conversation.

Distancing patterns and the course of interaction are affected by whether you are sitting or standing during a conversation. Standing interactions typically allow people more flexibility. Because knees are not in the way and because you can stand facing outward, partners may comfortably stay as close as 20-40cm (8-16in). When you are seated you can choose a similarly close arrangement if your conversation partner is next to you or a couch, but seated interactions typically involve more of a face-to-face orientation.

The result is that seated positions usually put the participants in a social interaction at greater distances from

▲ **Lining up for ice-cream** *in Prague, Czechoslovakia, people who are on their own stand out in contrast to family groupings whose members maintain smaller distances between themselves.*

► **Labor Day in Atlantic City, New Jersey,** *produces an array of temporary beach territories, all spaced approximately the same distance apart. This uniform pattern results from hundreds of spontaneous individual decisions.*

one another in order to make room for knees and for intervening desks or tables. Formal interactions such as business meetings, interviews or consulting sessions are almost always seated and usually the participants are arranged around desks or conference tables.

Seating options in homes are often severely constrained by the arrangement of furniture. For example, living room or family room areas are often inconvenient for casual interactions because the furniture arrangement is usually determined by the position of the television set. In many cases, family members and friends may prefer to talk in the kitchen or dining room around a table where they can face one another at fairly close distances.

By the way we handle distance we can also make it easier or harder to get involved in a conversation. For example, a

person wishing to join in can stand at the edge of the group and try to make eye contact with the speaker; or you can avoid unwanted conversation by keeping a greater distance and turning away.

When people talk, even when sitting side by side (say on a couch), they usually try to face each other. A third person coming in will probably sit opposite the first two: group members need a "common orientation space" in which to carry out their interaction.

With groups of up to six or seven people arrangements can be fairly stable, provided members sit in a roughly circle-shaped formation. But when the group reaches 10 to 12 people, opposite members are too distant from one another to carry on a comfortable conversation. At this point it becomes easier to talk to those next to you. This change induces a division of the large, unstable group into two or more groups which become stable in their turn, while the people at the ends reorientate themselves and make new circle-shaped formations that may grow and subdivide in their own turn.

Distance can also be used deliberately, as a means of

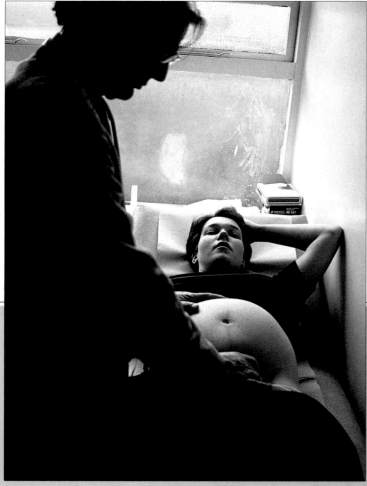

▲ **Professional detachment** creates an emotional distance between an examining doctor and his patient, allowing him to stand close to her and touch her in places normally reserved for intimate, even emotionally charged, interactions. Potential embarrassment is reduced by an impersonal manner, including the minimization of touching and eye contact.

Deliberate closeness can be used to advantage by a manipulative lover, a smooth salesperson or a crafty friend trying to put you into a mood to do a favor. Partners may be discussing a divorce but at a gathering stand close and hold hands.

exerting influence; for example, the boss may stand close to a subordinate, stare and look stern if he wants to intimidate. Police may do this to a suspect during an interrogation, or military officers to keep lower ranks in their place. Deliberate closeness can be used to advantage by a manipulative lover, a smooth salesperson or a crafty friend trying to put you into a mood to do a favor. Partners may cooperate (even unconsciously) to create a possibly false impression in observers: husband and wife may be arguing about the details of their divorce but at a social gathering stand close and hold hands.

A final function of distance relates to the way certain *services* and *tasks* are shaped. The doctor examining a naked patient, for example, takes a close approach, with much careful observation and some touching. However, this examination is not the intimate behavior of a lover or the intimidating behavior of a supervisor, but more like a mechanic investigating and repairing machinery. The poten-tial embarrassment of closeness is reduced by the impersonal meaning of the approach, touch and gaze.

Various other social situations use distances that are determined by the activity in hand rather than by the likes and dislikes of those involved. Working on a crowded assembly line, for example, or behind the counter of a fast-food chain means short distances and frequent touching. However, jobs needing concentration and privacy tend to keep workers apart. People may indeed choose their jobs to some extent according to whether they prefer isolation or contact with others.

Individual and cultural differences

People use and react to distance in different ways. Research on cultural differences suggests that Semitic, Mediterranean and Latin American people (the "contact cultures" – see *Ch10*) prefer closer distances than do the British and Northern Europeans. North Americans apparently fall somewhere in the middle. Even within a given country, racial and ethnic subgroups may differ in their preferences.

◄ **Apparent disorder** *in the arrangement of tables and chairs in a beach café disguises a pattern of social circles reflecting distance needs and ambitions that vary from group to group. The circle on the left attempts to unite 16 people but interaction can-* *not succeed at the distances created, and the main group has broken down into several subgroups. At top left a group of half that number succeeds at involving everyone in a single conversation.*

▲ **In the Tokyo Stock Exchange** *there is no room for personal space. The distances we allow sometimes reflect the nature of our activity rather than the need to be close enough to communicate in a desired way.*

When interaction between people from different cultures is unsuccessful, the reason often includes their differing expectations about distance. The foreigner who stands closer or farther away than we are accustomed will be viewed negatively. Such unusual behavior risks being put down to a deficiency in character rather than to the cultural difference it more likely is.

Sex differences greatly influence the use of space as well. Women generally prefer to be closer to other women than do men to other men, at least in North America and most of Europe. There is also evidence that personality offers clues to the individual choice or pattern of distance. Introverts and socially nervous people prefer greater distances than extroverts and those who feel at ease in company. Research on schizophrenic patients suggests they will generally choose greater avoidance of others than do nonschizophrenics. Violent people very often dislike the distances that other people tolerate well.

How to overcome distance problems

In determining the level of involvement between people, distance combines with other aspects of body language such as eye contact, facial expression, tone of voice and body orientation. These other tools can be used to cancel its effect when distance becomes a problem. The technical term for this is "compensatory adjustment."

For example, if you are sitting side by side with a stranger in a waiting room and the distance between you is only one meter (3ft), you would probably be quite comfortable, although this is the distance (within the "personal" zone – see below) that you would normally reserve for a close friend. That is because you can use other behavior to limit your involvement: you can turn away and avoid eye contact and touch. If you were to turn to the stranger, catch their eye and touch them, the level of involvement would rise noticeably.

Because these forms of behavior are dynamically related to each other, a change to one can be counteracted by compensatory adjustment of one or more of the rest. A too-close approach by a stranger may be met by turning away, decreasing the gaze and adopting a sterner expression, all of which lowers involvement. Then there is adjustment where the level of involvement starts out by being too low. For example, if the only available seats kept you and a friend several places apart, you would get "closer" by other means. You would look more, lean towards each other and be more expressive facially.

When people at a party are introduced to one another by a third person, a common arrangement involves the third person standing somewhat between and to the side of the other two, about perpendicular to their shared orientation. As the introducer leaves, the two people will probably move closer to one another. In doing so, however, they are likely to turn to a less directly facing arrangement which will probably result in a lower level of mutual eye contact. The decreased distance makes it easier to have a comfortable

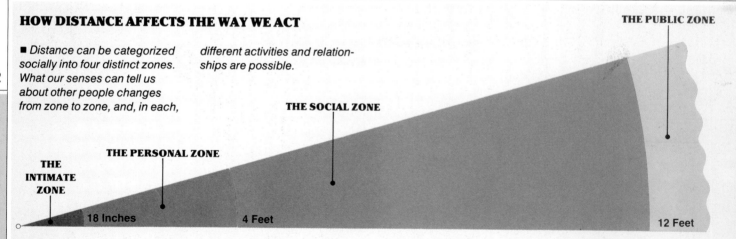

HOW DISTANCE AFFECTS THE WAY WE ACT

THE PUBLIC ZONE

THE SOCIAL ZONE

THE PERSONAL ZONE

THE INTIMATE ZONE

■ Distance can be categorized socially into four distinct zones. What our senses can tell us about other people changes from zone to zone, and, in each, different activities and relationships are possible.

18 Inches   4 Feet   12 Feet

■ **In the intimate zone**, within 45cm (18in) of each other, good friends and family members engage in activities like comforting, lovers make love and competitors in sports events wrestle and tackle. Not only can the partners touch and hug each other, but they are aware of each other's body heat and body odor. If people whisper, they can be heard.

■ **The personal zone**, from 0.5–1.2m (1.5–4ft), allows less intense exchanges. Touch is more limited, and body heat and odor are unnoticeable (unless the odor is strong). Speech becomes louder, and looking becomes more important than in the intimate zone: not only is it easier to focus but you can also see more of the other person.

■ **In the social zone**, from 1.2–3.7m (4–12ft), exchanges are more formal. Typical are those between business associates. They can touch, at the closer end of the range, and then only if one or both leans toward the other. Visual cues become more important, and voices become louder.

■ **The public zone**, 3.7m (12ft) and more, is characteristic of brief standing exchanges such as calling to a friend across a street, or formal exchanges between a speaker (perhaps teacher or minister) and an audience. Voices have to be loud, and it is impossible to see much detail of facial expression.

42

Eye contact, facial expression, tone of voice and body orientation can be used to cancel distance problems. If friends are seated far apart, they may get "closer" by looking more and by turning and leaning toward each other with expressive faces.

and relatively private conversation. At the same time, however, overall involvement is maintained at a comfortably low level because the decrease in distance is offset by a less direct orientation and a decrease in mutual eye contact.

Sometimes a change in distance signals an abrupt change in interaction. The touch of a lover, or a mother picking up her baby, are examples where the initial change in behavior is usually reciprocated. The partner responds in a way that increases involvement to a new and higher level. But the response (increased or lowered involvement) will depend on such things as the social situation, the relationship between the two people who are interacting, and the perception of why the initial change in behavior happened. It may be a smile and a hug, or a cold shoulder. **MP**

Crowding and crowds

Crowding reduces our opportunities to control distance. When people find the resulting intimacy unwelcome, there is usually physiological arousal, experienced as stress, anxiety or embarrassment. This leads to coping mechanisms such as rubbing the neck, which not only serves to reduce tension, but provide a barrier as the elbow points forward toward the source of the discomfort. Other barrier signals include averted gaze and closed postures achieved by folding the arms and crossing knees.

Crowded situations are frequently met in major cities and urban environments. When too much is happening around them, people experience "stimulus overload" and protect themselves by shutting out information. Trying to process all the available information is too stressful, and so low-priority inputs are disregarded. You can see this clearly when people walk down crowded streets. They pay no

43

◄ **Cultural and sex differences** *in distance behavior.* TOP *Women in a street in Rome engage in a physically much closer conversation than northern Europeans, and especially northern European men, would find comfortable.* BOTTOM *A more typically male, northern European pattern appears as members of a British charities committee mingle at a reception.*

▲ **In a crowded Amsterdam street** *a mother and daughter ignore the press of strangers about them and take a moment to exchange affection. Private displays of emotion in public – especially between adults – stimulate others to create extra space around the participants. Those who are not involved seek distance to emphasize their noninvolvement.*

attention to the drunk who shouts abuse at them and can even fail to recognize friends as they walk past. On busy subway trains, passengers avoid receiving signals from each other by looking out of the window or at the floor. Faces are expressionless, reflecting the desire to minimize any chances of becoming involved in interaction.

Stimulus overload significantly reduces social encounters. Compared with people who live in rural areas, city dwellers spend less of their time in conversations. While the small-town general store is a place for a chat, the city department store is just a building in which to buy things.

In crowded settings, people use "streaming" to avoid bumping into each other. Pedestrian traffic in streets splits into two parallel lanes, each going in opposite directions. Usually, these streams keep to the right, even in countries where the rule of the road is to drive on the left. This tendency to pass on the right also occurs in corridors. When two people approach head on, they will each move to the right giving the other room to pass. Attempts to pass on the left usually result in those embarrassing little dances, when neither person knows which way to move.

Passing movements such as these in high density conditions are usually accompanied by barrier signals, and there are differences between men and women. When men

■ **Coping with too little space**. TOP LEFT *Sharing a narrow seat in a subway train, two passengers each pretend that the other does not exist. They face and lean away from each other and ensure that eye contact* *does not involve them with anyone. Immobile faces signal an unwillingness to interact.* TOP RIGHT *The same strategies, as far as possible, are adopted by Japanese commuters packing themselves into the last* *available spaces in a Tokyo train.* BOTTOM *Three commuters in London, England, each find their own solution. One man buries himself behind a newspaper. Another defocuses his eyes and slips into a world* *of his own. The third uses a facial expression that positively signals unwillingness to be involved.'*

When too much is happening around them, people experience "stimulus overload" and protect themselves by shutting out information. Trying to process all the available information is too stressful, and low-priority inputs are disregarded.

are about to pass other people, they usually stretch out their right hand and move forward facing towards them. Women place their left arm across their chest and turn away from the other person as they pass.

In crowded public settings we practice "privacy regulation." During an experiment conducted in a civil defense shelter, for example, people tended to move around the shelter only when they had to go to the lavatory or to comply with shelter drill. Over time, the pace of the subjects'

movements slowed down further. Most people sat still, reducing the risk of coming into physical contact with others. Finally, some reacted by withdrawing from all social interaction – a process known as "cocooning."

The fun of being in a crowd

Reactions to crowding are not always negative and defensive. Quite often, we positively choose to be part of a crowd and welcome an involvement in close proximity with others. At football games, the theater, parades or open-air concerts, we are content to allow strangers physical contact. The effect of being in such a crowd can also transform behavior in other ways.

Emotions can be heightened in crowds and a feeling can become contagious. In many cases this emotional arousal leads to enjoyment, as when sharing in the exhilaration of seeing your team win. In other circumstances, however, it can erupt into violence and rioting.

Another effect produced by crowds is the reduction of personal constraints. In a mass of people, individuals can achieve a high degree of anonymity. For this reason, and because of the increased level of emotion, even those who are normally very meek can behave out of character. This can facilitate an enjoyable release from normal inhibitions, but also opens the way for manipulation. When emotions are high, and personal restraints low, it is possible to introduce models for behavior that would normally be rejected, and mass religious and political rallies can produce changes of attitude that would not be achieved in other circumstances. **PM**

■ **Crowd excitement** *can help us to express ourselves in ways that are impossible in smaller-scale interactions. Emotions are aroused and a feeling can become infectious. We achieve a high degree of anonymity that allows us to shed inhibitions. Great enjoyment can result, but the mood can easily be exploited by skilled manipulators.*

Using Body Language

IF YOU have ever been to southern Italy, from Naples down to Reggio di Calabria and Sicily, you may have been confused by a basic gesture used in the region. Ask a waiter for something which is not on the menu, and he is likely to respond not with a shake of the head, but with a quick upward head *toss*, often accompanied by a little "tsskk" sound. Once you get used to it, this small piece of body language is perfectly understandable, but it can cause confusion at first.

Why do people in the south of Italy have a gesture for "no" that is quite different from what Italians use in the north? Two thousand five hundred years ago, the area south of Naples was part of *Magna Graecia*, the ancient Greek world whose economic and cultural force was felt all around the Mediterranean. The Greeks were eventually ousted from Italy by the Romans, but along with their temples and palaces they left behind the "head toss." The spoken language changed quickly and today there are very few remnants of Greek in the local dialects. But this particular aspect of body language remains, linking the modern inhabitants of southern Italy with those in Greece, Turkey, Bulgaria and other regions of that once widespread culture.

Words change, and the way we speak can alter over just one or two generations. The way we use our bodies to communicate, however, is much more deeply ingrained. Like all animals, we signal to each other, and some of the signals may even be innate, meaning the same to any human anywhere. Most signals are learned, and they vary with culture, but not as much as spoken languages do. These include seemingly spontaneous displays of emotion and attitude, deliberate conventional gestures and innumerable body movements that we use to make our speech more effective. So fundamental is the contribution of the body language – also called "nonverbal communication" – that we rely heavily on it to understand not just foreigners, but our nearest neighbors and kin.

Getting messages across

Asked what someone has said, we still usually paraphrase the *words* they have used and leave it at that. Ignoring body language in this way does not matter, because it usually projects the same message as the one we say in words. Body language aids the communication process by providing emphasis and punctuation and sometimes by introducing a degree of redundancy. For example, you may say to a waiter in a restaurant that you have received two bowls of salad when you specifically asked for only one by holding up a single finger to

▲ **Physical self-expression**. Just as song and verse extend the expressiveness of the human voice and the spoken word, so dance and gymnastics make a creative extension of body language. As with poetic words, the form of a piece of body poetry may greatly outweigh in importance the content of any message that is conveyed. Dance, especially in the East, sometimes gives precise meanings to stylized movements of limbs, trunk, head and facial features, but we also respond to elegant deployment of the body simply because it arrests the eye.

▲ **An attitude of careful attention** takes more than words to express. You need to put the right tone into your voice and the right expression into your face, hands and posture. We are more conscious of our reliance on body language when trying to cope in a foreign tongue, but our reliance is almost as great even when speaking our native language.

Body Language **Voice**

Words

■ *Research identifies words as a minor contributor to the communication of attitudes. Voice qualities reveal much more about what we think and feel. Most important of all is body-language, especially facial expression and patterns of eye contact. Posture also conveys attitude, as can "leakage" through anxious movements of the hands and other parts of the body (see Ch14). We use touch to amplify expressions of sympathy or affection and sometimes of aggression (see Ch10), and even the distance at which we stand or sit from one another can convey an attitude (see Ch3).*

Before we speak, our gestures, postures and facial expressions are already broadcasting messages to those around us. And while we are speaking, they continue to do so, usefully clarifying what we say – or perhaps contradicting us in tell-tale ways.

accompany your complaint. There can be little justification for further misunderstanding.

However, there are also cases where body language contradicts the verbal message. A person says one thing and allows nonverbal communication to say something quite different. Which do we believe?

Studies have shown that in many cases, we trust the body language more than what a person actually says. In one experiment facial, verbal and vocal signals were combined in inconsistent ways. Negative vocal signals, for example, such as a hostile tone of voice, were deliberately combined with pleasant phrases, or a positive facial signal might accompany a negative verbal message. Subjects in the study were asked what they thought was the real attitude communicated. Weighting the variations in subjects' reactions to different combinations, investigators calculated that they relied only 7 percent on the actual words used. They relied 38 percent on such features as tone of voice and pace of speech. Most importantly, the remaining 55 percent was conveyed by facial expression and other body language. We show attitudes such as liking or disliking not by what we

actually say but by the way we say it and the expressions that accompany our speech.

Further studies have shown similar results for the communication of inferior and superior attitude. You might say things that sound quite humble and unassuming, but if body language conflicts with this message, people will perceive you in quite a different way. A haughty posture, coupled with oblique and infrequent glances will make you appear to take on an air of superiority no matter how much you might protest to the contrary.

Sometimes people feel obliged to refuse a generous offer out of politeness. If someone offers you a lift home, you might say "Oh, that's very kind, but I can get a taxi." As you decline the invitation, however, your nonverbal behavior may signal acceptance, even to the extent of a positive head nod and a facial expression that indicates your pleasure at the prospect. It is for this reason that your friend is likely to press the offer once more. Part of social skill is being able to recognize the occasions where such incongruities exist and respond accordingly. Most people would be disappointed if their first polite refusals were taken at face value.

We all meet situations in which our powers of communication are stretched. Adding easy-to-interpret body language to our words makes it easier for people to understand us. Often no amount of words will make up for absent or inappropriate nonverbal communication.

Body-language skills

Body language has been the subject of intense research by social psychologists in recent decades. Interest has been maintained not simply by academic curiosity but by a realization of the direct practical implications of research findings. Today, many people are being helped by social skills training (see *Ch* 15) which includes a significant focus

■ **Body-language cues** *tell us how close people are prepared to be emotionally, how relaxed they are with each other and how much they interest each other. ABOVE LEFT The postures and facial expressions of these lawyers in conference with a Rockville Maryland judge show a relaxed but calmly interested response to his words. Distance and a physical barrier keep intimacy at a low level. LEFT Tension, activity and intimacy are all higher at this dinner table, but the acceptance of intimacy – signaled by forward lean and intense gaze – appears one-sided. So does the interest shown by these cues and by facial expression.*

Body-language skills are indispensable to anyone who wishes or needs to assert their presence and point of view effectively. The secret lies in an ability to integrate appropriate cues of the right intensity and be responsive to your audience.

on body language. Managers and salesmen are put through intensive courses on appropriate styles of body language in order to increase their effectiveness. Social workers and those in the caring professions are taught how to adapt their postures and other signals in order to establish a closer rapport with their clients. Assertiveness training courses available to the public offer to help to improve effectiveness in everyday encounters (see p126).

The research that supports social skills training breaks nonverbal communications into several distinct "channels" of communication – for example, the face, the eyes in particular, posture and body-orientation, the use of distance and space, touch, nonverbal characteristics of vocal communication (such as tone of voice) and even personal appearance. Within each of these channels, researchers have tried to identify specific typical problems of nonverbal communication and to give a detailed account of the communications skills that we can usefully improve or acquire (see box opposite).

Communication channels provided by the different parts of the body do not act in isolation from one other. The really powerful messages are given off through combinations of signals, each expressing the same meaning. These combined signals are known as "cues," and although we sometimes respond to an individual nod of the head or a special kind of smile, in normal encounters it is the basic cues that shape our responses.

One particularly powerful combination of body signals is the "immediacy cue," which communicates our liking or disliking of another person. Here the extent to which we touch someone, the distance at which we position ourselves and the direction in which we lean are coupled with the degree of eye contact we maintain in the interaction.

48

"Relaxation cues" comprise types of arm and leg position, the angle at which the body reclines and the degree of relaxation of hands and neck. These change according to the status relationship between two people, the higher status being signaled by the greater degree of bodily relaxation and an asymmetry in leg and arm positions.

The "activity cue" signals one person's responsiveness to another. Various features of body language, including rocking movements, swiveling of the trunk, gesticulation and foot movements, together with facial expressiveness and speech rate, are combined to provide this broad type of message. Responsive people send these signals with great frequency.

These cues are important throughout an encounter. Active responses to each other by the participants are necessary to keep the encounter going – if you are unresponsive it will occur to others that there is little point trying to interact with you. But if you respond too actively they may feel overwhelmed. Immediacy cues have to be

◄ **A moment of triumph** *is marked by a spontaneous chin-chuck and shoulder embrace, as one French politician congratulates another and celebrates their joint success. Not only are words unnecessary: by themselves they could not easily convey, as the gesture does, the intensity of emotion being felt. In other contexts, this gesture is in some danger of being read as an act of over-familiarity.*

▲ **Driving home a point** *can seem that much more urgent when your audience seems to have no idea what you are talking about. Forcefulness, however, is usually the wrong tactic in such a situation. It may serve only to numb listeners into a sense of mute resistance.*

A SUMMARY OF BODY-LANGUAGE SKILLS

FACIAL EXPRESSION

Vary expression to fit changes in the emotions expressed. Make polite and friendly uses of the "social smile" but do not overdo. Use facial expression to show interest as listener and to be interesting – and qualify statements – as speaker.

Avoid underuse of facial expressions – especially a blank face, which may be seen as showing hostility or lack of interest. Avoid fixed, frozen expressions that do not vary with changes in the situation. Weak expressions that are badly timed and appear and fade quickly may appear insincere. Failure to use expressions to accompany your own speech, or to reflect what the speaker is saying, may also convey lack of interest. (See Ch 9.)

EYE CONTACT

A general rule is to look a lot, but with fairly long glances and definite looks away. Look more while listening, less while talking. Look away when taking up the conversation. Look back when handing it back. Add a lot of looking to smiling when conveying warmth. Add a lot of looking to a serious expression when trying to gain control of a situation. Avoiding eye contact, at one extreme, conveys nervousness and lack of confidence. Staring, at the other

extreme, conveys hostility and overintrusiveness. (See Ch 8.)

DISTANCE

Keep an appropriate distance and adjust immediacy cues to compensate when too close or too far away. Too much eye contact, forward lean and close proximity can give an overintrusive or domineering impression. Too much distance, too little eye contact, and turning away from the other can convey a cold impression. (See Ch 3.)

TOUCH

A brief touching on the hand, arm, shoulder or other conventionally accepted area of a person's body can convey warmth and emotional support, or it can be used to guide them or draw their attention to an important point that you are making.

Sudden and uninvited touching of a conventionally unacceptable part of another's body is too intimate. Too many touches to control direction and attention make you seem domineering. (See Ch 10.)

USE OF VOICE

Aim for a moderate volume, resonant tone, varied pitch and varied pace. High volume, a booming tone and an over-

varied or low pitch make you seem domineering. Low volume, a thin tone, and unvarying pitch and pace – especially a slow pace – convey a submissive, depressed attitude. Stuttering and some – but not all – other speech disturbances convey anxiety. (See Chs 12, 14.)

POSTURE

For an attentive posture, lean forward with a straight spine and with arms open. Turn toward the other. For a relaxed posture, lean back with head up and let your limbs take asymmetrical positions.

Avoid slumped shoulders, bowed head, folded arms and deflated chest. Do not turn your body away. These cues convey submissiveness, depression and lack of interest. (See Ch 5.)

GESTURE

Use gestures of emphasis to make your speech livelier and easier to follow. Also use gestures that clarify meaning (such as pointing), and those that convey meanings of their own (such as nodding to show agreement).

Do not overuse gesture when trying to secure a speaking turn. This appears aggressive. Too much fidgeting and hand-wringing conveys anxiety. Foot-tapping conveys irritation. (See Ch 4.)

APPEARANCE

To create a positive impression dress to conform to the standards that will apply to the situations you expect to meet. Looking attractive is an advantage in almost any situation. (See Ch 6.) PT

▶ Forceful gesturing takes a central place in the orator's repertoire of special speaking skills. When an audience wants a high level of involvement with a speaker, the distance at which he must position himself in order to address them presents an important problem. It can be overcome partly by the eloquence of words – especially words that strike an emotional chord. Probably more important in striking the right chord is a stirring tone of voice. In addition, emotional distance between audience and speaker can be reduced by powerful emphatic uses of the arms and hands and of a body that leans into each gesture. Distance from your audience can also be an advantage: men of physically small stature – considerably handicapped against making an impression in one-to-one encounters – seem literally to grow in stature as they address large gatherings.

49

adjusted as the encounter progresses to reflect the right level of intimacy, and relaxation cues to reflect what we discover about each other's status, or about how threatening or safe we are for each other.

The cues are especially important at the beginnings and endings of encounters – in the rituals of greeting and parting (see *Ch 11*). The degree of immediacy we bring to the ritual shows how intimate we each think our relationship is. Our activity shows how much it matters to us. Our degree of relaxation how much respect it involves.

Baton gestures

An important part of the activity that our body language contributes to social interaction consists of gestures that beat time to what we or another is saying. These "baton movements" are usually gestures of the hands and arms, but we can also add rhythmic nods of the head or shift from one foot to the other at points of emphasis, and speakers often put their whole body behind an emphatic pointing, fist-banging or thigh-slapping gesture.

These baton movements help to place emphasis on what

is being said and add a kind of punctuation to verbal communication. They can also act as clarifiers and remove ambiguities which are often present in everyday conversations. For example, "I'll speak to *you* first" means little, when there is more than one listener, unless accompanied by a well-directed nod of the head or a pointing gesture. Body movements and gestures of this kind can also maintain a rhythm in speaking which helps to hold the interest of the other person. What you are saying can be "projected" toward your conversation partner by making open-palm hand movements. Similarly, downward baton gestures can add specific emphasis to a point you are trying to make, while at the same time indicating the kind of mood in which it is hoped that the point will be received – with calm, rather than with alarm, indignation or enthusiasm. This is the hand movement to use when you are emphasizing that you do not want people to become overexcited by what you have to say.

Another useful gesture is the "precision grip," which involves small pincer movements of thumb and forefinger and steady movements of the pursed hand. It can be used to

HANDS AND ARMS IN ACTION

■ *Baton movements keep time as we speak. They are usually thought of as movements of the arms and hands, but we can also keep time by the way we shift our feet, nod our heads and sway our bodies. When we blink, we even do this in time with our speech. Both listeners and speaker keep time, creating an "interactional synchrony" that seems to be essential to having a sense of involvement. Arm and hand movements are particularly important for drawing attention to points of emphasis and for suggesting the speaker's attitude about what is being said. We are often conscious of "waving our hands about" when we speak, but seldom of how much we say with them. Distinctive hand postures show how we feel about what we are saying.*

1 *Arms fly out in the emphatic opening sequences of a chance encounter in the street. Two people are now locked into a joint rhythm.*

2 *A shadowy finger stabs across the wall as a public figure stresses his main point.*

3 *A palm-up baton gesture indicates the spirit in which listeners are to take what is being said – it is not to be underestimated.*

4 *In a characteristically French gesture of emphasis, a speaker demonstrates that the opinion he expresses is one he does not hold lightly.*

5 *One Englishman indicates to another the delicate intricacy of the concept he wishes to convey.*

6 *An American attempting to make his point precisely reaches out for an illusive precision.*

1	2	3
4	5	6

50

Baton movements help us to punctuate our speech, and to place emphasis on the words and phrases that matter. They can also remove ambiguities. Without supportive body movements, our speech can be dull, and attempts to interest others can fail.

emphasize a delicate point, or to encourage a concern for accuracy and truth. Various kinds of pointing can communicate hostility while clenched grips can signal a solid determination to achieve a particular goal.

The way to become familiar with these and other baton gestures is to watch skilled speakers in conversation with each other. The ability to establish rapport, develop interpersonal bonds or establish your influence comes not simply by knowing what to say but also by knowing how to say it. Without supportive body movements, speech can become dull, and attempts to interest others can fail.

The extent to which speech and gesture are closely bound together is most noticeable when people are speaking on the telephone. Even though the person on the other end of the line clearly cannot see the body movements and gestures, it is difficult to talk without making them. In one study conducted in Italy, psychologists obtained film of Italians in telephone booths. One clip shows a man holding the receiver in his left hand and gesticulating vigorously with his right. As the conversation becomes more agitated, he tucks the receiver under his chin in order to free both hands for gestural purposes, beating the air with highly expressive baton movements. Italians say that the way to silence an Italian is to tie his hands behind his back.

Body movements, however, can also be an obstacle to successful interaction. This is because they can reveal your nervousness and anxiety about the encounter in which you are engaged. The symptoms are easily recognized: hand-clasping movements, rubbing the palms and curling the fingers of one hand around the other.

One of the first things people are taught on presentation skills courses is to control distracting signals of this kind. They interfere with the presentation, thus making the content more difficult to follow, and the anxiety which underlies them can spread to other members of the group.

The solution is deliberately to replace the nervous movements with more expressive gestures. Anxious signals are nearly always what are known as "proximal" movements – they are directed toward your own body. Opposite "distal"

51

movements, directed away from the body, involve others in what you are saying, and making them can actually reduce your own level of anxiety.

Body language as punctuation

Speech is a more or less continuous stream. There are no verbal equivalents of the commas and other punctuation that make the written word so much easier to understand. Small-scale gestures using the hands and head occur at the ends of sentences. Larger units of speech, equivalent to a written paragraph, are accompanied by larger shifts of the body, particularly the legs and torso. Even bigger shifts mark the end of one person's utterance, signaling that it is time for the other person to speak. In this way an "interactional

synchrony" is achieved and the communication process is made much clearer and more efficient.

An ideal setting in which to observe the way body language punctuates speech is in a television newscast. The announcer passes through a number of distinctive and clearly identifiable topics and will use shifts of posture to mark out the transition from one to the next. Individual announcers have their own styles. One may join hands with the palm of one hand over the back of the other, while another interlocks fingers. Such hand positions are typically taken up just after the beginning of a new topic and occur at no other point in the presentation.

In normal conversation, it is much more difficult to observe this kind of body language, because it is often

▲ **Attracting the opposite sex.**
Two people dressed and coiffured to accentuate their sex roles also use body-language to create a hoped-for impression. He stands at an angle turning his head more than his body,

expressing an attitude of male dominance. Elbows held away from his body accentuate both the openness of his attitude toward the girl and the size of his body, while enhancing his expression of dominance. She

pulls her limbs toward herself, emphasizing the smallness of her body, and she leans back in a mainly open, submissively inviting posture. The smiles are recognizably smiles of attraction.

Body language provides conversational equivalents of commas and other punctuation. Small-scale gestures using the hands and head occur at the ends of sentences. Units equivalent to a written paragraph are marked by shifting legs or torso.

difficult to notice exactly when a topic change is taking place. People may backtrack to topics they have already discussed or jump forward to new topics. It may not even be clear whether there *is* a specific topic. Careful observations, however, have shown that people show more shifts of posture when introducing new information into a conversation than at other times. Gestures and changes of position typical of this moment include holding up one hand, pointing with one hand, drawing back the legs (if seated), raising one foot, shifting in your seat.

In successful encounters, interactional synchrony involves listeners as well as speaker. When movements of one person are reflected back by the other, a greater degree of rapport is possible than when body language is totally one-sided. This synchronization has been termed a "gestural dance" and some research indicates that movements may be in time with each other down to an accuracy of fractions of a second (although other research has failed to confirm observations at this time-scale).

This "dance" of course, normally occurs without conscious effort. It is, however, possible to become more sensitive to the speed and pattern of other people's body movements. This can be useful especially when a conversation fails to flow or other social obstacles seem to be in the way. By matching your style of body language to that of the other person you are much more likely to establish a relaxed and easy-going encounter.

Cultural body language

Not all body language is impervious to cultural change.

Some can change significantly over one or two generations or as a result of new cultural influences. A study conducted in New York City examined the gestures of Jewish and Italian immigrants, both of those who had been assimilated into American culture and of those who were striving to retain their cultural and religious identity. The differences between the assimilated and the nonassimilated groups were very notable.

Italian and Jewish gestures are distinctive. The traditional Jewish style is described as "ideographic." The hands, for example, trace out in the air the direction of thought patterns. Gestures reflect the general structure and progress of the conversation.

Italians, on the other hand, use gestures in a "physiographic" way. Southern Italians, in particular, use gestures to *illustrate* speech. Southern Italian hands are like metaphorical pencils while Jewish hands are as pointers used to link one part of the conversation to another. Consequently, the gestures of southern Italians allow you to follow the meaning of a conversation without speaking much Italian. In contrast, a full understanding of Hebrew or Yiddish is necessary in order to understand what is being expressed in a traditional Jewish conversation.

These differences between the two cultural groups were most apparent in the traditional communities – among Jews observed in the synagogues and yeshivas (schools for Talmudic studies) and among Italians in the district of New York known as Little Italy. In Jews and Italians who have assimilated to an American lifestyle, virtually all of these distinctions have disappeared.

In some cases, assimilated Americans still maintain contact with traditional groups. Then their body language shows a "bilingual" character. An Italian businessman in

■ **The compulsiveness of body language.** *Even when the person we are talking with is not in a position to see our gestural signals, the tie between speech and body language tends to remain as strong as ever. By assuming a hand-on-hip posture, the caller on the left bolsters her morale and reflects an assertive attitude toward the other person, yet this transmits no message. Nor can the hand of the caller on the far right convey the sweet reasonableness of what he is proposing. And no doubt the caller on the right, caressing the telephone cord, would be touching her man affectionately if he were only present.*

New York, for example, may normally act and speak like an assimilated American and show few expressive gestural movements. When returning home to relatives in Naples, however, or even at meetings with Italian groups in the United States, his style of nonverbal behavior is likely to change quite markedly.

Gestures with meanings

The rules of spoken language give us the power of speech by making it possible to utter sounds in a way that will be recognized as distinct acts of communication, for example, of *stating* that Paris is the capital of France, of *promising* to meet a friend in Paris, or of *warning* someone not to interfere with you. Acts of stating, promising, warning and so on performed in speaking are known to linguists and logicians as *illocutionary* acts.

Body language, too gives us the power to perform distinct acts of communication. These go beyond mere emphatic gesturing. Body language can even supplant acts usually performed in speaking. An act of giving (a complicated communication involving the abstract concept of a transfer of rights in personal property) does not need even the words "Take this." You can simply hand the item over with a smile and a bit of a bow. A nod by itself is an act of agreement – saying "yes" is redundant. Illocutionary acts such as saying

Gesture goes beyond mere emphasis. "Emblematic gestures" can supplant communication acts usually performed with words. Each culture has developed its own repertoire of emblems, many with original associations that have now been long forgotten.

"I salute you" in fact use words to *imitate* gestures.

Meaningful gestures such as the salute and a shake of the head are known as "emblems." Each culture has its own repertoire of emblematic gestures, some of which have very distant origins. The "middle-finger jerk," so common in the United States, was a sign of abuse much used by the Romans, who knew it as the *digitus impudicus*. In Britain, a similar abusive sentiment is communicated by the palm-back V-sign, which elsewhere in the world is used to indicate victory.

The "thumbs up" sign generally indicates in Europe and North America that all is well. In Greece and Turkey, however, it symbolizes anal penetration and is considered to be very insulting. So too is an open palm held facing toward a person with the fingers extended. It is known as "the hand of Moutza" and represents an ancient practice that most modern-day users of the gesture know nothing of. In Byzantine times, over 1,500 years ago, ordinary people used to participate in the humiliation of criminals and other prisoners by pressing handfuls of dung into their faces as they were paraded through the streets. You should take great care when ordering five drinks in a Greek bar.

▲ **The Threatening Monster gesture** is usually performed in fun, as here, for the benefit of a third party and at the expense of an unwitting accomplice – the "fall guy." Or could this tennis player be giving vent to secret feelings of real frustration in her relationship with her coach – possibly with her rate of progress – as she mimes behind his back? As with others of its kind, this emblematic gesture is an almost literal representation of a particular image or event.

■ **Very different meanings** can be conveyed by similar emblematic gestures in different countries. A notorious example is the Greek Moutza gesture (car-sticker version, right) – to a Greek a gross insult – which closely resembles a five-item-order signal.

Other emblem gestures include movements to indicate direction and also signals used to beckon and bid farewell. There are again a number of cross-cultural differences in the way these gestures are performed. People in Mediterranean countries, for example, use a movement where the palm of the hand faces downwards, while elsewhere the signal is made with the palm facing upwards. The Spanish beckon is often mistaken by Americans for a farewell signal, resulting in considerable confusion.

A linguistics of the body

Not all communications psychologists agree with his approach, but the American psychologist Ray Birdwhistell has attempted to construct a "linguistics" of nonverbal communications called "kinesics." It investigates how we build up meaningful units of body language from the simplest body movements.

Linguists who study the spoken language identify basic sounds called "phonemes." In languages that are phonetically spelled, there are just as many phonemes in the spoken language as there are letters of the alphabet in the written language, but English, for example, has 36 phonemes and an alphabet of only 26 letters. (For example, it uses "t" and "h" together to spell two phonemes – one voiced and one unvoiced – that most other languages using the Roman alphabet lack. It has five letters for 13 vowel sounds.) From phonemes we build up morphemes – units of meaning, such as "re," "place" and "ed" – from which we build up words such as "replaced."

Birdwhistell's kinesics identifies basic units of movement – "kinemes" – such as the four basic nose kinemes: wrinkled, compressed nostrils, one nostril flared, both nostrils flared. From kinemes we build up "kinemorphs" – expressions and gestures – that convey meanings. His observations in the United States led him to the conclusion that the vast variety of nonverbal messages that Americans know how to send and how to recognize are built up from only 50–60 kinemes. **PM**

▲ **A double emblematic gesture.** *Literally standing in a river (the Banga, in India) is a straightforward emblem of the washing away of sins, while opposed fingertips make an emblem of pious submission and supplication to a divine power. Although in this instance* *not directed toward a physically present recipient, the fingertip gesture reenacts a gesture used through the ages by feudal subjects to appease and plead for the indulgence of a feudal lord.*

▲ **The required response** *is produced by this small boy's emblematic gesture with its unmistakable message of "Make way, I'm coming through!" as he speeds along the sidewalk, on the outskirts of Las Vegas.*

Noticing Posture

PARENTS tell children and adolescents to stand or sit straight, not to slouch or stoop. They hope to teach them to project a better appearance – to use "the personal-appearance channel of communication" more effectively – just as they would by teaching good grooming and neatness. Partly, the postures that parents favor reflect the fact that some body shapes (see *Ch 6*) create a better impression than others: a straight body looks taller and slimmer than a stooped one. But more importantly, posture creates an impression of *attitude*.

Without necessarily being fully conscious of it, school-teachers and prospective employers base personal assessments partly on how interested, respectful and open to their own ideas a child or prospective employee looks, and these are three areas in particular where posture communicates loudly. Postural cues even help people to form impressions of who likes them and who does not.

The postures that reveal these attitudes, however, are not simply labels of personality or character, they are reactions to particular situations, events and people. Unlike grooming and style of dress, posture can change from moment to moment during a social encounter. Using it skillfully as a communications tool means understanding its versatility.

Showing interest and agreement

The illustrated sequence shown here records the results of experiments in which university students were filmed while watching talks on a television monitor. The students knew nothing of the purposes of the experiment except that they were to report, in the case of some talks, whether they found them interesting or boring, and in the case of the others whether they agreed or disagreed with what was said. Their unconscious body-language responses to the films were recorded as the postural expression of these attitudes.

When interested, the students spontaneously leaned forward and drew back their legs in greater alertness. When bored, they adopted more lethargic postures of leaning back, dropping the head, leaning it to one side, supporting it on one hand and stretching out the legs.

Disagreement and agreement showed a parallel between openness of attitude and openness of posture. Disagreement was shown by a vigilant posture, with head erect, arms folded and legs tightly crossed (so that the lower knee was visible). Agreement was shown by a more relaxed leaning to one side. It was as though the students were responding defensively to a threat when they heard talks that they disagreed with, while allowing access to a speaker whose views they accepted.

Asked what postures they would use to convey interest or boredom if they wanted to, randomly selected students were unable to give explicit answers. However, they accurately identified these postures when shown the drawings based on actual postures adopted by students who watched the recorded talks.

Earlier, while watching the talks, some students showed attempts to control their displays of boredom, but these attempts were confined to head posture. In one experiment the students were alone. They were inattentive during boring extracts, turning their heads away from the television monitor. In another experiment, when the experimenter was present with each student, this inattentiveness did not occur – presumably because the students were concerned about offending the experimenter.

This is comparable to "nonverbal leakage" (see *Ch 14*). According to the theory of nonverbal leakage, people control their facial expressions better than their bodies when lying, but fidgeting, increased self-touching and apologetic gestures commonly "leak" their feelings of

◄ **Postures of agreement and disagreement**. *When they disagree with what is being said, people tend to have "closed" postures – holding head and trunk straight and folding their arms. If they are seated, they are likely to cross their legs above the knee. A more neutral attitude is conveyed by folding hands on your lap and crossing your legs at the knee. When people agree, they are more likely to have "open" postures – leaning head and trunk to one side and leaving their legs uncrossed.*

How you hold your body can reveal feelings about events – how interested you are – and about people – how much you like them. It can show whether you agree with an idea, and it can help you to take your place in a hierarchy.

insincerity. Controlling the direction in which you turn your head when bored seems to have a parallel function to putting on a sincere expression when lying, while leaning back, dropping the head and supporting it on one hand seem to be "leakages."

Explicit awareness of the postural cues for interest and agreement can help to overcome the gap between reactions you want to communicate and the reactions you *can* communicate on occasions when you may need to show these attitudes – as a candidate at a job interview, for example, or when trying to give encouragement to a respected but boring speaker. Interviewers themselves – including personnel officers, counselors and doctors seeing their patients – are well advised to avoid postures of disagreement or boredom, as they are likely to discourage people from speaking freely. Interviewees are most likely to remember and openly divulge useful information about themselves when you adopt an attentive posture, combined with signals of agreement – not just nodding and smiling but arms unfolded and knees not crossed.

Even though we all seem to read these cues more easily than we can consciously produce them, an explicit awareness of them is also useful when we are gauging other people's reactions.

Taking in listeners' reactions is especially a problem in public speaking. At some prayer meetings and political rallies, sighs, shouts and spontaneous outbursts can be relied on for feedback in a similar way to the listener's "mmms" and "uh-huhs" of one-to-one conversation. The usual convention for listening to a talk, however, is to sit as silently as possible.

Even if the talk is informal, and listeners are supposed to interrupt with questions or objections, many people feel inhibited about intervening, especially when the group is large. Depending on distance and lighting, it may be impossible to see the fine details of facial expression and eye movement that normally inform us of reactions. However, audience posture, accurately read, can help a skilled speaker judge when to speed up, change topic, or otherwise heighten interest, or when to be more convincing.

■ Postures of interest and boredom. *RIGHT An interested listener typically leans forward with legs drawn back. When interest fades, the head begins to turn, while trunk and legs straighten. Then the head may begin to lean and require support by a hand. When completely bored, ABOVE people let their heads drop, and the body has a backward lean with legs stretched out. People who are concerned about what their bodies might be signaling try to lean forward.*

Even in one-to-one conversation or in small groups, you sometimes need to penetrate the polite reactions of listeners to be an effective speaker. Unconscious shifts in the positions of bodies and limbs can be the only early-warning signals available that you need to find something more interesting to say or need to overcome objections.

Showing and claiming respect

Orientation – the direction in which you point your body or parts of it, the head most especially – creates an impression of whom you are willing to give attention to and how much. Thus it can be a sign of respect. Obviously, if members of a group turn toward a leader – for example, if children pay attention to their teacher – then the leader can exert influence. What is less obvious is that the impression you create is affected by whether you orient both head and body toward the leader or just the head, and by how you hold your arms.

In a study of dominance, people were asked to comment on a drawing that showed one person standing, one seated and another three standing in the background. When the background figures turned more toward the standing figure, the commenters had a stronger impression that he was their superior, someone important who was taking initiatives. The effect of head orientation was more marked than that of body orientation.

As the background figures turned more toward the seated figure, the commenters had a stronger impression that he was haughty, important and taking initiatives. Again, the effect of head orientation was more marked than that of body orientation. The orientation of the background figures had no effect on how they themselves were rated; they were consistently seen as inferior.

Perception of dominance also appears to be affected by arm posture. People were shown a picture of six figures holding their arms in different ways. The figures with arm positions that made them appear bigger tended to be seen as dominant, while those with arm positions that made them appear smaller – for example, putting one or both hands behind the back – were seen as submissive.

The naturalist Charles Darwin proposed that making yourself smaller can appease and inhibit human aggression, and his observations have been supported in a recent study of fights between boys. The researchers examined the behavior of the child under attack just before the aggression ceased in a number of fights. In a highly significant proportion the victim made his body look small at this point – for example, bowing the head, slumping the shoulders, lying motionless on the ground, kneeling or shoe-tying.

In another study, fights that were ended by the interven-

◀ **Signs of affection.** *An open-arm posture suggests that an embrace would be welcome, and tilting head and body to one side is suggestive of laying them against another for comfort. Consciously or unconsciously, this posture signals a request, and it can strongly affect the mood of the person who receives the message.*

The direction you turn your head shows whom you like or respect – who has your attention. When you turn your body as well, this reinforces the signal. Liking is clearest when our postures match, dominance and respect when they do not.

tion of a third person were investigated. A significant proportion of these interventions occurred when the antagonist ignored some kind of appeasement display by the child under attack that made his body look small. Children shown videotapes of these fights were able to predict accurately whether and when an act of intervention was likely to occur, but they were not able to identify the specific cues on which their judgment was based.

Posture provides a system by which conflicts can be resolved or avoided through signaling acceptance of another's dominance. If you do not want to challenge someone's authority, or do not want to reveal a challenge before the moment is right, avoid expansive arm gestures and turn both head and body in a show of attention, rather than head alone. However, when you do need to assert authority, hands on hips and attention that is confined to turning the head will help to show who you think you are.

Showing whom you like

When people are equal, paying attention is a sign of liking rather than respect, and, once again, it matters whether you turn only your head, or both your head and your body. One experiment on liking involved pairs of American women students meeting and having a conversation with a third student, who was in fact a confederate of the experimenter. For half the pairs, the confederate turned her head and body mainly toward one of the students. For the other pairs, the confederate turned her head mainly toward one, with her body turned mainly toward the other.

The students were asked after the conversation to rate the confederate's attitude both to themselves and to the other member in the pair. They judged her attitude as significantly more positive to themselves only when she turned both head and body toward them. They judged her attitude as significantly more positive to the other person even when she turned only her head mainly toward her. In this case, they did not seem to notice the orientation of the body.

It has also been suggested that the direction a person's toes are pointing is a clue to whom they like (see *Ch 14*).

Similarity of posture – called "postural congruence" or "postural echo" can also signal liking. It often appears when people have similar views or roles, while postural dissimilarity often indicates marked divergences in attitude or status. It is especially mirror-image postural echoes – where one person's left side is equivalent to the other's right – rather than identical postures, where right matches right and left matches left, that appear to be related to interpersonal rapport.

In experiments, observers shown videotapes of a psychotherapist and his client saw them as getting on better with each other when they adopted more similar postures. When students in a college seminar adopt more similar postures they rate the seminar more favorably.

In a series of simulated interviews, the interviewee – a trained actor – was asked to mimic the postures of only one of each pair of people interviewing him. The interviewers showed no awareness of the mimicry, nor did the mimicked interviewers rate the interviewee as more similar to them in his use of posture and gesture. But the mimicked interviewers did rate the interviewee more favorably. In particular, they considered that he "thought more like they did" and said that they "identified" with him.

This would suggest that postural echo can be used as a means of furthering a relationship, establishing a feeling of togetherness and common identity.   **P B**

◄ **Signs of dominance.** *The man on the right seems to be the boss. He has a much more pronounced hands-on-hips posture than the man at left and faces him more obliquely. The man in the middle— attracting the least attention from the others – has a clearly respectful posture, facing his superior straight on and making his body small by holding his arms behind his back.*

◄ **Signs of harmony.** *This pair presents almost a mirror image of each other, as though the several decades of their marriage have made them into alternative selves. Studies have shown not only that people echo each other's postures when they know and like one another, but that a stranger can use this fact as the basis of a technique for putting others at their ease.*

Assessing Appearances

TRY AS WE might to avoid hasty judgments, at first meetings we assess people by how they look. Body shape, facial features, hairstyle, dress and adornment all influence our impression and affect the way we react. By influencing our assessment of personality and character, they may even affect the way we at first interpret what the other person says and does.

We may find later, of course, that our first impressions were wrong – the apparently straight-laced matron might turn out to be a fun-loving lady with liberal attitudes, or the seemingly radical young man with long hair may be a trainee lawyer with quite conservative views.

But we deceive ourselves if we think we can postpone our opinions about others until all possible information is in, and we presume too much if we expect others to disregard *our* appearance. You need at least a rudimentary impression of a person to begin interacting at all – for example, a sense that they are safe to be with – and stereotyped images inevitably influence first encounters.

The shape of our bodies

In the 1950s the psychologist W. H. Sheldon proposed that people's characters or temperaments were closely related to the shape of their bodies. His work, in fact, seemed to confirm some aspects of folklore. Short, fat people are often assumed to be jolly, sociable types. Tall thin people tend to be seen rather as neurotic and detached.

Sheldon defined three basic body shapes, or what he called "somatotypes." The "endomorph" is the potentially fat pear-shape while at the other extreme the "ectomorph" is tall, thin and fragile. In between is the "mesomorph" – muscular and athletic, neither too fat nor too thin. If we

DOES BODY TYPE AFFECT OUR ATTITUDE?

▶ **The three "somatotypes"** *approximated by vacationers in the south of France. People have been found to associate the slim straight-up-and-down figure of the "ectomorph" LEFT with a stubborn, pessimistic and quiet temperament. The "mesomorphic" figure CENTER, with broader shoulders (related to* hips), *is associated with an adventurous, mature and self-reliant character, and the pear-shaped "endomorph" RIGHT is seen as warm-hearted, agreeable and trusting. Investigations into the consistency of these associations have been inconclusive.*

◀ **The slim and the not-so-slim.** *Westerners would see the slender figure as the more attractive, but in some cultures custom decrees (and experienced men consider) corpulent women to be more desirable. The well-larded female form has also been idealized during some periods of European history, as evidenced in the paintings of earlier times.*

By the appearances we cultivate, we usually attempt to enhance our physical attractiveness, for an attractive appearance often influences people profoundly in our favor. We also use personal appearance to help us act out our social roles.

show people silhouettes of these figures, they attribute very different characteristics to each type. Endomorphs are described as shorter, even when all the silhouettes are the same height. They are also seen as less good-looking, but talkative, warm-hearted, agreeable and trusting. The ectomorphs are viewed as younger, more ambitious, stubborn, pessimistic and quiet. Finally, the muscular mesomorphs seem strong, adventurous, mature and self-reliant.

The interesting point about this kind of study is that although the people making judgments have no information other than the shape of the bodies, they are quite prepared to give detailed character assessments. We must assume that in real-life encounters similar judgments are made and that people act in accordance with them. Even though other sources of information are always available, body build communicates ideas in a relentless way of its own.

FACIAL ENHANCEMENT

■ *The urge to improve facial appearance reflects the fact that the face is the most important visual focus in social interaction. As the chief channel for body-language signalling of emotions, attitudes and response at close quarters, the face cannot help attracting our attention, and hence it cannot help profoundly affecting our impressions. Impressions are affected even by facial features that coincidentally resemble common facial expressions (see Ch 9).*

The advantages of being physically attractive

Most people like to think that physical attractiveness is a fairly small consideration when judging others. Numerous psychological studies have shown, however, that we respond much more favorably to physically attractive people, regardless of their gender. For example, it has been recorded that defendants in court cases are less likely to receive harsh sentences if the jurors see them as attractive people – unless, that is, they are believed to have used their good looks to conduct the crime, for example in a confidence trick. Even worse, attractive children, both boys and girls, tend to get better grades in school and receive better reports from teachers than their less attractive peers, even though their abilities, when measured objectively, are on average about the same.

From very early on in life, physical attributes play an important role in the way others react to us and the way we perceive them. We may protest that we do not care about characteristics that are only skin-deep, but the weight of evidence suggests otherwise. Consider a group of children, one of whom is responsible for some minor damage or slight offence, and none will own up. Who is going to get the blame? Sadly, it is often the overweight boy or girl with buck teeth and spots. Rarely will it be the clean, attractive, blond-haired and blue-eyed one.

Physical attractiveness is an important factor in a wide range of other social situations. In job interviews, for example, when other considerations are about equal, the most attractive man or woman will tend to be recommended for the job. Having secured a post in this way the attractive person's work will tend to be more favorably evaluated than that of a less attractive colleague. While this effect is seen for both males and females, it is women in particular who

61

To fit in with your social role – to be accepted as a valid actor of your part – you usually have to look the part as well as act it. Clothes are a kind of uniform that unwritten rules stipulate according to the occasion and the circumstances.

are judged on their appearances, not only by their male colleagues, but also by their female peers.

The implications of these findings are quite clear. Making a little effort to improve your physical attractiveness can make a great difference to the ways in which others see and judge you. The billions of dollars spent on cosmetics, plastic surgery, hairstyling and skin conditioners are perhaps not completely wasted. And this concern for appearance is not merely an aberration of the modern consumer society: the Greek philosopher Aristotle declared over 2,000 years ago that "beauty is a better recommendation than any letter of introduction." His words seem still to be appropriate today in our very different society.

For men, the attractiveness of their female partner is probably more important than their own physical appearance. A man with a physically attractive companion is generally perceived as being of higher status, wealthier and more intelligent than one with an unattractive woman. Presumably, people reason that if a male who fails to match

up in attractiveness can gain the attentions of a good-looking female then he must have other significant qualities which interest her.

However, women do not make the same kind of impression through a partner. In one study, people were shown photographs of allegedly married couples. "Husbands" and "wives" were arbitrarily paired to produce a range of matches, including unattractive men with attractive "wives" and unattractive women with attractive "husbands." While the men with attractive females were seen more positively than when paired with unattractive partners, "wives" gained little from having an attractive "husband." Females, it seems, are judged solely on their own looks.

If all this sounds depressing to the majority who do not consider themselves to be physically attractive, there are certain findings which might be of consolation. Attractive-

▲ **A conservative style of dress** wins influence through its association with social status. Through its somber colors it reveals ambition. The right style for business is harder for a woman to achieve than for a man. Women must not look frivolous, but neither must they appear too unfeminine (see p29).

THE POWER OF DRESS

■ *People who wear clothes associated with high status tend to have much more influence than those wearing low-status clothes. The man in a dark business suit, for example, or the woman in a sober but stylish outfit, are most likely to receive help from strangers. A number of studies have been conducted in Britain and the United States which show that* *people dressed this way act as influential role-models. A paid actor dressed in high-status clothes violated "Don't Walk" signs at a pedestrian crossing. When he did so, a number of other waiting pedestrians followed him across. However, when the same actor dressed in manual worker's clothes, fewer people followed his violation.*

AMBITION AND COLOR

■ *Colors in clothing are subject to shifts in fashion. Research has shown there is almost always a strong link between preferred hues and the "achievement orientation" of the wearer. No matter what style of clothing they wear, ambitious people – especially those with a taste for moderate risks, long-range planning and tasks that involve clear criteria of success and failure – tend to choose rather somber hues. They opt for grays, dark blues or browns. Those who lack this kind of ambition usually prefer brighter colors, especially greens, reds, light blues and even orange. The relationship is stronger in men, but it applies to women as well. This preference* *also appears in the colors of automobiles owned by ambitious people. Cars such as BMWs and Mercedes are rarely found in pale green or light blue. These shades are much more common among the cheaper Japanese or domestically produced cars.*

Porsches are a less obvious example. They are expensive enough to announce the achievements of their owners – and sales figures record more silver and gray versions on the road than other colors – but the styling draws them into the sportscar class, and racy reds are also common, driven in many cases by young men whose families can afford to provide luxuries for them.

ness is just one of many considerations which people use in evaluating others. Think of someone you first met recently (say a month ago) and have not seen since. Whether or not they were good looking, you will probably remember them as much for pleasantness of manner or warmth of speech as for any visual attractiveness.

Also, while we might often admire more attractive people we actually choose to interact with those who are only as attractive as ourselves. One of the hazards of being exceptionally beautiful is that it can sometimes make others ill at ease because they are aware of their own physical inferiority.

Finally, many experiments have shown that the same individual may be perceived as attractive or unattractive depending on style of dress, manner, cleanliness and other personal characteristics. Being attractive is not just a matter of having classically beautiful features.

The signals we send with clothing

Clothes have two basic functions. They protect us from extremes of temperature, rain and wind and provide a degree of modesty by masking sexual signals. What is also important however, is the way clothing transmits messages about the wearer's personality, attitudes, social status, behavior and group allegiances. Some people are more sensitive to dress signals than others, but there are very few who fail to take clothes into account at all when forming first impressions.

63

▲ **Signs of group affiliation.**
TOP LEFT Two regulars at the Henley Regatta on the Thames in England display rival rowing colors in their caps and ties.
TOP RIGHT Japanese team sup-porters spell out their allegiance with their headwear.
BOTTOM LEFT The "Sisters of Perpetual Indulgence" advocate gay liberation in the Haight-Ashbury district of San Francisco.
BOTTOM RIGHT The school uniform establishes group identity at the Kamuzu Academy in Malawi.

Hair on the head is a focus of creativity and expression, providing strong gender signals, with all cultures adopting different styles for men's and women's hair. These signals are arbitrary, reflecting cultural stereotypes of our sex roles.

To fit in with your social role, for example – to be accepted as a valid actor of your part – you usually have to *look* the part as well as act the part. Some eccentric managers and executives are able to dress in jeans and baggy pullovers, but they are very much in a minority. Clothes in the professional world are a kind of uniform and unwritten rules prescribe certain standards and styles for everyone in the hierarchy. The way to be accepted is neither to underdress nor overdress. If following the rules can be combined with a little individuality and personal flair, then

the effect will be greater. Silk scarves, ties and other items that have no real function can communicate anything from political allegiance to temperament.

Choice of clothes may betray personality. Men, for example, who are only interested in the practical aspects rather than the looks of clothes, tend to be rather cautious people with low social motivation and a sense of dissatisfaction. But women with this approach tend to be intelligent and confident, although they are reluctant to reveal very much about themselves. Men who are very interested in fashion and clothes design tend to be warm, helpful and often a little impulsive. Highly fashion-oriented women are rather different. They tend to have fairly low academic qualifications and generally hold conservative views; for example, strong belief in discipline and respect for parents. They tend also to be among the most religious.

Clothing, of course, is not an ideal personality test. What we wear is influenced by the situations we find ourselves in and by the styles of our families, friends and colleagues.

THE TALL AND THE SHORT

■ *In the movies, the romantic male hero is invariably made to look taller than other actors in the cast, even if this means digging foot-deep holes for supporting actors to stand in during close-up filming. In the United States, the taller of the two main presidential candidates has been the winner in every election since 1900 with the exception of Jimmy Carter. He managed to become President standing only 1.77m (5ft 9in) tall.*

Tall men are seen as more suitable for employment in a wide range of commercial and professional settings. In one study, personnel officers were shown the descriptions of two fictitious candidates for a job. These candidates were identical except that one was listed as 1.87m (6ft 1in) and the other as 1.66m (5ft 5in). Of those who read these information sheets, 99 percent favored the taller candidate.

Tallness in women, however, can be a mixed blessing. It can endow them with a more assertive and professional image, but

it can lead to their being judged as ungainly or overpowering by some males, especially by shorter men.

There is, of course, not much you can do about your height. Women can wear high-heeled shoes, which emphasizes the length of their legs and thus, in some cases, enhances attractiveness. Men can put on shoes with built-up soles in order to add an extra inch. But such devices only minimally change people's perceptions of how tall you are. A better strategy is to employ aspects of body language which either complement or weaken the signals given off by physical height. Short people, for example, can increase their dominance by adopting postures and patterns of eye contact that are linked with high status (see Chs 5, 8). Similarly, tall people can reduce the risk of appearing threatening by making more appeasing gestures than other people and by placing themselves in positions where they do not have to literally look down on them.

▶ **Forgetting your wig** can be a severe embarrassment if you are an English barrister and cannot properly appear without it to represent your client in court. However, the lawyer on the left, wearing a different collar from the others, is not a barrister. He apparently feels "undressed" in the presence of his bewigged colleagues. Wigs first became established as a part of courtroom dress in

England during the 17th century when they were a widespread fashion in Europe for men of rank – to improve height and enhance displays of status. Outside the courtroom, wigs, to disguise baldness, are used today as unobtrusively as possible.

Nevertheless, our impressions of a man in a double-knit sweater and flared corduroys will be quite different from those we form of someone in narrowly tailored designer jeans and an open-necked cotton shirt.

Part of women's dress style is to do with sexual attraction. The brassiere for example, supports the breasts and provides both comfort and modesty. At the same time, it accentuates and shapes the breasts. As ideas concerning the ideal bust shape change, so too does the design of bras. In the 1950s, bras were heavily reinforced and gave a pointed shape to the bosom, as in the classic pictures of Marilyn Monroe and Jane Russell. In the West, the modern attractive woman has smaller and more gently rounded breasts in line with the new desire for healthy bodies. The bra has changed accordingly and now contains little or no padding, gives gentle support and a more "natural" appearance. Its real function is still as much to do with providing signals as with support and protection.

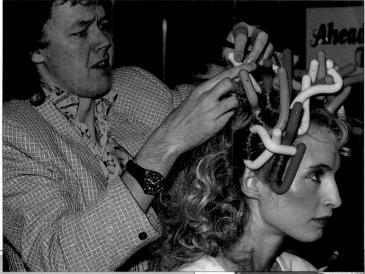

■ **Curly hair, straight hair.**
Whichever suits the needs of the look you are trying to cultivate, achieving the look probably matters enough to you to consume a significant proportion of your time. Hairstyle is one of the most personalized and sensual displays that we make to other people. The more hair, the more sensual the display.

Hairstyle expresses gender and affiliation

Hair on the head has long been the focus of creativity and expression. It provides strong gender signals, with all known human cultures adopting different styles for men's and women's hair. In Western cultures men part their hair on the left and women on the right, with a few exceptions. (Of course, there are also styles which have no discernible parting.) There is no particular biological reason for this – it is a quite arbitrary way of distinguishing between the sexes.

The arbitrariness of hairstyles is further emphasized by the way that men with long hair have been, and may still be, viewed with some distaste or derision. In earlier times it was considered quite normal for them to have long flowing locks, or even elaborate wigs.

In the 1960s, however, to wear long hair was to declare a set of political and philosophical beliefs. The style ran counter to the conservative norm and was therefore adopted by those with allegiances to countercultures and alternative lifestyles. The "long-haired radical" was considered an unsuitable candidate for responsible employment and was even refused service in bars and restaurants. Abruptly, however, long hair became the fashion, and it evoked less passion, but the fashion was short-lived and it once again became rare to find a bank teller or a policeman whose locks extended below the collar.

As a reaction to the dated "hippy" image associated with long hair, youth cultures of both sexes in the 1970s and 1980s reached the other extreme, shaving their heads or dying their hair to a multicolored display. Like the products of the 1960s, however, they used hairstyle and adornment to communicate their almost tribal affiliations, attitudes and lifestyles. Hair, largely a superficial remnant of our evolutionary past with little use, has become a means of self-expression – one that it is impossible to silence.

One other gender difference is the rate at which hair is lost by men and women. It is rare to find a bald woman, but bald men are commonplace. Male hormones, which start flooding the system immediately after puberty, can selectively kill off the roots of hairs growing on the crown of the head. Because this process affects only males, being bald can actually add to a man's image of masculinity and virility, especially when it occurs before other effects of normal aging have taken their toll. The Italian dictator Mussolini shaved his partially bald head completely shortly after seizing power in the 1920s, and Hollywood actors have also capitalized on this aspect of image enhancement.

Ironically, perhaps, the fact that hair is a focus of self-expression and sensuality means that in a different context – for example, in a monastery – shaving of the head is an act of self-humiliation. Not only self-humiliation, but the humiliation of others is possible: slaves were traditionally subjected to this treatment and the heads of prisoners are still shaved in many countries today.

Body decoration amplifies body signals

The adornment and decoration of the human body features in all known cultures and societies. It is also a practice that is as old as the recorded history of the human race. Figurines from southeast European Neolithic cultures show elaborate spiral skin decorations. The ancient Egyptians were skilled in the art of face painting and make-up, using substances and colors which would not be out of place today. Ancient Britons dabbed woad on their faces and hair, a blue herbal dye predating the blue rinse by several thousand years. The Greeks and Romans also used whatever materials were to hand in order to alter their physical appearance.

Some contemporary body decorations have the specific function of increasing sexual attraction. The British ethologist Desmond Morris has suggested that women use lipstick not simply to increase their prettiness or facial beauty. He takes an evolutionary perspective and considers the problems which arose when we became a bipedal species which stood up, rather than moving around on all fours. In apes, females signal that they are sexually receptive by a swelling and reddening of the genital labia, which are clearly visible to males from behind. In the standing female, however, such signals would be much less visible, and if they occurred now, of course, would be hidden by clothing. Lipstick, suggests Morris, is used to turn the lips into a "mimic" of the genital labia by emphasizing their fleshiness and making them redder. Males are more attracted to females with lips adorned in this way because they suggest a basic sexual invitation.

Decoration of the regions around the eyes using mascara and shadow has the effect of drawing attention to this region of the face. The eyes signal a range of emotions, not least those associated with love and attraction. The decoration of the eyes amplifies the signals and increases emotional communication.

WHY DO MEN SHAVE?

■ Body hair, and facial hair in particular, is a very basic gender signal. Because it is one visible way that the sexes differ, the presence or absence of hair is associated with masculinity or femininity. The male beard therefore communicates a positively masculine image while facial hair in women gives negative messages about lack of femininity. Why should men remove this strong signal of their gender by shaving?

The answer is partly to do with fashions and social conventions. There is, however, a more basic reason for shaving off the beard. Because it is such a strong masculine signal it also carries overtones of hostility and aggression. The deliberate reduction of facial hair may therefore signal appeasement, which has certain advantages.

However, shaving does not completely remove the gender signal. When women want to remove facial hair they generally opt for treatment which permanently destroys the hair follicles. Men, on the other hand, use a method which not only maintains the follicles but actually stimulates hair growth. The beard is gone, but everybody can see it could be grown. In the late 1980s there even appeared a fashion for designer stubble and a fashion for special razors that left the impression of two days growth. The basic gender signal is maintained and is more effective because it does not shout too loudly.

A study of beards by the American psychologist D. G. Freedman provides more information about the messages communicated by shaved and unshaved faces. He found that both males and females tended to view shaved men as more youthful than those with beards. Bearded men were seen by unbearded men as independent and extroverted, while women saw them as more masculine, sophisticated and mature.

▲ **Face-and-body paint.** A Yanomani woman in the Amazonian forest decorates her body and face for a tribal occasion. Decoration around the eyes is common to all cultures because of the powerful effect that the eyes can have in signaling emotion. Drawing extra attention to your eyes can have the effect of arousing the emotions of another (see Ch 8).

Make-up, shaving and hairstyling are ways of temporarily changing appearances to communicate messages about yourself. Some kinds of adornment, however, are more permanent. To display absolute commitment to a role, you need a tattoo.

Perhaps because of these sexual connotations, people have rather ambiguous reactions to women who wear a lot of make-up. In an experiment, volunteers were shown a photograph of an attractive woman. In one she wore no make-up, while in the other she was shown with lipstick and other cosmetics. When wearing make-up she was described as more frivolous and promiscuous and less reliable. It seems, therefore, that while cosmetics may increase a woman's sexual attractiveness, they can also lead to other more negative views.

Men might think that they are excluded from all this. Few men in the Western world wear make-up and most claim to be completely uninterested in their physical appearance. They might take considerable care of their clothes, but body adornment is not usually their style. This, however, is a fairly recent attitude. In past times it has been the men who were most lavishly adorned with exotic wigs and facial decoration. In many tribal societies this is even more evident, with male adornment expressing status in the hierarchy. But even today males go to considerable lengths to alter their physical appearance. Shaving is a good example.

Changing appearances permanently

Make-up, shaving and hairstyling are temporary ways of changing your appearance to communicate messages about yourself. Some kinds of adornment, however, are permanent, or at least semipermanent.

In tribal cultures it is common for both young men and young women to be subjected to ritual scarring or multilation. Many tribes have their own distinctive style of cutting or pricking the skin, or even reshaping parts of the body such as the lips or ears. Often this is conceived as a way of helping ancestor spirits to recognize their kin, but the actual function is to cement identities here and now.

The modern equivalent is tattooing, which serves a similar function. While tattoos may appear to be simply decorative, they are often quite deliberate statements of allegiance to certain groups or subcultures. To wear a tattoo is to say that you belong to a distinct sector of the population, and because the insignia is much more difficult to remove than, say, a badge or button, the message is far more distinct and meaningful.

In all cases of body adornment, from the most modest application of eye shadow to the gross disfigurations of facial tattoos, people are engaging in quite deliberate, although sometimes not admitted, attempts at image manipulation and enhancement. Along with the clothes we wear, we make statements about ourselves through such alterations to our appearance. It is useful, therefore, to think carefully about the kind of messages you are trying to communicate by considering how you would judge someone else using the same style and by trying to see yourself as others might see you. **PM**

▶ **The eagle triumphs forever** *over the serpent. This permanent display of the tattooer's art permanently advertises one man's sense of allegiance to the motorcycling subculture rallying here in a South Dakota town.*

▲ **A fingernail eccentricity** *highlights an already distinctive appearance in this Los Angeles newsstand operator.*

67

Reacting to Scent

BODY odor is something we rarely talk about. It is one of those taboo subjects that is avoided in everyday conversations. But smell is, in fact, an important feature of daily life. Not only does the absence of odors we consciously object to contribute to a person's attractiveness, so do positive chemical messages of which we are unaware.

Body odors

Some body smells are universally obnoxious. Odors that stem from poor personal cleanliness are considered unattractive in all cultures, even though ideas of what constitutes *visual* attractiveness differ considerably. In fact, throughout the world the only criteria common to notions of the physically attractive woman are lack of disease and a clean skin.

Sweating is an essential function, because evaporation of secretions from the skin helps to regulate body temperature. In most situations however, people who can avoid it strongly prefer not to show the inevitable wetness on clothing nor let sweaty odors offend the nostrils of other people.

A detectable aroma of fresh sweat in men can be attractive to women, but this has more to do with the associations of manly exercise and virility than with the smell itself. Every year both men and women spend billions of dollars on soaps, underarm roll-ons, body sprays and mouth washes in order to mask or replace perfectly natural odors with sanitized and artificial aromas. They are responding not simply to the huge advertising campaigns waged to encourage this spending, but to a genuine human preference for how other people will smell.

Chemical messages

Undetectable scents, however, can act as distinct signals and attractants. The ingredients in bodily secretions which provide this form of communication are know as "pheromones," from the Greek *pherein* – to transfer – and *horman*, to excite. In animals, these chemicals are consciously detected at considerable distances and serve, to some extent, in place of a spoken language. They help animals to recognize mates, give alarm warnings, mark territory and signal sexual interest and receptivity.

In animals and humans pheromones act as a kind of individual "olfactory signature." It is because each person has their own characteristic smell that tracker dogs, for example, are able to follow a given scent and ignore those left by other people. Even the most able bloodhound has difficulty, however, in distinguishing between the smells of identical twins. Something in our genetically ordered body

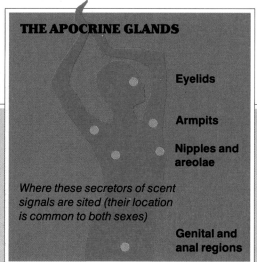

THE APOCRINE GLANDS

Eyelids

Armpits

Nipples and areolae

Where these secretors of scent signals are sited (their location is common to both sexes)

Genital and anal regions

SCENT AND SENSUALITY

▶ **A Marilyn Monroe look-alike** *promoting a perfume sends a visual sexual signal. A dash of perfume behind the ear is represented as making a face-to-face encounter more sensual. These images created for the perfume industry echo the importance of natural scents in sexual communication. Pubic hair and underarm hair both act as traps for pheromones from apocrine glands.*

Chemical pheromones that we do not consciously notice have a significant effect on our response to other people. We are aware of the offensive odors that make others repellent but not of the natural scent signals that make them attractive.

chemistry is probably at the root of our scent signatures.

Humans make very poor scent trackers, but they can still recognize certain aspects of body smells. An experiment conducted at the University of Pennsylvania showed that both male and female subjects could guess with 95 percent accuracy the sex of others from their breath, which was exhaled down a tube. Both sexes found it easier to identify the breath of the opposite sex, and male odors were generally found to be more intense and unpleasant than those of females.

At some point in our evolution we seem to have lost the capacity to detect pheromone signals consciously. Unlike other animals, we do not sniff parts of each other's bodies when we interact. This is because we have developed far more sophisticated and discriminating systems of communication.

In early infancy and childhood, however, body odor may be at the root of the attraction shown to the opposite-sex parent. It has been suggested that a pheromone signal triggers the Oedipal complex, in which boys, especially those between the ages of three and five, are supposed to be sexually attracted to the mother and feel a sense of rivalry with the father. At some point sensitivity to this female signal is switched off or repressed. Later, in response to hormonal activity, the sensitivity reappears as a powerful but unperceived influence, as adolescent boys and girls begin to be attracted to each other.

Pheromones can also alter basic biological processes, such as the menstrual cycle. Women who live in close proximity to each other, such as in prisons or dormitories, tend after a while to synchronize their periods and the length of the cycle. This is because chemicals in the odors produced during menstruation trigger its onset in other women. Although this effect is quite weak and usually has little direct influence, the build-up of the chemicals in a closed environment is sufficient to create a kind of biological harmony.

How perfumes attract

The role of pheromones in sexual attraction is highlighted in the use of perfumes. The pheromone exaltodile, the active ingredient in musk – so called because it was first isolated from secretions of musk deer – is a main ingredient in most. It is generally thought that women wear these musk perfumes in order to be more appealing to men. Perfume advertisements suggest that by wearing a particular brand of scent the women will develop an image of sophistication and will be transformed into an object of male desire. This, however, is only partly true. Men may find a scent pleasant and attractive because of its glamorous associations, but

APOCRINE GLANDS AND ECCRINE GLANDS

■ True sweat glands (the eccrine glands) occur over almost the entire surface of the skin. They produce relatively odorless secretions whose evaporation helps the body to lose heat and thus maintain a constant temperature. By carrying salts to the surface of the skin, these secretions also help the body to regulate salt balance.

Odorous "sweat" is most noticeable in the armpits, where apocrine glands secrete a slightly oilier, more persistent substance than eccrine glands do. It tends to ferment and become stale-smelling in the unnaturally confined environment that clothing creates, but its strongest communication effects are due to the odorless pheromones it contains.

Pheromones are released by apocrine glands when our emotions are aroused, and in turn they affect the emotions of those we are with. If we look dangerous, the pheromones we release may heighten their fear. If we look attractive, our pheromones may excite them.

the major effect of perfumes containing musk is to increase the sexual arousal of the woman.

Research has shown that normal women are sensitive to dilutions of one part musk to one million parts of solution. The sensitivity of the normal male is one thousand times less. It has been found that the maximum sensitivity of women to this chemical occurs around the time of ovulation and is influenced by the level of the female hormone estrogen in the body. At the menopause, when the estrogen supply drops rapidly, so too does musk sensitivity.

This simple aspect of female body chemistry begins to explain quite complex features of social behavior. Although they do not realize it, when men buy perfume for women, they are encouraging women to feel more aroused and to be more receptive to male sexual advances. The woman who has increased her own sexual receptivity in this way becomes, in turn, more attractive to her male partner, not because she smells nice but because she now signals her readiness for increased intimacy.

The presence of pheromones in perfumes increases the likelihood of sexual intercourse, as shown in a simple experiment conducted in the United States. Married women were supplied with perfumes. Some contained musk pheromones while others, which had identical smells, did not. Perfume was applied by all the women prior to going to bed at night.

Questionnaires were completed by both husbands and wives at the end of the trial period. These revealed that overall sexual activity markedly increased in about a quarter of those who had received the pheromones and that women in this group were much more likely to have intercourse

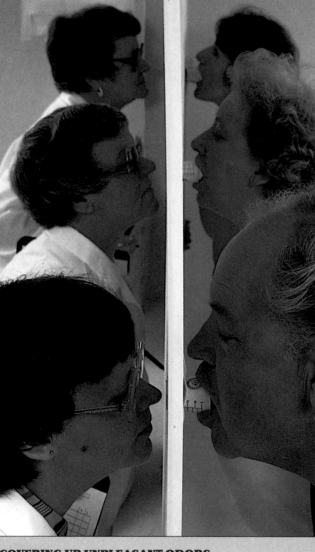

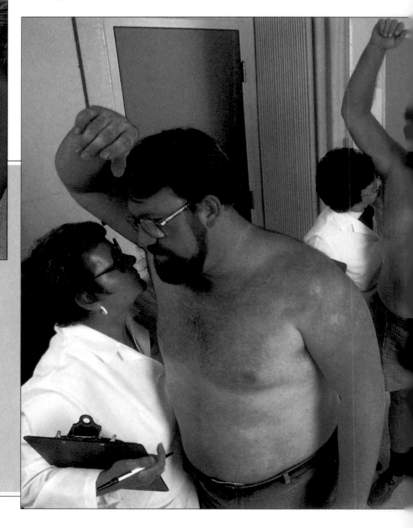

COVERING UP UNPLEASANT ODORS

■ *Industry spends enormous sums testing the underarm roll-ons and mouth washes that we buy to mask or replace natural odors. Underarm odors easily grow stale, and breath can turn sour when bacteria feed on food residues in the mouth or when infections develop in the digestive or respiratory systems.*

However, part of our motive for using underarm roll-ons is to *hide the emotional arousal that odorous sweating signals. By clogging the secreting pores and by making it difficult for secretions to adhere to underarm hair, deodorants can interfere with the pheromones that carry emotional messages, but since the pheromones are odorless the fragance of the deodorant does not itself block them.*

The major effect of a perfume containing musk is to increase the sexual arousal of the woman who is wearing it. Pheromone sprays for men also arouse women and can make men attractive in one-to-one encounters with the opposite sex.

during ovulation than those who had not received the pheromone-laden perfume.

Our perception of pheromones is not a conscious process, and human sexual behavior is complex, socially constrained and rule-governed. Nonetheless, we appear to respond to basic body chemicals in much the same way as other mammals and primates.

Pheromone sprays for men

Recently, recognition of the role that pheromones play has resulted in the marketing of special sprays for men. Male pheromone sprays usually contain a substance known as androstenol, a chemical obtained from boars, in the hormone androstenone, known to increase the sexual receptivity of sows.

Experiments have suggested that women, without being able to explain why, are more attracted to men who have applied the chemical. In one study, a seat in a dentist's waiting room was sprayed with pheromone, while others were left untouched. It was found that women were much more likely to sit on the sprayed seat even though it had previously been rather unpopular. Men, on the other hand, tended to avoid it completely.

In a further study of androstenol, researchers examined its role in influencing women's attitudes toward men. People wearing surgical masks were asked to rate the suitability of a range of applicants for a new job. Some of the masks were secretly impregnated with the pheromone. Women who wore these were found to favor assertive male candidates while women whose masks had no androstenol tended toward the quieter, less dominant applicants.

Androstenol can also make women appear more attractive to men. In one experiment, men rated women in photographs for attractiveness, before and after wearing masks impregnated with androstenol. The effect of the chemical was significant. Both men and women found the subjects of opposite-sex photographs more attractive after wearing the masks.

There is a practical problem for men attempting to become more attractive by using pheromone sprays. Because these sprays have very little odor, a man who uses one may not be identified as the source of the arousal that an affected woman feels. In a crowd – for example, at a party – he might succeed in increasing the arousal of women around him, but he will still have to compete with other men for the attention of a particular woman. The sprays are most effective in one-to-one situations.

In animals, there seems to be an inbuilt biological mechanism that causes a response to chemical messages. In humans, however, the link is probably much more complex. It could be that substances such as androstenol influence women in particular because they evoke memories of pleasurable sexual experiences. These positive associations, in turn, create a change of mood and, given the right circumstances, can lead to increased sexual arousal. Pheromones are by no means universal aphrodisiacs. **PM**

◄ **Which perfume?** *A difficult choice is offered by this perfumery in France. Ideally when selecting a perfume it should be tested on the skin – especially on the wrists – of the person who will use it. If possible, you should also check the reactions of the people you most want to smell nice for. Whether or not a scent pleases depends on a complex mix of the perfume's own chemistry, the idiosyncratic chemistry of the skin it is applied to and the associations aroused in the mind of the person who smells it.*

Making Eye Contact

EYES are usually thought of as *receivers* of information: we use our eyes to see the world around us. But they are also *transmitters* of signals that play a vital role in everyday social interaction. How we look at other people, meet their gaze and look away can make all the difference between an effective encounter and one that leads to embarrassment or even rejection.

To allow us to indicate exactly at whom or what we are looking we have acquired, through evolution, a special feature of the eyes: the eye whites. This area around the iris enables others to make very fine judgments about our gaze direction and the way our focus of attention shifts. In the complex world of human social interaction it is especially important to know when we are the object of another's gaze – and the whites tell us instantly.

Looking at the eyes of another person is such a powerful act of communication that it must be very carefully controlled. From time to time we may find ourselves gazing lovingly at someone close, in long intense bursts of eye contact – or fixing someone we dislike with a hostile stare. Normally, however we restrict our eye contacts to brief glances, and it is the precise nature of these glances that crucially determines what impression we make on others and how well we communicate.

Normally, too, we are hardly conscious of what is going on. Try talking to someone about gaze and mutual eye contact. You will probably find conversation increasingly awkward, as for a while you become self-consciously aware of those fleeting moments when two pairs of eyes meet.

How eye contact rules conversation

Knowing when to say your piece in a conversation is sometimes a particular problem. Sometimes both people talk at once, or else there are long pauses when neither knows whose turn it is to speak. The eyes help considerably to sort this problem out. Turn-taking is neatly arranged by a characteristic pattern of looking, eye contact and looking away. Other signals are also used (see *Ch 12*).

To start even the most trivial of conversations you must capture the attention of the other person by eye contact. Typically, you look at the eyes of the other person, and as soon as they look back you can begin to speak. Eye contact might need to be prompted by a remark such as "Excuse me."

As soon as the conversation begins, eye contact will be broken as the speaker looks away. Usually the person who is listening will look more than the person who is talking. To show responsiveness and interest as a listener, you need to

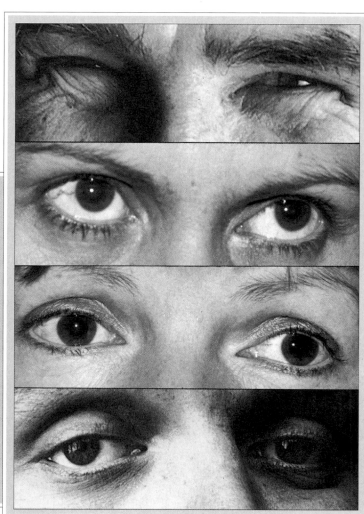

WHY EYES ARE WORTH WATCHING

■ *When we see another person it is often essential to know whether they have noticed us and, if so, what their intentions toward us are. It is most likely to be our social competence that is at stake – but it could be a matter of life and death, if the other person is hostile. Eye contact tells us at once that we are an object of attention. At the same time, the pattern of eye contact may convey warning or reassurance – and much additional information.*

◄ **As indicators of mood** *the eyes are the most reliable of all our facial features. The unself-conscious spontaneity of genuine eye signals is difficult to fake, and the smiling, darkly appraising, wistful and bored eyes shown here are easily identified without reference to facial expression as a whole. We can generally trust our readings of even subtler eye expressions. The same is not true of the mouth, for instance. Without smiling eyes, an*

apparently smiling or even laughing mouth is no proof of genuine amusement.

▲ **The eye whites,** *although having a stage-prop role in forming the eyes' mood signals, really come into their own as indicators of tell-tale shifts in gaze direction, especially in conversation. The way they are adapted to fulfill this function reflects the evolution of complex human social behavior. Significantly, even our closest animal relative, the chimpanzee (above), has no eye whites. Like most apes and monkeys, the corresponding parts of its eyes are brown.*

Most of us respond unconsciously to the eye signals of others. But with greater awareness of what is going on, we can learn to control situations more effectively and assess the moods and motives of others more reliably.

look at the other person's face for roughly three-quarters of the time, in glances lasting 1–7 seconds. While doing this, the speaker will look at you for less than half the time in order to maintain intermittent eye contact. These intermittent glances, however, rarely last more than a second each. Anything much greater than this will be found to be uncomfortable by either the speaker or the listener, or both.

Having listened, and signaled your interest in the conversation, you will need to re-establish eye contact in order to make your contribution. In easy relaxed conversations the speaker will readily detect your intention to speak and indicate this with a subtle nod of the head and a lowering of voice pitch. But things are not always this simple. Suppose you are making a point and do not wish to let the other person reply just yet. The simplest way of managing this is to avoid the other person's gaze. If eye contact cannot be established, your listener will find it much more difficult to interrupt. Such strategies, however, should be employed with caution, as they breach the unwritten rules of social encounters. You might make your point, but also make a bad impression.

On other occasions you might be faced with a person who just will not let you get a word in edgeways. The speaker avoids your eyes at the very moment when you want to signal that you are going to say something. There is a way to remedy this. First, switch off some of the support that you give by looking directly at the speaker. Look to one side, but in such a way that you can tell when you are looked at. Receiving less feedback, the speaker will eventually be drawn to look at you, hoping to find some sign of your interest and attention. At this point, meet the speaker's gaze and initiate your turn.

Holding your own in a group

In informal group discussions, without someone acting as chairperson, the role of eye contact becomes even more crucial than in one-to-one conversations. Here, in order to take your turn, you have to signal not only to the speaker but also to the other listeners that you want to speak next. Usually, such turn-taking is a relaxed affair and others in the group will actively encourage you to make a contribution. But what if you feel that you are being ignored or not allowed to say your piece? Getting into a group conversation is achieved most effectively by heading off attempts by others to catch the speaker's eye. If you can make eye

HOW EYES ATTRACT EYES

▼ The attraction of eyes and a need for eye contact show themselves early in life. Research shows that anything resembling the eyes tends to attract and hold an infant's gaze. Paired eye spots cause more smiling than single or treble spots, and a larger pair are more arousing than a smaller pair (see p79). Sustained mutual gaze between mother and child begins at four weeks, and by six weeks the two play at making and breaking eye contact in such games as peek-aboo. Eye contact not only introduces a baby to the world of social role-playing but also helps to ensure that the protective mother-infant bond is properly cemented.

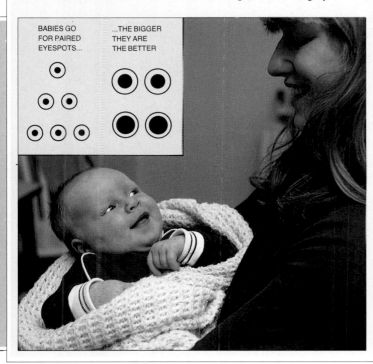

BABIES GO FOR PAIRED EYESPOTS...

...THE BIGGER THEY ARE THE BETTER

▶ **When looking at pictures** of people, we tend to glance first at and return most often to the eyes, automatically checking for mood cues and gaze direction. The way this influences the path the eye takes is used by many painters and photographers in working out their compositions, as the gaze track over this photograph suggests. After the eyes, the next most interesting features are mouths and then hands.

▶ **When looking at people** themselves, the eyes exert their usual attraction but sometimes we avoid glancing at them directly – perhaps because eye contact is emotionally loaded, perhaps also because of embarrassment or lack of confidence. The gaze track recorded here during a conversation came to rest 18 times

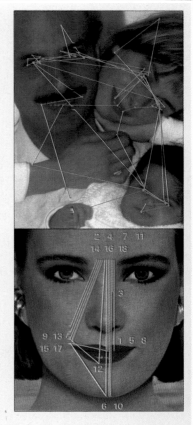

on the speaker's face in ten seconds of attention while the gazer was listening, seven times at a point between the eyes.

73

74

▲ **Looking while speaking** or listening. Whether answering questions at a public meeting or talking with friends at home, the same basic gaze patterns apply. If we fail to make use of them, our style of conversation will appear unnatural. Shown here are the three most typical patterns.

LEFT Pausing to choose words, we look away from our audience. (Stopping and looking at someone is a signal for them to speak.)

MIDDLE Attentive looking encourages the speaker to continue (but holding your mouth open suggests that you may already have formulated your reply and are waiting to speak).

RIGHT Speakers look directly at their audience especially when they want to emphasize a point (often accentuated by widening the eyes) and when they want to display conviction.

Accomplished public speak-ers learn to sweep their audience with their eyes, while they are speaking. Similarly acknowledging everyone's presence, the eye of a skilled conversationalist passes constantly from one face to another in a group.

■ **Which way do you look?**
Looking away during conversation can be self-revealing. If you ask someone a question, they will sometimes meet your eyes and then look away. Some will more often look away to the left, others to the right. It seems to depend in part on the anatomy of the brain. Those who look away to the right are likely to be more scientifically minded. Those who look to the left tend to be more artistic or religious.

But it makes a difference what kind of question is asked. In most people, the left hemisphere of the brain deals with verbal questions (such as how to spell a word), and such questions prompt them to look right. The right half of the brain deals with spatial questions (such as how to get somewhere), and these are associated with looking away to the left. **MC**

▶ **The intense speaker** – or the playful speaker causing momentary embarrassment – may reverse the usual pattern of looking by driving the listener's gaze away. The listener may look away to lower the level of intimacy or to express scepticism about a doubtful opinion or suggestion. A speaker may be impelled to look more often and more intently if the listener pays them less attention than they would normally expect.

How we use our eyes when speaking to others not only determines whether we hold their interest but also signals information about our sexual identity and social status. And where we look when listening can be just as significant.

contact with other listeners, perhaps by shifting your position slightly, you can not only signal your own intention to speak but also prevent them making that all-essential eye contact with the speaker.

Once you have taken on the role of speaker in a group discussion, you need to look at the other members in order to maintain their interest. When you want to stress a particular point, glance from face to face establishing brief eye contact with as many people as possible. At the end of your contribution make eye contact with the person who has signaled his or her intention to speak next. If nobody has made such a signal, glance again at each person's face and signal an invitation.

These basic components of eye gaze behavior in conversations and discussions are quite easy to master, once you know how they work. It is important, however, not to make eye contact appear deliberate or contrived. Skilled speakers use their eyes in a relaxed and balanced way, keeping in touch with people but never making them feel under pressure.

How eyes reflect status and sex

Eye contact and status are closely related to each other – but in two quite different ways. "Staring down" a person is often an effective way of putting them into a submissive role in situations of conflict. The person who looks away is forced onto the defensive. In normal conversations, however, the link between eye contact and status is more complex. Here, the inferior person tends to look and glance away more than the person in the superior position. When discussing something with your boss it is therefore you who

will probably glance most often. Your boss will tend to look at you in lengthy glances, especially when emphasizing a point or waiting for you to answer a question, and look away for longer than you.

This is known as "visual dominance behavior." In order to establish authority, a person needs to encourage the sense of respect which being looked at by someone else affords. Parents and teachers, for example, say "Look at me when I am talking to you!"

The relationship between status and eye contact in conversation is complicated by sex differences. Numerous studies have shown that women look at other people more than men, regardless of the sex of the other person. Similar differences have been found in studies of male and female children. It is perhaps partly for this reason that women often feel more at ease when talking with people of their own sex. More frequent occurrence of mutual eye contact and supportive gaze allows for more comfortable and close conversation.

Some psychologists have suggested that women do the most looking because they have been socialized into submissive roles. They have learned to be subservient and therefore show fewer signs of visual dominance behavior. However, at the age of six months girls already look at faces more than boys do, and it could be that more glancing by women during conversation merely reflects the fact that women are more interested than men in people and their reactions.

Women who need to establish authority over men in an organization may need consciously to limit the length and frequency of glances in conversations with them. Men who want to avoid inadvertently adopting a superior manner in conversation with women may need to practice a more supportive style of looking.

75

◄ **Dominant status** *may be signaled in different contexts by making and prolonging eye contact – or by looking away.*

TOP The classic withering look – a fixed stare, with eyelids half lowered, unmistakably designed to put its recipient in their place.

BOTTOM A reluctant object of public adulation must either risk an unwelcome increase in intimacy or look away in a display of superior indifference.

Effects of personality and culture

Some personality factors can influence the pattern of eye contact in both men and women. Extroverts, for example, who have an outgoing and sociable personality, look at other people more than introverts do. Some psychologists have suggested that this is because the central nervous system of the extrovert is less easily aroused than that of the introvert. Extroverts, they say, need more stimulation and emotional arousal, and this need is met partly by more eye contact.

People also differ in what is known as their need for "affiliation." Put simply, some individuals are more reliant on social companionship than others. Those who need to be with friends most of the time tend also to be extroverts, and they also tend to engage in a lot more eye contact than do people who are happy to be on their own. People who look at you a lot may appear to be, and may be, extroverted, but they may simply be using eye contact to seek your friendship.

Culture also influences styles of looking. Most of the Arab states, Latin America and southern Europe are termed "contact cultures" because people tend to stand much closer and touch more when they are having conversations (see *Ch10*). They also tend to exchange much more eye contact. This can be unsettling for foreigners not used to such an intimate style of social interaction, and it can lead to misunderstandings. The normal levels of facially directed gaze that are characteristic, say, of northern Europeans or Americans will be seen in the contact cultures as indicating insincerity, dishonesty or, at best, impoliteness. Typical contact-culture patterns will often be seen as threatening, disrespectful or insulting in northern Europe or the United States. There are also some interesting differences between Western cultures. Americans, for example look more at

To have another person fix their eyes on you can be disconcerting – or entrancing. It all depends on the circumstances. Either way, there are eye signals you can look for that will help you to judge the gazer's depth of feeling and sincerity.

strangers than do Europeans. This difference is also found in conversations, with the Americans looking at the face of the other person more than the British do.

If such national and ethnic differences make for awkwardness from time to time, bear in mind that there are much more extreme eye-contact customs to be found in some cultures. In the Lua tribe of Kenya, for example, it is forbidden to look directly at your mother-in-law; in certain parts of Nigeria inferiors do not look at superiors; and the members of some South American Indian tribes do not look at each other at all during conversation.

▲ **To be the object** of a baleful and unblinking stare can be disconcerting. In ancient Greek mythology, anyone who met the Medusa's gaze was instantly turned to stone. An age-old objection to being looked at persists in many cultures, and a superstitious belief in the "Evil Eye" – in the power of a stranger or evil spirit to cast a spell or bring bad luck simply by staring – is still found throughout the world, as are countless talismans intended to ward it off.

Even in California the mystique of the stare is acknowledged. A survey of students at Stanford University revealed that three-quarters thought they could tell if someone was staring at them from behind. Some insisted that they could feel staring eyes "boring into" them.

Few of us like being stared at. In another study, researchers posing as pedestrians stared at some car drivers who stopped at a red light, but not at others – and found that the stared-at drivers made quicker getaways when the lights changed.

▲ **The mutual gaze** of intense emotion can be an act of love or an act of hostility. To limit undue emotional stimulation, we normally avoid eye contacts of more than one second or so. Except between lovers and belligerents, exchanged glances decrease in number when people are forced into close physical contact – as in subways and elevators – or when conversation touches on intimate topics.

Looking, liking and trusting

The act of looking communicates meaning in its own right. One of the commonest signals is that of liking. Quite simply, we look more at people we like than at those we dislike. These looking signals will be decoded by others in a positive way. They will feel more attracted to people that they have detected, probably unconsciously, looking at them.

Looking at people and meeting their eyes are clearly first steps toward striking up friendships and winning positive regard. But the manner of looking is all-important. Sustained gaze in the form of a stare can be interpreted as an unwelcome sexual advance or as downright hostility. Like us, chimpanzees also use eye contact to signal aggression in hostile encounters, and staring at them in a zoo can induce agitated behavior. In order, therefore, to reduce the risk of signaling hostility in social situations, it is wise to make frequent but short glances.

If people consistently fail to look at us, in situations where it would normally be appropriate, we tend to become suspicious. This is because we feel that important signals are being deliberately masked, and we wonder why. Honesty and the ability to look someone in the eye are very closely related, and for good psychological reasons. Experimental studies have shown quite clearly that when people are required to lie, or have been encouraged to cheat, their deception is accompanied by averted gaze.

In everyday experience we similarly make judgments on the basis of a person's "shifty" eyes. Eye contact with another person, in any setting, increases the normal level of psychological arousal. In a tense situation – for example, when you are lying – eye contact may heighten your anxiety, and so you may avoid it. In experiments, however, avoided eye contact has not been found as consistently as may other tell-tale signs of deception (see Ch 14). In addition, some people are practiced at lying very effectively and still maintaining direct eye contact. These are people with "Machiavellian" personalities, who have learned through experience to control their levels of anxiety in order to manipulate other people. The mere fact that someone looks you in the eye is not an infallible indicator of their honesty and trustworthiness. **PM**

HOW YOUR EYES CAN GIVE YOU AWAY

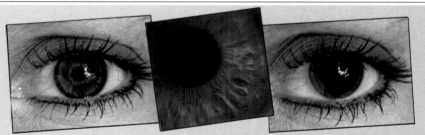

■ *Pupil signals. We find it difficult not to look at people who arouse our emotions. When the person is a stranger we usually look less often and more briefly in an effort to mask our real feelings. In this we are seldom entirely successful – and there is a further complication.*

Along with any emotional response comes a widening of the pupils of the eyes, even though the light falling on them remains constant. It is an involuntary reflex, and was originally an evolutionary adaptation that let more light, and so more information, into the eyes in an emergency. But it also acts as a mood signal. The sight of dilated pupils unconsciously triggers an emotional response and a corresponding pupil-enlargement in the person being looked at. It could be a signal of love at first sight, or one of simple like or dislike. (If it is love, the focus-softening effect of widened pupils may even help the emotion to take root.)

Returning another's open-pupil gaze with one of your own is almost certain to heighten their sense of arousal, which is why looking quickly away is important for discouraging both admirers and antagonists. Uninhibited gazing with dilated pupils is strictly reserved for lovers and people who are spoiling for a fight – as depicted opposite.

It is because pupil signals are involuntary that they offer lie-detector-like clues to what a person is really thinking or feeling – clues the student of human behavior will learn to look for. But the problem in ordinary situations is to spot them without staring – and without giving yourself away! You cannot easily learn to control your own pupils by practicing in front of a mirror.

There are tricks. You can always hide your pupils by wearing dark glasses; or they can be dilated chemically (not advised). At one time, Italian courtesans used to enlarge their pupils by putting the drug belladonna (Italian for "beautiful woman") into their eyes.

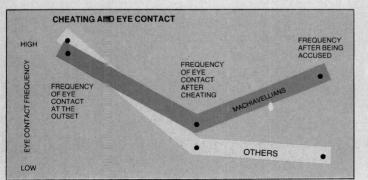

CHEATING AND EYE CONTACT

HIGH · LOW — EYE CONTACT FREQUENCY

FREQUENCY OF EYE CONTACT AT THE OUTSET

FREQUENCY OF EYE CONTACT AFTER CHEATING

FREQUENCY AFTER BEING ACCUSED

MACHIAVELLIANS

OTHERS

◄ **Good and bad deceivers.** We trust people more when they look us in the eye. Research shows that good liars know this. Unsuspecting students were tested for "Machiavellianism" (ability to hide emotions in order to manipulate others). They were then paired-off with "partners" who induced them to cheat in performing an unconnected laboratory experiment. Frequency of eye contact with an interviewer was recorded before cheating, after cheating, and after being accused of cheating. It was found that Non-Machiavellians looked less and so appeared normally "shame-faced." Machiavellians, however, looked the interviewer in the eye more especially after the accusation.

Reading Facial Expressions

USUALLY people's facial expressions seem a better guide than their words to what they are feeling. But sometimes they seem ambiguous or inscrutable. On occasion we may find this intriguing or even attractive, but it can also be irritating or disturbing. This is because we rely on facial expressions to show us how we are getting along with others, and how we should interpret what they say.

It is possible to read emotion and attitude from people's faces. Smiles and frowns are often spontaneous expressions of happiness and anger. Yet we also deliberately signal to one another with smiles, frowns and other expressions. We smile in greeting. We frown to show doubt or disapproval. We wrinkle our noses to show disgust. We do not necessarily have strong feelings when we use expressions in this way, but simply follow conventional rules for using the face as a vehicle of expression. In everyday conversation, we concentrate on our companions' faces rather than on their hands or feet, for the face is the major site of nonverbal signaling. Its spontaneous displays are the most informative displays, and its rules the most useful rules, of body language.

The great 19th-century British naturalist Charles Darwin circulated a famous list of 16 questions to missionaries and others in remote parts trying to discover whether body language, especially facial expression, is innate or learned (and thus governed by social rules). If expressions are learned, then in some cultures, he expected, there might be no smiling, not because the people were never happy, but because they used another expression for happiness. If expressions are innate, happiness or pleasure will everywhere show themselves in a smile, because that is the way the human nervous system and human face work.

Darwin asked, for example, "Is astonishment expressed by the eyes and mouth being opened wide, and by the eyebrows being raised? When a man is indignant or defiant does he frown, hold his body and head erect, square his shoulders and clench his fists? Do children when sulky pout or greatly protrude the lips?" He concluded from the replies that "the same state of mind is expressed throughout the world with remarkable uniformity." There were differences. For instance, "clenching the fists seems confined chiefly to men who fight with their fists." Among Australian aborigines, indignant men "wave their arms, while the women dance about and cast dust in the air." Nevertheless they

■ **Flushed with the effort,** an actress ABOVE simulates anger, a head of state CENTER puts on a display of mock concentration for photographers and an Italian street vendor FAR RIGHT shows with what vehemence he is prepared to defend the quality of his wares. Only in the case of the football supporter RIGHT can we feel certain that the flush is a genuine flush of emotion. Any facial expression that occurs spontaneously can also be closely approximated for a social purpose. With practice we can control our features and make our color rise – or become pale – at will.

Faces convey our most expressive body language. Reading them tells us how we are getting along. Spontaneous smiles and frowns are especially informative, but just as sincere words can be selected, so can sincere facial expressions.

hold themselves erect, and their *facial* expressions of anger are the same as everyone else's.

Studies of infant smiling have found how early it appears in a recognizable form and how much mothers see it as a sign that their babies are relating to them and responding socially. Even at a few days old, infants pay more attention to complex, face-like objects than to simple objects of the same size and color. At first, infants find other complex objects equally interesting, but within the first six months

they start to prefer faces. Furthermore babies *smile* at faces, and it is not the complexity of the face that pleases them – eyes, or even a pair of eye-like dots, elicit a baby's smiles just as readily as its mother's face (see *Ch8*). In contrast, the baby will not smile at a face with the eyes, or even one eye, covered.

The mother's response to an infant's smiles, as Darwin pointed out, makes them important for the bond she develops with her child. It is unlikely that an expression which has such survival value and which appears within the first month of life could be other than innate. Infants also show distinguishable expressions of distress, terror, disgust, surprise and interest. Studies of blind children have shown that, although they have fewer and less subtly graded facial expressions, they use the same facial muscles as sighted children in both posed and spontaneous smiles and in expressions of fear and anger. Blind thalidomide children also had the usual expressions, even when they were deaf and had no arms, and could therefore not readily learn by hearing or touch.

RECOGNIZING EMOTIONAL DISPLAYS

■ Emotional expressions may be innate, but it seems that we have to learn how to recognize them. In the first year of life children learn to distinguish between angry, sad, happy and neutral expressions, but only when there are acted out in a pronounced way. Children often fail to notice the facial expressions by which adults show that what they are saying is not meant seriously.

Recognition skills seem to improve with age. When children are asked to interpret expressions in photographs, the difference between the

abilities of three-year olds and 14-year olds is striking. There is some evidence that children (8 to 11) who are better at recognizing facial expressions are more popular, and that the recognition skill produces the popularity rather than vice versa.

Some, but not all, studies find sex differences in recognition skill, with women being better at it. But women's superiority does not extend to seeing through people's expressions when they are trying to hide their feelings. People who are good at deciphering facial

▲ **Mimicking a distressed look** can be a way of soothing someone. You show a comforting empathy at the same time as a comforting confidence about the situation. Here a Finnish mother gently mocks her baby's fear of a photographer.

expressions are not necessarily good at deciphering the body or the voice. Recognition of emotion is complicated, involving a reading in context of all body-language channels as well as what people say about themselves

There is broad agreement over six basic emotions: happiness, sadness, anger, disgust, surprise and fear. Their facial expressions are almost universally recognized, but elements of them are blended differently by different cultures.

Comparisons with animals also suggest that human facial expressions are innate – part of our evolutionary inheritance. Other mammals, unlike birds and reptiles, have the facial muscles to produce expressions, though these are more limited than ours. Dogs and cats, for example, snarl or spit while wrinkling their noses and baring their teeth. The origin of these expressions may be movements to display threatening intentions, such as showing the teeth – ready for an attack.

Darwin pointed out the detailed similarities between human expressions and those of several other animals. For example, orangutans and chimpanzees protrude their lips like sulky children when slightly angered or disappointed. He noted that monkeys raise their eyebrows when surprised, and draw back the corners of their mouths in a "smile" when pleased.

Modern researchers, relying on more systematic observations, have found that chimpanzees use open-mouthed displays of bared teeth to affirm acceptance of another's behavior, and they use horizontal displays of teeth to appease. The researchers have suggested that these expressions may have the same ancestry as human laughter and smiling. Some feel, however, that this is only true of the open-mouthed display, since the appeasement display is probably a grimace akin to human expressions of fear. Darwin also described similarities between animal and human snarls, although he remarked that snarls are not noticeable among monkeys. In fact, human threat displays and those of other primates look remarkably similar.

Universal expressions

Modern authorities such as the American researchers Carroll Izard and Paul Ekman have demonstrated that certain clearly distinguishable facial expressions communi-

cate the same emotions in every human culture studied. There is broad agreement about six basic emotions – happiness, sadness, anger, disgust, surprise and fear. Ekman showed photographs of the facial expression of these emotions to people from the United States, Brazil, Chile, Argentina and Japan and found that they were recognized in much the same way everywhere.

Ekman and his colleague Wallace Friesen also visited the Fore people of New Guinea, who have little contact with outsiders. They did not clearly distinguish fear and surprise, but otherwise the Fore who were interviewed agreed with the other nationalities. Other Fore people were videotaped posing the six expressions. American students deciphered them fairly accurately, except for the Fore representations of fear and surprise.

These studies use stereotypes of emotional expressions – the expressions are *posed* rather than occurring spontaneously. What they show is that there is a universal tendency to recognize certain voluntary expressions as appropriate representations of the emotions they signify. This recognition strongly implies that people in different societies spontaneously produce the same facial expressions for the same emotions. There is also direct evidence for this spontaneity.

Ekman showed a film of sinus surgery to Japanese and American students. Each student was videotaped while watching the film alone, and later while talking to a researcher about the experience. American and Japanese facial expressions differed in the interview. The Americans' expressions ranged from distaste to utter horror but the Japanese remained composed. When watching the film

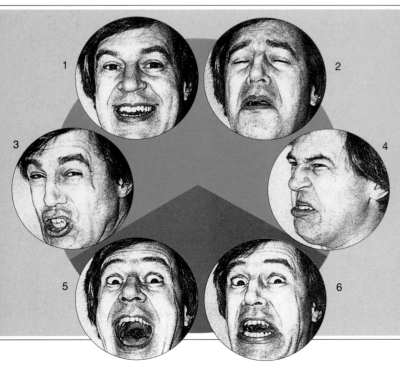

EXPRESSING THE SIX BASIC EMOTIONS

■ Universally, people express and recognize four basic emotions. Two others – fear and surprise – are distinguished by everyone except remote populations in New Guinea. Three independently expressive regions of the face – the eyebrows, the eyes and the lower face – are used.
(1) Happiness appears in a smiling mouth and wrinkles around the eyes. **(2) Sadness** has raised brows, lowered upper eyelids and a downturned mouth. **(3) Anger** gives the eyes a penetrating stare and causes the lids to tense. Sometimes the brows are lowered and drawn together. The lips of the angry mouth are pressed together, or opened and pushed forward as here. **(4) Disgust** shows itself in a wrinkled nose and raised upper lip. The lower eyelid is pushed up and the brows are lowered.
(5) Surprise raises the brows. The eyes are open wide and the jaw drops, opening the mouth.
(6) Fear raises and draws together our brows. The eyes are open and tense, and the lower lid is raised. The mouth is open and lips may be drawn back tightly. The different brow, eye and lower-face elements of the basic expressions may be blended to form angry disgust, for example, or surprised fear.

alone, however, students of both nationalities showed very similar distressed expressions. They also reported similar feelings and showed similar physiological responses, strongly suggesting that their emotions were the same, and that in both societies the same facial expressions accompany the same emotions when people feel no social pressure to hide their feelings.

Blending basic expressions

To categorize expressions accurately, Ekman and his colleagues developed their Facial Affect Scoring Technique. This divides the face into three areas (brows, eyes and lower face), whose muscle movements are largely independent. When expressions are broken down in this way it is clear that a basic emotion often appears in only part of the face.

▲ **Contrasting responses.** A mother and daughter make demonstrative spectators at the Wimbledon lawn tennis tournament in England. Behind them, a Japanese visitor responds mildly to the same events and a Western man displays little reaction. Different degrees of expressiveness occur in men and women, in members of different cultures and in different individuals. Our reactions on a particular occasion depend heavily, of course, on what personally interests and excites us and on how inhibited we feel.

There may, for example, be anger or fear in the brows, and a smile on the lips. Ekman calls such expressions blends of primary emotional expressions. There are other possible kinds of blend, such as a rapid sequence of two primary expressions.

Blending often explains why it is difficult to say just what emotion someone's facial expression reveals. We may be aware of the mixture of feelings a face shows, but not be able immediately to see what feelings are. It can be difficult to interpret them even from a photograph or videorecording that allows us to study the expressions again and again.

Despite Darwin's claims about the universality of expression, anthropologists and others have emphasized the differences in expressions across cultures. Part of the explanation for this is that basic emotions are blended differently in different cultures. The expression people from Britain and the United States call "smug" – an apparent mixture of happy and angry features – is not recognizable in many other cultures. The British "wry smile" one corner of the mouth up and and one down may be hard to find elsewhere. In New Guinea there is a common expression that mixes sad eyebrows and an angry mouth. This is not recognizable by Westerners.

Ekman and Friesen later developed the Facial Action Coding System. This catalogs the "action units" that the face is capable of producing, and the muscular movements that underlie them. Coding expressions on the basis of muscle action allows more detailed description.

Studies of the facial muscles support the view that particular facial expressions naturally accompany particular emotions. It is possible to record from electrodes on the surface of facial muscles. If people are asked to think of happy, sad or angry experiences, their feelings can be "read" from the electrical impulses to the muscles even when the face does not register a visibly distinguishable expression.

Rules for displaying emotion

Our ability to control facial muscles voluntarily (see box), however, makes possible a much more striking variable in facial behavior than the blending of basic expressions does – different cultures (such as the Japanese and American

82

► **Fierce faces.** *TOP A young girl produces a facial "emblem" of evil ferocity, playfully simulating elements of an emotion she does not feel. BOTTOM A member of the British royal family smolders in the hot sun and smolders at the intrusions of photographers, using compressed lips to help her give controlled expression to genuine anger.*

◄ **The simple and the complex.** *The straightforward and appropriate social smile TOP blends BOTTOM with a look of self-doubt. The two expressions combined tell us that their owner feels not quite right about the way she is using her face.*

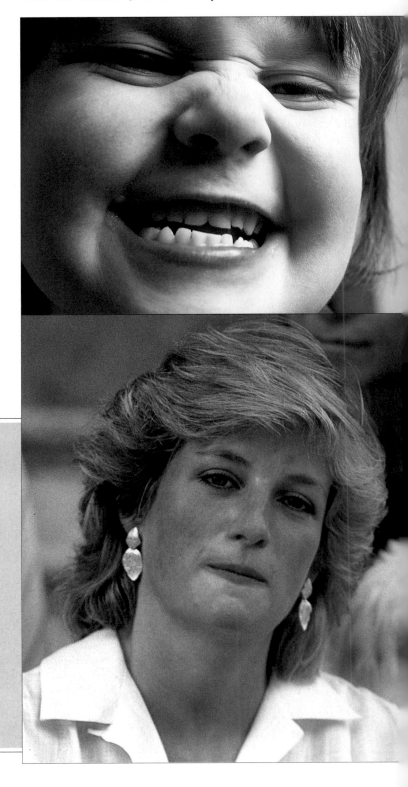

Facial muscles are only partly under voluntary control. With practice and effort, however, we learn to suppress the display of some feelings and to amplify the display of others. Social rules tell us how much to show.

students discussing sinus surgery), even different sexes, have different rules for how much emotion to display. Individuals, too, differ in their styles of emotional expression. Some withhold all. Others reveal all. Some people cannot stop themselves blushing.

A great effort may be needed to suppress spontaneous facial expressions. Our control over our faces is less complete than our control over our words (even if it is more complete than our control over other aspects of body language – see *Ch 4*). Social teaching of self-control can help. The British "stiff upper lip," for example, prevents bared-teeth expressions of fear or hilarity and eliminates tremble.

The tradition that orientals are "inscrutable" is not a mere Western fantasy. Studies of the Japanese show that their facial expressions are more difficult to interpret than European expressions even for the Japanese themselves. But there is also very good evidence that this is not because the Japanese are unemotional. Traditionally, they have had very strict rules about not displaying certain negative emotions, such as anger, sadness and disgust. The concept of "saving face" means not being caught out or shown up, but it also has a more literal meaning of controlling the front that one presents to the world. Some Japanese people associate these ideals with Buddhist dislike of emotion.

The Japanese are masters not only of suppressing emotions but of masking them with the apparent display of others. When afraid that they cannot keep a neutral expression, they traditionally resort to smiling and laughter. In doing this they are also following a rule of their etiquette that you should not inflict your sorrows on your friends.

The oriental's inscrutable face has caused Westerners discomfort, since we cannot tell what unexpressive people "really" feel, and Japanese use of the smile has led to gross misunderstandings. For example, the 19th-century writer on Japan, Lafcadio Hearn, tells a story of a Japanese servant who smilingly asked her Western mistress if she might go to her husband's funeral. She later returned with his ashes, saying, with a laugh, "Here is my husband." Her mistress thought her heartless, but Hearn suggests that her behavior was in fact heroic.

In recent times, the influence of Western culture has been undermining these conventions among younger Japanese, but even Westerners display the signs of emotions they do not feel – they smile when they pose for photographs or when greeting their mothers-in-law. People in some countries may intensify the display of particular emotions. The public expression of grief, for example, may often be exaggerated.

HOW THE BRAIN CONTROLS EXPRESSIONS

■ *Different parts of the brain are involved in facial expressions. Voluntary control occurs by means of the "motor strip" on the cerebral cortex, a muscle-controlling strip on the thin outer layer of gray matter that gives humans their distinctive intelligence.*

Nerve impulses pass from the motor strip through the "pyramidal" system of nerve fibers (so named because of the pyramidal shape they form where they bunch in the medulla oblongata at the base of the brain).

Emotional expressions, by contrast, come from the "extrapyramidal" motor system, an older group of neural circuits with fewer connections to the cerebral cortex.

Patients with damage to the motor strip of the cortex may be unable voluntarily to pose a facial expression that their faces nevertheless can produce spontaneously.

Patients with damage to the extrapyramidal system may be able to pose expressions that they never produce spontaneously.

▶ **Weeping over a coffin** *at a funeral in Kwangju, a South Korean politician makes a public gesture. Simulating feelings is not necessarily an insincere thing to do. It may be the most appropriate way – the one most easily recognized by others – of expressing a thought.*

Display rules often require us to produce friendly smiles but seldom to produce excited grins. It is easy to simulate mild feelings but requires more skill and energy to simulate stronger ones. There are tell-tale signs of even the most skilled unspontaneous smile (see *Ch14*), but lack of spontaneity does not matter when the smile is pleasant to look at and serves as an appropriate social gesture.

People tend to regard far more or far less expressiveness than what they are used to as deviant and unattractive. Comparatively unexpressive nationalities, such as the English, appear cold to southern Europeans. To the English, people from the Mediterranean often appear overemotional, insincere and perhaps childish.

Similarly, the rule that "boys do not cry" demands that males especially should put on a brave face. According to traditional northern European and Anglo-Saxon ideals, men should control their emotions and should perhaps not even feel fear, while women should not become angry. Studies have shown that people find it easier to recognize American women's facial expressions than American men's. This finding is common elsewhere, as well – at least for negative expressions. Women also speak of their emotions more than men. This sex difference seems learned, for the expressions of preschool boys are as recognizable as those of preschool girls.

Americans whose expressions are hard to recognize are found to be psychologically – and therefore perhaps emotionally – more aroused than those whose expressions are easy to recognize. This implies that American men learn to repress their emotional expressions, but that the effort to do so produces emotion and stress. This in turn implies that display rules may effect the amount of emotion experienced, and hence that culture may interfere radically in the emotional process.

Signaling with the face

Voluntary control of the face allows us, with practice and effort, to suppress emotional displays, even to mask negative feelings with imitations of happiness. And it allows many other social uses of the face.

The face is constantly informative during conversation, for example. Eyebrows rise to display surprise or disbelief. The corners of the mouth turn up or down to show amusement or a "shrug" of dismissal. The face (and the tone of voice) show us when we should take people's words literally, and when they are joking.

Many expressions used in conversation are not emotional. Winking is not part of any emotional expression. Raising the eyebrows is typical of surprise, but it is also used conventionally as a question-mark, or to emphasize

84

▲ **Hands fly to cheeks** *as a delighted surprise overwhelms an old man* RIGHT. *The hands move in an impulse to control what feels to their owner like too spontaneous a facial display.*

LEFT *The same action serves as part of a gesture of appreciation for unexpected attentions received. Here the hands serve to emphasize a facial expression. Security men watch impas-* *sively, maintaining an emotional invisibility that is part of their role.*

Is it insincere to pose our facial expressions? Even the most skilled unspontaneous smile can be detected. Lack of spontaneity does not matter however, when the smile is pleasant and serves as an appropriate social gesture.

particular words in conversation. Wrinkling the nose is a natural expression of a disgust, but it is also used for emphasis by some western women. We use "facial emblems" to mimic emotional expressions without wishing anyone to think that we really feel the emotion. Such expressions are parodies of the spontaneous ones, exaggerating certain features of them and omitting others. For instance, we drop our jaws in mock astonishment, or open our eyes unnaturally wide as we say "Wow!"

Conversational signals become habitual and just as automatic as emotional expressions. It is very difficult for an adult not to smile and nod when listening to someone's conversation. You will find it difficult to suppress eyebrow emphasizers during your own speech, or to raise your eyebrows when pronouncing a word you are *not* emphasizing. It is an interesting experiment for you to try this. But beware of doing it with someone whom you do not wish to offend. Others are likely to interpret your unexpressiveness as a lack of interest when you are listening, and when you are speaking they may find your facial misemphasis or lack of emphasis disturbing or bizarre.

Conversational signals do not necessarily accompany speech. In fact they are an important part of listening to someone else's conversation. Listeners employ nods and smiles, frowns of puzzlement, or the wide eyes and raised brows of surprise to encourage speakers and show them whether they are attending, have understood and are dismayed or impressed by what they have heard. People also yawn deliberately to persuade a speaker not to go on.

Young children do not use conversational signals properly. This is one reason why adults constantly ask children whether they are paying attention and have understood. Children take some time learning how to use these expressions, even when they are natural facial movements. Children may also have difficulty learning how to do expressions such as the wink, which do not come naturally.

Are social signals innate?

Particular parts of the face are used with different meanings in different regions. For Europeans and Americans, tongue protrusion is aggressive (held between pursed lips) or erotic (flicked between slightly parted lips), although it is regarded as neutral when people stick out their tongues while concentrating on a difficult task. But the tongue is protruded in greetings among Tibetans and Maoris. For the latter it is still rude, but not apparently for the former. In Chinese novels stretching out the tongue is an expression of surprise. In modern China it occurs as an expression of embarrassment.

In photographs, Americans from the southern states often have an expression in which the mouth is pursed, the tongue is shown, and one or both lips are drawn inwards over the teeth. This expression, rare elsewhere, is also seen in old paintings of southerners.

There is some suggestion of a cultural and possibly human impact even on primates' facial expressions. Chimps in one group had a vertical bared teeth facial expression which researchers thought "an idiosyncratic trait" of the group. Reports suggest that baboons in captivity

READING CHARACTER FROM FACIAL FEATURES

■ According to the pseudoscience of physiognomy, a high forehead is supposed to reveal intellect, a long, narrow face to show sensitivity. The chin is supposed to show weakness or strength. Lips are supposed to tell us something about their owners by being thick and sensual, small and prissy or thin and tight. These judgments have no factual basis – why are they believed? A large head suggests a large brain, which in turn (wrongly) suggests brainpower. Other beliefs about face and character seem to be influenced by the fact that some permanent features happen to resemble recognizable but passing facial expressions.

Listening to slow, intense music sometimes gives people an expression that stretches the lower face and raises the eyebrows, particularly above the bridge of the nose. It temporarily lengthens and narrows the nose and the whole face. Consequently, a long face may seem to have a permanent "sensitive" expression. Similarly, the chin sags in exhaustion or defeat but juts out when the jaw is flexed in determination – so a slight chin gives an impression of weakness. A tight, budded mouth seems to denote doubt, and thin lips suggest suppressed emotion. Thick lips seem sensual because pouts can be sexual.

▲ **Reading between the lines.** It is sometimes said that the face in repose reveals character, because habitual or recurrent expressions eventually leave the face with lines. Trying to work out the typical expressions of a really well-lined face is a special challenge.

have far more developed "cordial laughter" expressions than in the wild.

However, an expert on nonverbal communication, Irenaus Eibl-Eibesfeldt, has argued that basic emotional expressions are not the only innate and universal ones. He has found that various other expressions, such as the eye-play of flirting and bashfulness, are common across cultures, and appear in young children and even the blind. He has given particular attention to the "eyebrow flash" (raising the eyebrows for about one-sixth of a second) used in salutations among Europeans, Balinese, Papuans, Samoans, South American Indians, Bushmen and others.

Paul Ekman claims that the eyebrow flash is not universal, but a typical learned conversational signal. He explains it as mimicking the innate expressions of interest and surprise. Unlike the hostile frown, it is appropriate for different cultures to have chosen to use it in pleasant greetings.

In fact, raising the eyebrows has opposite meanings in different cultures. Darwin reported that it accompanied a head-toss and meant "yes" in Ethiopia and Borneo. Eibl-Eibesfeldt says it means "yes" in Samoa. In Greece and Turkey, however, a similar gesture means "no." The difference between the two expressions may lie in the eye-opening – wide for "yes," resembling the pleasure of a surprise; narrow, resembling a supercilious expression, for "no." Eibl-Eibesfeldt argues that where the eyebrow flash is not used, this is because people suppress it. In Japan, for instance, it has sexual connotations and decency requires its avoidance in Japanese greetings.

The varieties of smiling

An expression like the smile, which is common to all cultures, may appear more often in some than in others. One writer claimed that in the southwest Pacific you can draw geographical lines between "areas of Papuan hilarity" and areas of "Melanesian dourness." Another observed that New Englanders smile less than people from the Midwest, and that the highest incidence of smiling in the United States is among people from Atlanta, Louisville, Memphis and Nashville.

This might show that people in some regions or countries are happier than people in some others. But it is more likely to be because facial expressions are different in the two places. Similarly, laughter is used in Africa to express surprise, wonder, embarrassment. It is not necessarily, or even often, a sign of amusement.

People obey different rules for how much spontaneous pleasure to allow others to see, and they also have different rules for when and how it is appropriate to produce a "social" smile. Such cross-cultural differences create problems of communication and understanding. Regional differences in amount of smiling mean, for instance, that if a

■ **Facial accessories** *can profoundly influence social signaling.* TOP *Dark glasses combine with unwelcoming expressions – mouths compressed and postures angled away from us – to discourage our approach at this gathering in Dallas, Texas.* BOTTOM *Prompted by the photographer, the same group uses its lenses to accentuate the warmth and friendliness of a forward-leaning smile.*

Men who smile a lot count themselves sociable. Women who smile a lot describe themselves as feminine. People are rated more attractive with smiles than without, but the situation must be one where a smile is appropriate.

young woman smiles at a stranger in Atlanta, Georgia, her behavior cannot be interpreted in the same way as it might be if she were in New Haven, Connecticut. In the American South, a person walking down the street without a smile might be seen as angry or sad. In the North a smiler might be thought odd or considered to be showing a hostile mocking reaction.

Even in the same community, men and women smile differently. This is unlikely to be innate, as children's social smiling can been seen to change as they grow older. Their broad smiles do not change, but their "upper" smiles (showing only the upper teeth) become more frequent and selective. Boys of four reserve this type of smile almost exclusively for other boys. By this age children are able to simulate emotions quite well, though less able to hide them. Adults expect girls and boys to show different emotions. They see an expression as fear when it appears on a little girl's face and anger when it appears on a little boy's.

Women smile more than men. This is not because they are happier. They are (or have to appear) more pleasant, and often smile when uncomfortable or tense. One experimenter tried to induce expressions of pain by bending back people's fingers. Men looked suitably pained. Women had an amused expression. Women also show their teeth more than men in smiles of greeting.

Different smiles are used for different messages. For instance, women smile with a closed mouth to show that they are ready to be kissed, but show their teeth when they are initiating a kiss. There are many other sex-differences in facial expression. According to one researcher, for exam-

ple, men blink faster and more regularly than women.

Some individuals smile more than others regardless of gender. Men who smile a lot describe themselves as sociable. Women who smile a lot describe themselves as feminine. People in photographs with smiles are rated more attractive than without. But remember the different regional norms, and beware of overdoing smiles. Too much smiling, by the local standard, may seem aggressive or foolish. The important thing is that your expression should be suitable. Sad words with a happy smile may seem insincere. Defendants who look sad when describing their crime are viewed more favorably than those who look angry or happy.

Emotional feedback from facial expression

It is not possible to make a perfectly clear distinction between conversational signals and emotional expressions. Frowns and smiles are sometimes emotional and sometimes conventional. But a smile that occurs where a smile is proper may be a genuine expression of pleasure.

There is even some evidence to suggest that making a facial expression may cause you to feel the appropriate emotion. The explanation offered is that how your face feels gives you clues about how you are feeling. In "facial feedback" studies, people are either asked to move particular facial muscles or to exaggerate naturally occurring facial expressions. More expression tells you that you have more emotion.

There are reasons to doubt the facial feedback interpretation of these data (not least the fact that facial muscles of expression do not seem to have the nerve-rich organs called "spindles" that give feedback from other muscles). But they suggest that if you force yourself to smile at your mother-in-law you are actually likely to *feel* happier to see her than you would if you did not smile. **RL**

87

▲ **Friendly acknowledgment.** LEFT An open-mouthed smile and arched eyebrows are used almost universally in greeting from a distance. Only in Japan is it not part of the greeting ritual to make an eyebrow "flash". RIGHT A double row of teeth can express exuberant affection or admiration. Women often make a similar display when they feel like kissing someone.

POWER AND BLINKING

■ Men in general blink faster and more regularly than women, but those who gain a conscious control over their eyelids – and do not blink at all – can make a more powerfully masculine impression. A golden rule for actors attempting to achieve the screen presence of a Clint Eastwood or a Michael Caine is never to blink when the camera is on them. Another circumstance in which people try to control blinking is when they are lying. Here it is fear that excessive blinking will give them away, that makes them blink less than usual.

The Language of Touch

SOME touches carry no personal message. The doctor touches in order to examine, the hairdresser to cut hair and the tailor to measure. But most *communicate*. Sometimes much more powerfully than words, a touch lends support, asserts that we are together or shows appreciation, affection or attraction. By "control touches" we guide and steer people, or call for their attention and participation. Touching has ritual meaning in the handshake of greeting and parting, offering congratulations or sealing a contract.

Social rules that ban overly familiar or overbearing touches closely regulate these touches: how much and where on the body people touch implies how intimate their relationship is, and how power is distributed between them. You have to touch strangers, superiors, inferiors, mere acquaintances, friends and intimates each in the right way. But touch them you must, if you are to establish and maintain relationships. Touching strangers in the right way even helps the briefest of encounters to go more smoothly.

The influential touch

Despite concerns for their safety, political candidates know the value of walking into a crowd to kiss babies and "press the flesh" – a quick handshake can leave a lasting positive impression that may pay off later at election time – the voter's sense of personal involvement is enhanced in a way that words can never achieve. But you do not have to be a celebrity to exert influence through touch – celebrities in their turn need the demonstration of support and appreciation that an extended hand represents.

Frequently, the touch of a stranger is only accidental, but it affects us just the same. Momentary and seemingly incidental touches can establish a temporary but positive bond, with the receiver becoming more helpful, compliant and generous. In an experiment, staff in a library

"accidentally" brushed the hands of half the borrowers, most of whom were women, when handing back their cards. Those who had been brushed showed a noticeably more positive attitude to the library and its staff when interviewed, although they could not remember the touch.

Taps to attract attention are often the only kind of deliberate touch permitted between strangers. However, a polite request accompanied by a light touch on the arm can produce a surprisingly positive result. In another experiment, a coin was left in a telephone booth. As people came out, a young man or woman would say, "Excuse me. I think I might have left some money in there a few minutes ago. Did you find it?" Without the accompanying light touch, this request brought about fewer returns of the coin than when the touch was used.

Suppose you are out shopping, and agree to be interviewed by a young man or woman doing market research and holding a clipboard full of forms. Afterwards the interviewer thanks you, touches your hand, arm or shoulder and turns to go. Suddenly all the forms spill to the ground. What would you do?

WHEN TOUCH BECOMES ALL-IMPORTANT

■ *When it is difficult or impossible to express our deeper feelings in words, touch comes to the rescue. It can open an underlying channel of communication between two people that confirms and strengthens their relationship. Meanwhile, even small talk can safely go on without implying superficial interaction. This is especially important when long absences and physical barriers are involved. The elderly couple on the left are visiting their two daughters, both nuns in a closed order.*

How, where and when we touch others can make or break our relationships. If the message conveyed is appropriate, most people, most of the time, will respond positively to being touched. And on occasions it can be socially inappropriate not to touch them.

Whether or not you would help pick up the forms depends to some extent on *where* you were touched. The woman interviewer in this study was helped more by both sexes than her male colleague, and especially by men. However, even she found that her touch had to fall within certain body boundaries to be effective. Touching the hand or shoulder did not elicit help as often as when the touch was on the upper or lower arm. Hand touching was too intimate and shoulder touching overfriendly after such a brief encounter.

Only the arm offers what has been called a "neutral" or "nonvulnerable" body area. "Vulnerable" areas – head, neck, shoulders, hands, torso, lower back, buttocks, legs, feet – are only touched by intimates, while nonvulnerable areas are accessible to anyone, even strangers.

Nonetheless, a fleeting touch on a "vulnerable" area can bring a reward. It has been found that waitresses who touch their customers on the hand or shoulder as they return change receive larger tips. Even though the waitresses risk being thought too familiar, a respectful, ingratiating demeanor, with eyes averted, offsets any threat.

In one study, it was found that professional counselors seemed more expert to their clients if they began and ended a session with a handshake, physically guided the client in and out of the room and gave two brief touches during the meeting. In another, similar touches resulted in clients looking deeper into themselves and talking more openly about their problems to counselors they now judged as warmer, more understanding and more genuine than those who did not touch.

Polite and public touching

Politeness sometimes *requires* touching. You shake hands with someone a friend introduces and shake hands again later to show that you accept that a relationship continues to exist. The warmth of these touches can influence the other's attitude in a positive way, but politeness may also require you not to hold the handshake too long or touch in any other way, for the warmth of your greeting and your behavior afterward signal your expectations of the relationship (see *Ch 11*) and it is not polite to expect too much familiarity.

Because of its precise meaning, a congratulatory handshake can be offered with greater warmth than a mere greeting, and so can the handshake that seals a contract, since it symbolizes trust and expectations within a narrowly defined relationship, but how much warmth you can show

WHO MAY TOUCH WHOM, AND WHERE

■ There are in all cultures elaborate rules which specify who may touch whom, under what circumstances, and whereabouts on the body. Taboos generally reflect a culture's attitude to sex. In this study of American college graduates, which records how often different parts of the body are touched in different relationships, fairly distinct "go" and "no go" areas emerge.

Mothers and fathers

◄ Where mothers do or don't feel free to touch their grown-up sons and daughters.

► Where fathers do or don't feel free to touch their grown-up sons and daughters.

Same-sex and opposite-sex friends

◄ Where men and women tend to be touched by friends of the same sex.

► Where men and women tend to be touched by friends of the opposite sex.

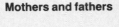

Seldom (0–25%)

Quite often (26–50%)

Often (51–75%)

Very often (76–100%)

in all three of these contexts depends largely on culture. In some cultures the polite way that people behave in public seems quite restrained and "cold" in comparison with others, labeled by social psychologists as "contact cultures." In the contact cultures, without feeling that it is presumptuous, people stand and sit closer (see *Ch.3*) and have more physical contact. One researcher observed 180 touches on average between pairs of acquaintances spending an hour together in San Juan, Puerto Rico and 110 in Paris, France. In Gainesville, Florida, the average was less than twice. In London, England, it was 0. When people touch each other during conversation, their contact commonly includes control touches such as tapping your listener on the arm to emphasize a point, as well as touching on the arm or shoulder to amplify expressions of support and appreciation.

Within contact cultures there can also be differences. Comparisons in Costa Rica, Panama and Colombia (three Latin American countries in close proximity) found the Costa Ricans touching and holding more than the Panamanians or Colombians did.

Patterns of touching can vary widely from culture to culture – and from context to context in a given society. There are "contact cultures" and there are relatively "cold" cultures. But even in cold cultures touch has an indispensable public role.

The types of touches used can also differ between cultures. For example, in greetings, Lapps, Maoris and Malays press their noses against another's cheek with a quick nuzzle-sniff – a far cry from the Western handshake, the distant bow of Japan and the bear-hug *abrazo* of Mexico.

The way children are brought up prepares them for these cultural differences. Observers visited playgrounds and beaches in Greece, the Soviet Union and the United States to study the frequency and nature of touches between children (aged two to five) and those caring for them. They found that the types and number of touches used to punish a child and bring a wandering one back were the same, whether the child was Greek, Soviet or American. However, when it came to the touches used for soothing, holding and play,

AMPLIFYING THE MESSAGE

■ A touch is rarely performed in isolation. It is usually combined with other forms of body language to give it a specific meaning and specific effect. When showing aggression in hostile encounters, for example, the facial expressions of the antagonists can be more important than their manner of touching. The angrier you look, the more aggressive is the act of tapping your finger on someone's chest, or holding onto an arm.

Because touch is so intimate to begin with, adding eye contact (another form of intimacy) can increase the effect too

much. This principle was seen in operation in a variation of the experiment described on the previous page. During interviews, some students were given ample eye contact or were touched on the shoulder, while others received both forms of body language. When the "interviewer" dropped some papers on the floor, those who had received only eye contact or a touch generally helped to pick the papers up, but those who had received both had more intimacy messages than they could feel comfortable with and, as a result, less help was given.

◄ Touch amplifies touch. The warmth of a simple handshake, whether of greeting or congratulation, can be progressively amplified by clasping the other person's hand, arm or shoulder with the free hand or, indeed, by performing a full shoulder embrace. In amplifying a handshake in this way, however, spontaneity is important and care needs to be taken if you do not wish to create an impression of undue familiarity or a patronizing attitude.

▲ Men touching men. Normal inhibitions in public often disappear in sports contexts – even off the field of play. Robust – and sometimes violent – body contact is a central feature of many male-dominated sports, and, especially in team games, exaggerated forms of mutual touching are common in expressions of camaraderie. But care is taken to parody by exaggeration behavior that might otherwise carry sexual overtones.

the American children received significantly fewer.

Another element in polite touching is respect for higher status, for this means allowing a greater liberty to the other than you claim for yourself. Research indicates that superiors more often touch subordinates, who do not, in turn, touch their bosses and secretaries (of either sex), teachers and students, supervisors and workers. Not only do superiors employ control touches that inferiors do not have the authority to use, but they may touch subordinates on the hand, the arm or the shoulder when lending encouragement or expressing thanks, while subordinates confine themselves to verbal expressions of these sentiments. When people are shown silhouettes of a pair facing each other, one touching the other on the shoulder, the toucher is judged more assertive and of higher status than the person touched. The toucher is also judged warm and expressive. If both silhouetted people are touching, impressions of status difference disappear.

Sometimes, however, the power of touch is used to achieve power. The status of male participants in a state legislative session in Missouri was rated according to committee leadership, tenure, service, age and other criteria. Then, observers positioned themselves in the gallery and recorded who initiated touch during the many conversations that took place below their vantage point. To their surprise, they discovered that *lower*-status individuals were the ones who initiated touch more.

Here, the men were more or less peers, with roles that were more diffuse and overlapping than, say, those of a boss and secretary. During social exchanges, the lower-status juniors tried to establish more intimate connections with their more powerful and higher-status colleagues by literally making physical contact with them.

Same-sex and opposite-sex touching

Even when culture and status are the same, men and women display notable differences in public touching: there is more touching between females than between males or between females and males.

Travelers at Kansas City International Airport in the United States, for example, were studied to see how they touched the people who came to meet them. Women greeted other women physically, with mutual lip kisses, embraces and other kinds of touches and held each other for relatively long periods. In contrast, the men just shook hands – and for them, this signaled that touching was over.

In American surveys, men agree less than women do with statements such as "I enjoy persons of my sex who are comfortable with touching," "I sometimes enjoy hugging friends of the same sex," and "physical expressions of affection between persons of the same sex are healthy." Men are more concerned about their sexual identity, and tend to avoid touching other men (except in sports) in case this is interpreted as having homosexual overtones.

Sports represent one special circumstance where exceptional public touching is permitted. Teammates pat each other on the back to encourage and applaud, and they give consoling touches of reassurance. Between men especially, the hugs, kisses, and slaps on the buttocks that would be unwelcome in a different setting are perfectly acceptable on the playing field. The intense enthusiasm of sport legitimizes tactile expressions of emotion between men that otherwise would be seen by many as homosexually threatening.

When a championship swim meet was studied, it was found that winners were touched an average of six times more than losers. The majority of touches were directed to

▶ **Women touching women.** *In the West, women are normally much less inhibited than men when it comes to touching each other in public. In mutual greetings or in giving expression to a sense of fellow feeling, they readily exchange unselfconscious embraces and kisses. Men are normally more watchful of their sexual identity and tend to shy away from behavior that is sexually ambiguous.*

EARLY RELIANCE ON BODY CONTACT

■ *Touch is necessary for infant survival. Premature infants are hyperreactive and must not be touched too much, but those given a medically supervised touch regimen develop more rapidly, leave hospital sooner and become healthier and more alert than other premature infants. Even healthy babies, if they are deprived of touch and handling for long periods, develop a kind of infant depression that leads to withdrawal and apathy; in extreme* cases, they may even waste away and die. On their own, food and medical attention are not enough to sustain life in these touch-starved children.

■ **The illustrations** on this page convey something of the pleasure that infants take in tactile sensations and in intimate contact with the mother's body, also the comfort that contact with the parental body brings, especially in moments of distress.

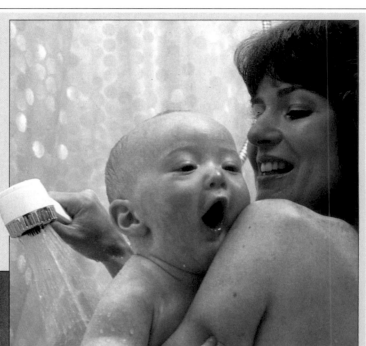

Our deepseated need to touch and be touched by other people, and the pleasure we find in tactile intimacy, are rooted in our need in infancy for protective, caring, reassuring body contact with a parent or caregiver – usually our mother.

neutral areas of the body, where they were less likely to be misunderstood as overpersonal or sexual: 60 percent to the hand, 23 percent to the back or shoulders and only 10 percent to the head and buttocks. There was no difference in the touches exchanged by men and the touches exchanged by women.

Men and women also feel different about heterosexual encounters. In a survey of 4,000 American men and women in their twenties, the women reported that they felt much less comfortable about touching and being touched by men than the men felt about being touched by women. This difference in attitude was widespread, occurring in men and women from every one of 40 different geographic regions of the United States.

Another study confirmed this. Both men and women

WHERE WE MOST LIKE WHOM TO TOUCH US

■ Universally, being touched by another person is a potential source of deep pleasure. But the pleasure is as much psychological as sensual: it depends primarily on who is doing the touching. If it is the right person – a close friend of the opposite sex – there are no "no go" areas, and women report that literally no part of the body is unexcited by touch. With other touchers the picture is more complicated.

Close Friends

▶ Where men and women say they would most enjoy being touched by a close friend of the opposite sex

◀ Where men and women say they would be most and least happy to be touched by a close friend of the same sex

Strangers

▶ Where men and women say they would be most and least happy to be touched by a stranger of the opposite sex

◀ Where men and women say they would be most and least happy to be touched by a stranger of the same sex

Very unpleasant

Not unpleasant

Very pleasant

93

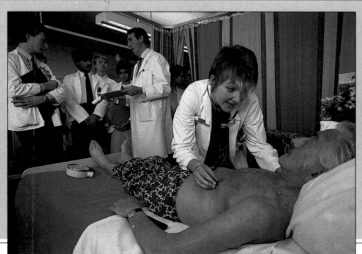

◀ **The soft toys** this little girl is holding are reassuring substitutes for the presence of her mother. Referred to by psychologists as "transitional objects," they reflect not a lack of parental attention or an unnaturally insecure child but the entirely natural process of learning to come to terms with maternal absences. It is a positive phase of growing up and not a "babyish" retrograde step.

◀ **Doctors are licenced** to touch us in ways we would not tolerate from anyone else with whom we were emotionally uninvolved. The doctor-patient relationship, some students of human behavior argue, has much in common with the infant-caregiver relationship – and explains why, for many of us, the sickbed is not always an entirely unappealing prospect.

reported that they considered the idea of being patted, brushed, squeezed or stroked by a girl- or boyfriend equally attractive. Men, however, were just as happy receiving this sort of touch from a stranger of the opposite sex, whereas women felt that, in this situation, it would be an invasion of their privacy. The results of these studies were particularly surprising because many others have shown no variations between the sexes in their actual behavior. It has been suggested that women feel uncomfortable about these touches because they sense that they are submitting to male dominance whereas men take a touch as an invitation to express dominance.

Women's inhibitions about cross-sexual touching seem to be reduced in a sport setting, just as men's inhibitions about same-sex touching are. Researchers visiting bowling alleys in the Kansas City area during a mixed league competition observed almost no differences between men and women in either giving or receiving touches. Public sports events – the immediacy and excitement of competition – seem to make the sexes more equal.

How we react to being touched when we happen to feel uncomfortably dependent or insecure may depend on our sex. Women tend to respond positively, men more warily. For courting couples, however, nothing is more important than mutual physical contact.

With a greater need for personal space than women, men find crowds much more uncomfortable and threatening to be in. In one study, the electrical conductivity of the skin (a physical measure of emotional stress, also employed in lie-detector tests) was used to assess the reactions of men, when placed in all-male crowds, and women when placed in all-female crowds. While most individuals, regardless of sex, showed arousal and annoyance in contact with others, the men showed the greatest stress.

When we feel dependent, vulnerable and afraid, our reactions to the touch of anyone, either male or female, can be quite different depending on our own sex. To accept touch at a time like that is to acknowledge fear and vulnerability – something many men find hard to do. For example, a reassuring touch from a female nurse shortly before a serious operation was enough to lower blood pressure and anxiety in women, but it *raised* blood pressure and anxiety in men.

The origins of sex differences are firmly rooted in childhood. In infancy, boys are handled more vigorously than girls, and are encouraged to engage in rough and tumble play. How parents perform as role models is also important: mothers touch their children more than fathers do (and the latter rarely touch their sons after adolescence), and fathers touch babies more for playing, while mothers do so more for soothing and grooming.

This pattern continues throughout childhood, so that by the time puberty arrives, the way each sex uses personal space and touching has already been learned by experiences with parents and peers. For example, boys tend to keep greater physical distances from each other than girls do.

In friendship, love and courtship

Warm and friendly touches – showing care and concern – occur most easily between relatives, friends and friendly neighbors and close workmates. The pats, holds and teasing touches that occur sometimes between friends are also characteristic of closer relations between family and friends, where closeness is signaled too, and constantly renewed, by embraces and kissing. The complete physical intimacy of a sexual relationship usually has to be achieved by passing through all of these categories of closeness, but even prospects of friendship can be affected by the way we touch.

The kinds of touch that are appropriate to establish a positive relationship in opposite-sex encounters are not the same kinds of touch that are appropriate for same-sex encounters. In one study, same and opposite-sex pairs met potential new friends at a series of three private meetings. After each meeting each partner privately recorded his or her impression of the other by rating how much they liked them.

By prearrangement, at the end of the second and third meetings, one of the partners touched the other with an arm touch or a back pat. When the partners were both male or both female, both types of touch were equally effective in

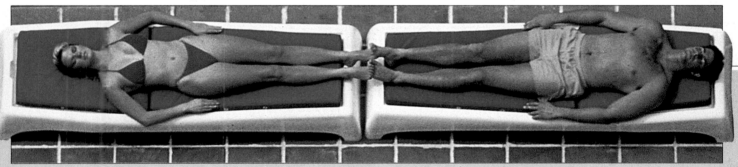

95

◄ **Touch is the principal language of courtship.** *It is through their hand-holding, kisses, caresses and embraces that courting couples express most convincingly their feelings for each other and pleasure in each other's company.*

So important does physical contact and the dialog of touch become at this time that it has been compared to the original state of infancy, and even described as a "second babyhood" phase. The thirst for con-stant physical intimacies among older adolescents and young adults can be almost as insatiable as a baby's, and many of the intimacies exchanged are noticeably char-acteristic of those exchanged between mother and infant. Partners expect or demand to be "held tight" as an expression of true love and commitment – and sometimes may even refer to each other as "baby." And, again like babies, courting couples may be uninhibited by the usual social conventions, as they exchange (often quite advanced) intimacies in public places.

▲ **The possibilities for tactile stimulation** *that the body offers are endless, and part of the joy of a developing close relation-ship is discovering new ones. An older couple may well have invented a subtle and sophisticated language of touch that is all their own. The couple here are probably doing no more than affectionately acknowledging each other's presence through gentle foot contact. But they could just as easily be stimulating each other in ways which exploit the complex sensitivity of the soles of the feet.*

cementing a positive impression. However, when the pairs were of opposite sex, the more intimate arm touch enhanced positive ratings more than the back pat, which seems to have been experienced as either overfriendly or superior.

Couples signal that they want to move to a higher level of intimacy by going through a predictable sequence. After initial visual and verbal contact, attraction expresses itself by a movement of the hand to hand or arm. Side to side contact is usually the first extensive touch. Arm to waist is a romantic bridge to a series of highly tactile stages that become increasingly erotic and sexual: mouth to mouth kisses, hand to face caresses, hand to body for sexual fondling, mouth to body, hand to genitals and then sexual intercourse.

Whether conscious of it or not, even at early stages friends and potential courting partners gain important knowledge of each other's personalities and their suitability for a long-term relationship, as attitudes toward touching and being touched become apparent.

What these attitudes reveal has been studied by comparing the results of personality tests with responses to statements such as "When I am with my girl/boyfriend, I really like to touch that person to show affection." "I enjoy my girl/boyfriend touching me when we watch television at home," "If I were to tell a same-sex friend that I have just got a divorce, I would want that person to touch me," and "I enjoy an opposite-sex acquaintance touching me when we greet or say goodbye or when he or she asks me out for a drink."

The results showed that individuals who like touching are more talkative, cheerful and socially dominant. They are also less bound by convention, etiquette and social image, showing an independence of thought, and are more inquiring, skeptical and nonconforming. By contrast, those who are least comfortable with touch tend to be lower in intelligence and, to some degree, emotionally unstable and socially withdrawn.

Other studies have concluded that men and women with more negative attitudes towards touching members of the same sex tend to have more authoritarian and rigid personalities. And, regardless of sex, those who are less comfortable with touch are also more apprehensive about communicating, less talkative and have lower self-esteem.

WHY WE CONSTANTLY TOUCH OURSELVES

■ Why do we all keep finding ourselves from time to time crossing our legs, clasping our knees, folding our arms, holding our own hands, resting our heads on our arms, stroking our chins, brushing our lips with a finger, or performing any one of a thousand similar acts of self-touching?

■ We first learn to touch ourselves when we carry out basic physical processes such as eating, eliminating and grooming. Such touching gratifies primary needs and this gratification releases tension. Later in life, self-touching continues to be associated with reduced tension and anxiety – it appears to calm us. In experiments involving mental tasks, those who are allowed to touch themselves perform better, apparently benefiting, through reduced tension, from a longer attention span and improved memory.

Touching yourself can give away the discomfort you feel when you form a negative impression of someone. In simulated job interviews, interviewers who touched themselves a great deal were more likely to report afterwards that they had felt a negative attitude towards the applicant.

■ Another approach to acts of self-touching that do not solely involve self-protection, self-cleaning or symbolic signaling explains them as "unconsciously mimed acts of being touched by someone else." They are supposed unconsciously to recall not so much the tactile gratification of primary needs as the tension-easing comfort of maternal body contact or the caring attentions of a close friend or lover.

▶ The teenager shown here, simultaneously hugging a thigh, arm and breast while intermittently touching her face, is conserving her body heat on a cool day in the best way she can short of curling up into a ball. But at the same time she is not merely allowing the parts of her body involved to rest in contact with one another: she is applying additional self-comforting pressures and touches.

Your attitude to touching may affect or reflect your personality. Surveys show that those for whom touch is important in their social repertoire are generally more cheerful, more dominating and less bound by convention than those who avoid touching.

Common traits found in those comfortable with touch include satisfaction with their bodies and physical appearance, less anxiety and tension in everyday life, a stronger, more confident and positive sense of identity and less fear and suspicion of the motives and intentions of others.

Touch and marital satisfaction

Greater physical intimacy in marriage is correlated with finding each other more attractive and companionable and with higher satisfaction about expressions of affection and sexuality. However, lack of physical intimacy is less strongly associated with separation and divorce than are the failure to feel emotionally close and the failure to communicate verbally.

Frequency of sexual intercourse for many couples

decreases with age and time although caring touch still remains a vital part of their relationship, and this affects the way they and other people assess its strength. Couples who are seen touching more, are judged to be more emotionally close, relaxed and attentive to each other than nontouching couples. Married couples who tend to sit closer and touch more report greater happiness in marriage, and dating and engaged couples who touch more score higher on psychological measures of romantic love.

One clinical study of women who sought help for feelings of depression showed that their need to be held was often so strong, that even though they were not in the mood, they sometimes engaged in sex with their husbands just for the comfort of being held. Women often complain that there is not enough reciprocal touching (such as cuddling) in their relationships with men, and some may find one-sided touches (being hugged while busy washing the dishes or being kissed on the cheek) "condescending." **ST**

▲ **Acts of self-touching** (sometimes termed "self-contact" or "auto-contact") are extremely common, as this group photograph reveals.

Almost everyone present is unconsciously performing some or other variation on the self-touching theme – finger nibbling, hand in pocket, head

on arm, tension grooming, wrist and knee clasping, self-hugging, arm folding, leg crossing and so on.

Greeting and Parting

A NATURAL and appropriate greeting can set the right tone for an encounter, and how we say good-bye may leave a warm impression that carries over to the next time. However, greetings and partings can occasionally be difficult to manage without embarrassment or offense. Doubts can arise, after greeting from a distance, about whether it is appropriate to approach, to amplify the greeting at closer range. In both greetings and partings there may be a question of how much respect to show and how to show it. Assumptions about the relationship may need to be reassessed during the ritual itself, in the light of unexpected coolness, familiarity or enthusiasm. Being introduced to people for the first time presents particular problems, because the way we greet them influences a first impression.

Acknowledging another's presence

Greetings do not necessarily open a conversation, nor are they necessarily planned or anticipated. Strangers who pass on a forest path, for example, may nod and exchange greetings without stopping or saying anything else. This gives reassurance that each has friendly rather than hostile intentions.

Most greetings are between people who already know each other; although even they may only be passing ones, for instance in the corridor at work. Passing greetings between friends and acquaintances may seem pointless, but they are important displays of recognition which affirm that a relationship exists.

In most public places – for instance, a bar, bus or a daytime city street – the majority of people you encounter are strangers. Their presence does not require acknowledgment. But when you catch sight of acquaintances or friends, you single them out with a "distant greeting." You exchange glances, showing that you are willing to greet them. A hasty look away would be a sign that you were not willing. You also toss or nod your head and raise your eyebrows, you usually smile, and you may wave or call out a verbal greeting or the person's name.

The main reason why people wait to catch acquaintances' eyes before approaching them is fear of being ignored or rebuffed. If they do not recognize you, either you are not worth remembering or they are deliberately "cutting" you because you are not worth knowing. Greeting may seem a trivial part of a relationship, but its importance becomes obvious in its absence – the cut is both rude and cruel.

Our greetings and farewells are not only symptomatic of the state of our relationships as we see them but are also powerful social tools: their style heavily influences people's impressions of us, and their neglect can cause deep offense.

It is the fact that greeting is a small and effortless token of acknowledgment that gives such force to a refusal to greet someone, especially if you keep a blank expression and do not even look the person in the eye. By not greeting or showing any sign of recognition you are treating someone as a stranger. You are denying that any relationship exists or has ever existed.

Familiar approaches and close greetings

When people meet, eye contact and an eyebrow flash may be all that occurs, as in greeting someone in passing. But such distant greetings are often followed by approaching for a "close greeting," within the personal zone or even the intimate zone (see *Ch 3*), involving touch – shaking hands, embracing or patting. There may be back-slapping, and a child may be touched on the head. Turning your body towards the other person at this point is a sign that you welcome such a greeting. (Ignoring someone's orientation toward you is an insulting rebuff.) We use

■ **The joy of greeting and the sorrow of parting** are vividly captured in these photographs. The fact that the greeting is directed at a father and husband who might never have returned, and that the parting involves husbands who may never return from the war zone for which they are bound, make these moments and the extreme reactions they elicit especially poignant.

distinctive phrases of greeting, and we each ask how the other has been. The warmth, familiarity or reserve of the greeting shows how we feel about our relationship. Understanding what the other's greeting expresses is something that often requires interpretation and we may have to modify our own manner in the light of it.

People do not look at each other much after initial eye contact until they are close enough to begin their close greeting. The person who covers more ground looks less. Perhaps this reflects only the fact that the greater distance involves more potential obstacles. But more probably it is because both approaching and staring suggest an invasion of personal space, giving the impression of either hostility or assumed intimacy.

This explanation is supported by the fact that people look at each other least in the two or three seconds before the close greeting begins, when there are presumably the fewest obstacles. At this point they often turn their faces right away, cutting off the possibility of any disturbing eye-contact, so they can prepare themselves and signal when they are ready. Smiles also fade or disappear – the aversion of gaze and reduction of smiling make the final look and smile a much warmer and more dramatic show of undivided attention.

Approaches often occur without an initial distant greeting – for example, when you go up to a friend who has not noticed you.

If someone hesitates before approaching in these circumstances or after a distant greeting, there is usually more politeness in this than genuine fear of being cut. Making an approach may be presumptuous, implying that your relationship is important enough to the other person to justify

ANIMAL GREETINGS

■ When pairs of nesting birds come together again after gathering food, they perform greeting displays to signal mutual recognition. Some penguins, for example, stand belly to belly, and, pointing their faces skyward, touch beaks. Social mammals, such as the hooved animals that live in herds, and pack animals, such as wolves, greet not only their mates but others as well. They employ their own particular displays, such as mutual head to tail sniffing in dogs and grimacing and nodding in zebras.

Greetings are common among chimpanzees – males touch each others' testicles and both sexes touch hands, hug and kiss. Chimpanzees also invite grooming with a "bow,"

by lowering their heads. Social animals of lower rank display submission in greeting higher ranking ones by lowering the body and making it small. Even a male giraffe will make itself less tall when approaching a more dominant male. This contrasts with the bristling and self-enlarging displays that animals use to show threat and dominance.

Lowering the body and offering the hands or touching seem universal features of greeting in humans too. The variety in the details of human ceremonies shows there is a strong cultural overlay, but the common features shared with the chimpanzee's displays suggest that some aspects of human greeting may be innate.

the inconvenience that it may cost to stop and show interest in you. Sometimes, questions of rank and privilege determine who will do the approaching and when they may approach. It is easier, for example, to feel comfortable about going up to an employer who stops and turns toward you with a welcoming smile after a distant greeting. Traditional etiquette books say that a gentleman should not approach a lady of his acquaintance until she makes a sign that she wishes to know him. It is the lady's privilege to decide.

Between family members such hesitation is out of place. People also approach without hesitation those whom they have a right or duty to greet, such as their hosts at a party. They may hesitate to interrupt, but hover in a way in which shows they expect attention.

Respectful greetings and salutes

Different cultures perform close greetings and partings in distinctively different ways. Polynesians rub noses. Tibetans stick out their tongues and in some parts of New Guinea males pat each other's buttocks. Embraces with back-slapping are common between men in Latin countries, but comparatively rare in northern Europe or the USA. The French shake hands at parting more than the English. An Englishman would shake hands with a Frenchwoman after a business meeting, but might find her offered handshake

SHAKING HANDS

■ *Shaking or clasping another person's right hand with yours is a traditional greeting in many, but not all, societies. Some, such as Polynesia, have acquired the handshake from the West. Others, such as Japan and India, do not use touch in greetings. Indians and Southeast Asians use the hands, but place their own palm to palm as if praying.*

Since the handshake involves physical contact, in traditional etiquette it is less formal than the bow. In the USA and Britain it is used as a fairly formal, business-like greeting or parting. People sometimes display more affection by including a kiss with the hand-shake, or by embracing the other's shoulder with the left hand. Adding your left hand directly to the handshake, however, or using the left hand to grip the other person's fore-arm can make them feel that you are trying to control their movements.

A strong, warm handshake is important in making a good impression. We often hear unpleasant handshakes being criticized as violent or viselike or mocked as "boneless," like a "dead fish." Categorizations of handshakes usually carry over to categorizations of personality – as excessively forceful, for example, or insipid.

According to etiquette books men ought to shake hands in greeting; for women it is optional. In Britain and the USA men do shake hands more than women, but in continental Europe the difference is less marked. Men often shake hands with women, although traditionally it was a woman's prerogative to offer a hand-shake to a man. There is com-paratively little handshaking between women except at a first meeting, or when one is congratulating the other. If women do touch each other they usually embrace and offer some version of the kiss.

"The French shake hands at parting more than the English. An Englishman would shake hands with a Frenchwoman after a business meeting, but might find her offered handshake after a relaxed social encounter disappointingly formal."

after a relaxed social encounter disappointingly formal. Among the most striking differences are the ways in which respect enters into greetings, but this is nevertheless an area of underlying similarity.

Greetings which involve lowering the whole body to the ground, as in the traditional Chinese *kow-tow* or the West African Mossi salute, seem extremely self-abasing to Western eyes. Even the Japanese bow behind a departing superior's back strikes Westerners as slightly degrading. But lowering the body or head is a universal sign of respect to a superior. In England it is proper to curtsy or make a low bow to royalty, and to kneel to receive a knighthood. People also kneel to pray.

Nineteenth-century etiquette books stressed status and precedence. Their rules concerning greetings and how they start are based on rank (lords to receive more respect than commoners, generals more than lieutenants), and notional rank (older people to receive more respect than younger, women more than men). The principles adopted are still sometimes employed today where rank is clear-cut; status-marking greetings, such as a servant's or a subject's bow or a GI's salute, should be offered unbidden; but in ordinary social encounters where the greeting is one used between equals, such as a handshake, an inferior should wait for a superior to offer his greeting rather than taking the initiative.

Status plays a lesser part in Western greetings today than it did in the 19th century, but there is a still a rule that inferiors should put themselves out more. They should stand up, perhaps to attention, when superiors enter the room. They should show respect by going to meet superiors, whether at the door or at an airport. These same actions, however, could also be a demonstration of love rather than a demonstration of respect.

First meetings and introductions

Greeting a stranger can be particularly awkward because the meeting itself may be a source of stress. Infants develop fear of strangers at between seven and eight months, when they begin to make the distinction between who they know and who they do not. We never completely outgrow this uncertainty about people outside our established circle. As adults we worry especially about the first impressions we make, finding ourselves at the mercy of someone who is bound to form judgments on the basis of very little genuine knowledge about us (see *Ch 6*).

The way we greet them is bound to be one of the few clues that will guide them. For this reason, etiquette books, when they were in fashion, stressed the importance of greeting correctly. Your greeting had to suit the circumstances and take into account the other person's status, sex and age. Showing that you knew the rules demonstrated your social worth. Performing graciously and without clumsiness, displaying deference but also self-confidence, said something about what kind of person you were. Even in our less consciously rule-bound age, we have not moved very far away from these principles.

Many greetings between strangers occur during introductions. Here a third party gives the names and often some

PUTTING THE RIGHT INTERPRETATION ON A GREETING

■ Greetings, like any signals, require interpretation. The personality of the greeter and the circumstances of the meeting may alter the way a greeting is made. These variables need to be understood in order to draw the right conclusions concerning the other person's assumptions and expectations about the relationship between you and the way the encounter that is beginning will go.

A kiss freely offered from someone who does not usually kiss in greeting means more than one from someone who usually does. The secretly love-struck, in particular, are prone to reading too much into greetings that are merely friendly, a squeezed hand or a lip brushing against the cheek exciting hopes that would not

be so easily fueled if objective observation of the love-object's greeting style were possible. Equally, it is possible to miss the special warmth in someone's greeting if you, but not they, take such warmth for granted.

Greetings after long separations are more elaborate and energetic than after very brief partings, though lovers who have been parted for 24 hours may be as energetic as friends who have not met for years. But even lovers usually greet each other less intimately on formal occasions or in the presence of outsiders. Sometimes, the sense of inhibition is not equal. Then it can rob a greeting of its expected excitement and introduce confusion into a relationship.

Obviously, kisses are warmer and more familiar than hand-shakes and nods, which we employ to signal a lower level of intimacy. Verbal greeting and forms of address also establish the character of the relationship – "Sir" clearly implies more respect than "Jones" which is less familiar than "Fred." "Hi" is more familiar than "How do you do?" used for strangers. "How are you" is used for friends and acquaintances.

Partners in greeting may negotiate to find the level of relationship that suits them, with, for example, "May I call you John?" or "Aren't you going to give your mother a kiss?"

Sometimes, negotiation is not so explicit. When one person offers a greeting such as "Hi," the response is usually at the

same level of formality or familiarity – for example, "Hello," "Howdy" or, of course, "Hi." In this case the first speaker does not usually offer any further greeting. Sometimes, however, the response is at a different level from the greeting: "How do you do?" or "Good morning," in reply to "Hi." If this happens the first speaker often greets again, usually at the new level, but sometimes at the original level.

Listen for adaptation when people are greeting. It does not matter whether the second greeter is more or less formal than the first – a similar pattern occurs. This act of coordination allows the ensuing encounter to reflect synchronized expectations for the participants' potential or existing relationship.

other personal details, in effect vouching for each of the strangers and confirming their identities and social worth. In former times you could not speak to someone to whom you had not been introduced – they needed a "reference."

The introducer helps to create the strangers' first impressions of each other. When you introduce people you often state your relationship to at least one of them, or show this by the way you name them – saying "Mr Jones," for example, instead of "John," or "JoJo." Your serious or your frivolous manner, your tone of voice and whether and how you touch either or both (see below) are all signs of your relationship to each person and your expectations about their possible future relationship.

The statements the introducer makes provide a topic of conversation, but also usually put the person described in a good light. Nevertheless people do not always like the way the introducer describes them or names them. They sometimes reply to "This is Mr Jones" with "Call me John," or to being described as a "personal financial consultant" with "I'm an accountant." Such corrections are easy if they

offer more friendliness or modesty than the introducer's remarks, but it is more dificult to change "John" to "Mr Jones," or to inflate your job description, without giving a bad impression.

Introductions go in one direction: one person is introduced to the other. Traditional etiquette says that inferiors should be introduced to superiors (and younger to older, men to women). To catch the attention of the superior, the introducer may first mention the name of the superior, then name and describe the inferior, who is therefore *presented* to the other. Nowadays status is less important, and at ordinary social gatherings the person presented is simply the new arrival – the one who has just joined the group, or been brought across by the introducer.

Greetings during introductions may present problems, especially if more than two people are being introduced. Generally the person to whom the other is presented greets first, following etiquette rules about the superior taking the initiative. When status does not count in introductions, the same initiative may be taken in order to welcome the

KISSING AND ITS ORIGINS

■ Some anthropologists believe that kissing originated in the act (still practiced in some cultures today) whereby a mother passed pre-chewed food to her infant during the weaning period. It was the strong association of this act with comfort, security and a loving relationship that conferred on kissing its special value.

■ In different societies, people kiss others' hands, feet, shoulders, cheeks, brows, eyes and

the hems of their clothing. In Europe gentlemen used to kiss ladies' hands. However, not all societies use the kiss or even approve of it. Some African cultures are revolted when they see foreigners pressing their mouths together. In France the president kisses men on both cheeks in formal ceremonies, whereas kissing is not much used in greetings between males in Britain or the USA except between fathers and young sons. ·

Kissing is an intimate greeting and is sometimes obviously sexual. It may appear so to the receiver regardless of the intention of the giver of the kiss. The anthropologist Raymond Firth describes an American woman's shock at her father-in-law's insistence on kissing her on the lips. But she may have misinterpreted his intentions. Social psychologist Adam Kendon described a father-in-law who placed his palms under his daughter-in-law's chin, and

used this same gesture when greeting children. A kiss to the mouth is non-sexual when greeting children, so the father-in-law's kiss may have been innocent, but misunderstandings can clearly arise from using the same greeting in different relationships.

When kissing is not mouth-to-mouth, one person usually gives the kiss, as a display of respect or affection, and the other receives it (on the cheek, the hands, etc). Kissing an

Introductions go in one direction. Traditionally, inferiors are introduced to superiors, younger people to older, men to women. Nowadays status is less important. At ordinary social gatherings the person presented is simply the new arrival.

newcomer into an established conversation group.

While all this is going on, you have to coordinate your greeting with the introducer's patter and with what the others are doing. You may also find it a problem to remember names, especially if you are concentrating on timing your handshakes, nods and hellos. One way to help your memory is to repeat the names – "Hello Julie." But, unintentionally, a list of repetitions like this may make you seem overly assertive.

Pleasure and sorrow at parting

People do not just leave each other at the end of a meeting. You do not even walk out without saying good-bye after sitting at work near a friend, although you may not have exchanged a word for hours. Like greetings, partings recognize the existence and nature of a relationship.

Unlike greetings, however, partings have an ambivalent character. You must show pleasure at what has just passed, but sadness at the forthcoming separation. You must leave people while at the same time protesting a desire for their company. Disentangling yourself may be especially difficult if you are trying to be sympathetic and supportive.

As with greetings, ceremonial actions in the parting ritual show the relative status of the person you are leaving and their value to you. The "close" demonstrations are much the same: standing up, shaking hands, embracing, speaking, kissing and waving appear in both greetings and partings. There are also parallel "distant actions," such as waving until the train rounds the first bend. Here you want to give the other person your attention for as long as possible, or to hold, rather than to catch, their attention. Putting yourself

out is again a sign of respect: following someone to the door or taking them to the airport shows you value their presence. It prolongs the time you can be with them and proves you are prepared to make sacrifices for them.

Just as the superior is supposed to take the initiative in offering greetings, so he or she should decide when an encounter is to close. The inferior may ask permission to leave, but the higher the status of your companion, the more difficult it is for you to provide a satisfactory excuse for leaving.

In parting ceremonies we typically state future intentions to meet, describe what we will be doing in the meantime, and express best wishes for these activities. "Farewell" and "Good-bye" – God be with you – proclaim these wishes when taken literally. Our "I hope"s and "Thank you"s parallel the "Missed you"s and "How have you been?"s of our greetings.

Again, different words mark different relationships – "Good evening" is for strangers and "Good-bye" or "Good night" for friends. Partings also give you a chance to reaffirm affection and avoid leaving on bad terms after a fraught meeting. Equally you reinforce feelings of coolness by declining a kiss or performing the formalities brusquely. Longer separations are preceded by more elaborate farewells, as comparison of drawn-out partings in airport lounges and brief good-byes from the breakfast table quickly demonstrates.

Interestingly, there seems to be no ritual of parting among other animals – they presumably do not have any conception of the future of their relationships and therefore do not need to reassure each other that there will be such a future or that the past has been worthwhile. They signal their intentions and attitudes at the outset of an encounter, but not at its end. **RL**

TENSION AND GROOMING

◄ The "air kiss" (far left) and an infant kissing its mother (left).

adult on the cheek or forehead out of affection may seem condescending, for this is what we do to babies and children.

In the "air kiss" two people put their cheeks in contact and each kisses into the air. This allows two women to protect make-up and avoid erotic overtones. But more fundamentally it may be a show of equality. Both parties receive affection: offering the cheek and not touching the other person with their lips.

■ Greetings and partings are moments of tension. You are on display. Your status or your expectations about a relationship may be brought into question. You may make a fool of yourself. The tension of all this is revealed by grooming.

In approaching one another, people adjust their glasses or stroke their beards. Women puff their hair or push it out of their eyes, and men sometimes hitch up their trousers. Sometimes they may be giving attention to their appearance deliberately, but more often these are unconscious ways of releasing ten-

sion. Like the toe tapping and finger drumming that we do in moments of frustration or indecision, these are "displacement activities" – activities that use up and so displace the energy that tension injects into us.

Tension-related grooming appears immediately before or immediately after interaction, not in the middle of conversation. In introductions the person who is presented grooms more often than the one they are presented to. The presented person is more likely to be described, and so is more obviously the center of atten-

tion. In some cultures (in Tibet, for example, and among the Ainu of northern Japan) stroking your beard or head has been incorporated into the formal actions of greeting.

People also try to reduce tension with laughter. Immediately after a serious greeting or introduction a light hearted remark will often occasion disproportionate amusement, though such "icebreaking" remarks may, of course, upset a stranger who does not share your sense of humor.

Making Conversation

CONVERSATIONS are such common, everyday events that we easily take them for granted and assume that they require no special skills. Yet at some time or other, most of us have had problems talking with other people. You may find yourself unable to get a word in edgeways, and feel foolish or inadequate. Sometimes you have to interrupt rudely to get the floor, and are left feeling that, to other people, you must seem unpleasantly aggressive. Or having been desperate to speak, you find that, once you have the floor, you do not know how to give it up, and you risk being considered boring.

People often speak of the "art" of conversation, usually when referring to particularly eloquent speakers, but some of the most detailed skills of this art are ones that all of us

have had to master. Frame-by-frame analysis of video-recorded conversations has revealed the complexity even of some of the most basic of interchanges. Even though the best conversations seem spontaneous, that is not because we are doing without *rules* – rather, we are following the rules automatically and with unconscious ease. Becoming more conscious of how these rules work helps people to achieve an even greater fluency.

Starting a conversation

Everyone sometimes finds it difficult to strike up conversations. The importance of doing so is obvious. To have relationships, you have to meet people and get to know them. To get to know them, you have to talk to them. At some point, there has to be an opening line, but how do you know what to say?

Conversations often begin when one person remarks, "Beautiful weather, isn't it?" or asks some other clichéd question. Conversation openers are rarely original – the anxiety of making the first approach is not conducive to creative thought – but this does not matter. What does matter is that these openers are recognized for what they really are – attempts at starting a conversation. They are a form of what the anthropologist Bronislaw Malinowski termed "phatic communion": "in which ties of union are created by a mere exchange of words." The words are unimportant – the fact that they have been spoken *is*.

There are exceptions. The livelihoods of confidence

CONVERSATIONAL SYNCHRONY

▲ **Beating out the rhythm**
A girl lying on a beach near Bordeaux, France, moves her hands, nods her head, even blinks, in time with what she says. A listening friend nods, blinks, shifts her body and makes sounds of attention and agreement in synchrony with the other's rhythm. It is obvious that of all the objects that might draw her attention on a sunlit afternoon by the sea, it is the conversation that holds her. An unconscious "interactional synchrony" like this occurs in all encounters that we feel right about (see Ch 4).

> The art of conversation involves intricate skills of social coordination. Showing interest and being interesting, starting conversations and ending them, taking your turn or interrupting, bring all our communication resources into play.

tricksters, for example, depend on their ability to engage a stranger's attention immediately. As a result, they are quite skillful at devising original openers. On hearing the Irish accent of a potential victim, one conman, who did not know that he was speaking to a researcher in communications skills, introduced himself by saying, "What wonderful poets the Irish are." Then he launched straight into Oscar Wilde's "Ballad of Reading Gaol," managing to get to the sixth verse before he could be stopped. This was a different sort of conversation opener.

Conversation is not simply the content of your speech; it is about timing as well – and this is often where the real art comes in. How you will know when an opening line is welcome will depend on the nonverbal clues you pick up from the person you want to talk to. The American psychologist Monica Moore has studied the nonverbal signals that women send – in situations ranging from singles' bars to university libraries – to indicate that they are

willing to be approached by men. (Unfortunately, she did not study what signals men send out to women.) These include "room-encompassing" and "short, darting" glances, "head tosses," "hair flips," and smiles. It is important to interpret such signals correctly and time your opening line as a *response*.

Once an opening line has been successfully delivered, a reply is needed. If the person who has been addressed wants a conversation, the reply must communicate this by being not too brief and by sounding enthusiastic enough. Enthusiasm is communicated more by the tone of the voice and by body language than by what is actually said. For example, if you reply in a monotone, even if what you say is exceptionally witty, you will sound both uninterested and boring – and not like someone with whom it would be pleasant to have a conversation.

Being a good listener

With the conversation opened, the next thing to do is to find out a few things about the other person – for example, by asking, "Do you live around here?" People usually like

◄ **Striking up a conversation** is easiest when it is obvious that we have interests in common. However, talk between this pair is likely to move on quickly to other topics than tennis. First conversations usually touch lightly on many subjects, as the participants exchange questions and answers that help them to compile personality profiles of each other and establish the range of similarities that they share.

▲ **Nonverbal signals**. Even when talking on the telephone, we rely not only on words but on pauses, rate of speech and pitch of voice in order to interpret the message. Here a speaker adds a forward lean and a serious facial expression to what is undoubtedly an earnest tone of voice. What she says seems to matter more to her than to her relaxed listener, and her folded arms suggest that she sees it as a point of disagreement between them (see Ch 5).

talking about themselves. Encourage them by being a good listener. The best way of doing this is to give a lot of feedback – lots of facial expression (see *Ch 9*), nods and other body-language signals (see *Ch 4*) and verbal signals like "mm-hmm" and "yeah." As well as helping a conversation along, these simple signals can also be used to control it in subtle and sometimes subliminal ways – by varying the intonation of, say "yeah," you can communicate anything from firm belief, to total disbelief. (Try it in conversation, and watch your partners adapt their speech accordingly.)

The anthropologist Ray Birdwhistell has analyzed the function of one type of feedback – nodding – in regulating conversations. He found that if a listener makes single brief nods throughout another person's speech, these act as simple signals of attentiveness, which "sustain the interaction without significant change in the level or content of the communication." However, if a listener employs longer-lasting single nods, these disrupt the flow of speech. Birdwhistell reported that, when he used one such single nod, the person who was speaking to him stopped, shifted his stance and said, "I was only joking." Double nods, Birdwhistell claimed, either modify the rate at which the other person is talking or bring them back to a previously established point. Triple nods usually stop speakers in their tracks, apparently because they are bewildering.

People generally like talking to those who give a lot of feedback because they appear interested and interesting. Feedback can result in even more concrete rewards – research has shown that, at job interviews, candidates who nod are more successful than those who do not.

Another element of conversational skill is paraphrasing what your partners have said – ". . . so there you were in the middle of the street. What happened next?" By virtually repeating their words, you show that you have been listening and are therefore interested. You pay the speaker the compliment of showing that it seems worthwhile to you to sum up what they have said. This encourages them to continue by making them feel confident that what they are saying is interesting, has worth and is being understood.

Questions and answers

What sorts of questions you ask and the answers you give are also important. As a conversation develops, partners will often disclose more and more about themselves. They frequently match each other – if you disclose an intimate detail, your partner will do likewise. But it is important that

▲ **Talking to the doctor** is easier if the doctor puts you at ease. Wearing ordinary clothing, seated in pleasant surroundings at an unimposing desk, the doctor is the woman at left. She has avoided the signals that usually give visual emphasis to the distinctions between her role and the patient's, and she has adopted a relaxed and open posture. These strategies make the patient feel less defensive, and they allow her to be more responsive to the doctor's questions and explanations. The doctor arrives more easily at an accurate diagnosis and the patient takes in more easily the doctor's advice and reassurances.

As a conversation develops, partners will often disclose more and more detail about themselves. It is important that neither discloses too much too early. They should aim for a balance and a gradual build-up in the exchange of information.

neither of you discloses too much too early. Aim for balance and a gradual build-up in the exchange of information.

The situation in which you find yourself can have a bearing on what kind of personal information you divulge. Traveling by air, sitting next to a stranger for a limited time, you may be fairly safe in saying more than you would if you knew that you would be constantly coming across that person in your everyday life. (You may, of course, wish to avoid saying too much because the flight is a long one.) Alternatively, when representing somebody else – your company at a conference or your child at a parent-teacher meeting, for example – you may have to be careful not to let them down by revealing weakness. However, divulging what may, on the face of it, seem like too much information can

have a beneficial effect when dealing with officialdom – by revealing your humanity, you become less of a statistic to the official and more of a person to be helped.

In the initial stages of any social conversation, it is obviously important to create a pleasant atmosphere. The type of feedback you give will help enormously – and it is just as important to use body language when speaking (see *Ch 4*) as when listening – but what you actually say can have a great effect. Compliments are particularly useful, and like opening lines, they do not have to be terribly original – "That's a nice dress you're wearing today, Jane – such a nice color for you." Linguists analyzing more than 600 compliments found that, in general, they kept to a fairly strict formula. For example, the word "nice" occurred in nearly one-quarter and the word "you" in almost three-quarters.

People like compliments, even if they have heard them before. They *can* be overdone – they can make you seem ingratiating – but of the nine most common ways that you may risk being a bore, this is one of the least risky – people rate it the second *least* boring.

Taking your turn

We usually take it for granted that we will somehow, effortlessly and efficiently, interweave our speech with that of everyone else. However, this can be a great deal more difficult than it at first seems. Remember, those wishing to take the floor must begin immediately from where the previous speaker has left off. In a two-person conversation, the main importance of this is to avoid awkward pauses. In

▲ **Are you boring your listeners?** *Signs of relaxed attention shade gradually into symptoms of boredom – there will be times when it is difficult to gauge reactions. In this case, soft furniture and an informal atmosphere encourage postures that would clearly show boredom only in a more formal context (see Ch 5). Listener responses in this scene are insufficient enough, however, that the speaker feels the need to lean forward to communicate his interest in his topic.*

ANATOMY OF A BORE

■ *People resent and dislike those who bore them, and it is not any easier being a boring person. If you are distinctly boring, you are at a distinct disadvantage in conversation and will probably be lonely and have a low opinion of yourself. Almost everyone has some boring traits, however, and it is worth anyone's time to consider the main characteristics of boring people that research has identified.*

If you are simply ingratiating and/or distracting, you are lucky – people answering research questionnaires rate these as the least boring characteristics of the nine listed here. Those who are constantly negative and banal are considered the most boring conversationalists of all. **PT**

Distracting. *Are you easily sidetracked? Do you become overexcited, engage in too much small talk, use too much slang?*

Unenthusiastic. *Do you use too little eye contact, lack expressiveness, and speak in a monotone?*

Ingratiating. *In order to impress, do you try unsuccessfully to be funny. Are you suffocatingly nice?*

Overserious. *Do you rarely smile and always use a serious tone of voice, even when your partner is trying to be light and amusing?*

Negative. *Do you only see the depressing side of things, and are you always complaining about the world and your problems?*

Passive. *Do you do fail to take a full part in conversations or express opinions? Is everything you say too predictable and do you continually conform to the other person's point of view?*

Tedious. *Do you talk too slowly, pause too long before replying, take too long to make a point, and make conversations drag on beyond their normal life?*

Self-preoccupied. *Do you show little interest in others and talk about yourself too much?*

Banal. *Do you only talk about superficial things or are you interested in only one subject? Do you repeat the same stories and jokes again and again?*

a conversation involving three or more people, you may not get to say your piece if you do not jump in promptly at the appropriate moment.

When conversing, people may disagree. They may squabble. They may argue. They may even shout at each other. But for the most part, their conversations will still display a remarkably orderly structure. This is because of turn-taking – only one person talks at any particular time, with changes from one speaker to the next occurring without any noticeable gaps or much overlapping. This order becomes all the more surprising when you remember that the length and content of each turn, the order of speaking and the number of times each speaks are all unknown quantities.

How can you tell when your turn has come? The simplest way is to be aware of pauses. Is the person finished speaking or are they simply stopping to think? The problem with this is that the delays between speakers are often shorter than the pauses within a speech itself. For example, in one study the average pause during speech was 0.807 seconds, whereas the length of the pause between speakers was 0.764 seconds. Other research has shown that, even in conversations involving a good deal of thought – academic discussions, for example – over one-third of the changes of turn take less than one-fifth of a second.

How can you take turns successfully when there is, literally, only a split second in which to decide that it is your turn? Anticipation is the key. Good listeners look ahead to predict and recognize their conversational partner's completion points. This is obviously quite easy when you have asked a question demanding a simple answer, such as "What is your name?" You can anticipate the kind of reply you will get (even if you cannot predict the actual answer) and then you can be ready to take the floor when you

receive it. The problem lies in longer turns, when there can be a number of possible completion points. Luckily, in such situations, speakers seem, quite unconsciously, to use intonation and body language (particularly gesture) to show listeners whether they have reached the end of their turns.

In one study, psychologists spent many hundreds of hours analyzing less than one hour of one conversation. In the end, they identified five "turn-yielding cues" by which speakers signal that they are ready to become listeners – a rising or falling intonation pattern; a drawl; expressions of little meaning, such as "you know," especially when accompanied by a drop in pitch or volume; the completion of a clause; and the termination of a gesture. The more cues that were present at one time, the more likely was the listener to take the floor unchallenged. If the listener tried to speak when these cues were not present, the result was interruption and a tussle for the floor. However, if the speaker made a gesture at any time during speech, this effectively overrode any cues that might be present, and listeners did not try to take over.

Other studies have found that people who are opening a passage of speech are much more likely to hold up or point one hand, draw back their legs, lift one foot or shift the trunk of the body than someone who is merely reacting to what has been said without the intention of speaking. When requesting information a person typically lifts the head or turns it toward the person who is expected to answer. Before replying, the person who thereupon takes the speaking role typically turns the head away briefly from the person who now becomes the listener.

Eye contact also affects turn-taking (see *Ch 8*).

FORMING IMPRESSIONS FROM VOICES

■ When people speak to us, we listen to much more than just their words. Recognizing the sound of a person's voice, for example, is one of the ways we identify who they are, especially on the telephone. Voices also influence impressions.

A deep tone tends to be perceived as a sign of sophistication, sexiness, security and a positive manner. Telephone receptionists, courtroom lawyers, political leaders and radio and television announcers often make a conscious effort to produce this effect.

Men and women are not judged in the same way on the evidence of their voices – we

tend more toward forming an impression of how humorous, sensitive or enthusiastic a woman is, and more toward forming an impression of how much physical and emotional power a man has.

Studies have compared the results of objective personality tests with the everyday judgments people make in response to voice cues. A large proportion of this research has found little basis for accuracy in the everyday judgments. Some studies, however, have correlated breathiness with being unassertive and correlated soft voices lacking in resonance with introversion.

▲ **A convincing tone of voice**. Can the witness be believed? Among "leakages" of deception consistently recorded in the laboratory are a raised voice pitch, a slower rate of speech and speech hesitation. These

deprive a voice of its convincing "tone." Other signs of deception include dilated pupils, reduced blinking and fewer head and hand movements (see *Ch 14*).

When conversing, people may disagree. They may argue. They may even shout at each other. But, for the most part, their conversations will still display a remarkably orderly structure. Turns and interruptions continue to be jointly managed.

Turn-yielding cues usually govern the form of a conversation without those involved being aware of their influence. However, there are always some who succeed by breaking the rules. Political leaders sometimes employ turn-yielding cues when, in fact, they are not finished speaking. When they do this during television interviews, they constantly have to fight off unwanted interruptions. This gives the impression that they are dominating impolite and inept interviewers, and it can make an important contribution to a successful political image.

When to interrupt

Interruptions are an obvious characteristic of conversation, even though they can be irritating and most people dislike them. There are a number of different types. First, there are "simple" interruptions, when two or more people talk at the same time and the person who had the floor stops in mid-flow (in what follows, italics represent people speaking both at the same time):

PERSON A "I think that Charlie was trying to pay you a compliment when he said that *and he...*'

PERSON B "*Yes but* it was a pretty back-handed compliment..."

Then there are "overlaps," when again people talk at the same time, but here the first speaker manages to complete what he or she is saying over the words of the other person:

PERSON A "If you mean he is being sarcastic with you, he's not. *He just isn't.*"

PERSON B "*That's just it.* He's always being sarcastic."

There are also "silent" interruptions: someone takes advantage of a pause (however slight) to interrupt the conversation:

PERSON A "When he says something like that he means..."

PERSON B "...that I'm always butting in where I'm not wanted."

There is also a fourth type of interruption, an unsuccessful

▲ **Speaking in turns formally.** At formal meetings, the person in the chair invites participants to speak in the order that their names appear on an agenda and invites comments and questions after each is finished.

If strict formality is followed, a listener interrupts a speaker only with the permission of the chair. All of this guarantees that important matters are more certain to be dealt with than in ordinary conversation, where

turn-taking is more complex and the direction of discussion less predictable.

one where someone talks at the same time as the speaker but does not manage to take the floor.

Dominant people use a lot of overlaps. In a study of university tutorials, it was found that, to control their course, tutors employed significantly more overlaps than students. The latter primarily used simple interruptions. The advantage of overlaps is that they are quite subtle, allowing speakers to complete what they are saying before control is snatched away from them. They therefore cannot complain. However, overlaps require good anticipation skills – listeners must be able to predict at some distance ahead where the speaker will most probably finish, in order to intervene at this precise point. Simple interruptions are much clumsier and ineffective: one person just barges into the middle of another's turn.

Men interrupt more and use more overlaps than women. A study carried out in California in the early 1970s found men responsible for 96 percent of interruptions. The researchers argued that interrupting is an example of men's dominance and control over women, and is also crucial in their control over conversations. Men's repeated interruptions prevent women from developing arguments and making points. Interrupting regulates which topics are introduced into the conversation.

Later research suggests that the difference between men and women in this respect depends to some extent on the social setting. However, it is a form of sexual inequality that should not be ignored. The best preventive measure for anyone who is a victim of too much interrupting is what is known to psychologists as "behavioral matching," and what ordinary people would call "a taste of their own medicine." If you interrupt back you will gain an equal say in the development and direction of conversation.

Ending conversations

Just as it is important to know how to time an opening line, it is also vital to be aware when a conversation has reached its natural conclusion. There can be few things

Anticipating what the other will do and say is fundamental to good conversation. It involves reading a whole series of signals, some in spoken language, others from intonation or pauses and hesitations, and still others from body language.

more annoying than talking to someone who ignores all signals and carries on when, to all intents and purposes, the conversation has long been over. This is particularly common when people talk on the telephone, perhaps because the person on the other end of the line cannot see your body-language signals and is insensitive to the verbal and vocal signals you must rely on.

Keep an eye out for cues such as sighs, increasingly longer pauses, "well...," and other open-ended verbal feedback as well as such body language as restlessness, less and less eye contact, and movement away. When you realize that a conversation is over, end it quickly but not too abruptly – even if both partners in a conversation know that

they have finished for the moment, you can still offend if you are too brusque when concluding. If the other person continues to cling to the last vestiges of talk take the initiative and firmly close the conversation, keeping it as friendly as possible.

Conversations are built and developed on complex structures. Anticipation is fundamental and involves a whole series of signals – some in spoken language, others from intonation, pauses and hesitations, and still others from body language such as eye contact, gesture and posture. We are aware of all these things when we work out where and when to speak, and of course, we also have to plan what we are going to say, try to understand what everyone else is saying and know when to finish. It is no wonder that most people have trouble at least sometimes managing all these different activities. **GB**

◄ Public speaking demands a special use of many of the same skills that we use in one-to-one conversation. Accomplished speakers try to catch listeners' eyes – as many of them as possible – to involve their audience emotionally. They use gestures of emphasis, moving from subtopic to subtopic in a coherent way, quickly enough to keep listeners interested.

They watch the audience for its reactions and adjust their pace and what they say accordingly. If listeners show signs of boredom or disagreement, the skillful speaker adapts, either by finding more interesting or more convincing words or by moving on to more promising points. Listeners whose faces are too distant to read for responses may still contribute their positive

or negative reactions through the attitudes that show in their postures (see Ch 5).

A SUMMARY OF CONVERSATION SKILLS

TALK

Avoid talking too much or too little. Make roughly an equal contribution to your partners' in informal conversation, reciprocating their amount of talking. In other circumstances adapt to the needs of the situation – for example, you should do most of the talking as interviewee, and avoid talking too much as interviewer.

If you are not sure of the appropriate level of seriousness and formality, follow the lead of others and bear in mind the nature of the occasion. Informal conversations require topic variety but not too much jumping around between topics. Use facial expression and other body language for emphasis and to show the spirit in which you are saying something (eg seriously or lightheartedly). (See Chs 4, 8, 9, 12, 15.)

DISCLOSURE

Disclose information about yourself, at least reciprocating the disclosure level of your conversation partner, if you genuinely want to be friendly. Avoid too much intimate disclosure, however, particularly of a negative kind, and do not get too far ahead of your partner. (See p 106.)

LISTENING

Use supportive responses such as nods of the head and vocal feedback such as "mm-hmm." Look frequently and allow the speaker to catch your eye. Use facial expression to show whether you have understood, are surprised, interested or amused. Use body language especially facial expression to respond to emphasis and the feelings that are being expressed, to show that you have

understood them. Make brief paraphrases of important points. Intersperse these responses with questions, including "open questions" that require more than a word or two to answer. (See Chs 4, 8, 9, 12, 15.)

TURN-TAKING

Contribute to the smooth synchronization of speaking turns by taking the floor during pauses. Avoid taking the floor too often by interruption. When you are offered a turn by others looking at you, take it promptly. Hand over soon after another signals a desire to speak – do not suppress challenges. Signal clearly whether you are continuing to speak or handing over (look away from listeners during a pause if you are not handing over). (See Chs 8, 12.) **PT**

Raising a Smile

HISTORICALLY, humor has often been seen in a very negative way. For example, in the 4th century BC Plato wrote about the "malevolent nature" of humor. For him, it meant trying to give yourself a sense of superiority by deriding lesser mortals, and he taught that only people of little worth did this. Other philosophers as eminent as Aristotle, Hobbes, Descartes and Kant took a similar view during the 2,000 or more years that followed, equating humor with ignorance and foolishness.

Modern psychology, however, regards humor with more respect. Sigmund Freud, the founder of psychoanalysis, saw laughter as a means of safely discharging nervous energy. It provides relief and self-gratification and renders potentially damaging conflicts harmless. While this approach is still very influential, more recent work in psychology has also focused on the *social* value of being funny – the useful role of the well-timed joke or light remark in everyday encounters.

What is a joke?

What, exactly, is a joke? Why do we laugh at certain kinds of stories and what are the essential characteristics of being funny? For humor to exist there must be an essential incongruity – an unexpected conflict or inconsistency between two ideas which is resolved as a joke. This may come about because the punch line bears an unexpected relationship to the opening part of the story, as in this well-worn piece of graffiti:

My mother made me a transvestite.
If I send her the wool will she make me one too?

An even cornier old joke has a similar form and relies on a simple double meaning:

My dog has no nose.
Then how does he smell?
Terrible!

Another regular feature of humor is "displacement." Here the most obvious interpretation of the situation is displaced by a less obvious or unexpected one. Take, for example, a typical psychiatrist joke:

Doctor, I keep thinking that there are two of me.
OK, but don't both speak at once.

The basic incongruities that lead to humor need not be expressed in the form of a spoken or written joke. Sometimes they occur naturally – for example, when a woman trips and falls into what looks like a romantic embrace in the arms of a man she does not know. Cartoons without any caption are often the funniest of all, relying on visual puns or unusual juxtapositions to achieve their effect.

Appreciation of humor depends very much on your reference point. Group affiliations, political leanings and ethnic background all influence the way a joke is received and how funny people find it. Because of this, a joke can

SHARING LAUGHTER

■ *When we laugh, we almost always laugh with or for the benefit of others. Laughter is not simply an explosion of feeling, but a form of communication. We use it especially to reduce the emotional distance between us although sarcastic laughter can be used to the opposite effect.*

▶ **Public levity**. *Members of the British Royal Family use posture – even the Queen's backward lean is composed – to show that they are in regal control of their responses. They are genuinely amused, however, and their responses communicate appreciation of the joke. By seeking eye contact, either with the cameraman or others present, they display a desire to share their mirth and use this as an occasion to be closer to people.*

▶ ▶ **Private levity**. *Maternity nurses in Texas do not need to maintain a public image. Their laughter can appear uncontrolled. In this informal setting, touch rather than eye contact is mainly what accentuates the sharing of humor. The standing nurse, otherwise the least demonstrative, uses both touch and eye contact.*

> *Humor can help you to influence people, and it can also help you to cultivate a more assertive self-image. In the relaxed mood that humor can bring to social encounters, people feel closer and relationships develop more easily.*

rebound on the teller. A conservative's joke about radicals or a left-wing joke about conservatives can make the teller an object of derision to the opposite camp. Some feminist jokes exploit this very nicely. The following story, for example, begins by making women the butt of a male-chauvinist observation, but the sting is in the tail of the joke: "Women were born without a sense of humor so that they can love men without laughing at them."

The advantage of being funny

Studies of persuasion have revealed that humorous people are perceived as more likable, and this in turn enables them to have greater influence. In one experiment, trained psychology graduates played the role of sellers in a bargaining situation. They were to haggle with people over the price of a painting. Some were instructed to take a humorous approach, while others made no jokes at all and bargained in a straightforward, serious way. It was found that dealers with the more lighthearted approach were able to get a significantly higher price for the painting. What

humor does, in this context, is to reduce the buyer's feelings of threat and anxiety and to establish a more relaxed rapport with the seller. Both trust and attraction are increased and the buyer feels able to make concession without losing face.

The implications of this study are quite important. If humor can aid the salesman, then it can also work in a similar way for the buyer. Making jokes which do not threaten the self-esteem of the person who is trying to sell you a car or a new refrigerator may allow you to win concessions. Humor can be used as a persuader in other social contexts and is useful in opening conversations with the opposite sex. Establishing a relaxed mood helps a relationship to develop quickly.

Men often use sexual-content jokes not only to amuse women but also to achieve an increased level of intimacy. The value of risqué jokes for men has been illustrated in a study in which male subjects were asked to rate the funniest of a number of risqué cartoons. Some of the men were to do this by completing a paper-and-pencil questionnaire, others by telling an attractive woman their choice. Those who made the direct responses to the woman experimenter found the cartoons significantly funnier than those who simply wrote down their choice. It seems that, because the

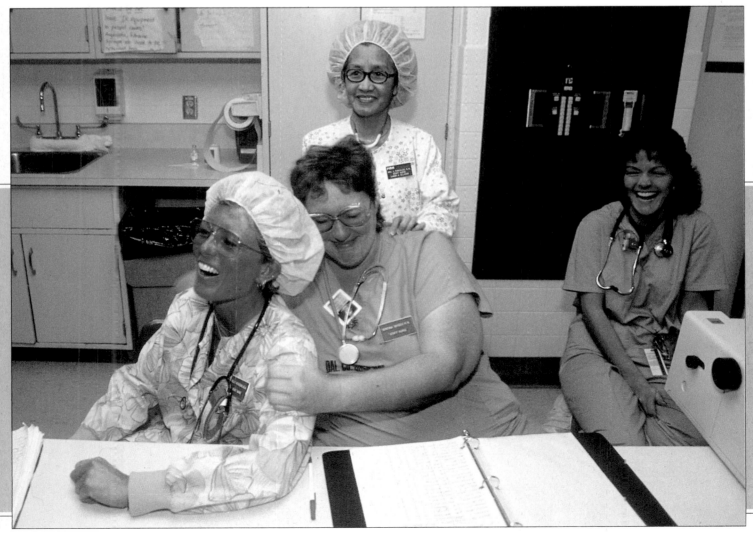

male subjects were trying to convey a sexy identity in order to appear attractive to the woman, the cartoon became more important and therefore seemed funnier to them.

Remarks or actions that people would often not see as very funny are sometimes found quite hilarious in group settings. This is the result of an effect known as "social facilitation." If one person laughs, then this greatly increases the likelihood that others will, and – because they are laughing – members of the group perceive the object of humor as funnier.

This illustrates one way in which you can increase your influence. If you can get people to laugh with you, then you have already established a degree of leadership that you can later build on. It can also improve your image and standing in informal settings, such as at a party, or simply in conversation with a group of friends.

Being uninhibited, overcoming aggression

Using humor can also increase your social prowess. A study in Texas of over 400 students revealed that those who saw themselves as humorous also regarded themselves as more dominant and assertive. The relationship between humor and these personal characteristics may be a clue to understanding why men dominate the world of professional comedy. Dominating and being assertive are still largely considered to be masculine attributes. In the 1980s, only about 12 percent of American comics were women.

Humor behavior begins to differ between the sexes early in the socialization process. Starting in the first school grade, boys suddenly seem to be the ones to tell jokes, do funny things and laugh, while girls tend to respond with a smile to the jokes of boys. Not only do young girls express a more restrained, "lady-like" appreciation of humor, they also want to know that it is all right to smile or laugh before they do. In a British study that highlighted these developmental differences, seven-year-old and eight-year-old children watched cartoons and listened to funny tapes. Even though the girls understood the jokes as well as the boys, they were more likely to look around in order to adjust their responses to match those of their companions.

Humor in adult life often develops best when inhibitions are lowered and there is a sense of social liberation. Jokes and funny stories attract the most laughter when told in bars. Researchers in California took the trouble to confirm this. Subjects in an experiment were given drinks of orange juice, some secretly laced with vodka. Those who drank the alcohol laughed much more at a selection of jokes and cartoons, but did not rate them as significantly more funny than those who had drunk unlaced orange. The slightly inebriated group also produced the funniest captions to go with the cartoons.

Even without drink, humor itself signals an easing of conventions and prepares the ground for closer social contact and discussion. It has been suggested that one of the qualities that made Henry Kissinger such an effective negotiator was his ability to use humor without detracting from the serious purpose of arms-limitation talks with Soviet negotiators. He was able to break through distancing rituals and encourage a more frank and open exchange of views by well-chosen and appropriately timed funny comments and stories.

A further important social function of humor is to reduce

114

▶ **Intentional and unintentional humor.** *Simple things make us laugh: when experience does not conform to our usual expectations, people feel tension; if the incongruity is harmless we may release the tension through laughter. Making a horse's tail into an unlikely wig is not a prize-winning joke, but such deliberate clowning provides an opportunity to laugh and feel more relaxed. A child's attempts to practice preschool conversation skills on an unusually urbane-looking monkey becomes an unintentional object of humor, and doting parents smile broadly in the background.*

Professional comedians make fun of taboo subjects without inhibition, encouraging us to laugh at everyday situations that make us feel anxious. This helps us to discharge bottled-up tensions and meet frustrations with a more positive mood.

aggression. Being angry and laughing are mutually incompatible responses, except where the humor is targeted in a derisive manner at a victim. In normal circumstances, hostility can be eased, and the probability of violence markedly reduced by persuading the antagonist to share in a humorous response. Skilled bartenders can use this strategy to very good effect in dealing with difficult and belligerent customers. Instead of confronting the aggression, it is possible to channel it away by creating a situation in which the emotion is quite inappropriate. Of course, the butt of the joke should not be someone with whom the other person identifies Telling a Polish joke to a hostile Pole is unlikely to be very helpful.

Releasing and displacing emotions

Some psychologists have taken a particular interest in people who make a living from being funny – the professional comedians. Many researchers in this field believe that being genuinely funny can only be achieved by regressing to a more childlike view of the world. This may be associated with the fact that comedians adopt humor early in life as a way of getting people to like them, and then use it to maintain their attention.

Many comedians have reported that their use of humor developed in early school days and was a means of coping with anxiety-producing situations. Such strategies were rewarded with laughter by classmates who lacked the confidence themselves to defy convention in the way that most humor requires. Defiance of convention continues into the adult life of comedians. The professionals tackle taboo subjects without inhibition and this gives them considerable social value. By encouraging us to laugh at the subjects that give rise to our anxieties, they help us safely to discharge repressed tensions.

Humor may also be a displacement of aggression. The professional comic is thought by psychoanalysts to be an angry person whose skills allow him to channel his aggression in a socially acceptable and productive manner. Another psychoanalytic view of the personality of comedians suggests that they are depressed people, but with enough strength of personality to transfer the depressed emotions into creative expression.

For all of us, humor is not only an invaluable social tool; it also provides a useful way of coping with personal frustrations and emotional difficulties. Making a joke about problems enables us to communicate the nature of our true feelings to others. By laughing about them we achieve a more relaxed mood, in which we are better able to understand and resolve conflicts. **PM**

▲ **Falling off your chair** at any time is funny – so long as no one is hurt. When t is especially out of place – for example, when your teacher is trying to give a serious lesson or a photographer has taken trouble to pose 28 girls for a group photograph – the result can be hilarity. How funny something is can depend on how excited you are to begin with and for this reason audiences for live television comedy are "warmed up" by comedians before the show. We are also affected by the tension we feel at having to conform to social conventions and the requirements of particular situations. Thus the joker in a group is often a well-loved nonconformist who makes fun of rules and the efforts of those who try to organize us, even when we would not seriously criticize these.

▲ **Humor is childlike**, allowing us to take a holiday from the seriousness of the roles we take on with adult life. It brings relaxation to a social situation by allowing us to put rules aside for the moment, forget our most earnest goals and indulge a pleasant mood.

14

Detecting Insincerity

IN 1905 Sigmund Freud declared: "He that has eyes to see and ears to hear may convince himself that no mortal can keep a secret. If his lips are silent, he chatters with his fingertips. Betrayal oozes out of him at every pore." Yet the ability to deceive others is thought by some psychologists to be a characteristic that has been genetically selected through human evolution. Comparisons have been made with animal deception, such as camouflage and mimicry. For hundreds of generations, it is argued, the ability to make others believe insincere remarks and promises has conferred advantages in struggles to control resources and win mating partners. The less cunning have, quite simply, produced less offspring, and a talent for creating false impressions has dominated the human gene pool.

Whatever the merits or shortcomings of this line of thinking, there are undoubtedly many occasions in everyday social encounters when people, for one reason or another, want to avoid expressing their true feelings. The ability to do this varies, and success tends to breed success. Those who lie effectively will tend to lie more often, perfecting their deception skills in the process. Those who fail are deterred from future attempts and get less practice.

In detection, however, the reverse is true. Once duped you will be motivated to increase your awareness of deception and of the cues that give it away, and most people are equally good at it. Some are called upon professionally to detect lying – customs officials, for example, trying to pick out likely smugglers from the travelers they interview –

but studies suggest that they are not as specially skilled as some people may imagine. A comparison between US customs inspectors and laymen found no significant differences in the ability to detect and expose deceptions. Researchers are attempting to make the principles of detection even easier to grasp.

How the mask slips

The way in which deceit "oozes" out of our bodies, as Freud described it, is now referred to by psychologists as "nonverbal leakage" – a series of body-language cues that indicate insincerity. Controlled observation has revealed just what these cues are.

One of the most reliable is the way we speak. People who are being deceptive make fewer factual statements, preferring instead more generalized and sweeping remarks. They frequently leave gaps in the conversation to avoid mistakenly saying something that would give them away. They speak with a higher pitch when lying, and at a slower rate. They hesitate more, and they are more likely to stutter or to make other speech errors (see panel below).

A more difficult cue is facial expression. People are better at controlling this than any other aspect of their body language. Slow-motion films of people engaged in lying, however, have shown that very short bursts of facial activity interrupt their deceptive expressions. These last less than one-fifth of a second and are known as "micromomentary expressions." They take on some of the shape of the angry,

---

HOW SIGNIFICANT ARE SPEECH DISTURBANCES?

■ People often give away anxiety by slips, stutters and other mistakes in speech. Although anxiety does not always or even usually mean that a speaker is lying, in some circumstances it can be a main clue. It is important, however, to distinguish different kinds of speech errors.

The chart below shows eight categories of speech error and the proportion of total errors that each category normally accounts for. When people are made anxious in experiments these proportions change, for there is an increase in each category of error except the

"Ers," "Ahs" and "Ums." These, known to researchers collectively as the "Ah" errors, appear not to provide any evidence of anxiety. However, more "non-ah" errors than you would normally expect in a person's speech are a sign that something is wrong.

Pace of speaking also seems to be affected. Some normally anxious people speak at a slower pace under experimental conditions of heightened anxiety. People not normally considered to be anxious speak more quickly than normal.

40.5% "Um," "er," "ah"
eg Well . . . um . . . it . . . um . . . happened on my way here.

19.2% Repetition
eg I usually . . . usually walk to work.

4.5% Word switch
eg I went back, to the mo . . . the hotel.

0.7% Slip of the tongue
eg I asked her to mate – I mean, meet! – me under the clock.

Others 0.6%

25.3% Sentence switch
eg Where's the key that . . . the key to the door?

7.8% Stutter
eg I really . . . c-c-couldn't stand it any longer.

1.2% Hanging sentence
eg I would have gone if . . . anyway I didn't go.

0.2% Incoherent sound
eg It's not something . . . ghl . . . I would choose to do.

Research has revealed principles for detecting lies and deceptions. Facial expression is least revealing, but the rest of the body may leak signs of insincerity, as do some speech patterns, tone of voice and even a reduction in blinking.

contemptuous, hilarious or sad face that is being masked.

Because of their short duration, micromomentary expressions cannot be consciously detected, but they can have considerable subliminal (unconscious) impact. Most people have experienced situations in which they have the strange feeling that a person really does not like them even though their expression seems friendly and positive. Similarly, we sometimes feel that others who appear cold and distant really have a positive attitude towards us. It is likely that these apparently illogical perceptions arise from the detection of tiny expressions of true feelings which leak out through the facial muscles.

The "social smile" is often produced for perfectly honest reasons (see *Ch.9*), and it can stimulate others to smile spontaneously, something that makes them feel good and quite possibly promotes their health through alleviating stress. It sometimes matters to know whether a smile is spontaneous or manufactured, however, and there are three ways of telling.

First, spontaneous smiles have characteristic wrinkles around the eyes, caused by activity in the muscle known as the *orbicularis oculi*, but these wrinkles do not appear when we force a smile. Second, unspontaneous smiles tend to be rather asymmetrical and are generally stronger on the left side of the face in right-handed people (stronger on the right side in left-handed people). The third difference concerns the timing of the smile. Often, unspontaneous smiles occur at socially inappropriate points in the interaction; and the build-up and the decay of the unspontaneous smile differs from the genuine expression – it switches on more rapidly, is held for longer and decays in an irregular way.

In general, people smile less when lying and they are slower to respond with facial expressions and other body

▲ **Hands and feet chatter** as much as voices do. Hand movements are expressive and so people reduce them when lying, in order not to give themselves away.

▶ **Three strangers** unconsciously maintain their distance while displaying polite, rather than a sincere, warmth. The lady on the right has created a buffered territory with her possessions. The lady on the left presents a friendly face but crosses her legs tightly away from the other two, while the lady in the center maintains a careful neutrality showing herself closer to neither.

▲ **Facial expression,** apart from the eyes, is the easiest channel to control when you want to look sincere. In experiments, trusting listeners pay more attention to the face and accept its signals as genuine. Suspicious listeners are more attentive to other body language and to the voice. Being a shrewd detector of insincerity means more than being knowledgeable about body language. It also means knowing when it is advisable to be on the lookout for insincerity and when it is reasonable to demand extra reassurance.

language to what you are saying. The eyes, in particular, are hard to control. Pupil dilation and reduced blinking are among the most consistently observed leakages in laboratory experiments. Surprisingly, however, 25 studies conducted over a 15-year period failed to find consistent support for our common intuition that only very good liars can look you in the eye as much as people normally do.

Give-away movements of the body

The hands are especially reliable cues for detecting deceit. A noticeable mannerism of people asked to demonstrate their lying ability is a decrease in simple hand movements. Most people seem to realize that hand movements have an expressive function and so they reduce them, in order not to reveal a deception. To curtail the messages of the hands they keep them still or out of sight. Fewer head movements are also very common.

When the hands *are* allowed to move, deceivers display an above-average frequency of what are known as "auto-contact behaviors." These self-touching movements are strongly related to high levels of arousal and nervousness. Telling lies increases this type of arousal, which is essentially what so-called lie-detectors measure. In everyday encounters you can act as your own lie-detector by being aware of people's hands when they keep touching

their noses, stroking their chins or brushing their hands across their mouths. But a person can feel nervous, of course, for other reasons than having something to hide.

When lying, we are also prone to use a gesture that appears to act as a kind of disclaimer for what has been said. It takes the form of a kind of dismissive shrug and normally appears just after a particular piece of false information has been communicated. It is interesting that politicians being interviewed on television about a contentious issue also sometimes use this kind of hand movement, and it is certainly one to watch for when buying a used car.

Postural cues are also important. Liars tend to make more postural shifts than nonliars. Although of their own they do not signal deceit, other postural cues give insincerity away by continuing to signal specific emotions and attitudes that only the face succeeds in masking. When in reality you are bored or full of disagreement with what a speaker is saying, it takes more than an interested or sympathetic *face* to hide the fact. Your bored posture can give away your lack of interest. The way you "close" your posture by tightly folding your arms and crossing your legs can give away your sense of disagreement (see *Ch 5*).

Similarly, showing respect or liking involves more than turning an attentive face in the right direction. If the body does not turn as well, the effect will be greatly weakened (see *Ch 5*). Even the orientation of people's feet is an indicator of whom they like and dislike. If you are sitting or standing with a group of other people, even when they do not know each other very well, you will observe that each person's feet will tend to point consistently in the direction of one or two other people. The pointing may result, for example, from the way they cross their legs.

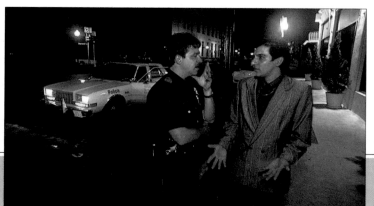

▲ Being stopped by the police, *as here in Dallas, Texas, or being questioned by a customs official at an airport, makes you feel ill at ease and defensive, even when — as this man's hand gesture protests — you have nothing to hide. Looking someone in the eye when you speak is commonly thought to be a mark of sincerity, and it is a technique that accomplished liars use readily. Looking at a policeman sincerely when he believes that he has heard it all before, however, may only provoke him to close his eyes.*

► Covering up laughter *with a hand over the mouth may seem a remarkably transparent deception, but its function is really to mute, rather than hide, the display of amusement. Children, especially girls, use this gesture as a signal that they are aware of social conventions calling the appropriateness of laughter into question. At one and the same time they feel and do not feel like laughing.*

118

> *We may not want to believe that we ourselves are skilled deceivers, but without this ability we would find even the most trivial of interactions a very unpredictable exercise. The social value of control outweighs some use of falsehood.*

This behavior expresses their sense of affiliation. Observe what happens when one person in the group is obliged to talk to another whom he or she does not like. You will see many superficial signs of friendliness and a smiling face. But increasingly, the feet will slowly swivel and point away. If you are at a drinks party and the feet of the seemingly friendly guest with whom you are having a conversation start pointing away, it is time to talk to somebody else.

Studies have shown that our attention to nonverbal leakage varies with circumstances. In an experiment, one set of subjects were warned to be suspicious of the sincerity of a speaker's performance, and another set were encouraged to be trusting of the same performance. The more suspicious observers gave more attention to the "leaky" channels, such as the body and the voice. The more trusting observers paid more attention to the face and accepted "honest" facial expressions as genuine. **PM**

SOCIALLY VALUED DECEPTIONS

■ Information about nonverbal leakage should help you to detect deception and insincerity more easily. But what should you do about it? Should you confront deceivers and expose their lies? It all depends, of course, on the situation and the motive the person has for deceiving you. In some circumstances the embarrassment which would arise from unmasking a lie might be more damaging than the lie itself.

For many people lying is a way of life. Years of practice have enabled them to perfect the art of manipulation. Car salesmen and professional confidence men immediately spring to mind, as well as lawyers, who have to keep other people's secrets, and politicians, who sometimes have to keep secrets of state and often have to inspire confidence and trust when the truth would not allow them to do this. Other professions deceive us with our own willing cooperation. Magicians make it seem as though empty hats contain white rabbits. Skilled actors on the theater stage or in motion pictures can similarly make audiences feel as though the emotions they portray are genuinely experienced.

Skill at deception is a very important attribute for nurses.

Anxious patients require continual reassurance that they are recovering, even when their condition is deteriorating. Similarly, they wish to hear that an operation they are to undergo is safe, even though the nurses may be fully aware of the risks involved. A study conducted in the United States found that the trainee nurses who got the best grades were also the ones who were the most skilled at deceiving their patients.

Being deceptive is often a tactful strategy that we adopt in order to reduce social friction and embarrassment. And detectors of deceit usually go along with the strategy from the same motive — as, for example, when someone refuses a second helping of your unpalatable homemade pickled herrings with the excuse of being on a diet. Often, we do not challenge a recognized deception because the truth seems likely to be a private matter. A friend, for example, may unsuccessfully conceal some distress or unhappiness, and we must judge whether probing for the truth will only make things worse than they are.

We may not want to believe that we ourselves are skilled deceivers, but without this ability we would find even the most trivial of interactions a very unpredictable exercise. We would not ever try to make people feel welcome or valued unless we happened to be in the right mood. We would not attempt to hide or contain our curiosity about other people's affairs, even when failing to do this would be rude or intrusive.

Controlling and managing our verbal and nonverbal displays may often cause them to appear planned, rehearsed or lacking in spontaneity, because we usually cannot control all communications channels simultaneously or equally well. Yet the social value of this control outweighs some appearance of falsehood.

■ **A display of political sincerity.** Pressing an open hand against your abdomen is not as symbolic as placing it over your heart, but by discreetly echoing that gesture former President Nixon sends a signal that associates him with the sentiments of trust and loyalty.

▲ **A doctor and his patient** and his patient's family need a relationship of trust and confidence, but the doctor may find it necessary to judge how much of the truth to reveal. Doctors and nurses, as part of their bedside manner, are required to develop skill at helping patients to look at their prospects hopefully.

Polishing Social Skills

SOME birds cannot sing the song that will win them a mate without first hearing it sung by another of the same species. In other words, they must learn this social skill. We too need to be shown *how* to interact effectively, but our song is an intricate body of accumulated know-how, habit and custom.

This social inheritance can be learned well or badly and can be skillfully or unskillfully used. The largely unconscious process of learning it and practicing its lessons (and perhaps adding a grain of wisdom to it) usually lasts a lifetime. We constantly meet opportunities to overcome our past learning failures and to refine our successes. And it is from other people's reactions to us – and the things friends will sometimes tell us about our behavior – that we discover what is successful and what is a failure.

Social science has also begun to help. The complex elements of social encounters are being unraveled as skills that can be learned more consciously than usually occurs in everyday life. Trained specialists can show people how to identify and polish the specific combinations of body language and speech patterns that they need in order to achieve their social goals.

Do you mix easily with others?

Social skill is the sum total of our ability to interact with other people. It is the ability to take appropriate social initiatives, and understand people's reactions to them and respond accordingly. This cycle (see box) occurs throughout any kind of social interaction – from ordinary, everyday conversations to special interchanges such as being interviewed or giving a talk.

Individual social skills include all of the various components of the behavior we use in these social interactions – the right patterns of eye contact, the right facial expressions, gestures and tone of voice, saying the right thing, using humor and so on. Like any skill, we can learn these and get better at them with practice.

THE SOCIAL SKILL CYCLE

■ *A boy sees a girl. A goal springs to his mind: "I'd like to meet her." He observes the way she glances at him and, concluding that he has a chance of success, decides to make a humorous comment to break the ice. He acts on the decision by turning to her, smiling and saying, "Nice day." The effect is a new cycle of observation, decision, action and effect – hers – including her action of looking out of the window at the rain, then at him, laughing and saying "You must be joking!" and the effect this has on him.*

As the ice breaks, the cycles become faster moving and more automatic. The pair seldom feel that either is thinking consciously of what to say or do. Yet interaction can continue only so long as each is taking in and interpreting the reactions of the other and making responses to them. To say they do this without thinking means that they do not behave in an overly self-conscious way – they are not hampered by doubts about what to do next. It also means that they probably do not even notice most of the adjustments they make in the complex and subtle process of social coordination that they achieve. They may unconsciously adjust their speech to

match each other's style of expression, for example, and modify their postures, eye contact and the distance between them to maintain a level of intimacy that feels right to both.

The repeating cycle of observation, decision, action and effect that makes this possible is fundamental to social skill. No interaction

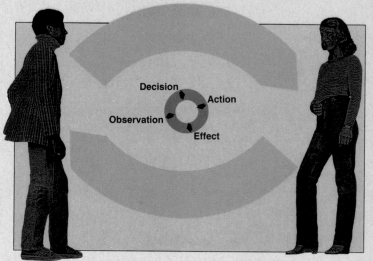

occurs without it, and it provides the framework for most of our learning of particular skills, as we constantly refine our behavior in the light of feedback.

Observation of people's reactions – for example, when you are telling a joke – lets you

know whether you are having the effect you are aiming at, and allows you to adapt future behavior accordingly.

Positive reactions, such as worked-for laughter, reinforce your confidence in the decisions you took about what to say and do. They also reinforce your confidence in your ability to perform the actions you

decided on. Not only have you decided correctly that the time was right to tell a joke, and chosen a good one, but you have told it well.

Unfavorable reactions – embarrassed or deadpan expressions, or unspontaneous laughter – sharpen your con-

sciousness of what is inappropriate and in what circumstances; or else they alert you to the need for a more skilled performance. Because of the range of possibilities – the joke itself was not funny, its subject matter was offensive, the occasion was wrong for joking or you told it ineptly – it may be difficult to pinpoint the problem. Often we cannot pinpoint it without advice from someone who knows better than us. In more daily encounters than we consciously take note of, however, we adjust our behavior experimentally. In subtle ways that often escape even our own attention, we decide first on this way of speaking, standing or setting a facial expression, then on that, until we find one that works for the present purpose, as evidenced by the feedback we receive in the reactions of others.

When you are not yet confident of a social skill you are practicing, the skill cycle may not work so smoothly. For example, if you usually shrink from taking the initiative in opening conversations at a party, then the first few times you force yourself to do it, your manner may betray some of the anxiety you feel about your performance. The person you

In the figure: **Decision**, **Action**, **Observation**, **Effect**

Like riding a bicycle, successful interaction is automatic when we know how, but all of us have times when we are not sure how to behave. Managing these situations means learning – from observation, from friends, even from specialists.

Once learned social skills are automatic. We do not need to rethink consciously how to carry out a greeting every time we have an encounter, any more than we have to think how to put one foot in front of the other when walking. In fact, it has been estimated that some 80 percent or more of our behavior is automatic, though we constantly monitor and adjust it, depending on the responses we are given. But we constantly learn new skills, giving conscious attention to what we only later use automatically.

Very few of us think that our social skills are perfect. In fact, the majority – over 70 percent – of young adults (a better-studied age group than others) admit that they have been shy at some time, and at any given time 30 percent or more report that shyness hampers them now (see *Ch 24*). In one study of students at Oxford University in England, 10 percent had "great difficulty" mixing, and further investigation revealed that most of these students had poor social skills. In addition, almost everyone at *some* time meets situations that their background has not prepared them for. The novice at formal dining may not know which knife or fork to pick up first. The brilliant cocktail-party conversationalist may find it impossible to make small talk with ordinary people.

It can happen to almost anyone that conversations with the people you are thrown together with in certain situations – the parties a new friend likes to take you to, for example, or coffee time at a new job – do not go well: people sometimes hold themselves away from you at an awkward distance, say little, look around when speaking and end conversations early. Highly skilled interactors quickly identify reasons for this: they realize that the unfamiliarity of the situation is making them behave passively for example – they are saying too little, and to others they appear

approach may fail to hide perfectly an uncomfortable reaction to your anxiety. But if you are willing to tolerate these imperfections, the conversation may well develop in a way that rewards your initiative and stimulates you to continue practicing the skill.

Practicing any skill – from driving a car to learning to play the piano – involves adjusting your performance in the light of feedback. From time to time, in order to improve performance,

we try to do things slightly differently. In the short run, this may seem to make it harder to play the piano, drive or interact socially. Once mastered, however, new skills become automatic, and performance may be easier than it ever was before.

▲ **Using social skills to learn social skills.** *When you are a tourist, people's speech – even some of their body language – may be difficult to understand: communication tools it has taken all your life to acquire can seem ineffective. However, there are universal signals – smiling, for example, putting the head on one side and gesturing away from the body – by which you can show a warm and rewarding response to those who try to help you to* understand local ways. When you lean forward with an attentive look, this also helps to make their efforts seem worthwhile. Even in very familiar settings, the best way to learn social skills is to make it rewarding for others to interact with you. This allows you to observe their own skills at close quarters and gives you opportunities to experiment – trying out things to say, for example – and learn from responses.

uninterested. Alternatively, they may realize that they are behaving in a domineering and overpowering way.

Remedies also come more easily to the socially skilled. They know how to correct their own reticence or how to check a domineering impression. But many of us find it less than easy to understand what we are doing wrong when social encounters do not go well, and, even when we do, remedies do not always occur to us.

How do we learn social skills?

The first and most important teachers of social skills are parents. Consciously, they give instruction – telling children, for example, to say "please" and "thank you." Unconsciously, they model social skills – giving their children examples to imitate simply by interacting with each other, and with friends, neighbors and strangers as they normally do. Parents help children to practice social skills by playing with them and asking them to talk about their experiences and their likes and dislikes. Parents' unconscious reactions as well as explicit praise and criticism of children's behavior provide an important part of the social feedback that further enables children to understand how to act with others.

Problems with social skill may well originate in the family. Some parents are poorer role models for their children than others, and none offer a perfect example. It is difficult for children to learn social skills from parents who do not play with them very much, or are unloving, unaccepting or inconsistent in their expectations. Excessive criticism can undermine self-esteem and with it the self-confidence that is essential to the uninhibited exercise of social skills. Any one of these factors can have an impact, and sometimes several apply at once.

Other important teachers are children's peers, particularly at times when they are not closely supervised by adults. Children learn much simply by watching others in the school playground and listening to what they say to each other. Children of the same sex especially are observed, to see on what terms you will be accepted as a girl or a boy. Those who are popular do not just watch and listen; they are good at making eye contact, smiling and starting conversations with other children, and they are sensitive to what other children want them to be like. Such is their importance that a child who does not learn these skills early enough can be seriously hampered later in life.

The reactions of other children can cause difficulties. Children who are rejected by their peers find it hard to assert themselves without being aggressive, and those neglected by their peers have trouble initiating interactions or responding to initiatives. A vicious circle can result: aggressive children becoming more aggressive, and withdrawn children becoming more withdrawn.

As children become adolescents, they follow the same learning strategy – combining principles learned in the family with the friend-making, courtship and job-finding skills they discover by observing and interacting with people outside the home. Entering the adult world of work almost always means learning new social skills, and it is now common practice to provide formal skills training for many kinds of professionals: health workers, teachers, police officers, managers, sales people, negotiators, diplomats (who need to understand cross-cultural differences in social behavior) and even politicians.

Airlines train their cabin crews to make effective use of body language in order to more easily convey a sense of warmth and hospitality to passengers who can often *see* busy stewards and stewardesses without having the opportunity to speak with them. Doctors are shown how to be a

LEARNING SOCIAL SKILLS FROM PLAY

■ *Lessons in how to interact begin with simple games that parents play with infants. "This little piggy went to market" not only teaches babies about their toes, it teaches anticipation of what comes next in a spoken sequence, a first step toward learning how to participate in conversations. "Peekaboo" teaches the use of eye contact in starting interactions as well as the art of taking turns. When parents show small children how to pretend to be a monkey or squeak like a mouse, they lay a foundation for the ability to act out the bewildering variety of childhood and adult* roles that constantly changing social situations will later assign to them.

■ **Games with other children** *help children to practice the ways that social situations give meaning to behavior – stepping across a line on the ground or saying a string of words like "Ready or not, here I come" mean something in one situation but not in another. Even playing different positions in a team game echoes the fact that people take different parts – such as listener and speaker, host and guest, buyer and seller – in a social encounter.*

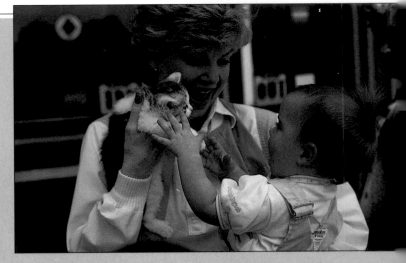

▲ **Exaggerated facial expressions** *stimulate babies to respond. They also give infants examples of how to make appealing faces on purpose.*

By the time they are toddlers, most children are adept at laughing and smiling for social effect.

In childhood, and throughout life, we need others to tell us what to do and to be models of social skill that we can imitate. We need them to give us opportunities to practice our skills and, by reacting to us, tell us how successful we are.

good listener, how to ask open questions (questions that require more than a "yes" or "no" or other simple answer), how to respond to others and how to summarize what a client has said. This helps them to diagnose illness more accurately, and their patients feel better understood and valued.

For professional help with everyday encounters, commercial social skills training programs – often called "assertion training" (see p126) are available to the public.

Throughout their lives, most people receive advice and criticism from friends and family in an informal, ongoing review of how they behave with others. Professional social skills trainers imitate this informal process and make it more precise.

Assessing social skills problems

Before social skills can be improved they must first be assessed and deficiencies noted. In everyday life, we evaluate our social skills through the feedback we get from other people's reactions. Politeness often prevents them from responding honestly and straightforwardly to things that they do not like. They may let us see by their uncomfortable behavior that something is wrong, but avoid telling us exactly what it is. An exception to this may be the comments of close friends – one reason why having them is so important to our social adjustment. When you find it hard to achieve a particular social goal – such as enjoying conversations at social functions, or getting people to take you seriously at work – you can ask a friend what you are doing wrong.

In professional assessment, trainee and trainer also begin by looking at unrealized goals. Often, part of the process is to identify a recent situation in which a goal was not achieved, and in which you could have used a particular sequence of skills more effectively – say, in a specific conversation that went wrong last week. So that the assessment will be based on evidence that is as realistic as possible, a video camera may be used to record a reconstruction of the event, with people taking the roles of those involved and using appropriate props.

Then trainee and trainer, with the help of a rating scale (and the trainer's professional expertise), analyze the videotape to pinpoint exactly which skills need improvement. On the one hand, you may discover that you are not smiling enough or making enough eye contact. You may need to stand closer, turn towards the other person more, speak more clearly and louder and ask more questions. You may be failing to give enough feedback – not showing that you have taken in what has just been said, not showing enough feeling or not revealing as much personal detail as the other. You may be failing to take your turn to speak and failing to take enough initiative. On the other hand, you might learn that your manner is overbearing: you do not listen enough or ask enough open questions. You may need to reduce your assertiveness by pausing more, reducing the volume and pace of your voice and handing over the conversation more readily.

Improving on past performance

Friends help us by telling us what to do to improve our social style and to follow social rules that we do not understand. They may even show us how, or point out as models skilled people worth watching. Similarly, professional trainers describe missing skills – breaking them down into components that are easy to understand and

▲ **Imitating adults** *helps children to learn adult roles. Parents with cameras who encourage conventionally masculine and conventionally* *feminine poses like these help boys and girls to learn how men and women interact.*

▲ **Dressing up** *stimulates children to practice the gestures and speech of role models. Cowboys, teachers, salespeople, waiters and waitresses,* *even kings and queens, are observed and imitated.*

learn – and they provide models by staging encounters in which someone shows how to handle effectively the situations that bother you.

The trainer or another person, together with a role-partner, models a single skill – for example, how to make effective eye contact when starting to speak – either live or on videotape. Performed by another, the skill is easier to recognize and its effects are much easier to judge.

Modeling the skill to perfection is often inappropriate. Professional trainers usually follow the principle that we tend to identify with and learn more easily from those who, rather than being social-skill "masters," are simply able to cope better than we are. This way, we learn that we can be effective without being perfect. For example, when refusing an unreasonable request your voice might not have as fully confident a ring as you would wish, but nevertheless, you have succeeded at the task. If you are choosing a model from your own circle of acquaintances to watch for useful examples of effective behavior, it is probably best not to focus on someone stunning, and there is little point in studying someone who seems so smooth that you would honestly prefer not to be like them.

Practicing what others have shown us and told us is an essential step toward applying their advice. We often practice skills by performing them in our imagination first. Parents sometimes prepare their children for visitors by rehearsing what they should do and say, and people often plan what they will say during a forthcoming telephone conversation by writing down a few points and going over them in their mind. Just as with learning lines for a play, you can rehearse a social skill until you get it right.

Practice and rehearsal also take place in formal skills training. Trainees try out demonstrated skills in a modified replay of the reconstructed event performed earlier, acting out the problem situation again, but in a more appropriate way. Your trainer may ask you to rehearse in your imagination first – to think the situation through and mentally plan what to do.

This is followed by coaching, feedback and reinforcement. During and after rehearsal, detailed observations of how you are doing will help you to monitor, adjust and improve your performance. This feedback can be given in the form of videotape or audiotape, providing a precise "action replay." Videotapes, especially, provide information

▲ **Making fun of a friend** can be a way of sending useful information about what genuinely fails to impress. Mockery can also signal a sense of superiority, however, and can be used to discourage others from interacting on equal terms.

▶ **Communicating a failure** to communicate. When listeners look baffled, skilled speakers try to find better ways of expressing themselves. When speakers look frustrated, skilled listeners ask helpful questions.

▲ **Being too assertive** brings a complex response. The listener in this scene feels confronted. Her smile announces self-control, but her lower eyelids have risen in anger. She looks at the speaker from the corners of her eyes in a warning gesture as her head turns slightly away. Her body is erect, tensed for conflict. To have his point accepted, the speaker may need to find a way of expressing it that provokes less hostility.

The most appropriate models are not masters of social skill. We learn most easily by copying people we identify with, especially those who are near enough to be partners in successful everyday encounters – the best lessons of all.

about body language that is very difficult to convey in any other way.

Good trainers give ample reinforcement, praising even small improvements, but ultimately the best reinforcement is found in feedback from successful real encounters. Trainees are given homework - told to seek out situations equivalent to the one they have rehearsed. However, situations are seldom exactly alike and trainees have to learn how to modify the skill in the light of each. Training continues with feedback from assignments and further rehearsal when necessary, before more skills are tackled.

How effective is social skills training?

Research has shown that social skills training can be very effective in some cases but only moderately so in others. Perhaps not surprisingly, it works best for people who already have quite good skills. Professional people such as doctors and police officers respond well to training in skills they need for their work. Many members of the public benefit from assertiveness training.

Those who are most lacking in social skills, however, include people with mental handicaps and many who go through life with psychological problems, drug and alcohol addictions and histories of criminal violence. In a study of psychiatric patients, 27 percent had social skills problems, and there is much evidence that a lack of these skills is involved, to a greater or lesser extent, in almost every type of psychiatric problem. Social skills training programs for the seriously disadvantaged have been developed by specialists and are now employed by nurses, occupational therapists and many others in the caring professions. People with milder problems respond to this training more successfully than those with severe ones.

In the course of psychiatric treatment, submissive *and* aggressive people are taught assertion skills – both "negative assertion," such as how to refuse requests or lodge complaints, and "positive assertion," such as paying compliments and showing interest in others. Those lacking the very basic skills – for instance, some sufferers from schizophrenia and people with mental handicaps – are taught how to start, maintain and end conversations, how to change topics and how to speak in turns.

An important factor in success is the relative isolation of the trainee. People who are isolated from others have little opportunity to consolidate their skills, and are more likely to fail than those who have a network of friends and family, or who have a good working environment.

Social skills training is being constantly improved. Researchers are trying to discover ways of preventing newly learned skills from deteriorating over time, and trying to learn how to help trainees apply them in the highly varied situations where they really count. When these techniques are known, they (and others) will form further steps towards giving those with serious problems what the rest of the world only *seems* to acquire automatically. **PT**

SOCIAL SKILL CHECKLISTS

■ Adapting and improving social skills becomes easier if you are aware of the elements that interaction includes. Checklists such as those that follow are particularly useful tools in focusing attention on specific elements. The answers to the questions in these checklists are not always immediately obvious. However, by paying attention to how you think you are doing on each point, by referring to the chapters listed and by asking the opinion of a close friend, you will probably be able to pinpoint areas worth working on.

NONVERBAL BEHAVIOR

Are you standing too close to your companion, or too far away?
Are you turning away when your companion is speaking?
Is there any way in which your physical appearance may be disturbing or otherwise inappropriate for the situation you are in?
Are you using facial expressions in the right way?
Are you catching the other person's eye too much for comfort, or perhaps too little?
Is your posture relaxed?
Are you using the right kinds of gestures, at the right time?
Does your body language match what you are saying?
(See Chs 3, 4, 5, 6, 8, 9.)

VOICE QUALITIES

Are you speaking too loudly or too softly for the circumstances or not varying your volume enough?
Are there varieties of tone in your speech, or is it expressionless and dull?
Is your voice pitched too high or too low?
Are you speaking unclearly – mumbling or cutting short your sentences?
Is the speed of your speech incorrect – too fast, too slow or too constant?
Is the flow of your speech interrupted by pauses, repetitions, stammering or omissions?
(See Chs 12, 14.)

CONVERSATIONAL SKILLS

Do you interrupt too often?
Are your statements too long or too short?
Do you generalize too much, or do you bore people by giving too much detail?
Is your speech too formal or too intimate for the situation you are in?
Do you reveal the same amount of personal detail, or do you remain remote or give away too much about yourself?
Do you include a good variety of topics? Do you move quickly to the next topic?
Do you show humor? Do you use too much or include it at the wrong time?
Do you look out for feedback, recognize it, interpret it and react to it correctly? (See p 120.)
Is your timing good? Do you react when appropriate?
Do you take turns at appropriate moments, or do you stay quiet for long periods or hog the conversation?
Do you ask enough questions, and of the right type? Do you listen to the answers?
Does your speech match your body-language signals?
Do you support the speaker with your reactions?
Do you spend the right amount of time on greetings and partings, and use the right words?
(See Chs 4, 11, 12.)

BECOMING MORE ASSERTIVE

■ The assertive person is not an aggressive one. Learning to be assertive helps you to be a better communicator. It enables you to say what needs to be said in a clear and confident way. Being aggressive on the other hand, is concerned with trying to dominate others, seizing every advantage and winning at any price. Becoming assertive means relating better to others and communicating with them on an equal footing. It includes being able to stand up for your rights effectively, while also being aware of the rights of others. It also means learning to be more effective without being aggressive.

Of course, becoming more assertive does not make you succeed at everything. For example, if you are just not up to your job, communicating about the problem more assertively may help you recognize that your true skills lie elsewhere. You may realize that your job is not for you and that some other area of work is. Your assertiveness skills may help you get a transfer to a different part of the company.

TWO KINDS OF ASSERTION

Sometimes the message you need to communicate is a negative one – refusing an unreasonable request, standing up for your rights by saying that you cannot accept a disadvantage or telling someone you have not understood what they are trying to say. Assertiveness training experts call this "nega-tive assertion." They try to help people to do it better.

They also help people with problems in "positive asser-tion." Many of us feel embar-rassed or awkward when we are paying other people compli-ments, accepting compliments or giving and receiving support and affection.

To become more assertive, a useful first step is to identify the basic rights you think you and others should have in encoun-ters – the rights to say no and not feel guilty, for example, and the right to change your mind. Then ask whether your own behavior is consistent with your belief in these rights. Do you claim them for yourself and do you allow others to exercise them?

Being able to say no – and mean it – is just as important as being able to ask to have your needs met. People lacking in confidence often feel uncertain of their right to refuse, and they make excuses instead. But an excuse is dishonest if you really mean no, and feeling resentful about being asked can be unfair to the asker. There may be no other person but you who can tell them what it is reason-able to expect.

Similarly, a positive assertion, such as asking for advice and help, is a right, providing that you recognize the other's right to refuse.

Assertiveness enables you to be yourself because you are allowing others to be them-selves too.

IDENTIFYING THE MESSAGE

■ Effective communication with others is only possible if we can accurately identify what messages they are sending. This can mean asserting your own need to know what other people mean.

Sometimes we are so over-whelmed by one aspect of a message – the emotional con-tent, for example – that we neglect other very important information. One useful tech-nique to learn is to distinguish the emotional content and the factual content in what is said, as well as to try to identify the need or wish behind the words.

A wife who says "You're later than I expected" to her hus-band when he arrives home may really mean "I am anxious about our dinner party and I wanted your help, so why weren't you back earlier?"

The emotion and need here are likely to be conveyed non-verbally in tone of voice, post-ure and facial expression. Only one aspect of the message, the factual element (his late arrival), has actually been stated, and this statement may or may not be true. The husband may have returned at his usual time but his wife's need – wanting help earlier in the evening – is only implied in what she said.

The way to identify these three elements is by "reflective listening." Simply restate what you think the real message is and ask the person who is speaking to you if that is what is meant. This technique can help you cut through to the heart of a problem. It also, of course, gives the other person a chance to correct your guess – "No, I'm not anxious, I'm angry." Once the message has been clarified it can be dealt with more effectively.

▶ Styles of self-assertion. Aggressive self-assertion means putting forward your own interests in a competitive way. This may be useful in some situations, such as getting your share of the bar-gains in a sale, but as a style of communication it will solve many fewer of your life's problems than cooperative self-assertion. This means being sensitive to what other people need you to say and do in order that they may understand your needs, purposes and opinions. It includes the con-fidence to express positive messages – such as compli-ments and thanks – without feeling embarrassed.

> *Assertive people give support and affection and pay compliments without feeling embarrassed. They communicate needs in a clear and confident way, allowing others to respond with openness and to communicate more effectively.*

BUILDING ON SKILLS

How do people learn to improve assertiveness skills? As with improving other skills they build on what they already have. Everyone has some area in their lives in which they are confident.

For example, a man lacking confidence in his career in a large company may be very confident where his hobbies are concerned, or in his ability to be a parent or make friends. Becoming assertive in his career means building from those areas of confidence and competence, becoming conscious of the reasons for that confidence in certain spheres and not others, and discovering how to transfer skills from one to another.

To build in this way, it is useful to compile an "assertive hierarchy." This is a series of tasks of increasing difficulty that you set yourself. The easiest task is one that you could do without anxiety, but one that you have not tried. Your ultimate goal, the task at the top of your assertive hierarchy, may be to know how to ask for advice and help from colleagues at work in areas where you have great difficulty, but fear of looking foolish holds you back. The first task in your hierarchy, however, should be something simpler, such as asking for help from a friend in one aspect of a hobby at which the friend is slightly more skilled. Confident in your hobby, you will find it easier to admit one small inadequacy and ask for help. When you see that most people are pleased to be asked for advice, the possibility of admitting difficulty in other more important areas may seem less alarming.

Assertive body language is also an essential ingredient in becoming more confident. Assertive posture, for example, involves making your body look big – you should not hold your hands behind your back when you want to be noticed and taken seriously. Rather, you might try planting them on your hips. It is not advisable to fold your arms across your chest, however, as this implies that you are unwilling to listen to what others have to say (see Ch 5). Tone of voice is equally important. A deep and resonant tone sounds more confident than a thin, a high-pitched or an unsteady voice (see Ch 12).

SEX-ROLE LIMITATIONS

Much of our social behavior is learned, without our realizing it, early in life. Women, for example, are typically thought of as submissive and men are typically described as aggressive. This difference is very much a matter of conditioning. It is often suggested that women's rewards in life mostly come from conforming to a feminine ideal of being passive, dependent and tactful. These characteristics prevent women from openly expressing their thoughts and feelings. Years of giving way to others often makes them feel that they really have less value than others – especially men.

Men's upbringing is often said to encourage an unemotional approach to life, but in fact it does encourage the expression of one particular emotion. Men are expected to be tough – their tender side is often stifled early in childhood. Men often claim that they never let emotion get in the way of decision-making, when in fact the emotion that often dominates them is aggression. Assertiveness training for men often involves learning to recognize their use of aggression and the effects it has on preventing others from having an equal opportunity in an interaction.

The aggressive approach in men is greatly rewarded, but both the typical male approach and the more submissive approach of women prevent open and direct communication. Not everyone feels a need for change, but many are beginning to seek more equitable ways of communicating. This is where assertiveness training plays a part. **JCB**

ASSERTIVENESS TRAINING

■ Courses are widely available. Many adult education and continuing education centers offer them to the public. These courses are often taught by psychologists who also run courses for professional groups. Trainers assess the existing assertiveness skills of participants and lead them in role-play practice of new ones. Follow-up studies of those who have participated in classes generally reveal that participants feel they and those who know them can see an improvement in their communication skills. Research is continuing into techniques of assertiveness training and a better understanding of effective communication.

2

HOW
RELATIONSHIPS
WORK

EYE TO EYE PART TWO

Why Relationships Matter

ARE you happy or unhappy? It can depend greatly on other people – on the help and emotional support they give you and the stimulation they bring into your life. Benefits such as these can flow in some degree from the most casual encounters, but they come especially from established successful relationships. Even your physical health can be affected by the level of emotional support you receive from friends, family and marriage partner in times of stress.

Stimulating company and support

Any company is enlivening to some degree. You can never be completely sure even of what your oldest acquaintances will say next, and this unpredictability contributes to their value, for we are creatures who need a particularly high level of stimulation.

Other creatures need stimulation too, and the penalties for having too little can sometimes be seen in zoo animals. Deprived of enough space to move about in and explore, or deprived of the social life that is natural to their species, animals suffering the stress of boredom pace mechanically back and forth in their cages, pull out their own feathers or fur or withdraw to sit in corners staring blankly. They can also receive too much stimulation – for example, in crowded conditions – and the symptoms are similar, but between the extremes there is a happy medium that, given the opportunity, each will find.

For humans too, there is a happy medium of stimulation, but individual differences greatly affect it. Extroverts are thought to have central nervous systems that are less easily aroused than those of introverts. As a consequence, to achieve an optimum level of arousal, extroverts choose brighter colors, listen to louder, more exciting music and mix more with other people. Only the most extreme introverts, however, shy away from all forms of social

contact (see *Ch23*). Age also makes a difference. An old person might find one or two friendly conversations in a day very refreshing while many an adolescent longs to be doing exciting things with friends in noisy surroundings.

Encounters with strangers, distant acquaintances, old friends and those nearest to us can all contribute to the stimulations we need. When we meet and interact with strangers, they are novel, and therefore interesting in themselves. The people we work with give us challenges that we must rise to and they share ideas and experiences. People we know also bring novelty into our lives by telling us jokes and bringing us news of themselves and of mutual acquaintances. The ones we know best know from experience what most amuses, entertains or excites us.

Stimulating activity can be solitary, and activity is a recommended therapy for loneliness (see *Ch24*). But generally people prefer to share it with others.

▲ **Social smiling** *does not have to be purely spontaneous to be pleasant, and by making it a part of the everyday encounters we have with strangers and the near-strangers that we deal with regularly, we stimulate them to smile at us. To be smiled at by them is in turn beneficial. In a sense you are receiving a mirror image of the smile you give. Unlike a mirror, however, the person sends a genuine social signal – that they are happy to be dealing with you. This cannot help but support your self-esteem and your morale.*

LENDING A SMILE OF SUPPORT

■ *We all like a good laugh and sometimes a good cry, and since these are ways of releasing tension, they probably contribute in a small way from time to time to our good health. Even a broad smile may put both sender and receiver in a less tense mood.*

It is best if both smiles are spontaneous, but a pleasant social smile can stimulate a spontaneous one in return. Smiling at someone on purpose may be a way of promoting their well-being.

When people smile spontaneously, they use two sets of

facial muscles – the muscles around the mouth, "zygomaticus major," which contract to pull up the corners of the mouth, and the muscles around the eyes, "orbicularis oculi." If we smile voluntarily out of a sense of its being socially appropriate to do so, we use only the muscles around the mouth – the eye muscles cannot be consciously controlled.

Nervous connections from the facial muscles extend to the hypothalamus. This part of the brain is, among many other things, intimately involved

with control of emotions.

The action of smiling is suspected of stimulating the hypothalamus in a way that has a positive effect on our mood (see Ch10), but the experimental evidence for this is weakest in the case of smiles that volunteers have been requested to pose artificially, using only the mouth.

Smiles are infectious, however. If you smile at someone, they will usually smile back, often involuntarily, with mouth and eyes. And returning your smile may thus alter their mood for the better. **RG**

The people we know give us stimulation, help and emotional support. Friends and those we love, especially, make a profound contribution to our psychological well-being. This in turn seems to promote physical health.

Perhaps the most pervasive and insistent of human social needs is for self-esteem. We all need our egos supported by receiving some combination of assurances that we are noticed, valued, liked or loved, recognized for what we have achieved and considered right or at least acceptable in what we think or have done. We also need to feel secure, to be reassured that the benefits we enjoy in life will probably continue at an acceptable level. Both security and support for our self-esteem contribute to the *emotional support* that we receive from others.

Very casual – even barely noticeable – relationships give some emotional support. These are "familiar strangers" who affect us simply by always being there. The same waiter standing by the door of the same restaurant that you never go into lends a comforting stability to daily life. This is a stability you may not even notice until one day he is no longer there.

People often make a social display to familiar strangers, a nod and a smile, and perhaps a "Good morning" between distant neighbors who do not know each other's names. If matters are to go no further, why do they bother? The point is that greetings are almost impossible to ignore. You are bound to get a response, and usually it will be a pleasant one. People like to be recognized and acknowledged by familiar figures – the mailman, newspaper sellers, neighbors. It gives a small but important fillip to their day which they return in kind. In the simple act of exchanging greetings we reinforce each other's self-esteem. So it is when people respond in a positive way to one another in everyday encounters of any sort.

Mostly, however, we turn to people we know well for emotional support. The potential of a person – through similarity of attitude, background and opinion – to make us feel right about ourselves is a main element in making them attractive as a friend (see *Ch 21*). For just the same reason, couples are drawn together by similarity (see *Ch 25*). For friends, husbands, wives and lovers, we tend to choose people who will reinforce our way of looking at ourselves

▲ **Local personalities** *add color to the neighborhood. They also help to give us some of the stability we sense in our lives, simply by always being there when we pass by.*

◄ **United in mirth,** *spectating neighbors in Amsterdam share a joke at the expense of a good-natured policeman as he helps to seal off a street during a protest demonstration. Humor allows strangers to feel closer and more relaxed with one another.*

and the world. Close friends and intimates also support us by giving sympathy when we are unhappy, by listening to troubles that we would not reveal to others and by making us feel liked and loved.

We are also dependent for emotional support on relationships that we do not choose. When you must work with someone, the work will be less stressful and more rewarding if you feel recognized for your contribution and liked, and if you receive reassurances when the job seems to be getting on top of you (see *Ch21*).

Family life is happier and children develop more confi-dence and more skills when they feel loved and secure and their self-esteem is strongly supported by parents who avoid excessive criticism and give them ample recognition for their achievements. Parents list the love and affection that they receive from their children as the chief value of having them (see *Ch17*).

Relationships also give emotional support by helping people to fulfill their role expectations and to have a sense of identity. We grow up expecting to be parents, for example – expecting not simply to have a biological relation to children but to be *like* a mother or father to them. Fulfilling this role makes people feel valuable, and it helps them to feel that they are an important part of the wider family and community to whose biological and cultural continuity they are contributing. Similarly, we maintain contact with kin and cultivate good relations with them, and we want to be friends with people at work, partly because this is what "belonging" to the family or the workplace means. **BM RG**

A helping hand

Almost always, having a relationship with someone involves mutual help. Some of the help we exchange is tangible. Children help their parents by doing chores around the house, workmates give each other lifts to the office, one sister looks after the children of another. Sometimes we help with information – a friend gives you a useful tip or a parent shows a child how to do a piece of homework. Others also help us by appraising us – they help us to understand, clarify and evaluate our problems so that they are easier to deal with. Out of concern, they may also help to motivate us to overcome problems such as smoking or excess weight. Utter strangers help each other, but

◄ **Working together, playing together.** TOP *A granddaughter helps her grandmother to bake cookies.* BOTTOM *The parish priest romps with a Basque refugee family in France. Two of the basic rewards of interaction with others are the material help they give us and the stimulation we receive from sharing experiences with them. When these two factors are knitted together by a sense of emotional rapport, built on emotional support, we have a relationship.*

We are better able to cope with stress when we have strongly supportive relationships. Others help us to appraise problems more objectively. They help us to release tension, show us they care and allow us to fall back on them.

usually when someone is in trouble and no one else is available. Neighbors do more, even when they are not friends. They watch out for the repairman, lend tools and cups of sugar and exchange gardening tips, but normally they do not feel close enough to ask for much more than this. Nor do circumstances usually justify it. Formerly, neighbors were more dependent on each other. In a rural community, there may have been no other way of getting a barn built than to ask for help from people who happened to live nearby. Before they had cars, people made more friends in their own street, and relied on them.

Work relationships also produce mutual help – more than neighborhood relationships do, because workmates spend more time together and the time is mainly devoted to getting something done. (Neighbors mainly talk when they are together, at the garden fence or in the street.)

Voluntary relationships can involve higher expectations of help, but these expectations are not uniform. Many friendships mainly involve socializing – the friends see each other for entertainment and seldom ask favors. Other friendships are centered on a shared activity, such as a team sport, and although there may be a high level of loyalty and reliance on one another during practice and play, the friends do not help each other, or meet each other very much, in other areas of life. Close friends, however, sometimes help each other significantly – lending money, providing useful introductions and helping each other and each other's offspring to get jobs.

When we need a lot of help, especially if we have no clear

STRESS AND SOCIAL SUPPORT

■ The various forms of help and emotional benefit that we derive from relationships are known as social support. This support, especially emotional support, and especially in the degree that we receive it from those closest to us, provides an extremely important buffer against the life-stresses that threaten our health.

Excess stress occurs when demands to adjust or adapt tax our emotional and physical resources. The demands can be external, resulting from events – for example, when you lose a job, move house, find yourself in serious financial difficulties or suffer a bereavement – or internal, resulting from feelings of discontent, depression or boredom.

Some stress is good for you. Our emotional response to healthy challenges and a bit of excitement corresponds to a state of physical arousal in which hormones and other

body chemicals stimulate the body's action systems – the heart and circulatory system, the nervous system, the muscles and the respiratory system.

However, the body gears itself to tackle problems that face us even when there is no action that we can take, and it gears itself up higher as our emotional response becomes more distressed. When there is too much stress and we do not know how to cope with it, the release of stress chemicals can reach damaging levels. Too much stimulation of the organs that make up the action systems can harm them, and excess stress has been implicated in high blood pressure, heart disease, asthma and a number of lesser disorders.

During stress, some of the body's organs function below their normal level. For example, blood flows away from the digestive system toward the muscles. The underperforming organs too can suffer. Excess stress has been implicated, for example, in the formation of ulcers, as too much digestive acid accumulates in an under-active stomach.

Also affected by changes in body chemistry during stress is the immune system. Research with laboratory animals and with humans has shown that the

white blood cells that attack cancers and invading micro-organisms are less responsive when we are under heavy stress. The cells are less able to divide and specialize for the specific tasks involved in combatting the disease at hand, and they are less able to divide and multiply in sufficient numbers to effectively eliminate it.

Research also indicates that too much stress threatens mental well-being. Depression and schizophrenia have both been associated with high stress.

People may experience equally stressful situations, but with different effects on their emotions and their health. Partly this is explained by the fact that we have different constitutions. Some people are not as easily aroused and so feel a less intense emotion and undergo more moderate changes in body chemistry. Also our bodies' susceptibility to the effects of excessive stimulation varies. The same levels of stress chemicals over the same length of time may produce high blood pressure in one person but not in another.

People also vary in their ability to cope. Those who are confident that they can overcome the challenge that a stressful situation presents

experience a less intense emotion than those who feel helpless. Similarly, if you can convince yourself that the crisis will soon be over or that it does not matter as much as it seems, the level of arousal may be lessened.

People are better able to cope when they have strongly supportive relationships. Friends and family may help us to cope by giving a more objective appraisal of the situation that faces us and of our capacity to deal with it than we can give in our distressed state. They may help us to release tension by making us laugh. They may provide a reassuring network of material and emotional supporters that we feel able to fall back on, at least to some extent, when the shock that we are experiencing is precisely that we have lost one of our main supports – a job, for example, or a loved one.

Those nearest to us are often people who are prepared to listen when we need the opportunity to release tension by complaining or by grieving aloud. Probably the most important support that other people provide when we are in need is to show that they care about us. Grief, anxiety and distress are all felt more keenly when they are endured in isolation. **IHG**

NEW THINKING ABOUT ILLNESS

■ *Only in the 1970s and 1980s did it become widely accepted that illness results from a combination of both physical and psychological causes. Ancient and medieval physicians had guessed that this is so, but scientific medicine had so far made all of its progress by concentrating on physical causes and effects.*

One early study that led to new thinking examined how social support can modify the effects of stress during pregnancy. All the women studied were facing, as well as their pregnancies, additional stress such as divorce, bereavement or moving house. Of those who did not receive much social support, 91 percent had complications in pregnancy and during childbirth. However, only 33 percent of the women who had good supportive relationships experienced complications. Women with inadequate social support systems and poor interpersonal relationships have since been found to give birth to smaller babies.

Further studies examined how supportive interpersonal relationships might affect specific aspects of our health. These produced remarkable findings.

When the effects of social relationships on the course of certain forms of arthritis were studied, researchers found that sufferers who received the least amount of social support had

ten times more pain and swelling than sufferers who received the most. Similarly, asthma sufferers with low levels of social support required almost four times as much medication as those who enjoyed a great deal. And men with partners, friends and families who gave them a lot of support had higher rates of recovery from heart attacks.

In Seattle, Washington, a study found the highest rates of tuberculosis occurring in people who felt isolated and lonely and lacked a supportive social network of friends and family. The absence of such a network has also been tied to a higher incidence and a more rapid course of cancer. Almost identical findings have been reported for multiple accidents, suicides and respiratory and cardiac diseases. It appears that there is no illness that is not influenced by the quality of our relationships.

Some studies have shown that people with a wide variety of social and community ties actually live between two and three years longer than those with few social contacts. One found, after taking into account and weighting such variables as the clinical cause of ill health, socioeconomic status, cigarette smoking, alcohol consumption and obesity, that the risk of dying is more than doubled for those who have inadequate social networks. **IHG**

▶ **Family life** *often creates tensions and strains. On balance, however, the enjoyment and the emotional satisfaction that we derive from being married and from being parents make it more likely that we will enjoy good health and live long lives. Parents tell researchers that they value children for their love and affection, for the fun and stimulation they provide and for the sense of role fulfillment that they make possible. Children*

depend heavily on their parents for their sense of self-esteem and security. This emotional dependence remains strong even in adolescents – who try to hide it – and does not disappear even in adulthood.

opportunity to pay the favor back – money to meet an emergency, or someone to look after the children while we go out of work – we tend to turn to our families, parents especially but also adult brothers and sisters. Mutual help is most intense in families living under the same roof, usually with some members contributing earnings and all sharing in different degrees the work of looking after the home and each other's daily needs.

The effect of close relationships

A consistent correlation has been found between marital status and reported well-being, and between marital status and mortality rates. Married people are healthier and live longer than people who are single, widowed or divorced, and this applies equally to every age group and to both men and women. And you do not need a marriage certificate to gain these benefits: those cohabiting or in similar long-term intimate relationships do nearly as well as married couples.

There are some simple explanations for this. Intimate partners tend to look after each other, make sure that they are properly nourished and care for each other when ill. Those living alone often develop bad health habits such as an inadequate diet, smoking and/or drinking too much.

However, researchers who have examined more closely the connection between marriage and health have found that not only is *being* married healthier than remaining single, but the *quality* of the relationship may further enhance its protective effects. In England, sociologists found working-class women whose husbands act as

Not only is being married healthier than being single, but the quality of the relationship may further enhance its protective effect. A wife or husband who is an intimate confidant helps you to manage life's tensions.

intimate confidants to be less susceptible to depression during stressful episodes in their lives. Of those who did not have a husband-confidant and were under stress, more than 40 percent developed clinically significant depression, while only 10 percent of those with a husband-confidant became so depressed.

Another study suggests that people who express their feelings are less prone to develop cancer. Women with breast tumors were interviewed before exploratory surgery. Women who spoke easily about their grievances and disappointments tended to be among those whose tumors were later found to be benign. Those who had more difficulty about communicating grievances were more likely to have cancerous tumors.

Couples with a good supportive relationship are less likely to suffer ill health if either partner becomes unemployed. Among men who lost their jobs as a result of a factory shutdown, those with wives who gave them emotional support had fewer symptoms of illness and lower cholesterol levels, and did not blame themselves for their unemployment. Although they did not find jobs any sooner, they did make a better adjustment.

The likelihood of a schizophrenic suffering a relapse and returning to hospital has been found to reflect the amount of sensitive support given by family members. Hostility and intrusiveness on the part of the sufferer's family results in a poor prospect of recovery.

It also seems that those with children tend to live longer than those with none. This is true despite the dangers to women of pregnancy and childbirth, and the fact that both young babies and adolescents produce a great deal of stress in their parents.

Life crises and support

A life-event or life-crisis – such as bereavement, divorce, job loss, or even the excitement of winning a lottery – can upset the balance of a person's life. This means a period of readjustment, a particularly stressful time in which the risk of illness rises.

135

▲ **A sympathetic ear.** *When a daughter comes to visit, or when your husband sits with you for a while, you can tell your troubles to someone you trust – someone who will see your point of view and tell you that it is all right to be concerned. Acting as confidante is the most common form of social support that adult daughters provide to their mothers. Husbands and wives who act as confidants to each other strengthen the bond between them every time they do so. Although part of the confidant's role is to suggest more realistic ways of seeing a problem, it is essential to allow the other to fully state their own view – to get it off their chest.*

The amount and type of support needed differs from one recipient to another, depending on their ability to cope. However, support may not be forthcoming, even from those closest to the victim. People in distress are often seen as threatening by others – perhaps because they feel that they, too, could share a similar fate. And the more severe a person's problems, the less likely they are to receive support. For example, studies show that it is more unlikely for those with the worst cases of cancer to receive support than those less seriously afflicted. People who show that they are coping well with a crisis attract social support. However, those in greatest need may be the least likely to get it.

Those who experience crises turn only seldomly to the professionals for help. They are much more apt to turn to informal support systems – family, friends and neighbors and people who have undergone similar experiences. As our need for social support has been increasingly understood, however, hundreds of support groups have come into being. Alongside the well-established ones such as Alcoholics Anonymous and suicide hotlines, there are those for migraine sufferers, battered wives, widows and widowers, parents of hyperactive children – in fact, there are support groups for those affected by almost every misfortune.

The effectiveness of social support is greatly enhanced when the victim can identify with the helper. For example, a woman with breast cancer may be more likely to accept emotional support and practical advice from someone who previously went through the same experience than from a well-meaning but uninformed friend.

Tending your social network

Generally speaking, women make the most of the support offered by family, friends and neighbors, whereas men depend almost exclusively on their relationships with their wives and with workmates. In fact, marriage and other long-term intimate relationships benefit men far more than women, and this may be because women tend to be the supportive partners within them. When men become widowers, they suffer far more illness and depression than widows – perhaps because they have lost more support.

While women have the social skills for generating and maintaining one-to-one relationships with a variety of different people, men tend to derive the rest of their social support from their colleagues at work, and identify more with groups than with individuals. This concentration of all

THE BROKEN HEART

■ *The loss of an intimate partner, close friend or family member can be an important factor in the onset of depression. This emotional impact of bereavement may in turn adversely affect physical health.*

Studies examining this possibility have produced some startling results. They have consistently reported a high death rate for widowers in the year following their partner's death – three to five times higher than that of married men of the same age. For widows, however, there is an increased likelihood of dying in the second or third year. It would seem that losing a partner has a powerful and relatively immediate effect on the health, and sometimes on the life, of the survivor.

The findings of a study on the causes of death in widowers are even more surprising. A sample of 4,486 men aged 55 years and over were identified and studied for nine years after their wives died.

The widowers in this study had a 40 percent increase in mortality rate during the first six *months of bereavement, compared to a sample of married men of the same age, but if a man survived the first six months after the death of his wife, he appeared to be at no greater risk of ill health than his married friends.*

By far the greatest cause of death for the widowers was heart disease. There was an increase of 67 percent over the number of deaths from heart disease that would have been expected under normal circumstances, and this accounted for about two-thirds of the increase in mortality during the first six months of bereavement. Cancer and infectious diseases also took a toll, and, in other studies, a reduced immune response has been measured in blood samples taken from widowers during the first few months of bereavement. But the stress of bereavement seems to act as an aggravating or precipitating factor especially in heart disease. Dying of a broken heart is more than a figure of speech. **IHG**

Studies have consistently reported a high death rate for widowers in the year following their bereavement. Cancer and infectious diseases take a toll but heart disease especially is a killer during this time of emotional adjustment.

social effort into a very small number of relationships can be dangerous – if, for example, a man loses his job or gets divorced, there may be no friends to rally round and fill the emotional gap.

Your social class will also affect your relationships. On the whole, the marriages of working-class people tend to be less resilient than those of higher classes and more often end in divorce. However, ties between family members are usually far stronger. Relationships among working-class workmates can also be more supportive than those between middle-class colleagues, who are more likely to feel a sense of competition with each other.

Given the association between happiness, health and relationships, it may be possible to have a happier life and reduce the incidence of illness by improving your own and others' levels of social support.

There are a number of ways that this could be done. An awareness of the importance of relationships and social support can make you more determined to create new support systems. This does not mean that you should go out with the express purpose of meeting dozens of new people. The average network of friends and relatives seen frequently is not particularly large – it generally includes some nine or ten people. Moreover, the effects of social support are not necessarily cumulative – having dozens of acquaintances may be far less beneficial than having two or three close friends or one intimate relationship. The best preventive medicine may be simply to strengthen your existing sources of support by enhancing the relationships that you have already. **IHG**

◀ **Expressing grief** *is a step toward coping with it. Others can help us to do it. Displays of strong emotion are discouraged in many cultures.*

In others, where public, self-expression is approved, displays may sometimes seem unspontaneous, but they help to make it easier for the genuinely bereaved to express themselves without inhibition.

▲ **In the company of her cat,** *an old woman sits on the stairway leading to their shared home. Humans of all ages have attachments to animals that provide some of the same emotional benefits as relationships with humans. Cats and dogs are the preferred species, because their natural patterns of social behavior are so adaptable to a human setting (see Ch19).*

Parents and Children

CHILDREN share their parents' home, and so physical proximity alone guarantees that they will interact with parents and form relationships. But these relationships develop as they do for more profound reasons. Children and those who care for them and play with them have a biological tendency to become emotionally attached. In addition, as children grow from infancy, they understand how they fit into the world by finding social roles to play. Usually it is the role of son or daughter that they meet first. In adulthood, achieving the role of mother or father will be a goal for most people. Social preconceptions about these roles help to shape the way that parents and children interact.

The complexity of family life creates strains and high demands. Members of a family have to play several difficult and potentially conflicting roles all at the same time, and, unlike friends, we do not choose our mothers and fathers and sons and daughters. If they fail to be what we need, we cannot easily find substitutes. If they expect too much, opportunities to get away from their needs and hopes are often limited. In spite of these hazards, parent-child relationships are a central part of our happiness.

Making the first contact

Many biologists believe that human infants, like other animal young, bond to their parents and other caregivers as a result of instinctive patterns of interaction. Physical care by itself does not seem to cause an infant to form an attachment. In an experiment, monkeys separated from their natural mothers at birth were offered a choice of substitute mothers. One was a wire dummy fitted with a feeding bottle. The other was a similar dummy that provided no milk but only the comfort of a soft covering that the other lacked. The monkeys fed from the one mother's bottle but habitually clung to the soft-covered mother and ran to it when frightened. Holding and touching infants in a way that comforts them undoubtedly helps human attachments as well to form, and other forms of interaction may also play a part from the very beginning.

As a mother's contractions push a baby into the world, the violence of its passage through the birth canal stimulates high levels of adrenaline and other hormones to be released into its bloodstream. One effect of this is to heighten sensory intake. The pupils, for example, are very enlarged, letting extra light into the eyes. Eyes signal emotion, and exchanged eye contact between people with enlarged pupils intensifies the emotions of each (see *Ch 18*). It is not known how much the dilated pupils of the emotionally aroused parents may affect the undeveloped infant – but the impact of the child's pupils on the parents as they hold it for the first time may help to reinforce their attachment to it.

In mother-infant bonding by other species of mammals, the role of scent in the first few days after birth has been

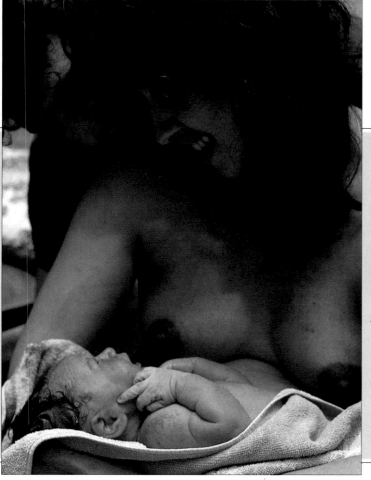

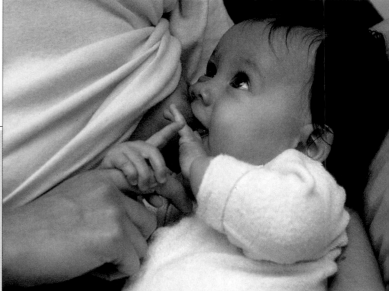

A MEETING OF MOTHER AND CHILD

■ *From the moment of birth it is difficult for mother and baby to take their eyes away from each other, or for parents to resist the urge to touch the new baby. This behavior and the baby's special responses – such as the dilated pupils of the infant* *above – lay the foundation for a relationship that in most cases will be an emotional focus for both parents and child for the rest of their lives. It will teach the child most of what it will ever know about relationships.*

Our first and, for most of us, our longest-lived relationship is the one we form from birth with our parents. From them, we learn our earliest and many of our most important lessons in how to be close to another person.

experimentally established. The newborn will bond to the mother partly as a result of already knowing her distinctive scent from the amniotic fluid in her womb.

If the distinctive scent of the mother is to have an influence on human bonding, the time of birth may be a particularly important moment – the human sense of smell is so underdeveloped that we do not consciously notice the scents of individuals, but while the infant's senses are temporarily heightened, it is possible that scent has an influence that it would not have in the days after birth.

When the birth is complete, mothers have a strong urge to hold the baby and put it to the breast. This intimate physical contact affects them both, and holding the baby at this point may also make a lasting impression on the father. The bonds depending on physical contact can also emerge, with equal strength, at a later date, when opportunities are better. For hyperreactive premature babies, touching may need to be limited at first, but when hospital personnel and parents do touch premature infants in moderation, they survive better than when not touched at all.

In some cultures, including many in India and Africa, mothers are expected to be in almost constant physical contact with the baby for the first year or so of its life. Most Western mothers, however, are quickly separated from their newborn infant – maternity staff in a hospital will care for it while she rests. After returning home from hospital, she is unlikely to sleep with the baby, keeping it instead in a crib by the bed at night. When still only a few months old, it may have a room of its own.

The Western pattern is changing somewhat. Maternity hospitals now encourage more holding by parents – including the father – at birth and earlier departures for home. Mothers who read about infant care cannot help being exposed to ideas about "natural breastfeeding," whose advocates argue that the relationship between mother and child is bound to be better if they sleep in constant contact side by side, third-world style. The infant finds the satisfaction of the breast – not simply an alleviation of thirst and hunger but a particular form of comfortable touching – whenever it wants to. This arrangement requires a husband's patience and conviction that it is worth the disruption to the marital relationship. In most families, scheduled feedings of a baby that sleeps on its own continue to be preferred.

By three months, the majority of mothers in most Western countries have stopped breastfeeding altogether, but they hold their babies for long hours each day, and produce exaggerated smiles with eyes opened very wide and

■ **Secure attachment to parents** develops out of positive and regular interaction. Stimulating play, comforting body contact, smiling and showing interest in its responses, and being there at predictable times, are what help parents to make a baby feel sure of whom it belongs to. Most parents will find them- selves doing these things spon- taneously. By the age of about eight months – when babies begin to distinguish strangers from those who make them feel safe – a secure attachment to the mother will be obvious.

During its first few months, a child becomes more or less securely attached to those who care for it. The more securely it attaches to them, the more confident, exploratory, independent and cooperative it is likely to be.

eyebrows raised as they speak in lilting tones to them. There is evidence that the distinctive tongue clicks and "shhhs" that adults use universally when attracting babies' attention and quieting them are understood from birth. Saying "shhh" causes an infant to stop moving and stop looking about. Neither tinging a triangle nor making a "pssst" sound draws attention like the tongue clicks that all mammals produce to communicate with their young.

Secure and insecure attachment

Infants first clearly display their attachments at about the age of eight months. A child begins to distinguish the people it knows from others, and it goes through a phase of being frightened by strangers. When frightened, it will go to the person who looks after it the most – usually the mother – to be held for protection, and it will protest at being separated from her.

Most children are "securely attached." They will explore a strange environment while the mother is present and display less fear when taken away from her (as measured by heartrate, pupil enlargement, hormone levels and the volume of crying) than "insecurely attached" infants, who will not leave the mother to explore. Some insecurely attached children behave ambivalently toward the mother in unfamiliar settings – for example, crying to be picked up and then crying to be put down.

Confidence to explore and interact promotes quicker development. At the age of two, children with secure attachments show better problem-solving abilities, and simply being close to an attachment figure is enough to

reduce fear. They play more confidently with other children at the age of three and a half and show more independence, while insecurely attached children are having more difficulty in overcoming their shyness of strangers (see *Ch 23*). Securely attached children are less obedient but better at cooperating in a joint activity that interests them. Less likely to be bed-wetters, they are nevertheless more likely to wet their clothing because stopping to use the toilet would disrupt what they are doing or amount to giving in to parental demands. A smile and a reassuring word from an attachment figure is enough to reduce the anxiety of a securely attached five-year-old.

In the case of adopted children, it takes longer for secure attachment to develop – especially if the child has had a number of previous caretakers – but it can be just as successful.

Positive interaction with parents who respond with sensitivity to its needs can promote improved development in an insecurely attached child. Stimulating play, comforting body contact, smiling and interest in what it has to say can all help. If the mother is working, it is important that the babysitting arrangements be stable and predictable. Uncertainty about who will be in charge can undermine the security of even the most emotionally robust child. **AC GGB**

141

■ **"Home base"** *for a toddler is mother's skirts. If this or another base is reliably available, the child will readily set out on independent explorations. Brushing away an annoyingly clingy child will not make it less clingy, but picking it up and comforting it regularly will. Working mothers can have confident and well-adjusted young children so long as they give them undivided attention at predictable times of the day and leave them in charge of caregivers who make them feel secure.*

Obstacles to secure attachment

Stress in mothers can put a strain on the developing relationship between mother and infant, and between mother and growing child, because of the difficulty she finds in interacting in a relaxed and spontaneous way.

An early hazard is postnatal depression. In most cases – two-thirds of all new mothers – depression amounts to no more than the "maternity blues" – feelings of tearful irritability that last from a few minutes to several hours. These may occur only once or twice or daily. Usually, they disappear completely by the end of the baby's second week, and many medical authorities believe that they are related to hormone changes. Up to 20 percent of new mothers, however, have feelings of depression and irritability that remain constant for some time. The mother may feel critical of herself as a mother, and blame herself excessively when things go wrong, especially with the baby.

Women who are dissatisfied with their marriage during pregnancy are more likely to be depressed once the baby is born. For most couples, the period after delivery puts a strain on the marriage, but if marital difficulties already exist, the couple may not be able to deal effectively with any additional stress (see *Ch 29*).

Also at risk are women who live away from their families or who do not have many friends – to assist them with the baby, give advice about child care or just hear about their feelings. Many new mothers feel guilty about negative feelings and need help expressing them. Almost all women, at times, have negative reactions to mothering. A woman who has not had previous contact with newborn infants may be disappointed, especially, to discover that they are demanding. One of the most important things that those close to her can do is to let her know that these reactions are both normal and acceptable.

Some babies are especially difficult. They have intense emotional reactions, crying vigorously when distressed, and they are difficult to comfort. If a child responds readily and easily, the mother is likely to interact with it in a playful and reassuring way. Mothers may gradually lose confidence in their abilities unless they receive emotional support from those close to them. A husband can be the most important support, but he may also feel anxious and powerless and blame his wife for the infant's behavior.

Many temperamentally difficult babies become hyper-active children. The strain of supervising them and the

▲ **Looking for trouble**. *Small children have to be watched constantly – a strain for parents. With conceptual development, children gradually learn responsibility. Research with pre-schoolers suggests that parents' wishes will best be taken to heart when children's wishes are frequently met too. In one experiment, mothers were instructed to comply with their child's every request during 15 minutes of play. Other mothers were told to play as they normally would. The compliant mothers received more cooperation from their children at the end of the play when asking them to pick up and put away toys.*

Children are stressful and demanding. First-time parents of babies and small children especially need to be prepared for a strain on family life. It is important for them to know that negative feelings are both normal and acceptable.

difficulty the children have in relaxing make it a special challenge for the parents to achieve affectionate and comforting interaction with them. Up to the third year, even mothers of normal children are especially prone to bouts of depression, often through becoming socially isolated on account of the constant demands of child care.

Strife within the wider family can also affect the mother and child. If the mother sees her parents as competing with her husband for her affection and the baby's, or if his family is seen as in competition with hers, she may react by trying to isolate herself, together with her child, as a mutual protection against conflict. This may establish a pattern of overprotectiveness which will restrict the child's ability to explore and develop.

All of these strains are likely to be more intense with a first-born or only child. Previously installed brothers or sisters make a less anxious – because more experienced – family setting for a new arrival. However, they too will depend on the adults for attention, and competition between them will affect each child's relationships with the parents (see *Ch18*).

Unequal attachment to parents

Instinctive urges to hold babies, smile and make nonsense noises at them are not confined to mothers, and so infants readily form an attachment to their fathers. In many babies it appears by one year and in most by 18 months.

Mothers are usually the strongest objects of attachment. Possibly, infants bond to their mothers partly as a result of experiences at birth (see above), but, without doubt, a reason for the intensity of the relationship is that a mother feels more committed to care for her baby than anyone else, and so she spends more time with it. In part, the mother's commitment may arise as a woman's instinctual response to the experiences of childbirth and breastfeeding, but there is also at least a very strong contribution from her learned sense of a mother's role.

The increased participation of women in the workplace has modified this role only superficially. After bearing a child, a woman stops working to care for it, often for several years and at least for several months. Even when they resume working, women feel that it is primarily their responsibility to keep their children clean, fed and properly dressed. They supervise the nanny or babysitter and take over more of her role than the husband does when at home. They take time off from work when their children are ill, but their husbands usually do not.

Fathers usually do not participate in bathing, changing diapers or feeding until an infant is at least six months of age. An American study found in the early 1970s that fathers of infants ranging in age from newborn to three months spent less than 40 seconds per day verbally communicating with them. Among fathers of infants from 9 to 12 months of age, only 25 percent gave any regular care.

Although fathers' participation in child care has increased since, their involvement still lags behind women's. They continue to see mothers as primarily responsible for child

◄ **More children mean more work for mothers**. *Opportunities for rewarding play and teaching activities diminish as the number of basic needs multiplies. Very simple tasks become frustratingly difficult to perform in the face of constant interruptions. At the end of a day full of concerted but only partially successful effort to keep the house tidy and the family happy, there may be few signs of concrete achievement.*

► **Fathers act as mothers' helpers**. *With very few exceptions, mothers are the main caregivers for children. Fathers almost always help, however, except where the mother role and the father role are rigidly distinguished. Paternal participation relieves mothers of some of the stress of child care and gives fathers extra opportunities to be emotionally closer to their children.*

143

THE VALUE OF CHILDREN

■ *Sharing love and moments of pleasure – rather than sharing the burden of supporting the family – is what gives a modern child its role. Historically, older children could help by hunting animals, gathering food, farming or earning money. Although they no longer have this role in industrialized countries, they still need to feel that they have something valuable to contribute to the family. Many parents value children, however, for giving parents a valuable role to play, and the majority value them for the relationship they provide. In a survey of American parents, only 5 percent of mothers and 8 percent of fathers considered that economic utility – including security in old age and help with chores – was a value of having children. (More than 85 percent of parents, however, thought that children should indeed help around the house.) Larger numbers valued their children for giving them "something useful to do" and making them feel adult and more mature (23 percent of mothers and 20 percent of fathers), and for giving them a purpose in life, learning experiences and self-fulfillment (36 percent of mothers and 32 percent of fathers). The largest numbers said that children were of value because they provide love and companionship (66 percent of mothers and 60 percent of fathers) and stimulation and fun (61 percent of mothers and 55 percent of fathers.)*

▶ **Seeing the world through the eyes of children** *and sharing their innocent delights and pleasures are among the rewards of parents who share time and love with their family.*

144

Children in industrial society have lost their role as contributors to the family's material well-being. Parents value them for the love, companionship and stimulation they provide and for the parental role they create.

care, and themselves as responsible for earning the family's way. An American survey in the mid-1980s showed that men were significantly less dissatisfied than in previous decades about their wives working, but they continued to be dissatisfied if their wives earned more than them.

Men who rate themselves competent to handle a baby when interviewed before their first child's birth are more likely to play an active role once the baby arrives. Women can encourage feelings of competence by showing their husbands what to do and by practicing patience when the new father seems clumsy or inefficient. The mother has acquired a sudden expertise – the first six weeks of her first child's life are often a very harrowing learning experience for her. She should bear in mind that her husband has had no such intense learning experience. He should realize that this – not necessarily a special care-giving female instinct – is the chief difference between them in ability.

The result of sex stereotyping in the division of child care can be that the father feels excluded while the mother feels overtaxed. She may feel trapped by her constant responsibilities, while he may feel diminished at having no relationship with the infant. As babies become small children, however, fathers find it easier to be involved with them through play. A 1982 survey in Britain found that this is the main way that British fathers interact with them – 76 percent with children under five played with them every day or most days.

Mothers give more affection and comfort to school-age children than fathers do. In another British survey of children aged seven, 39 percent of boys and 42 percent of girls felt closer to their mothers, while only 21 percent of boys and 18 percent of girls felt closer to their fathers. Boys, however, were more likely to share an interest with their fathers (68 percent) than with their mothers (33 percent), and girls were more evenly balanced between sharing interests with their mothers (49 percent) and with their fathers (40 percent). Fathers participated "a lot" in the lives of 50 percent of the boys and 31 percent of the girls.

Fathers may feel excluded from family life especially when efforts to involve children in their own interests meet frustration. Making contact through an interest is usually possible, however, when the child is allowed to enter the activity on its own terms – motivated by its own desire to have the father's attention – and is not expected to learn at a forced pace. It may help the father if he consciously makes the contact rather than the activity into the primary purpose of interacting. **IHG VEW**

Sharing a child's love

A mother usually welcomes the father's participation in child care as a relief from demanding work and as an opportunity to share an experience as a couple. Others may also be welcome, or may instead create conflict. Help from her own mother or her mother-in-law immediately after the birth is usually a boon. But if the grandparent and the mother have not yet resolved the question of which is the "executive generation" – which generation is now in charge (see *Ch 20*) – the mother may feel undermined in her attempts to assume her role, finding herself too often overruled in matters of how to care for her own child.

A working mother of an infant often feels anxious whether the person who cares for the baby in her absence has the commitment and the competence to do it properly. This is a concern worth having. In the mid-1980s, a survey in London, England, of registered child minders – women registered by

◄ **Mothers give most of the comfort** *that children receive from parents. Both daughters and sons feel closer to them emotionally as a result – especially daughters.*

► **Fathering can be awkward** *when you feel you lack the expertise. However, there are no skills of child care that a husband cannot learn.*

the local authorities as being free of tuberculosis and having homes safe enough for small children to be in – concluded that 17 percent were causing physical or emotional harm to the children they daily babysat. The difficulty of finding economic but reliable child care is often the main obstacle to quick resumption of a career.

Working mothers sometimes fear that someone may be stealing their babies' affections. This is a matter to feel easier about, for there is room in any child's life for several attachments, and children gain confidence and versatility from forming them. To fulfill a mother's role, a woman may need to feel that her child is not *more* intimately attached to another person. In the 15 hours per day or more plus weekends and holidays that most jobs allow an employee to spend at home, however, there is time to be the person who behaves in the most motherly way the most often.

There is no one "natural" arrangement for child care. What matters is that children receive proper nourishment, are protected from harm, receive affection and stimulating attention and develop a secure sense of identity. Different cultures and different families achieve these objectives in a wide variety of ways.

Children's family roles

At an early age a child begins to understand who it is in the family, and how to be that person. It learns that the children of the household have a different status from the adults, who control resources and provide for the children and control their behavior. Each child learns also that there are male and female categories in the family, and that it belongs to one of them.

No matter how many adults care for them, children will understand that their mother and father have a special social status in relation to them – others only claim authority over them in the name of the mother or father or both, to whom they refer important decisions about the children.

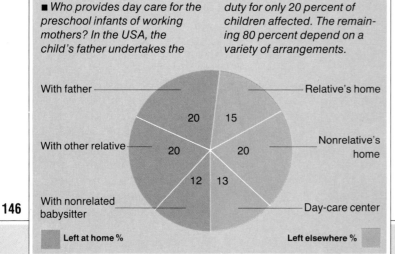

WHEN MOTHER GOES OUT TO WORK

■ *Who provides day care for the preschool infants of working mothers? In the USA, the child's father undertakes the* duty for only 20 percent of children affected. The remaining 80 percent depend on a variety of arrangements.

With father — 20

Relative's home — 15

With other relative — 20

Nonrelative's home — 20

With nonrelated babysitter — 12 / 13

Day-care center

■ Left at home %   Left elsewhere % ■

► **Outside help** *enables a working mother to resume a career. This young Italian has taken up residence and child-care duties in a British family in return for a salary and the opportunity to practice his English. Children form affectionate links with nannies and babysitters, but this does not dilute the intensity of the relationship they have with a loving mother.*

▲ **Working and caring for a child**. *Opportunities to combine paid work with successfuly looking after your own child are almost nonexistent. For hundreds of thousands of years, however, women with swaddled babies on their backs were a mainstay of hunter-gatherer and primitive agricultural economies.*

Working mothers sometimes fear that their child will become emotionally more attached to another caregiver. But there is room in a child's life for several attachments, and it can gain confidence and versatility from them.

Parental status will be socially reinforced in the neighborhood, at school and in innumerable laws – such as Article 371 of the French Civil Code, for example, which formally decrees: "At all ages the child should honor and respect its father and mother.'

To be reassured of its own status in relation to each parent – to feel that it is fulfilling its role – a child will desire recognition from each. Its self-esteem will be profoundly affected by whether it seems to be fulfilling parental expectations. Partly because of the parents' status, partly because of their sense of attachment to them, children follow them as their most important models when developing their sex roles.

Parents feel a social responsibility to teach children their roles and set standards of behavior for them. Also, in all families, there is some insistence on obedience just to make it easier to organize children's activities and care. The majority of mothers spank or hit small children as a punishment or to bring them to order. Few fathers spank very often, but they are usually seen by children as figures of greater authority, because they overrule mothers and mothers defer to them. Fathers hit boys more often than they hit girls, and are seen by boys as stricter and more aggressive than their mothers. An authoritarian father is usually regarded more favorably by children than an authoritarian mother, and a permissive mother more favorably than a permissive father.

Research shows that children internalize rules of behavior best when parents are affectionate and explain reasons for the rules. Physical punishment and depriving children of things they want – especially threatening to withdraw love – do not produce resistance to temptation or the capacity to understand and accept blame.

147

■ **Fathers like to involve sons** *in the activities that interest them. In many cases this will be a main focus of the relationship between them.* TOP *A famous American tennis star and the father who fostered his career.* BOTTOM *An English father shares with his son a national obsession for the game of cricket.*

▲ **Sex-role models**. *By acting out our sex roles as we see them, we give our children models to imitate in adult life. Here parents demonstrate that* *a mother's role is to look after the family's household needs and a father's role, when he is not at work, is to play and be entertaining. Especially for a* *son, the role of your father is likely to involve an activity that he shares with you.*

Conflict between caregivers about who is in charge can disrupt a child's relationships with them. A child will notice disagreement between the mother and father about principles for helping and disciplining children, or between a parent and a strict grandparent or a permissive nanny, and it will take sides. In the discord that accompanies divorce, one parent may try to set children against the other, and step-parents may be resisted by children as attempting to displace a natural mother or father by claiming authority and other rights without entitlement. In any of these situations adults can save children distress by cooperating to maintain consistent discipline.

Maintaining contact with both parents after divorce eases the distress of separation from someone they love and helps their self-esteem by making it clear that they are not rejected. It also helps children significantly in sex-role development. Boys, especially those separated before the age of five, tend to grow up less masculine if they have no father. Adolescent girls who have grown up without fathers have more difficulty than other girls in forming relationships with the opposite sex. Being treated as feminine by a father is an important element in developing the female sex role. Boys who grow up *with* their father develop more masculinity if they have a warm relationship with him.

Adolescent role-conflicts

In Western societies adolescents are given adult roles and responsibilities only very gradually. This period of transition may be less prolonged in a one-parent family, as children often have to shoulder more adult responsibilities and participate in more family decisions. For most, however, uncertainty about learning the role of a young adult creates insecurity.

Throughout childhood children gradually develop less emotional dependence on parents and seek independent relationships with friends. At about the age of 12 this trend enters a crisis. Children are preoccupied with keeping separate two lives that they find themselves leading – they do not want friends to see the dependent role they still play within the family and they do not want parents to intrude on the bravado and self-assertion that they share with friends.

As adolescence proceeds, groups or gangs partly take

THE FAMILY-CONFLICT DANCE

■ *Every family has family conflicts, and they are seldom isolated events. A quarrel may begin with an exchange between just two people, but anyone present who is emotionally involved with the participants will be affected and will probably affect the way the incident develops. Thus the father or a sibling will typically get involved in a conflict between a mother and child, or a child will intervene in an argument between its parents.*

There is another sense, as well, in which scenes of family conflict are not isolated – they tend to repeat again and again. When people live in close emotional proximity, they readily set up characteristic patterns of interaction – little family dances. Among them are patterns of conflict.

Imagine a typical scene of

conflict in your own family. You can probably predict the kind of situation in which the next one will occur, one or two topics it might have, who will say what, roughly in what order, and two or three ways in which the sequence will "end." It might end, for example, with a senior member of the household banging a fist on the table, with someone bursting into tears, with someone making a joke to divert people's attention or – very commonly – a child becoming excited and misbehaving or even having an attack of asthma.

It is misguided to blame anyone for a sequence like this. Everyone present contributes their own steps to the dance in a habitual way, and by keeping in step, they make the dance possible. This may be frustrating, because it can make

the sequence seem like an inescapable exercise that cannot resolve any of the conflicts that it is supposed to be about. There is no real "end."

Sequences change naturally, however, as the family's life develops – for example, as problem adolescents become adults and their parents seem less to them like problem parents. Consciously to change the steps in a family dance is difficult. One possibility is to bring in someone else – such

as a counselor – who can intervene more constructively than can a child with an attack of asthma. Or you could attempt yourself to act out of character. This will be constructive if it means showing more recognition for the positive aims behind other people's steps, praising what you can agree with in the other's habitual stance and helping them to find ways of realizing these aims. (See also Ch31.) **AC**

▶ **A father's hand spurned.** *Among the shifting patterns that occur in families are the pairs that form and the pairs that do not. A mother and daughter might be on good terms, leaving the father out, for two or three months. The pattern can then reverse, with the father being preferred, and shift back and forth again several times.*

Adolescents lead a double life. The friendship group commands a highly visible but superficial loyalty while the family's emotional support continues to be an unvoiced need. Successful parents show concern without intruding.

---

over from the family as social bases (see *Ch22*). Young people may feel no more secure, but they begin to feel ashamed of any impulse to participate in the intimate life of the family – this now seems childish. And yet the desire for parental reassurance may be strong. Even runaways who do not reply to parental attempts to contact them take heart from these attempts and may feel despondent when they do not find their names on lists prepared by search organizations.

As children attempt to establish a separate identity from the family, they strive for independence, but frequently undermine any credible claim to it by appearing irresponsible and immature. Child-parent conflict inevitably increases, usually reaching a peak between the ages of 13

and 15. Rebelliousness is related to the type and extent of parental discipline. Authoritarian rules are ready targets for violation, but a lack of discipline may appear to the adolescent as indifference. The most successful parent-adolescent relationships are those in which the parents are able to communicate their concern and affection without being intrusive or too involved in their child's life. They are willing to set limits for their child, but are prepared to extend privileges that foster a sense of independence and self-confidence.

Girls have less favorable relationships with their parents during adolescence than boys. Mother-daughter relationships are especially prone to conflict, because mothers are more restrictive with their daughters than are fathers.

In young adulthood children have the confidence to grow closer again to their parents. It is now less important to them to emphasize superficial differences, and an underlying basis of shared attitudes and opinions usually becomes more visible in the adult's choice of career, marriage partner and life-style, but all of these will be heavily influenced by experience outside the family as well. **AC GGB**

IDENTITY PROBLEMS OF ADOPTED CHILDREN

■ Most adoption agencies consider it dangerous to tell adoptive parents much about their new child's family history. It is feared that the information might be passed on to the child and encourage an interest in natural parents that could interfere with its developing normal relationships within the family that nurtures it.

Yet adopted children inevitably wonder why they were given up for adoption and fantasize about their natural parents. Often these thoughts are kept secret to avoid hurting the adoptive parents.

However, adoptive parents need not be hurt or threatened by this interest. It does not represent an inadequate emotional attachment to them but rather a need for a fuller sense of identity. Allowing adopted children to freely air their fanta-

sies and questions can help them to live more easily with this need.

Adolescence is a time of particular difficulty about personal identity. When you are taking on and anticipating new roles and allegiances at the rate that adolescents do, it may seem difficult to know who you are and who you are becoming. It is comforting to have firmly rooted sources of unchanging identity in your past history – a clear family origin, for example.

For this reason, as adolescents and young adults, adopted children may become actively interested in tracing their natural parents. Interest groups such as the Adoptees Liberty Movement Association in the United States campaign for freedom of information about personal origins. **AC GGB**

149

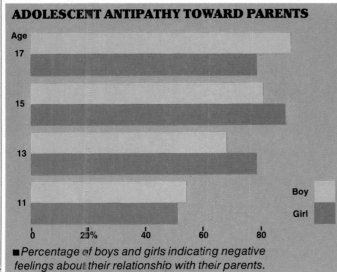

ADOLESCENT ANTIPATHY TOWARD PARENTS

Age		
17		Boy
15		Girl
13		
11		

0   20%   40   60   80

■ *Percentage of boys and girls indicating negative feelings about their relationship with their parents.*

◄ **Adolescent uncertainty** shows in the faces of two girls in the crisis mid-teen years. No longer willing to display an outward emotional dependence on their parents, children of this age are not yet secure enough in their own identities to establish mature relationships outside the family. Friendships are unstable and security is sought in membership of a temporary social circle.

Brothers, Sisters and Only Children

IN THE AGE of family planning, parents and prospective parents have it in their power to choose whether their firstborn will know what it is like to have brothers and sisters. This can be a difficult choice, because it involves trading off a potentially rich and supportive set of merely *potential* relationships against the quality of an already existing one. The larger the family, the less individual parental attention there can be for a child. Yet one of the most common reasons people give for starting a second pregnancy is to prevent a firstborn from being an only child – 78 percent of respondents in a survey in the United States believed that only children are disadvantaged. What balance can be struck between these conflicting considerations?

Bonds between brothers and sisters

The emotional tie between siblings is usually very strong. Older brothers and sisters have the same instinctive impulses to interact in caring and playful ways with babies and toddlers that adults have, and in a busy household they often have more time to indulge these impulses than the adults do. Drawn to a little brother or sister, the child becomes one of its first teachers of language and social skills. It is often the older sibling who is there to comfort it when comfort is needed.

The sense of attachment that grows in these circumstances later expresses itself in protective behavior toward little brothers and sisters in the school playground. A sibling also provides a ready confidant when you have problems to discuss without involving adults. In childhood and adolescence, you can conspire to keep each other's secrets from parents and to undo the restrictions they impose. In adolescence and adult life, a brother or sister can be a useful social contact, especially for meeting members of the opposite sex. In adult life people often turn to their siblings for emotional and material support in times of crisis.

Most people love their brothers and sisters and would feel a sense of loss if they died or moved far away. Judging from this feeling for a sibling we know, we are apt to assume that a part of our own children's lives will be empty if *they* do not have brothers and sisters too.

It could be said that the emptiness we fear does not have to be filled by a blood relation – if you lack a sister, a good friend can be like a sister to you. However, most family relationships are more certain and longer lasting than friendships. Sentimental ties and a shared sense of family identity hold adult brothers and particularly adult sisters together, and motivate them to rely more on each other than on friends (see *Ch 20*). If your child does not have brothers and sisters when you are gone, will there be a strong enough social support network to fall back on in adult years? This thought motivates many parents to think not only of new additions to the family, but to foster playmate relationships between cousins. Cousins who play together as children have more chance of feeling a sense of kinship and warmth as adults.

Sibling rivalry

It is a strain on the relationship between brothers and sisters that they have to compete for the limited resources made available by the family to its children, especially the time and attention of parents. Rivalry between them often appears strikingly in the early years. A firstborn joined by a younger brother or sister experiences conflicting emotions – excitement and curiosity, jealousy and anger. Often these emotions occur in children who are too young to really comprehend their feelings or to manage them adequately. A child who has a close and harmonious relationship with its

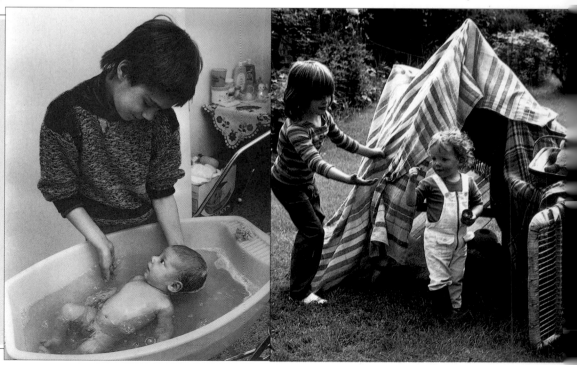

▶ **The birth of fraternal love.** *The impulse to interact in a caring and loving way with younger siblings is almost universal. When parental encouragement and a sense of family identity foster this impulse, it can become the basis of a life-long bond.*

▶ **Practicing for a later break** *from dependence on their parents, small children like to build dens (often expressly "for" a younger sibling) that create subterritories within the wider family territory. Parents may be invited to squeeze in for a visit, but they are also places where brothers and sisters meet each other's friends and share secrets.*

We use our ideal of the relationship between brothers and sisters as model for love between nations and races. It may seem wrong to deprive children of this highly valued experience. Yet only children are far from being disadvantaged.

mother before a new baby arrives is particularly likely to be jealous of the infant.

Sibling conflict between small children is more intense if they are less than two years apart in age. In part, this is due to the developmental level of the first child when the second is born. Children under two years of age are strongly attached to their mother and respond with distress when separated from her. While they may assert their independence in some ways – for example, by pitting their will against their mother's – they will still be fearful and insecure without her full attention.

Children younger than two years also lack the intellectual development to fully appreciate the arrival of the new infant and to understand their own feelings about the event. It is useful, however, to prepare young children for a sibling's birth – for example, carefully describing during the pregnancy what it will be like to have an infant in the family.

Parents should expect that their older children will show some negative or infantile reactions when the baby is born, imitating the baby's behavior in order to attract the mother's attention. Unless behavior toward the baby is aggressive, it should not be punished – reassurance and comfort are much more effective responses. Parents can also foster more mature behavior by having the older child help to care for the infant. Establishing a nurturing role for it will affirm the elder's importance, and will also form the basis for a caring and protective relationship in the future.

Rivalry is common throughout childhood and into adulthood. One study found it in 71 percent of adults interviewed. Commonly, siblings are unhappy about the way that another's achievements, physical attractiveness, intelligence, social skill or maturity seem better recognized by parents, and later by the world at large. Parents can seriously undermine the long-term relationship between siblings by playing favorites, whether unconsciously or as a strategy to motivate children's compliance with parental wishes. A son trained to resent his brother's successes at school or elsewhere – because they seem to diminish the love and acceptance available to him – may feel distant from his brother for life.

Unconsciously, siblings tend to attempt a reduction in the competition between them – or to find competitive advantages – by accentuating their differences. A firstborn may become more allied with parents in order to overcome the sense of being displaced in their affections by younger children – firstborns tend to be more conservative, reserved and achievement-oriented. Younger children often counter an elder's greater sense of importance in the family by being more rebellious, outgoing and socially charming. Often, if the first child identifies with the more dominant parent, a second child will identify with the less dominant.

Only children

In the 1920s, psychologists argued that being an only child is a disadvantage that parents should not impose on their children. Without brothers and sisters, a child was thought to be deprived of important learning experiences, such as sharing toys, learning to cooperate and learning to nurture younger children. Intellectual development was suspected of being affected by the lack of siblings to teach things to or learn things from.

The parent of an only child is a more anxious one. Although all first children experience a high level of parental concern, once parents have a second child or more, they become more relaxed about children, and lower

◀ **Learning from a sibling.** *A younger child can learn much simply by watching and listening to older ones and by filling in as the sole person free to share an activity. Studies suggest, however, that only children, eldest children and those from small families interact more with parents than younger children in large families do, and that this is a richer learning experience.*

Only children and children from small families benefit from greater parental concern and more ample family resources than younger children in large families. In all sizes of family, parents tend to give firstborns high levels of attention.

their expectations of them. Parents of an only child, however, remain concerned and protective, even growing more concerned as years pass and the likelihood of ever having another child diminishes. Unfettered attention and concern were thought to encourage dependency and timidity in the child and to promote selfishness.

Psychologists have taken another look at the only child, however, because of new population trends. In past generations, only children were born mainly during times of economic hardship or war. Today they appear more frequently, because parents divorce more often before another sibling is born, and because mothers more often delay having another child until their careers are firmly established, and then consider it too late.

Studies reveal that the only child's intelligence, aspirations and successes are, in fact, superior to those of children with siblings. However, this superiority appears in a comparison of only children and *all* other children counted together. It is not particularly noticeable until family size increases to more than four children. Only children do not differ from children in two-child families or from firstborns. Again, they do not differ from them in studies of such character traits as leadership ability, maturity and cooperativeness, but younger children from middle- and large-sized families score lower in spite of the greater opportunities to practice social skills with other children.

Only children do not differ from any other children in levels of anxiety or misbehavior. They do seem to differ from other children in sociability, but the difference is not what you might expect. Only children tend to *see themselves* as less sociable than do other children – they prefer solitary activities, such as intellectual or artistic hobbies, and they feel less of a need to be accepted and liked by their peers. However, they are not any lonelier than other children and their peers do not perceive them as being less sociable. From this we may infer that only children are more independent than children with siblings, but not to the extent that it makes them unpopular or unsociable.

Only children, children from small families and firstborns all tend to have more positive relationships with their parents than do other children. This is apparent whether it is the parents or the children who are interviewed, or whether the families are observed by outsiders. One possible reason for this is that parents are more anxious and attentive. The legendary anxiety that accompanies new parenthood really does not abate until the birth of the third child. Parents of one or two children appear to be equally anxious about their children, and to be concerned whether they are doing the right things as parents. Anxieties about the firstborn also never really diminish, because this child is always the first to enter new developmental stages.

Parents with only one or two children will also have more financial resources and time to spend with their children. The greater parental attentiveness that these children receive, and the greater speed of response from parents, communicates the message that the children are valued.

Parents of firstborns and those with small families tend to have high expectations for their children. Although these expectations are often unrealistic, setting high standards does promote achievement. The combination of high standards with a positive relationship allows firstborns and children in small families to attempt difficult tasks, but not at the cost of their self-esteem. **VEW**

153

◀ **A change in social role** can have far-reaching effects on feelings and behavior. Until now an only child, this girl is having to face up to a new status as one among siblings – and she is having to readjust her self-image accordingly. The fact that the new arrivals are twins – attracting special interest and demanding twice the usual attention – will make the delicate transition that much more difficult for her.

HOW MANY CHILDREN TO HAVE?

■ The lesson for family planners seems to be the fewer children the better. Having siblings is not usually as beneficial as having the undivided attention of your parents. The positive parent-child relationship in small and one-child families provides a better basis for emotional and intellectual growth than the companionship of siblings does, and there may be less parental attention espec- ially for the younger siblings if there are many of them. From the point of view of future social support, if you do not provide brothers and sisters this may limit the size of your child's future family network. One parti- cular strength of only children, however, is self-reliance. This may mean that an only child will not need as large a family net- work to fall back on during adult life.

◀ **The bond between twins** can be so strong that one twin will feel guilty for not sharing the other's misfortune when ill. This emotional closeness reflects an intensity of shared experience more than it reflects genetic closeness. Fraternal twins, who are genetically no closer than any other brothers and sisters, may be just as close emotion- ally as identical twins.

Family Pets

AS THE MOST intensely social and gregarious of all living mammals, humans crave association with other beings, and the other beings need not always be human. In the early 1980s, 40 percent of American households had a dog as part of the family. Not far behind were the Australians at 39 percent and the French at 35 percent. The millions of dogs, cats and other pets that people keep in their homes represent an important extension of the human social network, not merely extending families, but in many cases providing the only family-like contacts that a person has. How is this possible, and why, out of the innumerable species available, are we mainly attracted to only a few?

The human nature of dogs and cats

Dogs and cats are overwhelmingly the most common pets, and they are very well suited to join human families. Small enough and clean enough to be kept indoors, they are themselves social animals, adapted to fit in with a group. Wolves, the wild ancestors of dogs, live in packs that vary in size from about seven to about 20. In each pack, one pair – the dominant male and the dominant female – breeds. The rest help to defend the group's territory, kill game and care for young. This requires a cooperative and willing nature that domestic dogs have inherited and that humans value.

Wild and semiwild cats can live seemingly solitary lives, but their territories overlap in complex patterns, and they live in colonies – often only about five or six on a farm, but up to 60 in docklands and some other industrial settings – where small rodents and other prey are concentrated. Some of their social behavior can cut across the dividing lines between species to involve them with humans.

From a dog's or cat's perspective, humans make excellent dog and cat substitutes. Our behavior toward them stimulates dogs and cats to bond to us. For example, a mother

wolf or cat and her helpers carry food to her young, just as members of the human family do to a pet. Humans also play with pets in much the same way that mothers and helpers play with young .

The pet remains somewhat infantile for a lifetime – 10-30 years for a cat, 7-20 for a dog – being played with and depending on the human family for food without helping them to catch it. This is partly because it has been bred to be a pet, partly because it is always treated as a pet. If allowed to run wild and fend for itself, some can survive. Stray dogs, however, rarely live more than two and a half years, compared to a wolf's 8-16 years in the wild.

Human behavior toward pets parallels not only the pack or colony's care of young, but the way dominant animals treat subordinate adults. Humans groom their pets from above – scratches and pats on the head come from the same direction as a dominant animal's licks and nuzzles would. A pet dog rolls over and lies prone on its back to receive scratches and rubs on its exposed underside that are similar to the nuzzles a dominant wolf would give in response to this display.

Dogs usually groom humans from below, jumping up and attempting to lick the face, for example, as a subordinate

▲ **A cat's playfulness** *keeps its hunting and killing skills in tune and gives it a way of interacting with and bonding to other members of a group. Because of our behavioral flexibility – and the cat's – the group can be a human family.*

▶ **Canine companionship** *is reliably supportive. Whatever impression you may wish to share, your Red Setter will never contradict it. Here man shares with dog a peace-instilling view of Lake Tahoe, on the California-Nevada border.*

CAT OWNERSHIP AROUND THE WORLD

■ *For every 100 households, how many are cat-owning?*

Australia	32	Belgium	19
Canada	27	Britain	19
USA	26	Denmark	16
Austria	23	Finland	16
France	22	Italy	16
Netherlands	20	Sweden	16
Norway	20	W Germany	9
Switzerland	20	Japan	6

Keeping a pet extends and enriches family life. Our pets are usually members of social species whose natural repertoire of behavior allows them to substitute humans for their own kind and to form mutually supportive relationships with us.

wolf would a dominant wolf's. Humans hold dogs down by the scruff of the neck when they assert their dominance, just as dominant wolves hold down subordinates – except that they use teeth rather than hands to get a grip.

Human responses to animal signals

Human interpretations of pet behavior humanize the pet. For example, we see a dog with wagging tail, open mouth and lolling tongue as "friendly," while the natural function

of these signals is to display submission. A purring cat kneading your lap with its paws seems to be expressing love. (The fact that its claws are slightly extended and its nose is dripping slightly with a clear thin mucus may detract somewhat from your enjoyment of this effect.) In fact, kittens in the wild use this behavior to stimulate their mothers to feed them. Exaggeration of this and other natural patterns that humans find ingratiating has been selected for in the several thousand years of the cat's association with us as a mouser and companion.

We are sometimes helpless in the face of appealing signals from animals. Historians of domestication suspect that when we first domesticated the dog more than 25,000 years ago, we had not even conceived yet of the work that dogs might do for us as hunting partners, pack animals, herders or watchdogs. Possibly, all that motivated us at first was the attractive appearance of abandoned or orphaned wolf pups. This appearance aroused instincts to play and provide care as though for human infants, which almost all mammal young resemble in some respects.

People become involved with other species besides cats and dogs. Many a family that has set out to fatten a pig or a lamb in the back yard has found itself with a long-term attachment and an extra mouth to feed rather than an extra meal. Animals that humans have traditionally worked with in partnership are more likely to become companions, however, than the species (such as cows and pigs) that we have simply exploited.

Horses and riders, for example, are as responsive to each other as dogs and their masters. Adolescent girls are more likely than adolescent boys to be attached to a horse, and boys who are animal fanciers are more likely to be involved in a more impersonal way with tropical fish or cage birds, as a hobby activity. But man and horse do share a long and

155

DOG OWNERSHIP AROUND THE WORLD

■ *For every 100 households, how many are dog-owning?*

USA	40	Finland	22
Australia	39	Italy	20
France	35	Sweden	20
Canada	33	Austria	17
Belgium	30	Norway	16
Denmark	26	Switzerland	14
Netherlands	26	Japan	13
Britain	23	W Germany	13

romantic history, because of the intensity of feeling of men who have depended on their mounts in warfare and other dangerous pursuits. The Koran, for example, instructs on the love and care that should be given to a horse. Caligula, Emperor of Rome from 12-41AD, even arranged for his horse Incitatus to be elected to the highest religious office in the Empire – Pontifex Maximus of Rome.

Small caged animals such as hamsters and budgerigars often find a place in the indoor life of human families. There is even room for stick insects and tarantulas in some people's hearts. When goldfish die, parents often find themselves digging graves in the garden as children stand solemnly by. The more caged or otherwise confined an animal has to be, however, and the more distant it is biologically from humans, the harder it will be to have humanlike interactions with it. Any sense of attachment there may be between a lizard fancier and a lizard can only be observed with certainty in the human.

Psychological benefits of pets

Humanlike animal behavior has a striking effect. Dogs and cats bolster our morale and make us feel special, because they offer us intense loyalty and do not criticize us. They do not lay down conditions for continuing to love us.

Many people need a caring role in order to feel that they matter, and pets make them feel needed. No matter what arrangements the humans in your life may have made for themselves, if you have a pet there is always someone who will miss you if you do not come home tonight.

Taking in a pet can help children to have a greater sense of a contributing role in the family if they take responsibility for the pet's care. Similarly, a dog or cat can help parents whose children have grown up and left home – it can be an antidote to the "empty nest syndrome" (see *Ch 28*). A pet can also provide an outlet for those who have *never* had anyone to care for.

Better self-esteem from pet ownership and having someone to care for are of benefit to the lonely. Pets also combat the understimulation that lonely people suffer. They are something to watch and something to keep you busy. Even when the animals you keep are not very human, they can help to combat the effects of loneliness by providing positive "solitary activity" (see *Ch 24*).

Pets can also bring lonely people into contact with others who share an interest in animals. Even by simply walking your dog in the park you are more likely to become involved with other people. Like babies in strollers, dogs on leashes are conversation ice-breakers – they are appealing, and it is socially safe to question strangers about them.

A dog, cat or cagebird is someone to talk to. Most pet owners do not really look upon these companions as other species but rather as unique individuals, not quite as "animal" as their wild brethren. They talk to their pets and feel that there is a reciprocal understanding of moods – a mute communication. And they feel free to say to pets what is really on their minds, thus releasing many of their everyday tensions and anxieties.

We need to exchange touch but have inhibitions about doing so. The inhibitions are greater in some cultures than in others, and in all cultures men touch less than women do (see *Ch 16*). With pets, however, we are not constrained by

◄ **Our closest animal relatives** *fascinate us but make impractical pets because they are difficult to keep: too much like us, they are far more independent than dogs and far less predictable than cats. Reinhold Kasten's poster advertises "men from the primeval forest seen as never before."*

► **Biological distance** *makes a reptile an unlikely pet, because it does not have the ability to interact with us in a humanlike way. Tortoises or box turtles in the garden or house are more like mobile ornaments than companions. However, human behavior is versatile enough for even this aquatic turtle to win a lady's heart.*

Pet animals boost our morale by making us feel special and by giving us someone to care for. They make us more active, help us to meet other people and they are someone to touch and talk to. All of this contributes to our physical health.

politeness or worries about misinterpretation of our touching behavior. Petting is one of the things that owners of cats and dogs like to do best, and observations have recorded that men pet their dogs and cats every bit as much as women do.

Dogs, in particular, can also provide a sense of security. Even a small but noisy dog is as effective at keeping burglars out as many sophisticated electronic systems. Its inherited urge to join in the cooperative defense of territory makes it the classic watch animal.

Health benefits of pets

University students raised with pets have been found to be more sociable, self-reliant and tolerant, and to feel more self-worth. All of these are good indicators of a sound social support network.

Do these students have these positive attributes because they were raised with pets or are they the way they are because *parental* support was sound? No studies have proven that owning a pet affects your personality, or that it can be a long-term substitute for a human relationship. There is some evidence, however, that interacting with pets is an advantage to our physical health. A study of recently widowed women found that those who did not own pets were more anxious and experienced a greater decline in their physical health.

It is possible that one of the most important ways in which pets benefit us is by making us laugh when we play with them. This releases tension, as do so many aspects of interaction with pets – telling them about our troubles, for example, watching them or caring for them.

Overstressed people have dramatically higher rates of illness than others, and so a relaxed *feeling* of well-being seems to be *physically* good for you (see *Ch 16*). More obviously, our health is served by the fact that a horse's or a dog's need for exercise induces us to take exercise.

Studies in the 1970s revealed that stroking your pet reduces your blood pressure. (It reduces your pet's blood pressure too.) Another study concluded that pet owners were more likely to be alive a year after a major heart attack than nonowners. In 1986, it was observed that when both the coronary-prone and the nonprone experience a mild stress they respond to it with a smaller change in blood pressure if a dog is present. **BF**

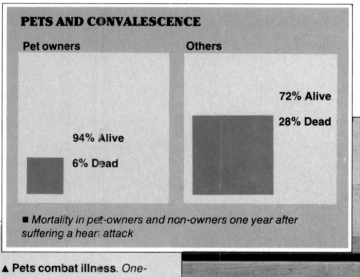

PETS AND CONVALESCENCE

Pet owners

Others

72% Alive

28% Dead

94% Alive

6% Dead

■ *Mortality in pet-owners and non-owners one year after suffering a heart attack*

▲ **Pets combat illness.** *One-year survival rates following a heart attack are significantly higher for pet-owners.*

▶ **Regular acquaintance.** *It is not necessary to be a pet-owner to enjoy the benefit of contact with animals. By feeding these pigeons at the same time on the same bench each day, this woman has formed a special relationship with them. Their daily welcome helps maintain her self-esteem.*

Keeping in Touch With Kin

SOCIAL rules make some relationships more or less obligatory. Neighbors, for example, may resent being ignored, taking this as a denial of a common courtesy due to them. The fact that someone is *related* to you creates an even greater expectation that you will be interested in them, and after leaving home we are expected to maintain relatively intense relationships with our parents, brothers and sisters.

The relationships we have with kin are influenced by psychological factors as well. Growing up in your parents' home with your brothers and sisters – and receiving their love and attention from infancy – creates a powerful bond (see *Ch17*). And the psychological need for an *identity* also draws us to our families. Distant cousins whom we have never met before receive our spontaneous attention – sharing family stories and news with them reinforces our sense of belonging. Adopted children may be fully attached emotionally to their adoptive parents but still feel a need to establish a connection with their origins, to know at least what their natural parents are *like*.

We like at least to keep in touch with kin. This is partly because we are fond of many of them, partly because we are interested in them, partly because we feel a duty to them.

Contact between kin

In underdeveloped countries with poor social services, little mobility and harsh prospects, it is not surprising that people rely heavily on their families for social support. And it is not surprising that frequent and close contact with kin – which makes this exchange of support possible – is such an important aspect of people's lives.

However, although industrialization modifies this picture, it *only* modifies it. In Britain, for example, 38 percent of single people over the age of 65 live with relatives, 28 percent of married couples over 65 live with their adult children and 54 percent of widowed or divorced people of this age live with children or other relatives. In all countries, old people living in institutions tend never to have been married or to be widowed and without children.

A survey in Toronto, Ontario, found that 50 percent of the strongest ties outside the home were to relatives. In all industrialized countries, adults tend to maintain close outside relationships with their parents and with brothers and sisters.

The bond between mother and daughter tends to be stronger than between father and daughter or between father and son, and the bond between sisters tends to be stronger than that between brother and sister or between brothers. Women are brought closer together because they are more intensely involved in the day to day business of child rearing and other family activities, and they also tend to form stronger, more personal relationships in general.

The intensity of our bonds to parents, brothers and sisters is reflected in frequency of contact – people see less of their grandparents, aunts, uncles and cousins – but frequency of contact is also affected by distance. In one American study, it was found that 60 percent of brothers and sisters who live more than 250 miles apart see each other once a year or

> *We keep in touch with kin mainly because we are fond of them. Also, feelings of family identity prompt both duty and spontaneous interest. Duty, interest and fondness typically draw us more strongly to some kin than to others.*

less. The members of working-class families tend to be less scattered than middle-class families, see each other more often and form fewer close relationships with friends. Working-class friends tend to be seen outside the home – for example, at a local bar or club, while family, including cousins who may have been close childhood playmates, are entertained in the home.

Much contact between adult brothers and sisters is at family gatherings at their parents' home. Frequency of contact tends to fall somewhat after the parents die.

In all countries, there are particular occasions, especially weddings and funerals, when more distant relatives are expected to come together. Christmas, in particular, is a family festival. Those without families, or who are separated from them, report acute feelings of loneliness at this time of the year. Although it is mainly close family that gather, they make special efforts to visit or invite isolated relatives during the season. Research confirms that gifts of more than token value exchanged at Christmas are given almost exclusively to kin.

Social support in families

The social support that kin give each other includes much more mutual help than we exchange with friends. Family members also give each other considerable emotional support and social stimulation.

Domestic help – and often accommodation – for elderly parents or help for a sister or a daughter who is having a baby are among the most common benefits. The help is almost invariably supplied by a mother, daughter or daughter-in law. Retired fathers visiting married children often work in the garden. More rarely, an adult son will travel to the home of parents or another relative to help with household or car maintenance, garden weeding or cutting the grass.

Money or goods often pass between parents and adult children in times of need, and parents often help children to set up house when they are first married. When children are more prosperous than parents, parents receive more than they give. Help to brothers or sisters in the form of money or goods is much less frequent.

Informational support is a form of help in which the family may take more advantage of the wider network of relationships within it. A study in London, England, for example, found that 25 percent of young people choosing a career were influenced by kin who had information about the career, had knowledge of how to get into it or could provide introductions.

An important form of emotional support in families is to act as confidant to someone who needs to talk about troubles. Usually, the confidant is a daughter listening to a mother, or a sister to a sister – but anyone can help another in this way. Family members are also the most important sharers of grief during a bereavement, and we depend on close family to reassure us of our worth during crises.

◄ **Events that change families** bring together their more widely scattered and more distantly related members.

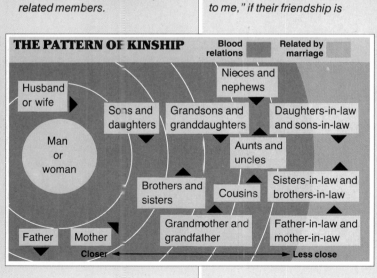

THE PATTERN OF KINSHIP

Blood relations Related by marriage

Husband or wife

Man or woman

Sons and daughters

Grandsons and granddaughters

Nieces and nephews

Daughters-in-law and sons-in-law

Aunts and uncles

Brothers and sisters

Cousins

Sisters-in-law and brothers-in-law

Father Mother

Grandmother and grandfather

Father-in-law and mother-in-law

Closer ◄———————————► Less close

THE FAMILY AND THE LANGUAGE OF RELATIONSHIPS

■ The concepts that we have of kinship roles make words like "father," "sister" and "uncle" useful for describing some of our nonkin relationships. For example, a woman may say of another "She is like a sister to me," if their friendship is particularly warm and intimate.

We expect brothers and sisters to have an equal and shared commitment to the family, and so "brother" and "sister" become appropriate forms of address within religious orders and at union meetings. Brotherhood is an ideal of race and intersectarian relations.

However, in American slang, when there is no context of shared commitment, it is depreciating for a man to call woman "sister," because this reflects the traditionally superior status of boys to girls in the family.

Priests are called "father" and the heads of convents are "mothers superior" because parents have moral authority and responsibility concerning their children. But aunts and uncles are less severe figures, and we can turn to them for help in delicate matters. Thus in Britain the term for a writer of advice to the lovelorn is an "agony aunt," and there is a slang term "uncle" meaning "pawnbroker."

The term "uncle" (French "oncle," German "Onkel") derives from the Latin "avunculus" – the mother's brother (the term for a paternal uncle is "patruus") The kindliness and geniality of the relationship that was expected between a Roman and his sister's children are still echoed in the modern word "avuncular."

Although our expectations of their roles are no longer so sharply different that we have words for two kinds of uncles, the fact that women are closer to their families and have more frequent contact with them than men do makes it more likely that the uncles (and aunts and cousins) you know best are maternal ones. **PR**

Keeping in touch itself is an important form of emotional support. Even when what is said is in itself trivial, both the caller and the person who receives contact may benefit from the opportunity to reaffirm their family identity and reassure each other that they care.

People are motivated by the *pleasure* of helping and keeping in touch with members of their family and also by a sense of obligation to do this. In an American survey, 50 percent of adults who felt close to both of their parents felt a mixture of these motives. Only 46 percent said that they acted out of pleasure alone, and only 3 percent out of obligation alone. Among adults who did not feel close to their parents 12 percent still helped them and kept in touch simply for the pleasure of it. Obligation alone motivated 38 percent, and 24 percent felt a mixture of motives. Obligation was stronger in working-class people, because of their parents' greater need, and in those with a widowed parent.

Parent-child conflicts

Strains can arise between parents and adult children when there is uncertainty about which generation is in charge. Some children establish a sense of "executive"

160

▲ **Three generations of women**. *Female kin tend to keep up closer relationships than male kin do.*

▶ **Godparents** *stand by at a royal christening in Luxemburg. Traditionally, the christening ceremony creates a spiritual bond between parents and godparents, who become a kind of kin. In medieval times, this was used as a way of creating alliances between families. Today, godparents are more commonly chosen from friends and family, and the link serves to strengthen existing bonds.*

BLOOD IS THICKER THAN WATER

■ *In most prescientific cultures, blood has been regarded as a mysterious and powerful substance, and "consanguinity," the notion of "shared blood," has traditionally symbolized the binding and unbreakable strength of family relationships.*

"Blood brotherhood," practiced in ancient Europe and in many other parts of the world, involved drinking each other's blood or mixing blood by pressing freshly cut wounds together. This was done to establish a bond of trust with the intensity and the reliability of a family one.

In the eyes of the medieval Church, marriage made the marriage partners themselves of "one flesh and one blood." Since the wife's sister was of one blood with her, she became a sister of the husband and thus marriage between a widower and his sister-in-law was banned as incest.

In some countries, this ban has been law up until recent times. It is also only in this century that adopted children received equal rights with those who "share blood" with other members of the family by being biologically related. **PR**

Some children establish "executive" independence in early adulthood. However, family tradition, temperament or genuine concern about children's executive abilities moves the parents of others to assert control or at least exert influence.

independence in early adulthood. They simply announce to their parents decisions about careers, marriage partners, where they will live and how they will bring up their children. If the parents are now ready to give up their own role as carers and become merely interested and supportive observers, this will not lead to much conflict. However, family tradition, temperament or genuine concern about their children's executive abilities moves some parents to assert control or at least exert influence over adult offspring.

When children are sensitive to a parent's need to be needed, and do not see it as a threat, they can often share family decision-making in a harmonious and mutually satisfying way. Inviting advice and giving it fair attention is often enough in itself. People who have to fight simply to have their concern heard are more likely to become interventionists than those who are secure in the knowledge that such wisdom as they have is not being ignored.

Parents who want to be taken seriously and to have a positive influence need to avoid threatening the self-esteem of a generation which equally wants to be taken seriously. It can especially undermine a child's husband or wife if the prospects for being recognized by in-laws as competent in the husband or wife role appear dim. Of particular importance is to avoid dwelling on the younger generation's faults and past mistakes as a justification for intervening.

Parental offers of tangible help are sometimes resisted as an attempt to buy influence or encourage children to be dependent. However, studies show that help from parents in setting up house is reflected in higher marital satisfaction. Children who receive such help from parents even plan larger families – perhaps because of feeling more economically secure – than those who do not receive help.

The most difficult situations to manage harmoniously when the question of executive status has not been decided are those in which responsibility is shared for a joint task, such as caring for a third generation. Disciplinary style and other aspects of child-rearing are often a point of disagreement between parents and grandparents, one that can lead to conflict especially when a grandmother is put in charge of small children while a mother goes out to work.

Conflicts between brothers and sisters

Brothers and sisters can feel life-long resentments as a result of rivalries that have a psychological root in childhood experiences (see *Ch 18*). Displays of favoritism by

▲ **Three generations of men.** There is no set time when an older generation hands over to a younger one the responsibility for its own affairs. Some transfer of responsibility occurs throughout childhood and adolescence, but many men continue to take a lead from fathers who have reached retirement age.

parents can continue to fuel these rivalries during adult life.

Conflicts can also arise if the burden of supporting the parents is not fairly distributed. Fairness can sometimes be very difficult to achieve. A widowed parent usually prefers to live with a daughter rather than a son, because the daughter is emotionally closer than the daughter-in-law who would probably be the person in the son's household they would most burden by moving in. In any event, it is impractical to rotate aged parents from one household to another, and so one household is likely to provide most of the accommodation and care. When aging parents live on their own, the children who live closest or have the least demanding careers or family lives have to take more responsibility. An unmarried, widowed or divorced daughter without children may be expected by others to move in and provide constant care, suffering considerable social isolation as a result.

A very typical cause of family strife is disagreement about dividing an inheritance. In a study conducted in London, disputes over wills arose in about one-fifth of middle-class families. Especially,in farming families, or families owning business, turning an inheritance into cash and dividing it equally may mean breaking up an asset that an eldest son has labored most of his adult life to enhance, and on which he depends for his livelihood. Even where a cash settlement is feasible, some of the children may feel that the proportions should reflect the unequal care and attention they have given to their parents, and this can be difficult to determine fairly. Parents can help to prevent conflicts by finding as fair a solution as they can and announcing it early, rather than leaving it as a surprise for their heirs to adjust to during a period of family crisis.

Distance in family relationships

Strains arise between adult family members when their status and lifestyles do not provide a continuity of family identity. An American study of brothers and sisters whose social mobility differed found that 59 percent of brothers and 23 percent of sisters felt less close to their same-sex

▲ **Distant in years**, *but close in spirit. Mothers tend to be closer to their children than fathers, and so do grandmothers tend to be closer to grandchildren. It is they who are more likely to help the mother with child care. Because of the close bond between mother and daughter, a child will probably know its maternal grandmother especially well.*

162

Children learn traditions from grandparents that their parents might never have been told. This contributes to their sense of family identity - all the more strongly for giving a more direct and independent glimpse of the family's past.

sibling as a consequence. Fathers are often proud of a son who climbs the social ladder through career success, but contact tends to be reduced. In a London study, 70 percent of children who remained in the same social class as their parents had seen them in the previous week, but only 60 percent of those who were upwardly mobile had done so, with mother-daughter contact least affected by this difference. Only 40 percent of downwardly mobile children had seen their parents in the previous week.

Most upwardly mobile women are married to upwardly mobile men or men who started with a higher social status than their wives' families. The women adopt the traditional role of wife and mother and, although more affluent, they continue to have much in common with their mothers and sisters. Men who are socially mobile, however, find less to share in life with their fathers and brothers.

In some families, standards of success are not shared by the generations. A young man may achieve success in business but still find that his parents are disappointed in him, because he has not been accepted into a profession such as medicine or law. Parents may be unable to understand or identify with creative or academic work that brings their child recognition only from an initiated circle. A young woman who has done well in a career may find that parents and other family members regard her as unwomanly. **AC GGB**

GRANDPARENTS AND GRANDCHILDREN

■ *Grandparents often have time and freedom that parents do not have to give relaxed attention to children. A grandchild can be a comfort in turn, ready to appreciate a grandparent's wisdom and playfulness.*

Children hear stories from grandparents and learn family traditions that their own parents might never have been told, because there was no time. This helps children to establish a sense of family identity that is all the stronger for its representing a more direct and independent access to the past than provided by parents.

Disagreement between grandparents and parents about how to care for the children may lead to conflicts that are distressing for everyone concerned. About a third of grandparents find their role at least difficult because of such disagreement. However, in families where both partners work or there is only one parent, grandparents brought in as extra parents are usually both comforting and supportive.

Only about one-quarter of grandparents feel distant from their grandchildren, but almost all derive more of their total satisfaction not only from their relationships with their grown children but also from friends outside the family.

When children are still young

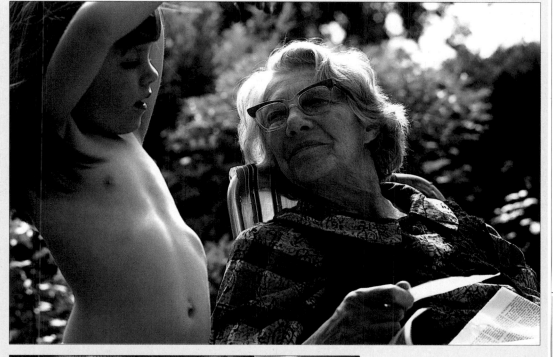

■ **A granddaughter** *can provide stimulation and emotional support.*

enough to be at home, their grandparents' home is often the main site for family gatherings. It is here that they have much of their contact with cousins, aunts and uncles.

Living under our own roofs, however, we visit grandparents less often than our parents, brothers and sisters and may see more of our grandparents at our parents' home than in their own. **AC GGB**

163

Friends and Acquaintances

FOR MOST of us, family relationships and the relationship with an intimate partner account for a major portion of our happiness, but even they can leave many of our emotional and social needs unfullfilled. This is particularly true when families are scattered by pursuing jobs and careers in different regions, and when intimate relationships break down and leave us on our own.

Self-esteem, even for members of close-knit, tightly concentrated families, benefits from the knowledge that there are others who value you not as a matter of family commitment, but voluntarily, as their friend. Families are not capable of giving the support we need in every situation – for example, at work – and they do not necessarily include the people with whom we share our most stimulating and rewarding interests.

We also need to make the acquaintance of people beyond the family in order to meet prospective romantic partners and prospective marriage partners. Even once established in a mutually supportive relationship with a partner, our best interests are served by maintaining a social network that enhances that support – and is there to help in case of bereavement or a break-up.

Yet, making the acquaintance of other people and forming friendships are events that are often taken for granted. People tend to assume that having friends and acquaintances, like falling in love, is one of those things in life that just happens – you are lucky if it does and unlucky if it does not. Personal well-being is served, on the contrary, by actively developing social contacts.

These may range from a large pool of acquaintances through progressively more intimate associations, including a personal social network that comprises, in addition to close family, some friends, a few close friends and perhaps one or two best friends.

164

Among familiar faces

If you wrote a list of people you could greet by name, you would probably think of hundreds – perhaps as many as 1,000 or so. Most of these acquaintances make very little difference to your life and only a small minority are ones you could turn to when you are in trouble.

Nevertheless, on occasion you meet, show each other recognition and take polite or even friendly interest in each other. The stimulation and the boost to self-esteem that encounters of this sort provide make them less inconsequential than they might seem.

▲ **Becoming acquainted**. *The demands of child care can isolate young mothers from friends who are not as tied down. It is important for them to make new contacts with women who share their new interests.*

◀ **Familiar strangers**. *A young commuter and an older railway employee cross paths daily, exchange greetings and sometimes a joke. The relationship remains casual, but the daily routine is more satisfying because of it.*

Personal well-being is served by social contacts. A wide pool of acquaintances can be beneficial, but our most important social network is a small circle of relatives and friends, including a few close friends and perhaps a best friend.

Even barely noticeable relationships with people you do not know by name contribute to the whole. "Familiar strangers" (see *Ch16*) can have a regular place in our lives by commuting daily in the same bus or train or by being part of the neighborhood where you live. Some may nod to you and smile. Some may stop a moment and chat. Someone who makes regular deliveries to your department at work or cleans the windows on a particular day of the month might always exchange a few words about the work with you, and perhaps a joke. This is more stimulating and enjoyable than ignoring each other, and you probably get a cleaner window as a reward for giving recognition.

People are strongly motivated to become acquainted when thrown together frequently. Good relationships at work are essential to a happy and productive working environment (see p174). Near neighbors are expected to be friendly in certain ways (even though they do not have to become friends) or else they will not live up to social expectations of what it means to be "good neighbors." In the country, someone may live miles from you, and you did not choose that it should be they who live there, but because they are your nearest neighbor you have a reason to call on them and call on them for help.

If you are a city-dweller, the "stimulus overload" of being too often in crowded places with too many other people may make you content not to have any contact at all with the person on the other side of the wall between your two apartments or the fence between your homes. The incentive to become involved will be even lower if the apartment block is badly designed for relationships, with doors opening into long impersonal corridors. People are more likely to get to know one another when doors open into small common areas that create a sense of community for ten or fewer households.

Being on good terms with close neighbors can make an important difference to how well you enjoy the privileges of

◄ **Neighborly conversation** *flourishes in the street and over garden fences. It is usually close friends and kin that we invite indoors, but we tend to see the fact that someone lives near us as a reason for being attentive and cordial.*

A COMMON PATTERN OF FRIENDSHIP AND ACQUAINTANCE

Individual

Closest friends 1–5 (including spouse)

Other good friends 5–15

Social network 15–30 (including other family)

Named acquaintances 100–1000

Familiar strangers 5–10

▲ **At the center of a unique social system**, *we each gather to us in a social network our friends and close kin. Beyond lies a large pool of acquaintances, some of them people we could not name – virtual strangers but potentially friends.*

165

occupying your own piece of territory. Neighbors can be a useful source of help – keeping an eye on your property, for example, when you are away. Also, we do not like to be looked down on or disliked by those we see frequently. The stress of this is something to avoid, and so we want to make a good impression on neighbors and learn enough about them to avoid unnecessary conflicts.

In one study, asking residents of an apartment complex to say who they liked and disliked, researchers found that the great majority of *both* were people who lived very close by. For reasons such as these, meeting new neighbors is one of the situations that people most commonly report as provoking anxiety or making them feel shy. Normally, a very simple show of interest and willingness to help in small ways is all that is needed to make the right impression. It does not usually answer to anyone's need in a neighbor that you should be remarkably interesting, clever or attractive.

In large measure, the question of *who* our acquaintances will be is decided by circumstance. Children make their first contact with other children who are brought to the house by friends of the family, then with schoolmates, or fellow members of clubs organized for children (see *Ch 22*). In adult life we happen to be introduced to others by relatives, and by already established friends and acquaintances. We have little choice over who our neighbors or workmates will be. Students may have little choice over who will share

rooms in dormatories or whose doors will open opposite each other, but studies have confirmed that such physical proximity significantly promotes the formation of friendships between them.

However, not all contact is haphazard. We *ask* to be introduced to people we would like to know. Sometimes the main reason a person has for going out to work, or for choosing a certain kind of work, is the opportunity to meet people. Meeting people is often a motive for joining a leisure activity group, enrolling in adult education courses or going to church. And when we become *better* acquainted with someone we know, this is very often by choice.

Initial attraction

People are likely to become acquainted more easily if they are attracted to each other, and initial attraction depends very much on the first impression that physical appearances create. People who look attractive to us as acquaintances, however, are not necessarily the ones who seem most attractive in themselves.

We are *impressed* by the best dressed and most physically attractive people. We tend to attribute desirable qualities to them – they are seen as better, more interesting, independent, poised, exciting, sexual and successful. In experiments where students are asked to rate essays supposedly written by others whose photographs are

▲ **Opportunities are seized** by some – but not by others – to make new acquaintances as a meeting breaks for coffee and sandwiches. What you say does not have to be remarkably interesting or even on topic. Some of the conversation in this scene is probably about the lecture that has just been given. Some of it is probably about places that both people happen to have visited on holiday.

Similarity is the key to attraction. We become interested in people whose appearance makes it seem that they will support our self-esteem – people who will confirm our world view and tell us that we have worth as individuals.

attached, they give extra marks when the "author" is more attractive. Attractive children are seen by both teachers and other children as better behaved. Even friends of attractive people are seen by others in a more positive light than the friends of the less attractive.

We seem to like attractive people not just because they look good, but because of what we think it tells us about their personalities. This makes us respond so favorably to them that studies have shown them to achieve more social, educational and economic success. (See also *Ch 6*.)

When it comes to wanting to make someone's acquaintance, however, we tend to be drawn to people who are about as attractive as we are, who dress something like we do, who look like they are about our age, education, class and race and have about our abilities and values. Similarity, in other words, is the key. We do not look for relationships with people whose brilliance will make us seem dull.

We become interested, rather, in people whose appearance makes it seem likely that they will support our self-esteem – people who will confirm our view of the world and tell us we have worth as individuals. In addition, we are drawn to those who seem like us because they are more likely than others to share interests that we enjoy talking about.

In some situations, mutual help, another main benefit of relationships, can also be part of the initial attraction that leads to acquaintance, as when we try to make useful

167

◄ **Similarity of experience** *draws us together. Gondoliers at a historical regatta in Venice, Italy,* TOP *share an identity and share a lunch that helps them to express a sense of belonging with each other.* BELOW *Similar age, dress and social status and a shared religious experience help worshipers feel at one with each other during a prayer meeting in Tulsa, Oklahoma.*

▲ **At life's crises,** *we turn to someone who seems like us for emotional support. Those who have been through the same experience are especially supportive. We prefer their empathy to the sympathy of others who may not really understand.*

First conversations permit new acquaintances to speak about common tastes and interests. This exchange may help to prepare the way for future encounters, but much of the interest shown is not in the form of words.

contacts among neighbors or people who can help us in our careers. It can happen that what leads to first contact is the other's reputation for being interested in something that interests us or for having a useful benefit to trade. **RG**

Making first contact

First contact with a new acquaintance is often an introduction and an exchange of greetings. The words that are spoken may be unremarkable, many of them merely conforming to the ritual formulae for a greeting. But this exchange is in reality very complex because of the nonverbal communication it involves. When you face each other at a close distance like this, feeling the style of each other's handshake, the manner and appearance that you habitually cultivate have their most direct possible impact.

The way you look each other in the eye, the facial expressions with which you respond to what the other says and the length of time that you hold the handshake all

convey a degree of warmth and interest. If there is too little warmth, we signal a reluctance to become involved. If there is too much, we may appear to be demanding too much intimacy too quickly.

If someone else is introducing us, it matters how they do it. They may introduce us by first name, even by nickname, and that may make the whole exchange more relaxed and spontaneous. If they introduce us by surname only and "Mr" "Miss" or "Mrs," a more formal mood will be established from the outset and with it a more formal manner. The remarks the introducer makes about us by way of introduction may immediately open appropriate avenues of conversation – "Roger lives in the corner house with the attic extension you were asking about." (See also *Ch 11*.)

If you are introducing yourself, you will need an opening line. Again this does not have to be remarkable. Mention your name and some point of contact, such as a mutual friend or an interest that you have heard that your new acquaintance shares. If the person is completely unknown to you, comment on the weather or some other uncontroversial topic of universal interest. After a few minutes of chat, you may feel well enough established to mention your name, extent your hand and explain more about who you are. (See also *Ch 12*.)

Following an introduction there will usually be a conversation. This may be only short and polite, but if people are pleased or interested after the first few moments of greeting, the conversation will be longer and more committed, as the participants attempt to discover more about each other and to define the type of relationship they might have.

▲ **Pleasure in bringing others together** *shows in the face of the man on the right as two new acquaintances exchange a warm handshake. When our friends know each other, they give us a more stable social network.*

▶ **Introducing yourself** *can be easy when a mutually interesting activity gives you lots to talk about. In self-introductions we often talk for some time first about an impersonal topic, then say our names and mention more about ourselves.*

They will ask each other questions and exchange information about themselves that presents them in a favorable light. You should avoid mentioning points that might strike a negative chord.

You should mention what you do in life and any other points that give your partner opportunities to question you in ways that will reveal what is interesting about you. To be successful in this kind of conversation, however, you must reciprocate – you must ask questions that will allow others to reveal the selves they want to show.

The conversations that occur at this stage sometimes appear meaningless because of the triviality of the information that is exchanged. However, they give new acquaintances an opportunity to reveal common interests that may be the subject of future encounters and to show interest in each other and so open the way to further contact. Much of this interest is shown nonverbally.

People who have a lot of acquaintances and benefit from good relations with them are "friendly" – they are rewarding to be with – even when the relationship has little of the intimacy and commitment of friendship. They are likeable and warm, because they display "immediacy cues" (see *Ch 4*) – they do not stand or sit too far away. They adopt an "open posture," including leaning forward and directly facing you with arms and legs not crossed. If cultural rules permit, they touch you occasionally in a friendly but not too intimate way (see *Ch 10*).

Their faces show interest through frequent eye contact, smiles and other reactions to what you say. Giving information about themselves is balanced by asking questions and being a good listener. They create openings by initiating topics of conversation that reveal interests and so make future encounters more likely. **BMM PT**

From acquaintance to friendship

Good neighbors who do not become friends ask each other for help in small matters and they visit with each other – but in the street or over the fence rather than indoors, and in the winter in the cold countries they may consequently see less of each other. For more stimulation and support than this, we turn to friends and family. When family are not available or do not meet all your needs, how do we become close enough to someone to call them a friend? And what makes some of our friends not just friends but close friends?

Following initial contact, further encounters may confirm an attractive first impression. Then attraction may grow. Progressive stages of increasing openness can peel off layers of our outer selves like the skins of an onion. Communication becomes more intense when this happens, with a sharing of private thought and opinions.

A crucially important advantage of knowing that someone thinks well of you is that you can more easily reveal to them

169

▲ **Warmth and likableness** rely on "immediacy cues" – a smiling expression, eye contact, an open posture and sitting or standing near enough to others, or leaning close enough to them, to make them feel liked.

◄ **Sharing a joke about work** eases workplace tensions and makes people feel closer. We rely on good relationships with workmates for help with the practicalities of our jobs. Workmates also give us moral support.

self-doubts, weaknesses and emotional needs. To do very much of this, however, you need to feel a sense of trust as well as a sense of being approved of – you need to feel that support and approval will not dissolve when the burdens of being close to you are revealed. Trust such as this develops as people move closer by stages, each reciprocating the increasingly intimate emotional support that the other gives.

As we become close, we begin to refer to each other as friends as a way of declaring to each other and to other people that there is a commitment.

Progress need not always be smooth. Attraction can have different degrees of strength. The person you like might not permit anything more than friendly acquaintance. Or both of you may move back and forth between different levels of friendship as you learn more about each other and change your expectations. Most of these adjustments will be signaled nonverbally by the way you greet each other and part and by the way that you regulate the level of intimacy when you are together (see *Chs 4, 11*).

Exchanging rewards

The level of intimacy and commitment that we arrive at reflects the rewards that we offer to each other. These in the end are the basis of attraction. The differences in how close we are to various friends and acquaintances arise from the different kinds of emotional support, stimulation and help that we exchange with them.

We have different needs when coexisting with neighbors or workmates or when playing a favorite sport with casual friends, and what we do for each other reflects these needs.

Having these less intense relationships is a way of adapting to particular situations. Our close friendships, however, will more strongly answer to the needs that characterize *us* rather than any particular situation. Close friends make each other feel right about the way they approach life in general and reassure each other about doubts and concerns that they would keep private from other people. Variety in our relationships also arises because different friends support different aspects of our personalities – one makes us feel right about ourselves, another is more fun to be with.

Rewards exchanged in a relationship rarely match one for one. You may be better at bolstering your friend's self-esteem, your friend may be better at making life fun. Your friend may have some unattractive qualities or you may disagree on important issues. But a balance is achieved and a bond is created. Since friendships are not exclusive in the way that romantic partnerships are, people find it easy to fill in what they miss in one friendship by making friends with someone else who answers to the need. But, out of friendship, people usually try to understand the needs of their close friends and help them to meet them.

Forming a friendship or maintaining it can matter enough that you are prepared to change in order to be a more rewarding friend. For example, we make ourselves more open to the opinions of friends and become interested in new topics when they offer opportunities to share an attitude. This is often a two-way process of gradually growing more alike.

The explanation of friendship as an exchange of rewards is called "exchange theory." It represents the development

■ **Making each other feel right** is the chief reward of friendship, and this means agreeing on at least some important issues. LEFT During an overlap in their conversation, two friends give voice in unison to a shared impression. RIGHT Straightening out a disagreement between friends is a priority for others who value the relationship that has fallen under such a strain.

Rewards exchanged in a relationship rarely match one for one. While pleasing you in several ways, a friend may still have unattractive qualities, or you may disagree on important issues, but a balance is achieved and a bond created.

of friendship on the model of people trading with each other in a marketplace. In return for the desirable qualities we discover in another person, we offer our own rewards, seeking a "fair trade" (see *Ch 31*). It is important, however, to make a realistic assessment of how rewarding we are and to avoid trying unsuccessfully to attract someone whose reward level is too different from ours. **RG**

Advantageous limitations

In practice, most casual relationships remain just that. By unspoken agreement, they are restricted to particular times and settings. A study of friendships among horserace betting enthusiasts in Las Vegas, Nevada, for example, showed that even long-term friends who met frequently at the track and freely discussed their feelings and anxieties about winning and losing almost never discussed marital, family or work problems.

Several psychologists have suggested that the limited nature of many friendships is, in fact, one of their most

attractive features. There is none of the uncertainty and vulnerability that intimacy gives rise to. Both parties accept the relationship for what it is and expect no more. They help and support each other in the activities that are characteristic of the setting, and their shared experiences foster a sense of belonging to the setting – finding a sense of identity within it. Casual friendships are often very long-lasting. People may keep up a relaxed, mutually satisfying relationship for years, one that outlives numerous love affairs and even marriages.

Many of the contexts in which casual friendships arise – sports, hobbies, voluntary and professional associations, work settings – necessarily involve teams, committees, and other groups. Group loyalties emerge and within each group or clique, which may number from three or four to ten people, there are usually pairs of particular friends. It is rare for two friends to belong to different cliques.

Studies have shown that group membership brings with it a tendency to exaggerate the merits of the clique and correspondingly to devalue other cliques, even where there is little or no direct competition. Rivalry with nonmembers is seldom particularly intense and is usually good-humored, but nevertheless increases the feeling of belonging. Gossip is a main activity – about absent members of the clique, and, with greater enthusiasm and more malevolence, members of other cliques.

In workplaces, especially, the development of friendships and cliques is inevitable. Although friendly relations will often exist between superior and subordinate, most genuine friendships at work develop between people who have the same or almost the same status.

For those in lower positions, in particular, work friendships can bring a sense of solidarity and give access

171

■ **Shared fun and shared confidences** *are rewards we may find in a single friendship. Often, however, a friend who meets our needs in one way is not ideal in another. Even our most intimate relationship needs to be supplemented by further social contact.*

to information which helps to offset the lack of power that subordinates have within the formal structure. In most cases the organization benefits from the friendship networks within it – cohesive friendships make for high morale and enable efforts to be mobilized to help solve the organization's problems. In a badly managed system, however, the more cohesive the informal network the more effectively can the demands of superiors be resisted and their plans sabotaged.

Some work situations produce intense and binding male friendships, but most men are more distant from other men than women are from other women. Women's friendships are more "person-oriented." They tend to be warmer and more satisfying.

Work situations *can* produce extremely intense and binding friendships. This is particularly the case when the job is highly demanding, stressful or dangerous, where colleagues have to rely on each other's expertise and emotional support. Examples may be found in a wide range of occupations, from medicine to firefighting, and from professional team sports to police work. Warfare, probably the most stressful of all occupations, often produces such bonds of comradeship and mutual obligation within fighting units that the soldier's main motive for keeping going is his desire not to let his comrades down. Ties of this kind may acquire a greater psychological significance for the people concerned than they feel for their marriages or families.

Men's friendships, women's friendships

A common conception of men's friendships is that they are *characteristically* marked by these strong bonds of comradely loyalty and deep mutual understanding, whereas women's friendships are by comparison rather shallow affairs, prone to bickering and jealousy. The facts are quite different. Men's friendships more commonly tend to be "thing-" or "activity-oriented" – built around doing things together. Friendships between women, by contrast, involve more affectionate behavior and more disclosure of confidences – they are more "person-oriented". Women experience their friendships as warmer, more satisfying and more important than men do. Some writers have been moved to extreme pessimism about men's friendships, seeing them as relatively barren, aloof and unsatisfying. Several explanations have been offered for these differences. The two which

■ **Intense comradeship** *appears in situations where people have to rely on each other under extreme stress. Peacetime occupations such as policework and firefighting can have this effect, and it is especially common in combat troops.* TOP *American soldiers in Vietnam and,* BOTTOM *in a more relaxed pose at a training camp in Ethiopia, girl fighters for the Eritrean People's Liberation Front.*

have attracted most support are both based on the patterns of upbringing experienced by most males and females from infancy.

The first involves competitiveness. Men, it is claimed, are less able to form close friendships with other men because males are brought up to see each other as rivals or potential rivals in the contests of life. Since confiding in a competitor is not very advisable, men have little inclination to manage a close, trusting relationship (and so do not develop the skills). Women are much less likely to be involved in obsessive competitiveness and find it relatively easy to be open with another woman.

The second explanation is based on the notion of homophobia, or a fear and dislike of homosexual feelings and relationships. In most industrialized societies, at least, boys are brought up with a high level of anxiety about effeminacy and homosexual activity. Girls are not burdened with anything like the same pressure against masculine behavior or lesbian relationships. It is suggested that this powerful conditioning follows boys into adulthood, where expressions of tenderness or affection between males are accordingly avoided. Women friends in general feel much less inhibited in their expression of positive feelings, whether verbally. or in physical touching and cuddling.

Conclusive evidence is lacking for both explanations, although it is likely that each is of some importance. Recent studies suggest that, while the pattern of male unexpressiveness is still found, the distinction between men's and women's friendships is less clear-cut than was previously thought. It is possible that this is due to changes in society's definitions of maleness and femaleness, although whether this means that males are adopting a more traditionally female approach to friendship, or vice versa, continues to be unclear. **BM**

▲ **People and activities** interest both men and women. Women, however, tend to share much more in their friends' personal lives. Men are more likely to confine their relationship to shared activity.

▶ **Women rugby players and affectionate soldiers** contradict the stereotypes of female friendships and male friendships. In eastern Europe and the Muslim world, men more commonly express a personal attachment to each other that would not often be seen in American and western European men.

GOOD WORKING RELATIONSHIPS

■ Good working relationships improve both the health and happiness of people at work and the health of the organization they work for. Poor relationships put us under pressure and give rise to stress. Relationships with supervisor, subordinate or colleague each present different challenges, and men and women face particular problems about meeting each other in these roles. In all cases, good communication is at the heart of successful coping strategies.

BEING SUBORDINATE

In organizations where the supervisor is perceived by workers as considerate, there is likely to be friendship, mutual trust, respect and a certain amount of warmth between superior and subordinate. In those where the supervisor shows very little consideration, the workers are under more pressure. They report that the supervisor does not give constructive criticism, has "favorites," pulls rank and takes advantage of them whenever the opportunity arises.

Some of the stress women experience in dealing with male supervisors is caused by the common assumption that women are generally less well-qualified than men, and by women's own belief that in order to gain support from their (usually male) superiors, they must prove that they are more competent than male counterparts. However, a majority of women have reasonably good relationships with male employers. It is those who have female employers who are not as content.

It has been suggested that this occurs because today's female employers come predominantly from that group of women who were among the first to unshackle themselves of their "fear of power" and other inhibiting female traits and attitudes. In doing so, they felt that

they had to adopt male patterns of behavior at work. However beneath their acceptance of dominant roles lay an insecurity and a lack of confidence and assertiveness. The disparity between their outward behavior and their hidden feelings produced a first generation of senior women executives – rather frightening figures – whose outward behavior was determined, aggressive and, to the women who worked for them, terrifying.

Men increasingly find themselves with women bosses, who may have different managerial styles and expectations than their male counterparts. When these are not understood, male subordinates will feel the strain of adapting to them.

STRAINS OF SUPERVISING

Managers and supervisors have poor relationships with their subordinates sometimes because of the way their own role is defined by superiors. One of the central functions, as traditionally defined, of any manager or supervisor is to watch over other people's work. So it is that, in the past, problems with subordinates have been attributed mainly to a manager's inability to delegate responsibility. Today, however, managers are increasingly being urged to improve their interpersonal skills, and to manage by participating with their subordinates to get the job done efficiently.

Studies in Britain have shown that the current emphasis on participation may for several reasons cause managers to become resentful, anxious and stressed. Their actual powers are not as great as they are officially said to be.

Managers may resent the erosion of their sense of superior status. They may be under irreconcilable pressures – for example, to have the time to hear every subordinate's point of view and also the time

to achieve higher rates of productivity. In any case, their subordinates may refuse to participate.

Dealings with subordinates can be a greater source of stress for managers with technical and scientific training – those who are "thing-oriented" – than for managers who are more "people-oriented." People with backgrounds in technology are more likely to think that relationships at work have a low priority. They may see them as trivial, petty and time-consuming and therefore as an impediment to doing their job well. It can also come as an extra challenge for men to find the managerial sensitivity they need to have for the unique stresses that women subordinates experience in the work environment and outside.

Female supervisors worry more about their subordinates' expectations of them than they do about the expectations of their own superiors. Because female supervisors are inclined to act as counselors and confidantes to their subordinates, they often suffer conflicts of

▲▶ **Relations between equals** are less relaxed at managerial levels. For fear of appearing weak, managerial staff are less likely to share problems or seek emotional support.

▼ **Relations between superiors and subordinates.** Female supervisors, inclined to act as counselors and confidantes to subordinates, often feel a conflict of interest between loyalty to those above and those below.

People who mistrust their colleagues are likely to be unsure of their role in the organization. It can be extremely useful to ask a superior to make your responsibilities clearer to you and to everyone who works with you.

interest between loyalty to their superiors and loyalty to their subordinates.

COLLEAGUE RELATIONSHIPS

Relationships between colleagues are frequently influenced by rivalry. Another source of stress thus comes from a lack of mutual support in difficult situations. At highly competitive managerial levels, for example, it is likely that problem-sharing will be inhibited for fear of appearing weak or incompetent, and many studies highlight the isolated life of the top executive.

There is evidence that women managers in male-dominated organizations often have considerable difficulty in achieving social integration with their male peers. They therefore lack the cooperation of male colleagues in joint decision-making and teamwork. Many women feel that their male colleagues of similar or equal status are combative, appear to feel threatened by them and are generally a source of stress. Increasingly, men find themselves competing with women for jobs, promotions and transfers. This causes difficulty for many, because often they lack the particular male-female social skills that cordial competition between members of the opposite sex requires.

The rise of the career woman in many of the traditional male-dominated occupations such as management has meant that couples are experiencing more dual-career family stress. Both husband and wife face high demands of child care, in addition to the demands of their jobs. They face limitations on their careers during periods of major career activity by their partners and more limits to their potential geographic and promotional mobility. **CLC**

175

IMPROVING WORKPLACE RELATIONSHIPS

■ People who wish to improve their workplace relationships should first identify which relationships cause the most stress – that with the employer, those with colleagues or those with subordinates. Consider what courses of action are possible to change these relationships, and assess each one according to its costs and benefits, both personally and in career terms. Discuss the possibilities with a friendly colleague to have a more objective and independent opinion.

Being more supportive may well be worth the risk of seeming soft to subordinates or competitors for promotion. The sense of threat from a talented and energetic subordinate can often be transformed by handing over more responsibility and fostering the subordinate's career in a way that reflects positively on your own management skill. Research has found that poor relationships exist when people trying to work together feel a lack of trust and support. Each may feel that the other is not interested in listening to and trying to deal with the problems of others.

What are the risks of being more assertive in your relationships? How can you learn to do this (see Ch15), and in what degree would it allow you to make a more productive and more satisfying contribution?

It can be an extremely useful piece of self-assertion to ask a superior to make your role clearer to you, and to define it more sharply for everyone who works with you. People who mistrust their colleagues are likely to be unsure of their role in the organization – 48 percent of industrial employees were reported in one American study as not being sure of their responsibilities, usually through lacking proper communication with superiors. They gain less satisfaction from their jobs than people who feel that they understand what they are supposed to do, and they are more likely to feel that their well-being is threatened because of work difficulties. **CLC**

Child and Adolescent Friendships

A TODDLER has barely any concept of friendship, nor any ability to make friends and keep them. By about the age of 14, however, children who are socially well-developed become loyal, stimulating and understanding companions. By 18 friends may mean more than family. The stages by which we reach this level of social accomplishment are as much a part of child development as growing physically, or learning language and intellectual skills.

A developing grasp of friendship

As with other skills, learning to make friends depends on intellectual development and growth as a person. Friendship demands a sense of self-worth, an ability to comprehend the idea of cooperation, an awareness of the needs and rights of others and an understanding of the nature of trust. It also demands an ability to reciprocate favors and guard a friend's best interests.

The age at which a child advances from one stage to the next in developing these qualities will vary – some children grasp certain concepts quickly; others take longer to understand them and put them into practice. To some extent development also varies between the sexes. Girls tend to be more socially developed earlier, participating more readily in activities that children regard as more appropriate for girls, such as talking and being helpful.

Toddlers around the age of two play *in the presence of* rather than *with* other children. Later, around the age of three and over, they recognize and name as friends or even best friends children who live nearby or those who are brought by their parents to play with them. This type of friendship is very unstable and changes from moment to moment according to circumstances. A friend is a momentary playmate who is like an extension of the self, valued for what they have – toys, candy or similar material possessions

that might be enjoyed. Small children's descriptions of friends tend to be exhausted once they have said what is striking about their circumstances: so-and-so "lives in a nice house" and "has a big dog."

Around the age of four, the idea that "a friend has things I want" begins to be the idea that "a friend has personal resources or abilities that can be useful." Up to about seven the child looks for assistance from others who are friends, but does not immediately develop the parallel idea of helping the friend in return. A friend's toughness or skills may be admired but little assessment is made of character. When the child does begin to understand the concept of helping others, the help is often undependable, given only when convenient. At this age children are relatively unaware of rights or ideas of cooperation.

Between the ages of 6 and 12 there is more knowledge about give-and-take and cooperation, and an appreciation that friends do things for one another. Children have some idea that being a friend creates obligations such as loyalty – "You are my friend so you shouldn't talk about me behind my back." Yet it will be some time before the child understands that cooperation is mutually beneficial and not a selfish way of getting someone else to help you.

Around the age of nine the child can begin to see things from their friend's point of view and to undertake joint ventures for the benefit of both. Friends share secrets, are open and genuine with one another, show loyalty and self-sacrifice. They begin to understand that intimacy and mutual understanding are part of the role of a friend. However, children between 9 and 12 remain exclusive and possessive of their best friends and do not readily accept that best friends can also have other very good friends. They value loyalty and commitment only to themselves.

From about 12, children know that friends have indepen-

▶ **Babies and toddlers** *play in each other's presence, but do not develop friendships. They do not choose each other's company but are brought together by adults, and when together are attracted more by play objects than by each other.*

▶ **Boys' friendships** *are more activity- and thing-oriented than girls'. Riding bicycles (even your sister's) and climbing trees in a gang provide an outlet for energies that in part reflect the effects on metabolism of male sex hormones. Girls are more likely to play indoors, coming together only a few at a time. In conversation, girls compare experiences and their likes and dislikes, while boys compare how many blades their pocket knives have and how sharp they are. These differences also reflect socially conditioned expectations of how boys and girls will behave.*

Childhood friends give each other stimulation and enjoyment and they boost each other's self-esteem. What is most important is that together they practice the skills they will need later to build social lives outside the family nest.

dent needs and other friends that are equally special, and also appreciate that this does not detract from their friendship. There are the beginnings of adult-like friendships and an understanding of the friend's character.

Friends are now liked because of their capacity to be intimates, because they share common interests and have attractive personal qualities.

Among the disadvantages that families have to count when considering a move to a new neighborhood or town is the disruption this will cause to their children's relationships outside the home. How serious this disadvantage is depends on age and ability to make new friends quickly. Before the age of seven, children usually do not have any sense of enduring relationships and often form new ones as easily as they give up established ones. From about the age of eight, however, they are more likely to find it difficult to leave close friends, since at this stage they understand that friendships normally last for some time, and that some friends are special and irreplaceable. Popular children with a wide range of friends appear to have less invested in each particular friendship and therefore find it easier to cope with moving. Those who are most at risk are the children who are rather shy and who have one special friend with whom they play almost exclusively.

Popular and unpopular children

Some children learn better social skills and a better concept of friendship than others, mainly by observing successful interactions between the adults and older

177

■ **Children of the same age**
tend to be the partners in most children's friendships. They are brought together at the same age in schools and, given the choice, they prefer playmates who have about the same level of fluency in speech. However, boys' play is more likely to be out of doors and to involve competitive games, and for this reason boys have more acquaintances of different ages than girls do— to make up team numbers, boys' playgroups often have to include a range of ages.

children in their lives and by having good relationships of their own with these elders (see *Ch15*). These children are more likely to try to take the lead and be accepted as leaders when playing with those of their own age. Through their experience of leadership and popularity they learn self-respect and emotional security, rarely developing shyness or low self-esteem. This experience also helps them to develop their concept of friendship even further - they tend to treat other people as individuals at an earlier age and to have a greater number of friends.

Unpopular children fall into two distinct groups: those who are rejected by other children for being aggressive, and those who are neglected by other children because they are withdrawn and uncommunicative. Both types lack the ability to make themselves interesting to other children. They tend to come from families that suffer from greater conflict, disharmony and irritation among their members. The parents often follow authoritarian child-rearing practices. They are more likely to be socially isolated themselves than the parents of popular children and to provide their children with poor models of social skill.

Children who are rejected may try too hard to get attention by attempting to control other children. The most crucial skill they lack is being able to assert themselves without being aggressive.

Children neglect those who are unable to start interactions and who do not respond at all to initiatives from others or respond in an unrewarding way – not appearing to be interested. Socially neglected children spend a great deal of time on their own, look more than act and do not ask questions or ask for help. They daydream, stare into space and often hover outside a group, unable to gain admittance.

The parents of neglected or aggressive children may keep them away from other children in misguided protectiveness. Well-meaning parents and teachers often exacerbate the problems of shy children by being pleasant and comforting when the child is withdrawing from the peer group – rather than giving praise when the child interacts appropriately.

Deprived of the opportunity to learn better social skills and better concepts of friendship from their elders, unpopular children usually fail to learn them from peers as well, and they fail to develop emotional security. As a result many of them will suffer serious psychological problems later in life, become juvenile delinquents or run an increased risk of dependence on alcohol or other drugs. Their loneliness often lasts into adulthood. People who were unpopular as children are overrepresented in groups such as the divorced, the unemployed and even those who are dishonorably discharged from the armed forces.

Attempts to train unpopular children to become more popular are recent, but programs exist, mainly in the United States. The goal of many is to make neglected children more competent at attracting attention and holding it by asking questions, listening in a warm and friendly way and saying things about themselves that relate to the other child's interests. They are also taught to enter groups more assertively. Aggressive children are taught to listen to other children and to "hear what they say" instead of trying to

178

► **Children neglect other children** *who do not know how to join in, and a complicating factor can be race. Studies in England and Hawaii have found children preferring playmates of their own race, although this was a less important factor than sex. Among children and adolescents in these studies mixed-race groups of girls or of boys were more common than mixed-sex groups.*

To make friends, children need to join in games without trying to dominate them. They need to draw attention to themselves without trying to control other children. These skills come most easily to those with skilled models to imitate.

dominate conversations. They are encouraged to join in other children's play constructively, without trying to change the game that the group is playing.

Children may need to be persuaded that these strategies work well and are satisfying. In some programs the children are shown videotapes of other children behaving and interacting in appropriate ways; the children who watch the tapes are then asked to comment on what they have seen and draw lessons from it. In other training programs, popular children are taught to be more accepting of the rejected or neglected child.

When a child of your own has difficulty making friends the most useful help may well be to find some special times to spend together. Social interactions with a patient and interested adult can teach a child the conversational and relationships skills that are needed for peer-group success. Eventually, children should practice social skills with children, but by itself, simply arranging meetings with others of the same age may force the child into situations they cannot yet handle. Existing patterns of shyness or aggression may be reinforced. **SD**

Steps to maturity

In adolescence, children experience more loneliness, on average, than at any other time in their lives (see *Ch24*), and yet they have more friends, on average, than any other group except unmarried young adults. This paradox is accounted for by the intense adolescent *need* for friends. As physical development creates new sexual and aggressive urges, children have a growing need to share and explore feelings that they believe parents will suppress. They also need to talk about and develop new ideas and potential new identities that they encounter outside the home and fear their parents will not understand.

Children who are good at making friends do so energetically in adolescence. Those who do not have many friends, or who find themselves temporarily separated from them, are more likely than adults to experience this absence as loneliness.

By stages, adolescents develop styles of friendship that allow them to practice relationships that are more and more adult. The ages at which the different stages occur vary between individuals and also between generations. In the 1950s, for example, the change from having a same-sex to an opposite-sex confidant occurred at a later age than it does now – traditional barriers preventing close friendships between males and females have since then broken down considerably, partly as a result of more widespread coeducation.

A "pre-adolescent stage" occurs between 11 and 13. Friends are people who share activities, but the main emotional ties are still with the family and most leisure time is still spent with them.

Girls between 14 and 16 have friendships with other girls. They are very emotional and intense. Intimate discussions

◄ **Children reject other children** who are too aggressive. Those who are unable to assert themselves without trying to control other children or always want to change the game to one that they have thought of may find themselves physically pushed away from groups at play.

of the problems associated with puberty result in a high level of disclosure of personal feelings and a strong sense of vulnerability. Because of their intensity, these relationships are sometimes rather unstable, breaking down over fears of disloyalty or too much possessiveness. Most girls' friendships are close and tender by comparison with most boys' friendships.

By 17 or 18, girls have a complex understanding of friendship and are less intense and demanding with their friends. Some of their need for intimacy has been transferred to boyfriends.

Between 14 and 17, boys' friendships are with other boys and, like younger girls, they are based mainly on activities and companionship. Boys mainly seek company in gangs,

which tend to resist authority. Boys are usually older than girls before they begin dating. They often remain part of a male gang for many of their social activities.

In late adolescence and early adulthood friends are more numerous than at any other age, and the friendships formed at this time tend to last longer than those formed earlier or later. Some may survive a lifetime.

Belonging to a group

Group or gang membership helps young adolescents to learn the roles they will take as adults – for example, as leader or carer – and to establish separate identities from those provided by their families. Gangs provide members with the opportunity to talk intimately and receive support

180

STAGES OF ADOLESCENT FRIENDSHIP

▶ **Girls in early adolescence** *form emotional same-sex friendships. By the age of 14 they seek ties outside the home that are at least as intense as those within. The relationships formed with other girls are often not stable, but they make possible a joint exploration of new experiences and new identities.*

▶ **Boys between 14 and 17** *form group-based friendships strongly centered on activity and companionship. Interest in girls grows steadily, and girls begin to enter a boy's social network, but they still do not belong to the group that gives him his sense of identity and that now partially provides the emotional security for which he previously turned almost exclusively to his family.*

In early adolescence, some of a child's emotional dependence on family is transferred to a group of same-sex friends. Reliance on the group in turn ends as we emerge from childhood into adulthood able to form our own independent relationships.

for their developing sense of difference from their families.

Membership of a gang enables adolescents to participate in their generation's subculture. An outward manifestation of this is an obsession with dress, hairstyle and language. Rules are often strictly enforced and dissenting members may be teased, ridiculed or ostracized. Although highly visible, and visibly different from parents', these styles often represent only a superficial break from the values of the family. In one American study 83 percent of teenagers "had a lot of respect for their parents as people," 75 percent "shared their parents' values and ideals," 57 percent "got on well" with their parents and "enjoyed their company," and only 25 percent thought there was a large generation gap.

As members of the gang grow older, they begin to include members of the opposite sex (usually when the leader begins dating). It is then that adolescents begin to practice the rules of heterosexual behavior that they have previously only observed in adults and older adolescents.

The importance of group membership diminishes with age, as adolescents become more confident about their own destinies and about their abilities to make and maintain relationships themselves, and as they begin to feel less constrained by the pressures to conform to the group. By late adolescence, the larger gangs have been replaced by small cliques, consisting of a few couples. **DM**

◀ **A mixing of the sexes** *begins in earnest when girls are about 17 and boys 18. Group membership becomes less important as adolescents become surer of their personal identities and more confident of their abilities to interrelate one-to-one.*

◀ **The transition from adolescence** *to young adulthood is a time of intense interest in relationships. Attraction between the sexes is high as we practice intimacy and consider a choice of life-partners. Same-sex friendships are also intense. Young adults have established an independence from their families but have not begun new ones of their own. They make friendship work hard to fill the emotional gap.*

181

Coping with Shyness

IN SOCIAL interactions, we often have to cope with shyness – if not our own then other people's. Everyone feels at least some shyness on some occasions, and surveys ranging from Japan to Germany to the United States suggest that at least 30 percent of young adults everywhere consider themselves too shy. More than 70 percent say that at some time in their lives shyness has hampered them socially.

Only between 2 and 4 percent of people are shy all the time – in every situation, and regardless of who they are with. For the great majority, shyness is a difficulty in meeting particular kinds of strangers they are anxious to be accepted by. Often the difficulty is specifically that of lacking confidence in interactions with the opposite sex. The most important consequence of shyness is that it impedes the formation of relationships. Shy people have fewer friends, fewer close friends, fewer people they can talk to about private feelings and fewer dating partners. They are less satisfied with their relationships. They belong to looser social networks, in which few of their friends know each other, and they receive less social support (see *Ch16*). Not surprisingly, shy people tend to become lonely.

Shyness and social anxiety

Ask yourself what shyness is and you might think of shy behavior – of someone blushing, for example, when given a turn to speak, and glancing down with an embarrassed smile instead of looking at listeners; or, less dramatically, you might think of the behavior of a somewhat reserved person, reluctant to take the floor in conversation, to speak for long or make eye contact.

However, though embarrassment and reserve are typical of shyness, they do not define it by themselves. Almost anyone can feel embarrassed – for example, if you suddenly ask them a question about an intimate matter or mention an indiscretion they are ashamed of. Similarly, when someone's behavior is reserved, numerous possibilities compete with shyness as an explanation: they might be tired, distracted by personal worries or tragedies, calmly waiting to see how people customarily behave in a setting that is new to them, or for some reason they may think you an unattractive person to be involved with.

What matters is *why* people are embarrassed or reserved. When the reason is that they feel unconfident about how well they will perform socially, it is shyness. Shyness is the tendency to behave in a particular way because of a self-conscious anxiety about an encounter, sometimes vague and unspecified, but often centering on a key apprehension – that events will not go well, for example,

▲ **Shying away from the teacher's gaze** is a hard thing to avoid when you receive a dressing down. We find it difficult to resist the urge to minimize interaction with those we displease or think we displease.

▶ **Shyness is reinforced** by repeated social failures that are partly due to shyness itself. One step toward breaking out of this cycle is to become aware of it.

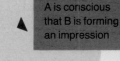

THE SHYNESS CYCLE

A's self-image is of an unattractive or socially unskilled person

A assumes that people like B are favorably impressed only by very attractive or very socially skilled people

A is pessimistic about making a good impression on people like B

A's pessimism is reinforced

A is conscious that B is forming an impression

A believes that B has a poor impression

A behaves shyly or anxiously

A feels anxious

A wants to make a good impression on B

Some shy people may have a genetically inherited tendency to shrink from social encounters. Most shyness, however, is a learned anxiety about particular kinds of situation. Unrealistic self-criticism is a major part of the problem.

because people will think you are unattractive, or not clever enough, or socially inept.

Some psychologists distinguish what they call "public shyness" – social anxiety that shows itself in behavior such as embarrassment or avoidance – from "private shyness" – feeling shy but hiding it by making yourself appear to enjoy social encounters you find difficult. Even very extroverted television personalities have described themselves as shy – reporting to psychological researchers that not only did they have to mask their stagefright in order to enter their profession, but they continue to hide attacks of nerves when

they interview people they hold in awe. But not all social anxiety is shyness. Concern that her guests might not amuse *each other* may give an ambitious hostess a racing heartbeat and set butterflies fluttering in her stomach, but we would not say she was hiding *shyness* when she kept these feelings private. Similarly, people feel socially anxious if an argument breaks out and threatens to spoil an otherwise enjoyable social occasion.

Self-conscious anxiety, of course, does not always show itself in shy behavior when it shows itself. Hands may tremble. People may speak more rapidly and stammer. A tendency to show anxiety in this way can by itself contribute to shy behavior, however, by giving people a reason for not wanting to draw attention to themselves.

▲ **Camera-shy girls** *hide their faces in Morocco. Some of the situations from which we shrink are determined by culturally defined concepts of modesty. Thus many women would feel shy about swimming topless at the beach, and most would feel shy if they were the only one to do so.*

SELF-CONSCIOUSNESS

■ "Self-consciousness" has a bad name because we almost always use this phrase to refer to anxiously counterproductive self-awareness, but on its own, being conscious of yourself is not shyness, and usually it is beneficial.

Settings where people seem likely to scrutinize us will stimulate anyone to think about their appearance or behavior – formal social occasions, for instance, where people are concerned about special rules of dress and conduct. People

meeting you for the first time take note of your name, your appearance, what you have to say and how you express it, and you cannot help observing how they react. Job interviews are held for the very purpose of scrutinizing candidates, who inevitably watch personnel officers for clues about the impression they are making.

You cannot assert yourself in any way – for example, by complaining about the food in a restaurant or by taking the initiative in starting a conversation –

without being aware of the attention you draw from at least one other person. Both men and women feel conscious of what they must look and sound like when dating someone for the first time, and men especially when asking for dates.

Being conscious of ourselves in these special settings allows us to take in people's reactions as reactions to us, and to particular things about us. We receive social feedback that teaches and fine tunes our social skills (see Ch15). **DP PT**

Is shyness inherited?

For some cases, especially those 2 to 4 percent of the population who are shy with everyone, and not just when meeting people they do not know well, the definition of shyness needs a qualification. Sometimes public shyness reflects introversion – the desire simply to limit the amount of stimulation your environment provides. The nervous system of an introvert is more easily excited than an extrovert's and the two types of personality find enjoyment only at different levels of stimulation. For example, introverts prefer quieter colors. Since social encounters are stimulating, introverts seek fewer of them, and enter into them in a more reserved way.

Being introverted also means experiencing higher levels of anxiety in anxious situations. Anxiety may well be one of the symptoms of overstimulation for an extreme introvert, and going away to live alone in a lighthouse may be a way of avoiding it. But introversion not social anxiety is the main key to understanding this display of shyness.

Of course, there are degrees of introversion, and it can be a secondary factor in the behavior of someone who is shy *primarily* because of social anxiety.

Researchers find some tendency for shy parents to have

▲ **In an unfamiliar place,** *waiting for a worrying medical encounter, out-patients whose tests have turned up the possibility of illness wait their turn in the corridor of a Spanish clinic. The impulse to stay close to someone you know and to seek an extra distance from strangers easily comes over us in surroundings that we find menacing.*

▶ **The situations that make people shy** . *Shy people were asked which of 14 typical situations were particular problems for them. The percentage of respondents identifying each is shown at right.*

People can become shy both by underrating themselves and by overestimating the expectations of others. Anxiety may result from thinking that you must be exceptionally clever and attractive or else feel like a social failure.

shy offspring. This may be due to the environment that shy parents create – for example, by giving their children unconfident models of social behavior to imitate – or possibly there is a genetic component of shyness that we can inherit with the rest of our physiological make-up. To assess this possibility, researchers have studied both identical twins (with identical genetic inheritances) and fraternal twins (with nearly the same inheritance) who happen to have been separated at birth and raised in separate families. In these twin studies, there is an even stronger similarity than between parents and offspring in the amount of shyness observed. It is possible that the genetic element is inherited introversion.

Social anxiety can be observed in infants. By about eight months, after they come to recognize familiar people, most babies will begin to be afraid of strangers. This is a normal part of development and most children grow out of it by learning to see unfamiliar events as nonthreatening. However, about 10 percent remain fearful. This "early-onset shyness" is especially suspected of having an inherited element. But psychologists also believe it to be influenced by the infant's sense of attachment to its mother: this may be partly determined by the mother's own behavior, but it is not known how.

Children can be *more* or *less* securely attached to their mothers. Those who are securely attached communicate easily and quickly when in need of comfort. An insecurely attached child will not readily express its needs and may fail to go readily to its mother for comfort; or it may be difficult to comfort, crying first to be picked up then to be put down. There are indications that some children are more difficult

WHAT MAKES YOU SHY?

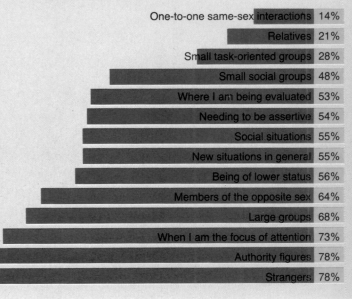

Situation	%
One-to-one same-sex interactions	14%
Relatives	21%
Small task-oriented groups	28%
Small social groups	48%
Where I am being evaluated	53%
Needing to be assertive	54%
Social situations	55%
New situations in general	55%
Being of lower status	56%
Members of the opposite sex	64%
Large groups	68%
When I am the focus of attention	73%
Authority figures	78%
Strangers	78%

to comfort from the moment of birth. Researchers have found that insecurely attached children are more likely to show high levels of fear when confronted with unfamiliar situations than securely attached children.

Learning to be shy

Not all shyness arises in infancy. "Late-onset" shyness, which appears in children who have already successfully overcome an infant's normal fear of strangers, is thought to result more exclusively from social influences. It is focused more precisely on anxiety about specific personal characteristics, such as being unattractive or a having little to say that will impress or interest others. Early-onset shyness tends to persist, while late-onset shyness is more likely to be resolved successfully.

People can become shy about a particular characteristic both by underrating themselves and by overestimating the expectations of others. Thinking that you are physically unattractive, for example, is only part of being shy about your appearance. The other part is thinking that it matters crucially and detracts from your social acceptability. You feel *ashamed* of your appearance and, although it only makes you gloomy when you are alone or with trusted friends, it makes you anxious when you are with people who you think might reject you.

Perfectionistic beliefs – for example, that you have to be extremely skilled socially, that you have to make only scintillating or very informative or witty remarks, if others are not to judge you socially inept – can sometimes cause

extreme shyness, making it hardly possible to speak. The problem is not that you cannot think of anything to say but that you cannot think of anything *good enough* to say. Anxiety results especially when every encounter is viewed as a potential disaster, on the assumption "I must behave perfectly or else I will be a complete failure," or "I must have practically everyone's approval or I will feel worthless."

Sometimes we are conscious of not *knowing how* to behave: we may know that special expectations about conduct, and possibly dress, are associated with a situation we are in – for example, a visit to a private club – but we do not know what these expectations are. Everyone feels at least some of this kind of shyness in new situations, but most overcome it by watching others and carefully experimenting.

People who have difficulty learning social skills, however, are bound to find such situations much more trying, and some view whole classes of encounter as unlearnable: "I will never know how to behave with men" or "I will never know how to behave with women."

Many of the experiences that cause late-onset shyness occur in childhood. Parents and teachers may carelessly describe impressionable children in negative terms, training

185

◄ **Practicing how to be coy.** Imitations of the modesty and timidity that is supposed to be part of the feminine role are a typical element in a feminine role-player's repertoire of gestures. Here a small girl dressed up in her mother's clothes practices the art of shrinking playfully from contact.

▲ **Holding back,** a small boy touches his lip for improved concentration on the question of how he should conduct himself. In so doing he momentarily embodies the self-doubt that characterizes shyness. The girl at the fence has unselfconsciously given all of her attention to what lies beyond. From her posture, it appears that her partly hidden companion is doing the same.

them in low self-esteem. The same sources may too readily reserve praise for only the very attractive or the very skilled.

Differences in parental attitudes towards girls and boys may influence the way in which a child handles a shyness problem. Researchers in England have observed that shyness is often treated by parents as an acceptable trait in girls, but not in boys, and that shy boys tend to have more difficulty in their social encounters than shy girls. The anxiety of parents to push boys out of their shy behavior may be partly responsible for this, by in turn making the

boys more anxious about how they handle situations.

Other children can be particularly influential. In one study, men whose shyness was severe enough to interfere with dating reported childhood backgrounds with common characteristics. They had lacked friends. In school sports, they were left out during team selection. They disliked contact sports such as football. Instead, they preferred golf and volleyball. When bullied, which was often, they never fought back. Rather than coming to associate peer-group interactions with pleasure and happiness, they learned to be

LIMITING THE DAMAGE OF DISAPPOINTMENT

■ *Many of the irrational beliefs that inhibit our contacts with others take hold of us during the stress of disappointments. Out on a date with a particularly desired partner, for example, you seem to make a poor impression, and afterwards tell yourself that the evening was disastrous and that you have no future with the opposite sex. Failing to make a good first impression in a new job on which almost everything in your life seems to depend can lead to pessimism about your ability to work effectively with other people.*

Even when the disappointment is long past, it can continue silently to reinforce negative self-judgments that persist. One group of professional counselors (called "rational-emotive therapists") help people to overcome these effects by helping them to take a more rational approach to self-appraisal.

First, the disappointments in your life are identified, along with the negative beliefs they have precipitated. There is often a widening circle of unhappy thoughts: "I made a poor impression because I said stupid things. I always say stupid things. I am useless. No one will ever think anything of me. It is awful."

The next step is to make the victim see the damaging consequences of these beliefs. The resulting depression, with-

drawal from friends and staying home sick from work are brought into focus, and not as consequences of the event but of the way the event has been understood.

With the benefit of rational appraisal, the beliefs are assessed from the point of view of the victim's own common sense. How sure can you be of the impression you made on someone? Even if you did do badly,

is it really fair to judge your potential from a single piece of behavior?

More helpful beliefs are encouraged: "The only way I am sure to get nowhere with the opposite sex is to shun them. Making one bad impression is not awful – it is just unfortunate." This way of thinking can encourage positive steps such as talking to friends about how to do better next time. **PT**

▲ **Breaking the ice** *is the hardest part of going to a party. Here guests at Magdalen College in the University of Oxford touch themselves anxiously and struggle to make conversation. Social anxiety may be heightened by how much an occasion matters to us and by exaggerated expectations of how difficult it will be to make the right impression.*

186

It is worth remembering how much more there is to successful conversation than cleverness. The most important purpose of speaking is to make us feel at ease about being together. It is not to convey information, amuse or impress.

anxious and apprehensive about other children. As they grew up avoiding social encounters, they missed out on opportunities to learn and practice social skills.

Overcoming shyness

Making yourself more attractive and improving your social skills (see *Ch15*) helps you to think of yourself as the type of person that can succeed in social encounters. The reduced anxiety that comes with this increased self-esteem probably does as much to improve interactions as any objective increase in your ability to meet other people's standards. A team of researchers staged a series of short social interactions between shy university students and a confederate. Through the confederate's behavior, the researchers made sure these encounters were successful and satisfying for the shy students. The students reported overcoming some of their shyness – simply by experiencing these encounters and achieving a more confident impression of their capabilities.

Social skills training techniques applied especially to shy people include "rhetoritherapy," which teaches speech effectiveness. "Interpersonal process training" teaches people how to relax in anxiety-provoking social settings. Trainees are shown and allowed to practice skills for handling specific problem situations, such as making telephone calls, and they practice general communication skills such as listening to others, responding empathetically and talking about themselves in a less inhibited way. An underlying philosophy of interpersonal process training is to help shy people to focus their attention on a positive impression of their partners rather than imagining a negative impression the partners might be forming of *them*.

Another step toward the self-confident use of social skills is to understand that everyone else has also had to *acquire* these same skills at some time in life.

Since so much social anxiety results from unhelpful beliefs, an important strategy is to be less critical of yourself and more critical of what you *think* about yourself and about what you *think* you should feel ashamed of. Ask people you trust to tell you what you are really like, and try to base your image of how attractive you are, for example, on a more objective assessment. If objective comment just confirms what you always thought, then consider the possibilities of self-improvement, but consider too whether your unattractiveness really matters as much as you have always thought. Physical appearance has an important effect on impressions, but it is only one of many factors. Whether you are a likable person in other ways matters more.

If objective assessment of your conversation skills confirms that indeed you are not a notable wit, it is worth remembering how much more there is to successful conversation. Usually it is more important to make a mundane remark – about the weather, for instance – than a clever one, or than none at all. The most important purpose of speaking is to show friendly intentions, not cleverness. Speech in humans has replaced the grooming that can be observed in other higher primates, such as chimpanzees, and many of our common expressions are designed to make us feel at ease about being together rather than convey information, amuse or impress.

One professional procedure that tries to help anxious people learn that they are fallible but acceptable is called "cognitive therapy," from the word "cognition," meaning the processes of knowing. The object is a more realistic self-evaluation, and positive self-image. **DP PT**

◄ **Rolling her eyes** *away from the sea of other eyes upon her helps a schoolgirl get through her performance at the microphone. Feeling yourself at the center of other people's attention is a main element in many of the situations that prompt a shy response.*

THINKING ANXIETY AWAY

■ *A helpful technique for reducing social anxiety involves muscular relaxation. To use it, construct a list of the situations that make you anxious, from easiest to most difficult. Then imagine as vividly as possible the least difficult situation, and allow all of your muscles gradually to relax one by one, starting from the tips of your toes and the tips of your fingers until you reach the muscles of your face and neck. Allow yourself to feel as though you are floating in space. This relaxes away the anxiety that the image brings. You then go on to the* *next situation. By practicing it is possible eventually to reduce the anxiety that the real-life situation habitually brings. Approaching it with lower anxiety can permit you to be more effective, and this experience teaches confidence, further weakening the link between the situation and a counterproductive emotion. The technical term for this technique is "systematic desensitization." It is systematic in taking on all of your problem situations one by one, and it "desensitizes" by making you less emotionally sensitive to them.* **PT**

Overcoming Loneliness

PEOPLE seem to be everywhere. Recently the world's population surpassed five billion. While it used to take centuries for the earth's population to double, now it does so every 35 years. A curious paradox accompanies this population explosion: despite the multitude around us, we seem to feel more cut off from other people than ever before. In the most crowded cities, relationships can be harder to establish than in thinly populated countryside, and, even when established, networks of social support may be fragile.

We have become the "lonely crowd." Surveys reveal just how widespread loneliness has become. For example, when pollsters asked Americans if at any recent time they had felt lonely or remote from others, about 25 percent of respondents said they had.

Missing friendship and missing intimacy

Loneliness is a painful awareness of not having the relationships you need. The kinds of contacts you have can sometimes be an important part of the problem. Some people are "socially lonely," missing a set of friends – a social network. For example, immigrant Italian-speaking housewives in North America and Australia who have fulfilling relationships with their husbands and children sometimes know almost no one else. Unlike other members of the family, they do not go out of the home and do not learn to speak English.

Many other people, however, are "emotionally lonely" – they miss intimate relationships, and simply having more contacts will not necessarily bring them close to people in the way they need. Some people, however, lack both closer relationships *and* a network of friends.

Loneliness may be only short-term – a passing phase following, for example, a bereavement or move away from

friends and home to start university. For some people, however, it is a central, persisting feature of life, maintained by isolating circumstances such as those of the immigrant housewives, or by a lifelong difficulty in forming friendships or intimate attachments. Both social and emotional loneliness are distressing, but of the two, emotional loneliness is thought to be more painful.

Besides distinguishing short-term and long-term and emotional and social loneliness, some psychologists distinguish "negative" and "positive" loneliness. Positive loneliness would correspond to romantic images of isolation. The 19th century English poet William Wordsworth, for

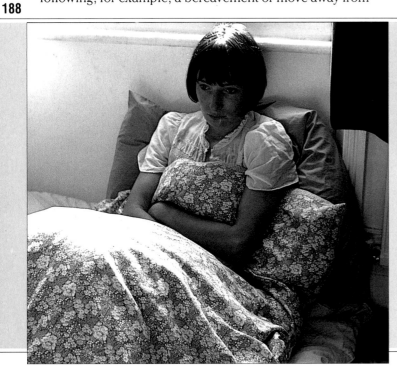

◄ **No one to be with** *can also mean no where to go. Young adults and adolescents, in particular, feel ashamed to be seen alone, and avoiding this embarrassment contributes to their loneliness by keeping them away from places where they might meet people.*

▲ **The pain of losing someone close**. *Emotional loneliness, here a central part of the grief of a widow with her orphaned daughter, is the unfulfilled need for an intimate relationship – in this case a particular intimate relationship that can never again be. Friends are a valuable support in coping with the stress of emotional loneliness.*

Loneliness, whether an absence of friendship or of love, can be temporary or persistent. We may be isolated by circumstance or lack of social skill. In both cases, the most useful strategies involve thinking positively about other people.

example "wandered lonely as a cloud" when he saw the host of golden daffodils that were later to

...flash upon that inward eye
which is the bliss of solitude...

Solitude is often seen as an ingredient for creative activity and self-growth, and periods of social isolation may well bring benefits (see box), but it seems unlikely that geniuses in the midst of their creative endeavors, or solitary hikers at one with nature, are in fact feeling very *lonely*. People who say they are lonely almost inevitably speak of the pain and discomfort of being without others.

Who is most vulnerable?

Loneliness can be found in every section of society, but, in some groups, more people are lonely than in others.

Studies challenge the assumption that we are most apt to be lonely in old age. They point to adolescence as the phase in the life span when loneliness is greatest. Having fewer contacts will not necessarily *make* you lonely, and even though old people have fewer friends and spend less time with them, they do not usually want or need as much social contact as younger people.

Another common belief, that loneliness is associated with widowhood, has more truth in it. With 42 percent reporting themselves to be victims, loneliness is most common among the widowed and divorced (including single parents), and least common among married people (only 20 percent). Those who have never been married typically fall in the middle at 38 percent of those interviewed.

Yet marriage is no guarantee of avoiding loneliness. The married people who are most at risk are dissatisfied with their marriages, dissatisfied with their sex lives or dissatisfied with being homemakers. The wife who stays at home all day is often bored and cooped up by herself, sometimes frustrated with having to discipline her children and having to wait for the family's one car so she can get out.

Not surprisingly, lonely husbands and wives describe their relationships as lacking intimacy: they do not touch each other and do not tell each other about their feelings. They may take psychological or even physical jabs at each

---

THE BENEFITS OF SOCIAL ISOLATION

■ *Being alone means loneliness only when we want other people's company – and often we do not. Simply to avoid too much stimulation, and to perform tasks that require concentration, everyone seeks solitude sometimes.*

Great political and spiritual leaders including Jesus Christ, Gandhi and Martin Luther King went through important periods of prolonged solitude. During these times they discovered more completely their own sense of mission and formulated important aspects of the message they would carry to followers.

RESTRICTED STIMULATION

The religious retreat has a centuries-old appeal to ordinary people too, and psychologists have also found that social isolation can help to achieve important changes in our lives. Therapies that aim at "restricted environmental stimulation" have been shown to be more effective for example, than many other programs for helping people to lose weight and stop

smoking. The most effective method requires the patient to lie in bed quietly in a dark and soundproof room for a day or less. By removing people from the complex of daily cues and reminders that other people unconsciously give them to think and behave in their usual way, these therapies seem to unfreeze existing attitudes. People become very receptive to suggestions for change, and new values can more easily take root.

ENHANCED RESPONSES

Besides affecting our attitudes, isolation affects how we react to other people. Just as hunger enhances our enjoyment of a meal, periods of isolation make others more attractive. So if you want to have an especially pleasant evening with a friend, each of you should spend the afternoon by yourself.

Going out to a special restaurant to rediscover the intimacy in a marriage can be money well spent, especially if you do not both spend most of the day beforehand interacting intensely with other people in busy office work.

Even when going away for a brief weekend without the children, the time spent as a couple together may in fact be better if time is also found for one or two solitary walks in peaceful surroundings.

other, misinterpret innocent remarks and be irritated by their partner's habits. Conflicts escalate disproportionately. Such a couple may share a house but not their daily lives – read the newspaper during dinner, go on separate outings at weekends, have different friends.

Asked simply, "Are you lonely?" women are more likely than men to say yes. On other, more subtle measures of loneliness, however, men often have higher scores than women. Women are found to be more lonely when the questions ask them to admit their feelings or to label themselves. Men reveal more loneliness when the questions – like those in the questionnaire below – tap the quality of their relationships. Thus studies showing women to be

more lonely seem to reflect the greater openness of women and the greater sensitivity they have to their own feelings. Studies showing men to be more lonely seem to reflect the greater difficulties men have in forming intimate bonds.

The painful consequences of isolation

Lonely adolescents are apt to run away from home and they are more likely to become involved in delinquent behavior. Some lonely adults are problem drinkers. Studies show that, as a group, lonely people drink much the same quantities as any other, but people who are lonely experience a greater than average number of drink-related work, legal, social and health problems as a result. The lonely, not surprisingly, are apt to drink to drown their sorrows rather than to be sociable.

Lonely people often report psychosomatic complaints such as insomnia, feeling tired, appetite disorders and a low sexual appetite. Their sense of isolation expresses itself in their higher-than-average tendency to report in question-naires that they experience episodes of feeling "vulnerable," "abandoned," "without hope," "afraid," "helpless," or "desperate panic." Because they *appear* desperate, lonely people often frighten away potential friends. The lonely may behave in a disconcerting, hyperalert way in company, vigilantly appraising others for their potential to fill the relationship gap in their lives.

One of the predominant features of loneliness may be a set of negative, self-deprecating feelings. Lonely people are

---

HOW LONELY ARE YOU?

■ To get a sense of how psychologists would assess your own degree of loneliness, answer the following four items. They are taken from the most frequently used research measure of loneliness, the University of Los Angeles Loneli-ness Scale. For each question in the list, indicate how often you feel as though the statement applies to you.

	Never	Rarely	Sometimes	Often
I feel in tune with the people around me	4	3	2	1
No one really knows me well	1	2	3	4
I can find companionship when I want to	4	3	2	1
People are around me but not with me	1	2	3	4

Total your score for all four items. The average total for 250 Los Angeles respondents was 4.2; higher scores reflect greater loneliness.

▶ **Going out to be alone.** As many as 20 percent of married people say that they are lonely. They describe their marital relationship as lacking intimacy, and often the mar-riage partners find it difficult to communicate their feelings to each other except in ways that create conflict. When conflict is intense, getting away from each other can seem more important than being with anyone.

Because they appear so desperate, lonely people sometimes frighten away potential friends. They may behave in a disconcerting, hyperalert manner in company, too eagerly appraising the opportunity that each person present represents.

more inclined than others to describe themselves as "unattractive" or "stupid." They are more likely to report feeling ashamed of things they believe they have done wrong and to report feelings of insecurity. From time to time, many lonely people have a sense of agitated boredom that can interfere with concentration as they become distracted by feelings of uneasiness or anger and the desire to be elsewhere. They are almost always unhappy and pessimistic, tending to be bored and apathetic, and to select terms like "alienated," "melancholy," "sorry for self," "isolated," "empty," "depressed" and "sad," when asked to describe their feelings.

Perhaps most serious of all, loneliness threatens life itself. One of the most clearly identified characteristics of potential suicide victims is their sense of loneliness. Lonely people also make more use of health services. An explanation for this could be that, when they become ill, they turn to professionals because they have no one else to care for them – and they may see doctors and nurses just to have a form of social contact. In addition, however a lack of the social support that relationships usually bring seems genuinely to undermine the lonely person's resistance to disease (see *Ch 16*).

In a study carried out in areas of rural Iowa in the United States, the loneliness of senior citizens was assessed and their health was monitored for two years. Among the most lonely group, 22 percent moved to a nursing home during the two years; among the least lonely group, only 4 percent moved from their own homes to an institution. Partly this must be accounted for by the fact that the nonlonely people had friends and family who could care for them at home,

▲ **The vicious circle of loneliness**. Loneliness is dispiriting. It encourages negative, self-deprecating feelings. This pessimistic attitude about your own worth makes it difficult for you to present yourself in ways that others will find appealing. You tend to see other people, too, in a more negative light when none of them are your friends. When you feel critical of people as a matter of habit, it is all the more difficult to convey to them the sense of liking on which friendship can build.

but the higher stress of a lonely life was probably a factor in their needing *more* care. Even more striking is the fact that, during the two years, four times more of the loneliest people died than of the least lonely.

What causes loneliness?

Why do we become lonely, and when is loneliness most likely to occur? Sociologists see its roots in social condi-tions. Urbanization creates a more impersonal environment – to protect themselves from overstimulation, city-dwellers become very adept at limiting involvement with people they

do not know, and so it is difficult to make contact with them when you need to establish new relationships. At the same time, a high divorce rate and high mobility both create a continuing *need* for new relationships.

Some people are more vulnerable to these conditions than others. Psychologists have observed, for example, that lonely people tend to have lonely children. Perhaps in part this inheritance is genetically determined, but there are undoubtedly important environmental influences: lonely children describe their families as cold, disagreeable and distant. They spend less time with their parents. Finding time to talk to your children and do things with them can doubtless help you to protect them from growing into lonely adults. The passive television viewing that features so prominently in family life falls far short of the joint participation in shared activity that children need in order to intensify their relationships with parents and to develop socially. Lonely people tend to be low in self-esteem,

192

URBAN LONELINESS

■ *Being alone in a big city is harder than being alone in a small town or in the country. City-dwellers protect them-selves from "stimulus overload" by avoiding social interactions. In public places, they avoid making eye-contact with each other, make their faces blank, put on the earphones of their personal stereos and retire into private worlds. Not only those* *who are already well-supplied with relationships do this. The same behavior occurs in migrant young adults who have left their family and friends behind and in single parents isolated from social contact by the full-time demands of looking after an infant.*

To protect themselves from overstimulation city-dwellers become adept at limiting involvement with people they do not know. It is difficult to make contact with them when you need to establish new relationships.

introverted, shy, self-conscious and lacking in assertiveness. They say they have difficulty making friends, getting along with others, initiating social contacts and enjoying themselves socially. These personality problems may reflect both environment and heredity (see *Ch 23*) and may both cause loneliness and result from it, thus contributing to a vicious cycle.

It might be expected that lonely people are so eager for friendship that they would go out of their way to promote future contacts with new acquaintances. This does not seem to be the case. When they do meet new people, they tend to harbor critical thoughts about them, to talk about themselves more, make fewer references to the other and do less to keep the conversation going when pauses do occur.

It is possible to conclude from this that lonely people

have only themselves to blame – that their personalities and behavior are the root of their problem. However, such events as moving house, the death of a spouse and disappointments in school or at work can all generate feelings of loneliness and the negative attitudes that go with them. Thus, loneliness can be a result of both individual vulnerability and environmental pressures.

Coping with loneliness

Almost everyone who suffers from loneliness simply gives in some of the time. They cry, sit and think gloomy thoughts, in their own words "do nothing." But all have at least some coping strategies.

Sometimes, these offer temporary escape, and they can be harmful if used too often – going to sleep for example, for longer hours than are necessary, overeating, taking tranquilizers, watching television and drinking alone. Some people, whether they have it or not, spend money to cheer themselves up. A more effective strategy is found by those who try to take their mind off loneliness, or redefine the problem to minimize its magnitude by telling themselves it will not last forever. This can contribute to a more optimistic frame of mind and to behavior that fulfills the prophesy.

Needless to say, positive coping *actions*, such as calling on a friend or inviting someone to visit, are crucial. Those

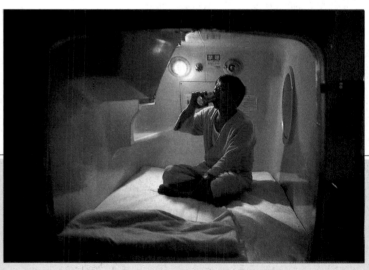

▲ **Alone in front of a television set** *a commuter who has worked too late to catch his train settles in for the night in a Tokyo "capsule hotel," where the emphasis falls on economy of space. Some television viewing can be a stimulating way to pass time when you are on your own, but it is a passive activity and does little to help lonely people to make acquaintances. Watching television with someone else may be a waste of an* *opportunity to interact in a more rewarding way. Too much family television viewing, for instance, can deprive children of the intensity of interaction they need with their parents and of the opportunity to learn the social skills from them that will help to protect them from loneliness in adult life.*

who take the most effective advantage of these occasions understand the importance of signaling to other people that you are interested in *them*, and of controlling any pessimistic tendency to be critical of them. Asking questions, finding ways of keeping conversation flowing – to help the other person retain interest in it – and interpreting other people's personalities positively can all help to improve the chances of forming relationships. Individual encounters will be more satisfying and other people in general will seem more pleasant and less threatening.

Many victims of loneliness want very badly to establish romantic attachments (see opposite page). Experts who have studied loneliness, however, tend to say that improving friendships is a more appropriate first step, as the turmoil of

romance can involve high emotional risks. Even those "emotionally" lonely people who are not "socially" lonely are advised to approach the problem by way of their social network. If this network does not already include possible candidates for a more intimate relationship, it should be expanded to do so. In this way, closer relationships may be attempted from within the network, building on an established foundation of friendship.

Some people turn to religion, hoping to overcome loneliness by reaching out to a personal God. There is no evidence that religious people in particular are less lonely than the nonreligious, but there *is* evidence that people who find meaning and purpose in their lives, whether it is religiously defined or not, tend to be less lonely. Religious

194

▲ **Waiting to be picked.** *The traditionally passive role assigned to women in the rituals of courtship sometimes makes it seem to them that there is little they can do but wait helplessly. The wall-flower look that can result, however, is worth avoiding. Two girls at a dance will seem easier to approach and more attractive if they are chatting in a friendly* *manner and seem to be enjoying each other's company. One of the reasons why friendships help us to meet potential intimate partners is that people who obviously have friends appear more likely to be easy to get to know and to be rewarding to talk to.*

Many lonely people want very much to establish romantic attachments. The best way to do this is to improve friendships. Intimate involvement usually happens through getting to know someone you meet when you are with friends.

people have been found to interpret and react to loneliness in characteristic ways. For example, they are more likely to invoke religious explanations of why they became lonely, often because they believe that it is God's will that individuals should experience loneliness to help them grow in faith. They are also more likely to use prayer as a way of overcoming their loneliness.

Psychologists differ in their opinion of constructive solitary activity – such as reading, or playing a musical instrument – as a strategy for combating loneliness. Some believe that to overcome loneliness, you must tackle the root of the problem: you must form social bonds, and active solitude does not accomplish this. There is much evidence, however, that keeping active enhances your mood – and happy people are rarely lonely. Advocates of contructive solitude also note that, for some severely lonely people, social contact may be so stressful that it only serves to intensify their feelings of isolation.

In employing constructive activity to overcoming loneliness, it is best to select intrinsically enjoyable and only moderately difficult challenges. Given a choice between trying a new idea for your garden this weekend or starting a 14-volume history of the western world, you would be advised to take the garden.

Expert psychological help in overcoming loneliness is available from private practitioners, from life-crisis support groups (see *Ch 16*), from psychological clinics, from social skills training workshops and from student counseling centers. Properly conducted programs bringing sufferers together with well-qualified professionals for as few as six two-hour sessions have been effective in diagnosing personal problems, correcting misunderstandings and suggesting new ways of behaving.

Whether they seek professional help or deal with their problems alone, there is encouraging news for most lonely people. Like many of life's other difficulties short-term loneliness, especially, runs its course. People usually get over it. Long-term loneliness, too, can be alleviated by changes in attitude and behavior. **DP**

DOING SOMETHING ABOUT LONELINESS

■ *The first step in overcoming loneliness is to resist the passive outlook that can so easily result from being always alone. People for whom loneliness is a temporary condition get over it because of the constructive actions they take.*

WHAT TO DO
Accept invitations when they are offered.
Call on someone or invite them to visit.
Be responsive in conversation. Show people that you are interested in what they say by smiling and nodding.
Ask questions to keep the conversation flowing. This will help others to find it rewarding to talk to you.

Ask questions that help people to present themselves in their best light.
Be open to the interests of other people.
Draw attention to interests you have in common.

WHAT NOT TO DO
Do not stay away from people to hide your loneliness.
Do not make negative remarks about yourself.
Do not harbor critical thoughts about the people you meet.
Do not think that you have to be exceptionally clever or attractive to be liked.

◄ **Religion offers comfort** to a visitor to the Iona Abbey in Scotland. All major faiths offer insights into the positive experience of solitude, and they also bring the faithful together in a sense of community. The idea of drawing close to a personal God inspires many lonely people to adopt a religious commitment.

THE LONELINESS BUSINESS

■ *The millions of people trying to escape loneliness are an important market for businesses such as dating services, "personal" classified advertisements in newspapers, singles bars, cruise organizers, ski clubs, groups for single-parent families, and commercial therapy groups.*

The primary and explicitly stated purpose of dating services is to foster romantic attachments. They promise to do the work for you of finding your perfect match.

In one way or another, all the other businesses also aim to help people form close relationships. Do they really provide a shortcut to intimacy? While a few people form close, long-term relationships this way,

others are often disappointed.
What might be called the first law of close relationships is that similarity, especially similarity of outlook, promotes friendship (see Ch 21). If a dating agency's pool of other clients who are genuinely similar to you is big enough, and their system for sorting files really is efficient enough, their services may be worth the investment.

THE SIMILARITY FACTOR
But the romantically lonely should bear in mind that one item of similarity for all clients is likely to be that they have difficulty forming relationships. Your own initiatives may offer a better prospect of meeting someone who is similar to you in interests and has social skills

that you can learn from and that will help you to relate.
It may be helpful to join a political club or history-preservation society, precisely because socializing is only a secondary purpose of the group.

ROMANTIC FEELINGS
When businesses aim to help people feel as though they are in love, it is important not to get swept up by the situation. A cruise, ski trip, or even a singles bar might well provide the right atmosphere for romance, and you may feel this is worth the money. But falling in love is very different from forming a relationship, and romantic feelings often cloud the judgment that sound relationship formation requires (see Ch 25).

Finding a Partner

IN BOTH dating relationships and in more serious courtship, people play for higher emotional stakes than they do in other cases of making someone's acquaintance or becoming close. Becoming a couple makes us feel conspicuous. We are more strongly aware of what other people think of our choice and of whether we are in favor with or whether we are being rejected by the person who attracts us. Almost everyone goes through the remarkably exhilarating experience of falling in love during one or more relationships like this – and most of us also more than once go through the sorrow of breaking up with someone who mattered to us.

Finding someone to fall in love with, however, is not really the point of seeking this kind of relationship, and breaking up is not a failure of the process that the relationship belongs to. Experts are agreed that finding a life's partner depends on investigating potentials and testing suitability in a way that is impossible during the excitement of being in love. Breaking up, furthermore, normally means that the courtship process has successfully identified a relationship as an unlikely long-term prospect. The highest emotional stake involved is long-term happiness, and our chances of this are best assessed during our less romantic moments.

Initial attraction

Attraction to potential dating partners is very similar to the process of attraction that leads into friendship. That is, attraction is more likely when people are in frequent physical proximity to each other. Physical appearance is often the first quality of the other person to arouse our interest. However, we are not drawn to those who are strikingly more attractive than we are – we do not expect to be found attractive by people who look better than us. An introduction through friends or a self-introduction leads to conversation, and talking affects attraction by revealing whether we have joint interests or attitudes that could make us rewarding and emotionally reinforcing company for each other. (See *Ch21*.)

In addition, a number of special features affect attraction between the sexes. One effect of physical proximity, for example, is that we do not tend to be sexually attracted to anyone with whom we have been intimate while growing up. The person need not be a blood relation, such as a brother or sister, to be excluded in this way. Studies of the communally raised children of Israeli kibbutzim, for example, reveal that they have very little inclination to marry each other when they reach adulthood; a partner is almost always chosen from outside the home kibbutz.

It often requires special effort to achieve the proximity required to meet potential dating partners. Adolescent boys and girls may attend separate schools. Men and women may be streamed into separate male and female occupations. This helps to promote the popularity of dances, parties and other events organized to help them to meet.

Friends and relatives are particularly important. They help by providing introductions to their own friends, and this is the way that most couples meet. Relatives of the opposite

196

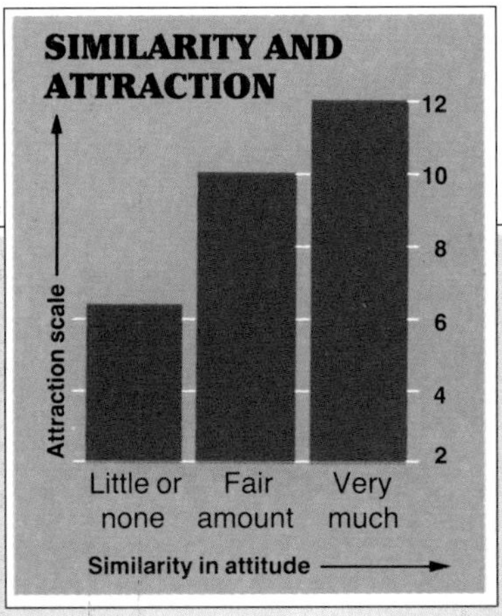

▲ **Think-alike couples** *attract each other. When they share little or none of each other's views, volunteers in experiments are attracted only half as much to otherwise attractive people. The impact of disagreement is still significant even when we share a "fair amount" of the same thinking.*

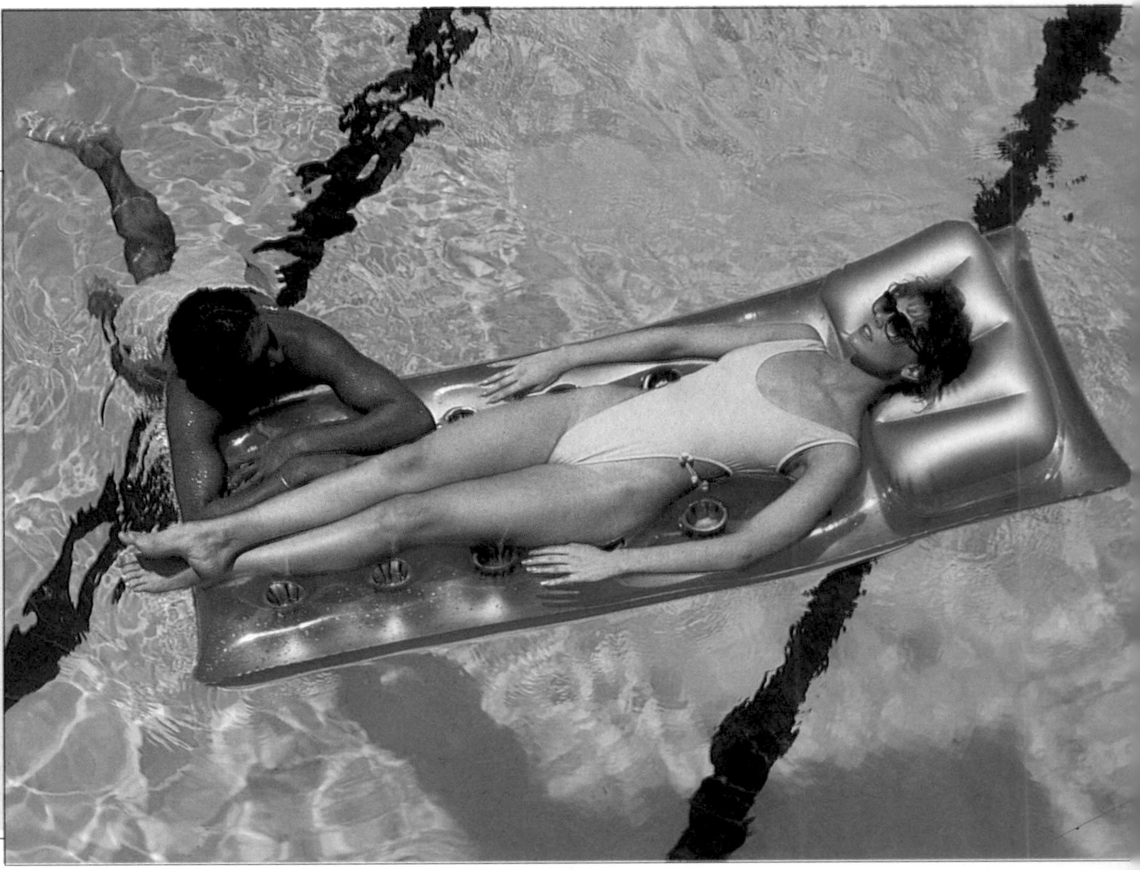

Falling in love is not an essential step toward forming an intimate relationship. A satisfying long-term relationship is founded on mutually controlled stages of courtship that permit two people to know and adjust to each other.

sex, or friends with relatives of the opposite sex, can be especially helpful. A sister, for example, may bring her girlfriend to the house at least partly with the intention of seeing whether her older brother likes her. A social network is instrumental too in helping you to create the right impression when meeting potential partners. The fact that you are with friends who seem to be enjoying your company makes you appear more attractive – a more likely prospect as a good companion.

Your attractiveness to a potential partner will greatly depend on how closely you match their preconceived personal ideal. We each have an image of the sort of person we are likely to want. It is usually heavily influenced by the sexual role modeling that our opposite-sex parent has provided. If our relationship with the parent has been rather distant, pop images may have a stronger effect on us.

For men, the physical attractiveness of a female partner is more important than the physical attractiveness of a male partner is for women. There is a statistical correlation between extroversion in men and a liking for big breasts. Introverts tend to prefer small ones. Women are attracted by a slim physique, including small buttocks, in a man 12–15cm (5–6in) taller than they are. More important for both sexes, however, is manner and self-presentation. A great range of immediately apparent qualities are available to both sexes for comparison with their ideal images of a partner – style of dress; tone of voice; the assertive or unassertive, inviting or uninviting way they hold and move their bodies; not only facial features but subtleties of facial expression. The power of similarity to attract can be notable when you meet someone whose face resembles yours.

◀ **Physical attraction** *is a starting point for many relationships. We are attracted to those who are about as attractive as we are. An imbalance of attractiveness may undermine a relationship in the long term. The more attractive partner may develop a sense of dissatisfaction or the less attractive one may fear such a development.*

▲ **An attractive similarity of appearance** *includes more than physique and our facial features. We are attracted to those whose similarity of style suggests a similarity of background and attitude. They look like people who will agree with our way of thinking, share our interests and understand our way of expressing ourselves.*

DESIRABLE AND NEGATIVE QUALITIES

■ *In a survey in the United States, young men and women asked to select and rate potentially desirable attributes in a partner produced entirely different "top-ten" lists. In order of importance, what women most sought in a man were:*
a record of achievement
leadership qualities
skill at his job
earning potential
a sense of humor
intellectual ability
attentiveness
common sense
athletic ability
good abstract reasoning.
Most sought by men in a woman were:
physical attractiveness
ability in bed
warmth and affection
social skill
home-making ability
dress sense
sensitivity to others' needs
good taste
moral perception
artistic creativity.

Looks were thought to be very important by 40 percent of young men in a survey in Britain and by 23 percent of young women. Personality and faithfulness were, however, rated as more important by both sexes, especially having a good sense of humor and being considerate and reliable.

NEGATIVE ATTRACTION

Some psychologists argue that the classic studies of mutual attraction are actually better understood in terms of repulsion. What happens, they say, is that when people meet they do not so much select initially for qualities they are positively attracted to as pick out what they dislike and would prefer to avoid in others. Once we have screened others for disliked characteristics (such as an unattractive appearance, dissimilarity of attitudes and disagreeable mannerisms) we are inclined to be attracted to them. **EG**

197

Becoming acquainted

If no mutual friend is at hand to make the introduction, you can always introduce yourself. This is often preceded by nonverbal signaling. "Preening gestures" – acts of self-touching followed by or combined with glances at the person of interest – are used to display attraction and invite interest. For example, a teenage boy may unnecessarily and ceremoniously comb his hair while allowing the reflection of his eye in a store window to fix on the girl he wants to approach. If she touches her hair – even in mild confusion – and glances away and then back, he will feel emboldened to approach. An older man might straighten his tie or brush something from his jacket and glance with interest at a woman. If she smiles in response he will feel more at ease about starting a conversation. A very innocuously humorous remark or comment of appreciation about something they can both easily relate to – about the way their host has arranged the party, or even about the weather – is all that it usually takes to get started.

First conversations are usually just as superficial when you are meeting a potential dating partner as they are when you are meeting a potential friend, and they are just as important to the process of relationship formation. Talk does not usually touch on intimate topics or your most deeply held beliefs, but the participants allow each other to know enough about each other's backgrounds and interests to form an impression of how similar they are in personality and attitude. They are selective in what they reveal about themselves, responding each to what the other says with comments that seem likely, in the circumstances, to make a good impression. Attraction may increase as a result of what is said, because the couple feel that they fit in with each other, or it may cool because they feel they do not.

Equally or even more important than words during the conversation will be the participants' nonverbal signaling. A significant source of attraction is attraction itself, and in a first conversation we will show this mainly by how much we smile, how much eye contact we seek and how close we are prepare to stand or sit.

In starting a dating relationship, in particular, we will be attracted to someone who makes us feel that we are handling our sex role – as we conceive it – successfully. A man with a strong sense of his masculinity will be attracted to a woman with a strong sense of femininity who makes him feel admired for striking a dominant pose. A woman who does not feel at home in a submissive role will be attracted to a man who finds it appealing that she asserts herself on an equal footing with him. At the same time she will probably be pleased at being found sexually attractive. He may show his attraction, for example, through involuntary dilation of the pupils of his eyes.

Falling in love

Where should we go from this initial contact? Some would say, date for a time and then either you will fall in love or you will have to keep on looking for the partner who will make this happen. Falling in love, however, has surprisingly little to do with forming a *relationship*.

▲ **Moving too close** too quickly will cause the other person to put up barriers, such as seen here in arms tightly folded, legs crossed and a slight turning away of the body. The effect will be the opposite if you speak from a distance that is slightly too far away for comfortable conversation, or lean back slightly. This will draw your new acquaintance toward you, if the person is genuinely interested in you.

▶ **Drawn together** by dim lighting, a couple test the potential for a closer relationship. Arousing colors may help to precipitate romantic feelings.

Falling in love is an exciting dream come true. The object of love seems like an ideal that has turned into reality. The feelings that we have for this person are ones we have only imagined experiencing as our own.

Although it can happen to almost anyone at any age it is most common in late adolescence. At this age we are still only on the threshold of a capacity to form fully adult relationships, and although, on the face of it, our romantic episodes are very much concerned with the other person, we are almost entirely preoccupied with our own feelings.

It is true that the love-struck are obsessed with the object of their love. They are able to think and are often able to talk of little else. This person comes to seem like the only one in the world who matters. But we conceive of the person in such an idealized way that the object of obsession is more accurately identified as an image – one that has little correspondence to a reality. The beloved's real virtues are exaggerated and many more are imagined. The lover's mind is closed to any possibility of finding fault.

The object that obsesses us is an ideal image of the person we would like to love and be loved by. What excites us is the notion that the dream of being so loved is coming true or is about to come true. The feeling itself is part of the dream and the feeling too preoccupies us. We are restless

and agitated. We feel an irregular heartbeat and a raised blood pressure and pulse rate. Our palms may feel clammy and we may have sudden flushes and feelings of momentary weakness. We lose our appetite, lose sleep and lose the ability to think straight. It is all part of the expectation that we have formed by going to the movies and reading paperbacks about love – and it is exciting and fascinating to feel it really happening.

You might seek love as an end in itself. Although falling in love is often likened to an illness (we are said to be "sick with love") it can be a time of pure elation. Being in love can create a sense of euphoria that makes us optimistic about every aspect of our lives, makes us give up inhibitions and act, sometimes appealingly, out of character.

Must we fall in love?

There seems to be no solid evidence that this *has* to happen, however, in order for us to learn eventually how to form a more mature loving relationship. Indeed it does not seem to happen very much in many cultures. Western culture has a belief in the idea of romantic love and this seems to be one of the main reasons why Westerners have the experience.

Psychologists identify several preconditions for falling in love. One is our belief in the phenomenon – the expectation that it *will* happen and the assumption that it must happen in order for an intimate relationship to occur.

A second precondition is that we should have a fantasy image of the person we will one day fall in love with. Popular stereotypes propagated on television and in the movies will make some contribution to this image. So will our opposite-sex parent and other models who influenced us as we grew up. The fantasy image encapsulates everything that has been said above about what we believe

199

◄ **A sense that they belong together** – *perhaps it is for the first time that they realize they share this feeling – makes an intimate distance seem right to an intimate couple. The question of whether they really do belong together will arise again and again as their relationship develops. Both they and their friends and families will watch to see if apparent similarities of attitude are genuine enough to hold the couple together in the long run. Will their values and role-expectations prove compatible and remain so? Are their shared interests broad enough and likely enough to remain shared? Is the commitment they feel of a quality (intensity is not enough) to sustain the relation-* ship when the first excitement of romance wears off and when they become less rewarding company for each other? The danger of the romantic phase of partner selection is that we will fall in love with our partner's superficial resemblance to a fantasy image. Then romance may incite us to make too early a commitment – before we have had the opportunity to know the reality behind the image.

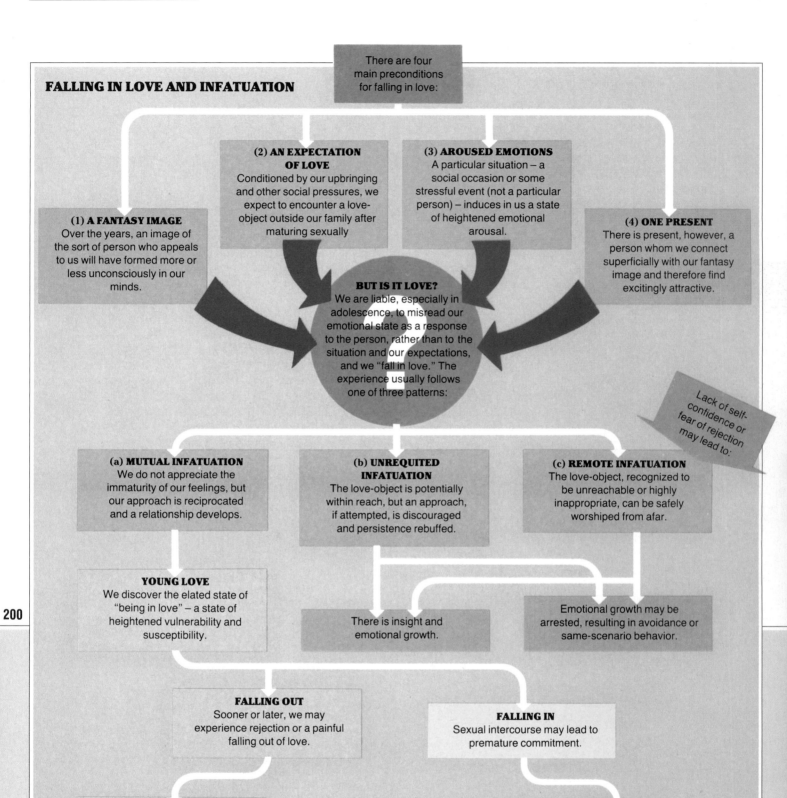

FALLING IN LOVE AND INFATUATION

There are four main preconditions for falling in love:

(1) A FANTASY IMAGE
Over the years, an image of the sort of person who appeals to us will have formed more or less unconsciously in our minds.

(2) AN EXPECTATION OF LOVE
Conditioned by our upbringing and other social pressures, we expect to encounter a love-object outside our family after maturing sexually

(3) AROUSED EMOTIONS
A particular situation – a social occasion or some stressful event (not a particular person) – induces in us a state of heightened emotional arousal.

(4) ONE PRESENT
There is present, however, a person whom we connect superficially with our fantasy image and therefore find excitingly attractive.

BUT IS IT LOVE?
We are liable, especially in adolescence, to misread our emotional state as a response to the person, rather than to the situation and our expectations, and we "fall in love." The experience usually follows one of three patterns:

Lack of self-confidence or fear of rejection may lead to:

(a) MUTUAL INFATUATION
We do not appreciate the immaturity of our feelings, but our approach is reciprocated and a relationship develops.

(b) UNREQUITED INFATUATION
The love-object is potentially within reach, but an approach, if attempted, is discouraged and persistence rebuffed.

(c) REMOTE INFATUATION
The love-object, recognized to be unreachable or highly inappropriate, can be safely worshiped from afar.

YOUNG LOVE
We discover the elated state of "being in love" – a state of heightened vulnerability and susceptibility.

There is insight and emotional growth.

Emotional growth may be arrested, resulting in avoidance or same-scenario behavior.

FALLING OUT
Sooner or later, we may experience rejection or a painful falling out of love.

FALLING IN
Sexual intercourse may lead to premature commitment.

EMOTIONAL GROWTH
Insight gained through perhaps several episodic relationships leads to a "courtship phase" in which our feelings are tempered by greater realism. We learn how to discover and respond to the person, not the situation.

INSTABILITY
We rush into an inherently unstable marriage or state of living together. But learning, adjustment, growth and a stable outcome are still possible in many cases.

LASTING LOVE
There is progress to a mature love relationship and probably courtship, with a stable marriage a likely outcome.

Adolescents are vulnerable to falling in love, especially at times of looming decision about careers or education, or when friends fall in love. Postadolescent men are susceptible as a part of their mid-life crisis.

we would find most attractive in an intimate partner. It is a fantasy because it has not yet been tested in a real-life experience of intimate partnership.

We also need to be *ready* to fall in love. Exactly when we do can depend on unsuspected factors. Some people go cheerfully from one superficial relationship to another with hardly a thought of long-term involvement. Until, one day, they suddenly fall in love. The timing is often significant:

they may just have completed a course of study, or reached a crossroads in their career.

Once past adolescence and early adulthood, men are more likely to fall in love during their mid-life transition than at other times; women just before menopause. Those facing redundancy or retirement are similarly vulnerable. Adolescents and young adults often fall in love just when it will affect education or career-path decisions – it may, for example, lead to abandoning a career plan urged upon them by over-concerned parents.

The things friends do, especially if most of them belong to the same social group, can be powerful triggers of "copycat" behavior: one couple falling in love can prompt others to do the same in quick succession (similar copycat behavior can also determine when engagements, weddings and pregnancies happen). Our desire to conform – to identify with our social equals, hold onto their approval and grow with them – is especially strong in adolescence. It can affect the behavior of even the most independent-minded.

Another precondition is a moment of emotional arousal – a situation in which our adrenaline is flowing. What has aroused us need not be the attractiveness of a person. In a famous experiment conducted in Vancouver, Canada, the arousal factor was the Capilano suspension bridge swaying an alarming 90m (300ft) above a rocky gorge.

A final precondition is the presence of a suitable other person on whom we can focus our emotional state – someone who reminds us of our fantasy image – and call

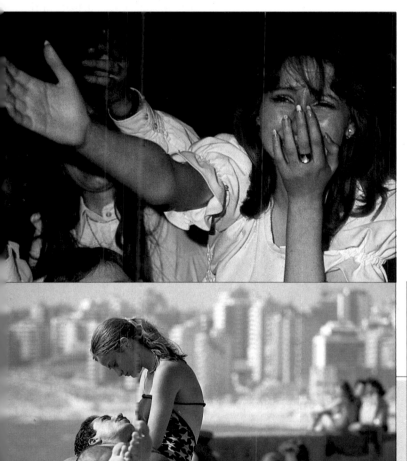

■ **Being in love** can mean an infatuation felt from afar, as in the case of this overwrought pop fan TOP or it can mean an intensely shared experience, as in this scene BOTTOM of Beirut in a quiet moment between the bombs. Tumultuous feelings of love depend on high levels of emotional arousal, and often the object of love is not the only, nor even the most important, cause. Thrilling music, romantic settings, even danger, can contribute.

THE TENDER TRAP

■ *Why do we fall in love? The biologist answers that falling in love is a stage in the formation of a "pair bond." For humans, pair bonding is a complex emotional process whereby a man and a woman are impelled to secure a stable base for the prolonged nurturing of children. Another stage in pair bonding is mutual experience of sexual intercourse and orgasm. Either stage, in fact, can lead on to the other.*

It is easy to see how falling in love leads to sex; but it is not as widely appreciated that sexual intercourse can by itself trigger the falling-in-love experience. Realistic judgments may be hard to form once the shared emotional impact of orgasm has been experienced. The symbolism of this moment, reinforced by hormone surges that act directly on the brain, is sometimes powerful enough to tie

together two people quite unsuited to each other. This is why it is often argued that adolescents should delay sexual intercourse until well into the courtship period. They should give themselves time to explore each other's personalities before, perhaps prematurely, locking themselves into a pair bond.

In the United States, the average age at first intercourse is 17.7 for females and 18 for males, mostly in a steady dating relationship (25 percent of girls and 12 percent of boys report that they did not enjoy the experience).

In Britain 56 percent of young people think that premarital intercourse is "all right," and 69 percent "would have it."

In another survey, 36 percent of the adolescents surveyed thought i wrong to marry someone you had not slept with.

it love, or at least sexual arousal. In the Vancouver experiment, men were met by an interviewer after crossing the suspension bridge. Other men were met after crossing a lower, solid footbridge standing only a few feet above the stream. In some cases, the interviewer was a man. In others, it was an attractive woman. All of the men were given some questions to answer and a brief story to write. The interviewer also gave them his or her telephone number, with the invitation to call in case they wanted more information. Men meeting the female interviewer in an aroused state – coming off the suspension bridge – tended to write stories with a higher sexual content than men meeting her after leaving the solid bridge. They were also more likely to telephone her later. When the interviewer was male these differences between the two groups of men did not appear.

If you believe in falling in love, if the time is right, if the moon is high or passionate music has quickened the pace of your heartbeat and the right sort of person happens to be there, showing an interest in you, you will almost certainly be struck by Cupid's arrow.

The perils of romance

Falling in love is not always a happy experience. It can be associated with bouts of anxiety and depression. Love may even be experienced as agony and yearning. People can, and often do, fall in love with someone who is not able or is unwilling to return their love, someone they will never see again or someone whom social conventions do not allow them to love openly.

Falling in love often does not *end* happily. Sooner or later, the excitement wears off. It cannot be sustained indefinitely and when it no longer fuels our admiration for the love object, disenchantment may set in. In fact, a part of growing up and maturing psychologically and sexually is usually that we *do* not marry our first love object. Self-preoccupation and extremes of emotion are not consistent with the mundane problems of organizing a life together. Because there is no progression to a more realistic frame of mind, first love usually founders.

With the belief in romantic love so deeply rooted in our expectations, however, many are vulnerable to falling in love and marrying precipitately. Adolescents whose parents are divorced, who are at odds with their parents or with authority in general, or who are low in self-esteem, are most at risk. Many married couples who are less seriously affected, however, are nevertheless affected. Most newly-weds or young couples preparing for marriage expect or at least hope for married life to be romantic. One of the

◄ **Fun to be with**. TOP *Sharing a sense of humor and finding entertainment in the same situations is one of the bases for a sound relationship.*

◄ **Mutual self-disclosure** *paves the way for mutual commitment. Courting couples learn something new about each other every day. When the discoveries reinforce the relationship, there is a sense of excitement and progress.*

► **Passing the separation test.** *How does your partner react to being together again after you have been apart?*

> *Past the initial sampling stage of courtship, we enter a "bargaining stage." We "negotiate" for a closer relationship with one of our dating partners. This may lead at first to a private and then to an institutionalized commitment.*

greatest perils of romantic love is the strain it puts on those marriages that have to face the disappointment of its inevitable loss.

Building a foundation

Sound partner selection involves moving from initial attraction to a closer acquaintance with several dating partners, and then when someone promising is found, discovering whether a closer relationship can be built out of the realities of each other's personalities, experience and ability to adapt.

The first stage is sometimes called the "sampling stage." While dating more than one person at once and meeting new potential partners all the time, you try to learn enough about others to know with whom it would be possible to enter into a more committed relationship.

When you find a partner who has enough in common with you and who is interested in a more serious dating relationship, you may begin a genuine bargaining stage. There is more self-disclosure, more expression of need and desires. With sufficient trust, the partners confide in each other what rewards they would expect within a long-term relationship and what expectations they think they could meet. Much of this bargaining may be indirect, through expression of opinions and attitudes, including communications of these through the way you behave – for example, through the degree that you each give and seek affection, or through the control that one of you takes in the relationship and the other accepts, or, alternatively, through the equality that you establish together.

If, as a result of bargaining, you both see the prospect of a rewarding future together, you may decide to commit yourselves to spending time and energy on the relationship and to excluding other potential partners. You might reach this stage without speaking of it in words. Finally, however, partners will have to decide whether their commitment is great enough to be institutionalized – for example, through the public announcement of an engagement.

The courtship now enters a stage in which friends and family have more explicit opportunity to scrutinize the relationship, adjust to it, advise on its suitability or protest about its implications for the partners' wider network of relationships. Now the partners' attention will be focused more clearly on such questions as whose family will be advantaged or disadvantaged by such decisions as where the new household will be established. It now emerges how well each partner will adapt to in-laws and which friends will become shared friends. **RG**

The courtship period

The processes of partner selection and assessment are demanding for both partners. Because marriage involves not only liking each other but actually living together, a sexual relationship and forsaking all others, there is much that each person needs to test in the other before a final commitment can safely be made. This will lead to tension and conflict. Conflict may be beneficial to the relationship or destructive, depending on the issues.

On the one hand, conflict about personal matters – such as persistent habits, strongly held beliefs or basic traits of personality – is likely to be destructive. This reveals to the partners the limits of their compatibility and the limits of the support they will be able to give each other's self-esteem

JUDGING THE STRENGTH OF A RELATIONSHIP

■ We regularly employ covert strategies to gather information about our partner's feelings toward us and our relationship. These "secret tests" are popular because they do no require that we directly talk about such risky topics. Thus, our egos are less likely to be bruised should our partner fail a test by signaling a less than desired commitment. See how many of the following secret tests are familiar.

ENDURANCE TESTS

Note your partner's reaction to time-consuming demands. For instance, he or she passes by enthusiastically agreeing to look after your pet while you are away for a few days.

TRIANGLE TESTS

Note your partner's reaction to a potential rival. For instance, he or she fails by not showing jealousy when an attractive friend is extremely attentive to you.

INDIRECT SUGGESTION

Note your partner's reaction to your jokes or hints about having a close relationship. For instance, he or she passes by squeezing your hand after you say, "Some people I know are very special to me."

SEPARATION TESTS

Note your partner's reaction to extended time spent away from you. For instance, he or she fails by saying "Three

weeks! Seems just like yesterday!" when you telephone after a three-week trip.

QUESTIONING OTHERS

Note what your partner's friends and family report about the relationship. For instance, he or she passes if a brother discloses that the family has been told to "be especially nice" to you.

PUBLIC PRESENTATION

Note your partner's reaction to a public declaration or demonstration or affection. For instance, he or she fails by pulling away to talk to someone else when you approach at a party and put your arm around his or her waist. **BMM**

and world view. Although such conflict may not benefit the relationship, it may benefit the partners in the long run by impelling them to abandon their courtship.

On the other hand, conflict about how to organize the relationship is probably beneficial – such questions as how to use leisure time or frequency and style of sex. If the problem is resolved then not only will the couple feel a shared sense of competence, but their relationship may benefit from the adjustment in their behavior that they negotiate. If problems cannot be resolved, the partners have at least learned that their relationship will not work.

Courtship is particularly prone to stress some 15 to 18 months after the relationship has formed. This seems to be

due to the expectations of the couple and their friends or relatives that the courtship must now be judged a "success" or a "failure."

Four types of courting couples have been distinguished – in terms of the length of time from the first meeting until marriage, and also in terms of the extent to which the couple share their lives.

"Accelerated couples" move very rapidly from their first meeting to being very confident that they will sooner or later marry. In some cases this only takes a few days. "Accelerated-arrested couples" initially have a sharp rise in confidence about marriage but tend to take a little longer to reach absolute certainty. "Intermediate couples" steadily increase in confidence about marriage without any particularly startling or sudden leaps. "Prolonged couples," on the other hand, are those whose confidence in the likelihood of marriage stays rather low for a long time, even though they may court steadily and exclusively for several years. Then it increases, often quite sharply, when they make a quite sudden decision to marry.

Accelerated couples (contrary to popular belief about rapid romances) are actually more close emotionally than the others in the marriages that result, and they genuinely share many of the trivial chores of life such as shopping and washing the dishes.

Prolonged couples are often not very close, do not spend much of their leisure time together and usually separate the chores on the basis of "his" and "hers."

Arranged marriages

The practice in Eastern cultures of parents arranging their children's marriages implies a belief that marriage and childrearing are too important to be left entirely to the whim

▲ **Arranged by mail**. *A bride-groom and the Philippine bride he has selected from a mail-order catalog contemplate their future life together.*

▶ **Measuring up**. *Customers at a bridal store in Los Angeles, California, prepare to look the way they think a bride should look on her wedding day.*

Courtship is particularly prone to stress about 15 to 18 months after the relationship has been formed. Now the couple, their friends and their relatives are inclined to judge the courtship as either a "success" or a "failure."

of the individual, and that the state of being in love is too unstable and unreliable to be a basis for a marriage. It also suggests that courtship is not always a necessary preliminary to marriage.

If the divorce rate is used to measure marital satisfaction and success, then studies would appear to bear this out. The divorce rate among a group of Indian couples with arranged marriages was compared to the divorce rate in a group of Indian couples who had Western-style marriages, and to a group of American married couples.

In the traditional Indian (arranged) marriage, the divorce rate was very low (around 1 percent). In the Western-style Indian marriage, by contrast, it was much higher (around 40 percent). In the American group it was higher still (around 52 percent).

Yet to what extent are marriages in Western cultures *not* arranged? Most people like to think they have complete freedom to choose their own partners, without taking social expectations or the wishes of parents or friends into account. How true is this? It has been found that the majority of partners in a marriage have many of the following features in common: they are of the same race and religion, have the same economic and educational background and income level, and come from the same town or even the same neighborhood. They also share the same pastimes, are members of the same club, vote the same way, read the same types of book and look rather similar. Few of them married partners their parents or friends did not approve of.

It would appear from this that marriages in Western cultures are determined by social factors, and by parents and friends, and that courtship – by virtue of its being a period in which practical information is exchanged – is the accepted way of arranging a marriage. However, whatever it is that brings two people together initially however much family and friends approve or disapprove, the success of their relationship is something that only they can achieve for themselves. **SD**

ROMANTIC RELATIONSHIPS AT WORK

■ Romantic involvements at work are becoming more common as more women are employed in the same occupations as men. Both the unattached and those more or less bored with marital sameness gain access at work to a large and often constantly changing pool of potential sexual and/or romantic partners. Regular exposure to attractive people frequently leads to romantic liaisons. Work also allows us to demonstrate skill and competence, and we are attracted by success. Challenges and demands requiring cooperation help to bind co-workers together, and this increases the likelihood not only of ordinary friendships but also of love affairs.

OFFICE AFFAIRS

Some researchers divide office love affairs into categories depending on the motives of the participants. There is the love category, in which the goal is to find and establish a close, long-term relationship, while in the ego category the main desire is for excitement and sexual adventure, in other words, a "fling." In the job-related category the participants are motivated by the desire to improve their situation – to gain promotion or achieve an easier workload. Since each person who is involved has their own motive, there are nine possible combinations within the categories. However, an American study carried out in 1977 found that in practice only three of these possible combinations actually emerged. In the first, both partners were in the love category, seeking a long-term loving relationship. In the second, both were in the ego category, having a fling, and in the third, called a "utilitarian" relationship, the man was having a fling and the woman wanted a promotion.

"MUTUAL USERS"

A more recent study, which reflected the growth of equality between men and women in the workplace, also identified these same three combinations of motives but in addition found a complementary type of utilitarian romance, in which the man sought job advancement and the woman a fling, and a fifth type, labeled "mutual user," in which both participants were primarily motivated by hopes of job advancement. It seems likely, however, that these investigations have oversimplified the motivations that underlie involvement in close personal relationships. It is possible, for example, that a person may simultaneously desire love, excitement and job advancement from their affair, and it may be very difficult to decide which of these motives is uppermost at any one time.

EFFECTS ON WORK

Scientific evidence as to how romance at work may affect job performance is mixed. A recent study found that both the lovers themselves and the onlookers in general agreed that usually romances at work had little influence, one way or another, on performance. However, there is some evidence that inefficiency may occur when the lovers are in positions of relatively high responsibility, but not when the lovers are lower down in the organizational hierarchy. On the more positive side, both participants and onlookers have reported actual improvements in work output by participants who are motivated by a mutual desire for genuine love. The relationship seems to give a boost to their morale and efficiency.

EFFECTS ON COLLEAGUES

Contrary to what some writers claim, evidence also indicates that those fellow workers who are aware of the romance do not make excessively simplistic or predominantly hostile judgments about it. The people who are perceived as searching for love are generally regarded favorably by their co-workers, while those out for a fling are judged rather neutrally. Whether the love-affair involves marital infidelity or not seems to be less important than the extent to which the participants were liked before the love affair came to the notice of the co-workers. Only those seen as motivated by job advancement are likely to get clearly negative evaluations. And these judgments may be particularly hostile when the person concerned is a woman, suggesting that a sexual double standard still survives in this aspect of personal relationships, as in so many others. **BM**

Thinking About Love

LOVE is the most talked about, sung about, read about and worried about of all human concerns. Yet despite this attention – or perhaps because of it – love remains one of the most misused of words. The popular media, tend to identify love with romantic passion – and the result is widespread confusion, particularly among impressionable teenagers and young adults. For some, love means little more than sexual attraction; others find themselves wondering if their love is "true" – whether it conforms to some romantic ideal. And most of us are probably still inclined to think of love as a feeling before we think of it as a relationship.

But is it helpful to invoke love at all in trying to talk usefully about relationships? Traditionally psychologists have thought not, preferring to steer clear of a term so widely associated with subjective feeling. It is only quite recently, in searching for ways of describing the pattern, quality and changeability of certain kinds of relationship, that they have begun to look again at the concept of love, trying to understand some of its subtlety and trying to find measurable elements for study.

The American social psychologist Zick Rubin started by distinguishing between loving and liking. He developed a scale to reflect the difference between the two (see box) – and in a study of dating couples was surprised to discover that although partners felt they loved each other, some did not like each other tremendously, and most liked certain of their friends as much or more. Loving, he pointed out, differs from strong liking. It involves three important characteristics: caring (being as much concerned about another's needs as about one's own); attachment (needing to be with and cared for by the other person); and intimacy (having a close bond with the other person through privileged communication, whether of an intellectual, emotional or physical kind).

But Rubin's attachment, intimacy and caring, while perhaps reflecting the essentials of mature love, seem to do less than justice to the stormy emotions – the agony and the ecstasy of being in love. Psychologists Ellen Berscheid and Elaine Walster accordingly reinstated "passionate" love, distinguishing it from what they termed "companionate" love – in three ways.

First, passionate love is romantic and very intense – the joy and the sorrow of it are both stronger. Our relationship

---

LOVING, LIKING AND FEELING

■ *Love is not a special kind of liking. Just as it is possible to like someone without loving them, so it is possible, though unusual, to love them without liking them particularly. Questions of the kind used by Rubin in framing his loving and liking scales are given below in the form of a simplified self-assessment test.*

■ **To measure your regard** *for a friend, dating partner, lover or spouse in terms of loving and liking, imagine that you have inserted his or her name in each of the following statements; then give each statement a rating from 1 to 9, depending on how strongly you would agree or disagree with it (for example: disagree completely = 1; agree completely = 9; agree to some extent = 5). For scoring instructions, see below.*

  1 I feel responsible for -----'s well-being.
  2 If I could never be with ----- I would feel miserable.
  3 I have great confidence in -----'s good judgment.
  4 I feel I can confide in ----- about virtually anything.

  5 If I were lonely, my first thought would be to seek ----- out.
  6 I think ----- is one of those people who quickly win respect.
  7 I think that ----- is unusually well-adjusted.
  8 ----- is the sort of person who I would like to be.
  9 I would do almost anything for -----.
  10 In my opinion ----- is an exceptionally mature person.
  11 It would be hard for me to get along without -----.
  12 ----- is one of the most likeable people I know.
  13 I would forgive ----- for practically anything.
  14 Most people would react favorably to ----- after a brief acquaintance.
  15 I would highly recommend ----- for a responsible job.
  16 One of my primary concerns is -----'s welfare.
  17 It seems to me that it is very easy for ----- to gain admiration.
  18 I would greatly enjoy being confided in by -----.

■ **Scoring.** *The total score for statements 3, 6, 7, 8, 10, 12, 14, 15 and 17 is the measure of liking, the total for the others is the measure of loving.*

■ **Love and one's feelings.** *Having distinguished loving from liking, Rubin also distinguished loving from the feeling of being in love. The essence of love, as his three factors imply, is action: love is reflected not primarily in feeling but in the dynamics of a relationship. The feelings with which love is so often identified are better viewed as side effects. And often they are side effects not of love but of infatuation (see Ch25). But surely an adult relationship without strong passionate feelings and expressions cannot be love? Rubin disagrees. The widespread supposition in Western society that a passionate, rapturous, emotionally involving kind of love is the only proper basis for commitment and marriage leads to difficulties as passion fades. On the one hand, there is disappointment and a feeling that the very foundation of the relationship*

has been undermined; on the other, there is a danger that the essential, enduring features of love may be overlooked. We need to accept the evidence that love can still be very much alive in a relationship even though the passionate feelings that may once have inspired it have long since subsided.

Rubin's critics, however, suggest that he may have underestimated the long-term importance of a passionate dimension in loving relationships or has failed to acknowledge that there is more than one pattern of love deserving the label.

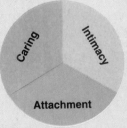

▲ **Rubin's model of love.** *Always present are the factors of attachment, intimacy and caring. They remain after the nonessentials of love have been stripped away.*

The popular picture of love between man and woman emphasizes romantic passion – and all too often gives rise to unrealistic expectations. The wider picture revealed by research suggests there are more satisfying ways of thinking about love.

with the object of our love becomes our primary interest in life – we think constantly about the person concerned and want to spend all our time with them. Companionate love, on the other hand is much less intense, is calmer and more relaxed; it leaves room for other people and other pleasures than romantic ones.

Second, companionate lovers can be quite content with less frequent and less intense sexual contact than passionate lovers

Third, passionate love rarely seems to last. Companionate love is more stable, resting on a less fragile attachment based on respect, admiration and trust. Trust is probably the most important characteristic of the relationship. Companionate lovers are more careful to honor their promises to each other and protect each other's feelings.

The passionate and companionate are, of course, not mutually exclusive. Almost invariably, both factors are present. It is simply a matter of which predominates in a given relationship.

Love is multifaceted

The sociologist J. A. Lee, considers that these two factors can be usefully distinguished in their turn from several others. He proposes six in all, each with its corresponding love-style. His friendship love (*storge*) and passionate love (*eros*) take in the main points of Berscheid and Walster's pair, but he also identifies possessive love (*mania*); selfless love (*agape*); practical love (*pragma*) and game-playing love (*ludus*).

For Lee, passionate love focuses strongly on physical attraction and sensual satisfaction. Those who are most in

its grip look for rapidly developing, emotionally intense relationships – and they tend to idealize their partners.

Friendship love is a caring, concerned love growing out of friendship based on similar interests and pursuits. For those who love mainly in this way, the best part of love consists in making a home and raising children together, in a long-term relationship founded on mutual trust.

Possessive lovers are insecure and dependent, and so tend to be anxious and fearful of being rejected. They feel physically upset when things go wrong and may even use illness as a way of gaining attention. They become jealous very easily.

Selfless lovers are content to sacrifice their own interests in favor of their partner's, to give without expecting a return. They cannot be happy unless their partner is also happy. They are prepared to share all they have, and are vulnerable to exploitation.

Practical lovers take a hard-headed view of relationships, seeing them as based on satisfactory rewards rather than romantic attraction. A typical partner will have a suitable background, a good job and the makings of a good parent. Game-playing love is seen as fun, as a game, not to be taken too seriously, and involving little real

207

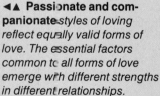

◄▲ **Passionate and companionate** styles of loving reflect equally valid forms of love. The essential factors common to all forms of love emerge with different strengths in different relationships.

■ **Giving and receiving love.** *Mature and immature love are often distinguished in terms of the extent to which a partner actively contributes to a relationship or passively accepts its benefits. For a child, love is being loved, and many adults apparently continue to think of love in this way. For mature adults, however, love means giving love, as well as receiving it. At least one partner in a love relationship must be prepared to give. In failing relationships, people who feel unloved will often come to discover that they themselves are not giving love, and that their partner feels similarly unloved.*

DISCOVERING YOUR OWN LOVE PROFILE

■ *Using Lee's six-factor analysis of love (see main text), Clyde Hendrick and his colleagues asked people questions designed to show the relative prominence of each factor in an individual's "love profile." An abbreviated version of the questionnaire is given here.*

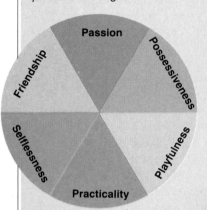

■ *By rating each of the following statements on a 1–5 scale (1 = strongly disagree; 2 = disagree; 3 = neutral; 4 = agree; 5 = strongly agree), your own love profile should begin to become apparent – at least in rough outline. Scoring instructions are given after the list of statements:*

1 *You cannot love unless you have first had a caring relationship for a while.*
2 *The best kind of love grows out of a long friendship.*
3 *Kissing, cuddling and sex should not be rushed into; they will happen naturally when intimacy has grown.*
4 *Love is really deep friendship, not a mysterious, mystical emotion.*
5 *I believe that "love at first sight" is possible.*
6 *We kissed each other soon after we met because we both wanted to.*

7 *Usually the first thing that attracts my attention to a person is a pleasing appearance.*
8 *Strong physical attraction is one of the best things about being in love.*
9 *When things are not going right with us, my stomach gets upset.*
10 *Once when I thought a love affair was over, I saw him or her again and the old feelings came surging back.*
11 *If my partner ignores me for a while, I sometimes do really stupid things to try to get his or her attention.*
12 *When my partner does not pay attention to me, I feel sick all over.*

13 *I try to use my own strength to help my partner through difficult times, even when he or she is behaving foolishly.*
14 *I am usually willing to sacrifice my own wishes in favor of my partner's.*
15 *If my partner had a baby by someone else, I would want to raise it and care for it as if it were my own.*
16 *I would rather break up with my partner than stand in his or her way.*
17 *For practical reasons, I would consider what he or she is going to become before I commit myself.*
18 *You should plan your life before choosing a partner.*

19 *A main consideration in choosing a partner is how he or she reflects on my family.*
20 *I would not date anyone that I would not want to fall in love with.*
21 *At least once I had to plan carefully to keep two of my lovers from finding out about each other.*
22 *I can get over love affairs pretty easily and quickly.*
23 *My partner would get upset if he or she knew some of the things I have done with other people.*
24 *What he or she does not know about me will not hurt my partner.*

■ **Scoring.** *Divide your total for statements 1–4 by 4. This is your score for the friendship factor. Recent surveys indicate that the average score for women is 2.9. For men it is 2.5.*

Similarly, divide your total for statements 5–8 by 4. This is your score for the passionate factor. The average score for men is 2.9, for women 2.7.

To get your score for the possessive factor, divide your total for statements 9–12 by 4. The average for women is 2.6, for men 2.2

To get your score for the selflessness factor, divide your total for statements 13–16 by 4. The average for women is 2.5, for men 2.3.

To get your score for the practical factor, divide your total for statements 17–20 by 4. The average for women is 2.1, for men 1.8.

To get your score for the game-playing factor, divide your total for a statements 21–24 by 4. The average for men is 1.9, for women 1.7.

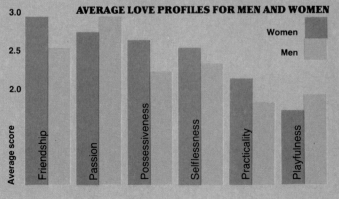

AVERAGE LOVE PROFILES FOR MEN AND WOMEN

Women

Men

Average score: Friendship | Passion | Possessiveness | Selflessness | Practicality | Playfulness

(3.0, 2.5, 2.0)

■ **The average love profiles** of men and women differ in interesting ways. Surveys testing for Lee's factors show that women tend toward a more caring, practical love than men, with an element of possessiveness. Men are more interested in the passionate, game-playing kinds of love. Profiles of the average male and female responses to the questions related to each kind of love are shown in the chart. The common view of women as romantic and of men as practical seems to be wrong: men are the romantics and women are the practical ones.

Research also shows that women fall in love earlier and more often than men before the age of 20. Once past this age, men fall in love more easily than women, while women fall out of love sooner than men. Women are much tougher when it comes to ending a relationship.

Thinking of love not as one thing but as several factors interacting, each of which can be assessed separately, makes us more aware of our own pattern of loving, of the fact that it changes with time, and of how it might be changed for the better.

commitment. Ludic lovers like to flirt, to keep their partners guessing, and they tend to move in and out of love affairs quickly and easily.

Love is dynamic

Yet another way of thinking about love has recently been proposed by psychologist Robert Sternberg. He returns to a three-aspect approach. What he calls his "triangular model" of love (see diagram, below) has intimacy at one corner, passion at another and commitment at the third.

Different styles of loving and the changing character of love are then visualized as a shifting center of gravity within the triangle, depending on the shifting balance between intimacy, passion and commitment. Lee's friendship love, for example, is weighted heavily toward commitment and intimacy. It can be balanced by passion, but it does not need to be. An almost wholly passionate love, on the other hand, weakly weighted toward commitment, would be highly unstable.

People are not tied to only one kind of love. With one partner a person may encounter mainly friendship love; with another the same person may discover more romantic passion. Neither pattern of loving is closer than the other to being "true" love: they are simply different, and so are all of the infinitely many other combinations.

Most love changes over time. A relationship may start as a passionate attraction or as a flirtatious game, depending on the lovers' personalities. As matters progress, elements of possessive love (high both in passion and commitment) may start to emerge. After this, passionate and possessive love may give way to a calmer, more relaxed relationship, as friendship love develops. Then care for long-term stability may focus attention more on shared concerns in a flourishing of practical love, an intensification of commitment.

This, of course, is just one possible progression; an arranged marriage might start with a strong concern for practical considerations and later move on to show passionate and possessive qualities. The unique character of each experience of love unfolds through time.

Passionate love, when initially present, provides the strongest possible motivation to form a relationship; but the companionate forms of love are more likely to sustain it in the long term. More than 50 percent of young couples in Western countries express the expectation that their own love will continue to be romantic throughout life. But this dream does not usually come true. We need to be aware of and prepared for changes in our feelings for our partners, and in their feelings for us. If the original sense of passion fades or changes, the relationship is not necessarily dying, for the original sense of trust and commitment may grow and flourish. **RG**

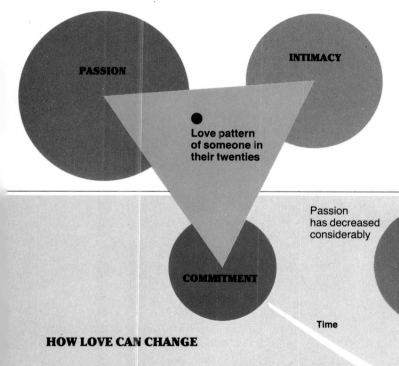

HOW LOVE CAN CHANGE

▶ Sternberg's model of love stresses the dynamic nature of love – how it can change, as time passes. It also gives special prominence to the dimension of commitment. A sense of commitment, which may only be weakly present in the early stages of a relationship, can fluctuate widely as it develops. A point may come, however, at which we decide that we really do love somebody and feel very strongly committed to keeping the relationship going. A strong sense of commitment is one of the tests of mature love and is a major factor in love relationships that endure in later life.

PASSION **INTIMACY**

Love pattern of someone in their twenties

COMMITMENT

Passion has decreased considerably

Time

PASSION **INTIMACY**

Love pattern of the same person in their forties

Intimacy has increased slightly

Commitment has greatly increased

COMMITMENT

Patterns of Jealousy

LOVE and friendship bring out many of our best and most positive emotions, but they also have a possessive element that can lead to feelings of jealousy. These feelings are so common that when respondents were asked if they were prone to jealousy, 50 percent labeled themselves as jealous people. We may be jealous of potential romantic rivals or of the demands that a partner's family makes on their time or affections. A child may be jealous of the attention a parent pays to other family members, or jealous of a friend's friends. Very few of us fail to display these feelings at some time in our lives.

Jealousy can have devastating effects on relationships. In a survey of lapsed friendships 57 percent of respondents gave their former friend's jealous or critical attitude toward the respondent's other relationships as a "moderate to very important" reason for the break-up. A further 22 percent said these were of some importance in the break-up. Couples usually expect an exclusive commitment to each other and some jealousy of potential rivals is often taken as a healthy sign of this commitment. However, many couples, as well, break up because one partner becomes so jealous that the other is unable to tolerate it. In addition, jealousy may lead to violent behavior; violence is an issue for nearly a third of couples who seek counseling.

Who is prone to jealousy?

For an event to provoke a jealous reaction it must first be seen as a threat to the relationship. The threat does not even have to be real – an imaginary threat can produce the same effect. To take an example, suppose that you pick up the telephone and accidentally overhear someone of your own sex speaking in what could be an intimate fashion to your partner. How is this event to be interpreted? Some people might see it as talk between friends or colleagues, while others might see it as evidence of a romantic liaison. Depending on the interpretation that the event receives, the same incident may create feelings of jealousy in one person but not in another. Which interpretation you make may reflect your personality, your current state of morale, the state of your relationship or all of these at once.

The study of personality suggests that, except for rare extreme cases, few people are chronically jealous. Some may be slightly more prone to jealousy, but there is very little evidence that jealousy is a personality trait apparent in all situations and relationships. There are, however, some personality traits that appear to make jealousy more likely.

Of these characteristics the most prominent is low self-esteem, or feelings of inadequate self-worth. People with low self-esteem are usually more dependent on their friends and intimate partners than those with high self-esteem. They will therefore feel more menaced by potential threats to their relationships. They will also react to a perceived threat by being more protective of the relationship.

The more materially dependent we are on the other person, the more likely we are to be jealous, but the dependency effect is stronger still in the case of emotional dependency, where there is little self-esteem to fall back on

Jealousy can undermine friendships and intimate partnerships, and can put a serious strain upon family relationships. It is less likely to arise in those who have self-esteem, feel secure and do not feel excessive emotional dependence.

if the relationship breaks up. This leads us to watch our partner's actions more carefully and to see more occasions as threatening; we are also less likely to give the benefit of the doubt in interpreting these situations.

The jealousy that a small child so easily feels about the attention that its parents give to its brothers and sisters (see *Ch18*) also reflects dependency. Parents can combat rivalry between their children by giving them reassurances that there is room for all of them to achieve their needs within the family. Giving an older child a valuable role to play in the care of younger ones helps them to feel confident that they are contributors to the well-being of the family and are not *merely* dependents.

Insecurity about how the other person views us will usually make us more jealous. The fact that jealousy decreases as we spend more time in a relationship is probably due to an increased sense of security about the other's feelings for us.

Those with high self-esteem are usually less jealous. However, self-esteem is not simply a trait of personality. Anyone's morale may be temporarily deflated. In such a situation, an overheard telephone call would be more likely to provoke jealousy. During the crisis mid-teen years, when their reported self-esteem is lowest, adolescents feel very dependent on their same-sex friends and are prone to break up over feelings of jealousy.

The threatened relationship itself may affect how dependent, and so how jealous, we will feel. If our relationship with the other person is equitable – that is, if we are about equal with them in what we put in and get out of the relationship – then jealousy is much less likely to occur (see *Ch31*).

Attitude and trust

With couples, sexual attitudes and behavior influence jealousy. If sexual exclusivity is not important, then a perceived threat to the sexual exclusivity of the relationship will not cause jealousy. What is not clear is whether a strong belief in or desire for sexual exclusivity makes a person more jealous or less.

An important part of the answer to this question concerns previous relationships and their link with current expectations and feelings. If you strongly desire sexual exclusivity and your partner has had an affair in the past, you are more likely to interpret events as threats to your relationship and to feel more jealous. It has been found that people who believe firmly in monogamous marriage experience less

◀ **Tempers flare** at a dance on the Isle of Lewis in Scotland. A man who believes that his partner is being pursued by another man is more likely to take action – including violent action – against the interloper than a woman would, but either may feel an impulse to assert their rights. If he believes that she is pursuing another man, he may respond by seeing other women, to raise his self-esteem.

▲ **A skeptical reception** for words of reassurance. You are less likely to perceive a situation

LOVE AND VULNERABILITY

In our relations with most people, we preserve a certain distance and maintain our separateness. It is one of the devices by which we unconsciously protect our self-esteem. But the caring love relationship differs from all other relationships on precisely this point. Partners reject this separateness and seek as full as possible a sharing of experience. The stance of self-revealing openness they are impelled to adopt, however, exposes them to special injury. Their defenses are down and their self-esteem is acutely vulnerable. If one partner loses faith in or is betrayed in some way by the other, the emotional consequences can be disastrous. Even a predominantly caring love has its passionate and possessive sides, and the notoriously fine dividing lines between love and jealousy and between jealousy and hatred are all too easily crossed.

in a jealous way if the trust you feel in a partner prevents you from seeing the situation as a threat to your relationship. Trust depends partly on how well you know your partner, and it increases with time – the longer you are together, the more secure you feel. Trust may be more difficult to extend if you are going through a period of low self-esteem or if you are very emotionally dependent on your partner.

jealousy. However, if they are confronted with a cut and dried instance of infidelity that threatens their relationship beyond all doubt, they will be more jealous than will people whose belief in monogamy is less firm.

Finally, people whose partners encourage them to have an affair with the opposite sex by maintaining that they would not be jealous should be skeptical. They can even take it as advance notice of their partner's likely infidelity. Research shows that those who intend to become involved with someone else often claim that they would not feel jealous if their partner were to have an affair.

Trust appears to play a major role in determining feelings of jealousy both in intimate and in other relationships. Couples whose mutual trust is high are less jealous – anyone with a firm belief in monogamy may be so trusting that it is unlikely they will view any situation as a potential threat to the relationship. However, once that trust has been broken by undeniable infidelity, jealousy will occur. In a similar fashion, the knowledge that your partner has had an affair in the past may increase the likelihood of jealousy because you will be less trusting and more likely to interpret ambiguous situations as a threat.

Sex differences in jealousy

While there is no difference in the total amount of jealousy displayed by men and women there do appear to be differences in what makes people jealous, and in their responses to it. In evaluating threats to their relationships, women are more threatened by their partner's lack of attention and by time spent away from them. Men are most likely to feel jealous of their partner's positive attentions to another person.

Men and women not only differ in their responses to the events that make them jealous but also in their interpretations of why the events occurred. Women are more likely than men to blame themselves, and, consistently with this, to react with depression. Men tend to blame their partner and are more likely than women to react with anger. Men are also likely to deny that a threat exists or that they are, in fact, jealous. Once they admit to being jealous, they are likely to follow strategies designed to raise their self-esteem, such as seeing other women. Women more often respond to jealousy by attempting to improve the relationship.

The responses that men and women display when jealous have implications for those who might use the tactic of inducing jealousy in order to improve a relationship. Women are more likely to try this than men. But given that the response of men who are jealous will generally be to pursue other partners, the effect might be the exact opposite of what was intended.

Responding to jealousy

People respond to jealousy in any of three ways. For some, it is by withdrawal or avoidance. Others opt for an interpretation of events that play down their importance. And the third way is to make greater efforts to bolster the relationship.

Those whose answer is to interpret the situation often deny that there is in fact a problem or that what they are experiencing is jealousy. One example of this comes in a

212

◄ **Sibling rivalry.** *Different families afford different levels of material support for their children, but one benefit that every child looks for and may envy a brother or sister for receiving is a mother's reassurance and affection.*

► **An angry rebuke.** *Has it appeared to the one partner in this relationship that the other has not been paying him the right kinds of attention? Jealous males tend to blame their partner for not behaving correctly. Jealous females blame themselves for failing to hold their partner's attention. They are less likely to react with anger.*

Couples with a high degree of mutual trust are less jealous. Those who are confident that they share a firm belief in monogamy may be trusting enough to view almost no situation as posing a threat to their relationship.

recent study. A woman stated that she had never felt jealous during the ten years she had spent in an open relationship with her husband. When the researchers asked her what she experienced when her husband was with another woman, she replied that she only felt "a stabbing pain in her heart, not jealousy." Those who take the third way of responding seek to increase communication with their partner. This they do usually by being as open as possible in addressing outstanding issues and by attempting to set up new lines of communication.

While these strategies are fairly common, not all of them, and particularly not withdrawal, do much to reduce jealousy. Other ways may be more effective in helping us

cope with the emotion. One might be to assess whether the perception of a threat is in fact accurate. Another might be to decide that, in spite of the situation, the relationship may still be worthwhile pursuing.

It is also important that self-esteem and self-assessment should not be made totally dependent on the results of one relationship. The more we rely on a single close primary relationship as a source of self-esteem, the more jealous we are likely to be. If it is another who suffers from unreasonable jealousy, your own efforts to give them better self-esteem and to feel more confident may help greatly.

Engaging in activities that will rebuild trust can both protect relationships from jealousy and help them to recover. Unfortunately, perhaps, the rebuilding of trust may involve placing yourself and your partner in similar situations to that which originally provoked your jealousy. **BE**

213

Enjoying a Sexual Relationship

A COUPLE'S sexual activity is one of the most powerful expressions of the intimacy they share. Thus the state of their relationship as a whole will tend to affect this activity, and in turn the sexual satisfaction they provide to each other will influence their relationship. Thus sexual satisfaction can be an indicator of the health of the relationship, but caution must be used in measuring satisfaction. Frequency and style of lovemaking are elements in a *particular* relationship. They are matters that should be negotiated by you and your partner and not decided by social standards.

Frequency of sexual activity

How often a couple have sexual intercourse depends on each partner's individual preferences and circumstances as well as on the state of the relationship itself. The appetite of each partner has nothing to do with gender – the average man and woman have equally powerful sex drives.

There is evidence that sexual activity may decline somewhat as a relationship continues. The novelty wears off. In addition, physical and psychological demands – such as the arrival of children and increasing responsibilities at work – can influence the desire and ability of a couple to have sex as frequently as they once did.

Contrary to popular opinion, sexual interest does not decline with age. The well-known studies by Kinsey and,

later, Masters and Johnson found that older people were still sexually active, although it was suggested that they may become less so as they grow older. More recently, Americans between the ages of 50 and 93 were asked to fill in a questionnaire about their sex lives. When the results were examined, researchers found that the middle-aged and elderly have an interest in and openness about sexual activity that is unrestricted by age. In fact, they are sexually active right through the age-range and in as wide a variety of ways as the young.

It appears that whether or not we continue to have a satisfactory sexual relationship as we grow older depends less on the physical consequences of aging than on our attitudes toward sex, and on our belief that sex can continue to be a perfectly natural and enjoyable part of the relationship as long as we want it to be. It can also be a renewal of intimacy that hard-pressed couples with demanding children and demanding careers may look forward to at a later, more relaxed time of life.

The meaning of sex within a relationship

Is there any way in which the sexual quality of a relationship can be measured? While it is possible to assess the frequency of intercourse, this does not always reveal a couple's satisfaction with one another. Since feelings about

Sexual satisfaction can be an indicator of the health of a relationship. What is satisfying, however, is a matter to be negotiated by you and your partner. It is not a question to be decided by social standards.

sex are often a direct indication of satisfaction, it is more productive to look closely at the meaning of sex within the context of a couple's whole relationship.

Sex has a different meaning for different couples. For example, in the United States it has been found that unmarried people who live together seem to make sex a more important feature of their relationships than married couples do, yet they see it more as an essentially physical function and less as an expression of emotional attachment.

Many married couples regard their sexual activity as prompted more by love than by pure sexual desire.

What sex means to a couple is influenced by other nonsexual aspects of their relationship as well. Sex may be seen as a reward to be given or withheld depending on satisfaction of other needs. It may be seen as a solemn duty to perform or a privilege to receive by right. These views will vary from one person to another and from time to time within a relationship.

When partners differ in their attitudes toward their relationship and their expectations of it, or in their needs, sexual relations may be unsatisfactory and put a further strain on the relationship.

As in other aspects of relationships, a very useful way of looking at and evaluating dissatisfaction is to view it in terms of rewards. If partners feel that they do not receive enough pleasure and reward from sex, or are not compensated for a lack of sexual rewards by other things within the relationship, they are likely to feel dissatisfied. Partners need to feel not only that they as individuals are being sufficiently rewarded, but also that there is a balance in the rewards for both of them – that what they give is valued.

It is important to ensure that, on the whole, sex provides mutual and comparable satisfaction – that both partners' needs, wants, likes and dislikes are taken into account. This in turn means that couples have to be able to express and explore their sexual preferences and interests safely and comfortably within the relationship.

Dissatisfaction and the balance of power

Problems that cause sexual dissatisfaction often concern the balance of power in a relationship – whether one partner makes most of the decisions or whether both have an equal say. In the sphere of sexual activity, this usually involves the

215

▲ **Sexual dissatisfaction** *arises when partners do not share the same attitude to sex and have different expectations of the relationship*

◄ **Each sexual relationship is unique.** *Frequency and pre-ferred style of lovemaking can vary enormously from one mutually satisfying relationship to another, and there is no common prescription for sexual happiness. Interest in sex does not necessarily decline with age, and is not necessarily stronger in the male partner.*

▶ **Making life's adjustments.** *Throughout a relationship there will be changes in the partners' lives that have repercussions for their sexual satisfaction. The arrival of an infant, extra pressure at work or any other form of stress will contribute to a decline in the couple's ability to express themselves sexually. Both frequency and enjoyment may be affected. At other times, changes will work in favor of a satisfying relationship.*

question of initiating and refusing sexual advances. In a good relationship, the balance of power is about equal – both partners feel able to initiate or decline sex. Problems arise when the balance of power is not equal *and* one partner feels that their rights are not being recognized.

If a more dominant partner initiates sex, the other may feel that they cannot refuse to participate. If a more submissive partner tries to initiate sex, the other may feel free to reject the invitation if they do not feel like taking part. However, people will quite often deliberately refuse such a request in order to express their power over their partners.

In what way an imbalance of power is harmful to the participants depends to some extent on how each of them views sex. If it is seen purely as a physical act, a partner who feels compelled to take part against their will is likely to feel used, but when it is seen as an expression of love, a refusal to "make love" may be taken as demonstrating a lack of affection.

It is, however, preferable for partners to recognize one another's rights while asserting their own – "You have the right to refuse me, but I have an equal right to make the request" and vice versa. Equality of initiation and refusal reflects a balance of esteem.

People who are emotionally sensitive are more capable of initiating sex successfully. Because they are more likely to be aware of the other person's emotional state, they are more likely to use the right approach at the right time. In the same way, their sensitivity enables them to recognize when *not* to impose on an unwilling partner and when not to refuse because their partner would view this as rejection.

Expressiveness and attractiveness

The way we express ourselves physically during sexual activity seems to be associated with how much satisfaction we get from the relationship. For example, it appears that the amount of kissing during sexual intercourse is a good measure of the strength and quality of a relationship. About 80 percent of couples regard kissing as an indispensable part of intercourse. In addition, people kiss far more during sex if their overall relationship is working well. If one or both partners are experiencing tension at work or in some other aspect of their daily lives, the amount of kissing during intercourse declines, but it increases again when tensions are reduced.

The way in which couples achieve orgasm also appears to have implications for a relationship. Once a decision to make love has been taken, men are more likely than women to seek an orgasm by any available means. Women usually prefer penetration and full sexual intercourse.

This may be because intercourse demands more involve-

216

▶ **Emotional sensitivity** *is an important factor in initiating sex successfully. Being aware of your partner's emotional state helps you to know what is the right approach and when to use it. It is important to recognize when not to impose. Knowing when not to refuse – because, for example, your partner's self-esteem may suffer from what they see as a rejection – also requires emotional sensitivity.*

People kiss more during sex if their overall relationship is working well. If one or both partners are experiencing tension at work or in some other aspect of their daily lives, kissing during intercourse declines.

ment from both partners than some other sexual acts. If both partners are involved and physically united, they may also feel united in a more metaphorical way that particularly expresses their love. Thus for many people – and especially for women – the act of intercourse as a whole, rather than just orgasm, is at once physical, emotional and spiritual.

How often and in what way you express your sexuality can depend on how physically attractive you seem – to others and to yourself. And this also seems to be associated with sexual satisfaction.

Physically attractive people tend to lead more varied sex lives. They have a larger number of partners, and within the confines of a given relationship, they experience and practice a wider variety of sexual techniques. For example, oral sex and the female superior position are more likely in couples where one or both partners are judged very physically attractive.

Just how physically attractive we find our partners can affect the frequency of intercourse. Some 80 percent of people who are satisfied with their sex lives also find their partner appealing, and there seems to be a correlation between these two findings – in a significant number of cases in which a couple has little sex, one or both partners attribute this to the fact that they do not find the other physically attractive.

Improving the relationship

There are several strategies that a couple can use to improve the role that sex plays in their relationship. For example, by participating in your partner's preferred sexual practices, you can show your concern for them and for the relationship. Simple matters such as taking good care of your body will enhance your attractiveness and your enjoyment of each other. Allowing yourself to accept and explore a range of physical sensations will also increase pleasure and satisfaction.

A sexual relationship can often be improved if a couple are more open to emotional contact. For instance, you can be more willing to express your feelings openly, more ready to reveal your deeper self, to share your thoughts, fears and concerns and to show your partner how much you value them. As a relationship develops psychologically, both partners will usually become more physically intimate and, therefore, even closer emotionally. **SD**

217

◄ **Physical attractiveness** depends partly on the gifts of nature. Within a sexual relationship, however, it is largely a matter of body care and self-presentation. Simply by accepting your body the way it is, you are more likely to behave in a sexually attractive way toward your partner. Feeling good about your physique may mean doing exercises and changing your diet in order to lose (or gain) weight to bring yourself closer to an ideal of the attractive. It may be worthwhile, however, to find out first exactly what is your partner's ideal of attractiveness. The stereotyped physical ideals that we see in television commercials and in magazine photographs do not necessarily match everyone's personal taste. Surveys show that about 80 percent of people who are satisfied with their sex lives also find their partner physically appealing. In only a minority of these cases do people meet exacting standards of beauty.

The Married Couple

A GREAT majority of adults in the industrialized world – in fact, about 90 percent – will be married at some time in their lives. Of those who do not, some may choose to remain single, but others will have no choice. An alarming number who marry will divorce, but this is not because marriage itself has lost its attraction – instead people give up on particular relationships and try again. For example, of the four out of ten American marriages that end in divorce, 80 percent are preludes to further unions.

The "perfect" marriage

Every society has its own definitions of what a perfect marriage should be. In the Western world, it seems that a husband and wife have a perfect marriage if they love each other, have no other sexual partner, display trust, loyalty and intimacy, confide in each other, show mutual respect, are willing to listen to their partner's concerns, and agree on their children's upbringing.

However, from time to time the balance of social expectations shifts. For example, a study carried out in 1986 showed that 74 percent of American couples rate "equality in the relationship" as an important component of marriage.

We can be fairly sure that their great-grandparents (and particularly their great-grandfathers) did not place the same value on this.

Despite such changes, there does seem to be almost universal agreement about what marriage should be, as demonstrated by such common statements as "You shouldn't let him/her treat you like that." In addition, Western society, unlike many other cultures, almost always expresses its expectations of marriage in terms of love and romance – rather than in practicalities such as "Will he/she be a good parent/provider/homemaker?" However, there is evidence that, when considering marriage, men and women are more willing to opt for something other than the intensities of love than our marital folklore would seem to suggest (see box p219).

Despite this, throughout daily life, our friends, our families, and the media all reinforce an idealized image of marriage, and this can affect our thinking as to what we should put up with or demand. Such influences are remarkably stable. For instance, in spite of the fact that today it is not unusual for both partners to have careers, a majority of working wives still record the greatest marital

THE COHABITING OPTION

■ Of those people who decide not to marry, some will decide to live together, or cohabit – that is, share a bedroom with a person of the opposite sex for more than four nights a week. By this definition 5 percent of the entire population of the United States cohabits, but in special populations (such as college students), almost one in four cohabits or has done so in the past.

For some, cohabiting is a test of the prospect for a successful marriage – a tryout before they get married; for others, it replaces marriage. Between 47 and 70 percent of all American couples who marry will cohabit for at least a short while beforehand, while 15 to 30 percent of those who are "replacing" marriage will eventually marry anyway – especially, it seems,

when the woman becomes pregnant.

Those who cohabit are more independent and aggressive, and they tend to value nontraditional relationships (although, in practice, the division of household tasks is about the same as for married couples). Although cohabitors who eventually marry are somewhat more likely to get divorced than those who do not live together before the wedding, this may be because they are simply more nonconformist as people. One study has found that cohabitors are practical rather than romantic and less attracted to the idea of marriage. This would mean that the marital relationship is a smaller part of their lives, and they would not be as likely to put up with it "for better or for worse." **SD**

► **Borrowing the symbolism** of a confetti wedding, a young couple express commitment to each other in a strikingly more informal setting. Participation in a social rite such as a wedding gives both the couple and others a focal point at which to begin the major phase of their adjustment to the new relationship.

We all desire a perfect marriage but all have to adjust to a reality that can never fully match the expectations we begin with. Some realities of marriage are unexpectedly stressful. Others are unexpectedly rewarding.

satisfaction when they perceive their husbands as superior to themselves in intelligence, competence, professional success, and income – just as their own mothers would have done.

Expectations and reality

Given the importance of marriage in society, and its significance in personal terms, it is not surprising that people approach it with some anxiety. A recent study shows that steady couples of college age who are about to get married for the first time are nervous about living up to their (and others') expectations about marriage. This anxiety centers specifically on two things. First, they are worried that they will not have both security *and* excitement in marriage; and second, they doubt the possibility of having a fulfilling experience that will also live up to popular culture's ideal of romantic marriage. Couples like these are unsure about whether they will be capable of providing and receiving all the expected undying love, intimacy and support in the real circumstances of a real marriage – after the honeymoon is over.

Courtship prepares you for becoming married, but it does not prepare you for *being* married. "Being married" involves more than just loving each other; there are further requirements.

Each couple begins marriage with a variety of explicit and implicit expectations about the role each partner will play – what they think a husband or wife *is* and *does*. These expectations are influenced first and foremost by how each partner views their own parents' relationship and second by what each partner perceives as socially acceptable.

If the husband's and wife's expectations differ substantially from each other's, the satisfaction either can derive from the marriage will be diminished. If, for example, the husband expects to have a traditional marriage in which he works and his wife stays at home, and the wife expects a more liberal relationship in which all responsibilities are shared equally, conflict is bound to arise.

Role expectations may, of course, change over the life of a relationship. Thus, both partners may begin a marriage with similar expectations – say, for a traditional relationship

▲ **Equality in the relationship** is rated by three-quarters of Americans as an important part of a happy marriage. Achieving it is an ambitious undertaking and success contributes to how much a husband and wife are admired as a couple, especially if they combine this with setting an example of long-term harmony and lasting stability.

NOT FOR LOVE ALONE

■ *In the past, marriage was considered to be so important that, according to a survey of American men and women carried out in 1967, over two-thirds of women would have married a man they did not love, as long as everything else about the relationship was satisfactory.*

Attitudes have changed somewhat since then. While one recent study gives figures of only 4 percent of women and 1.7 percent of men stating that they would marry for reasons other than love, others have come up with around 16 percent for both sexes. However, even if we take the most conservative position and accept the 4 percent and 1.7 percent figures, this would add up to some 2,850,000 adults who approach marriage from a purely pragmatic viewpoint. They are not alone in taking this attitude. For a variety of reasons, many cultures look on the practical rather than the romantic side of marriage (see p228). **S D**

Each couple begins their marriage with implicit and explicit expectations about the role a wife or a husband will play. These expectations are influenced by social standards and the example of the couple's own parents.

– but changes in the needs or desires of one partner may put pressure on the other to adjust to a new role. This might occur, for example, when the wife tires of being a housewife, and goes against her husband's expectations of wifely duties by pursuing a career.

Most couples enter marriage (or other close relationships) with the expectation that romantic love will continue throughout its duration, that the powerful, pleasurable feelings that were part of the initial courtship will last. This unrealistic hope is constantly emphasized on television and in films and romantic novels, at the expense of the less romantic but equally important adjustments and sacrifices that couples in successful relationships are required to make in their daily lives.

The idealized cultural image of marriage also includes unrealistic beliefs about the qualities of the partner.

However, the illusion of perfection is often shattered within the first year of marriage, and disappointment with a partner often blurs into disappointment with the marriage.

It is important to be aware of the powerful effect our expectations can have in determining how satisfied we are in our relationships, and how much effort we must expend in redefining them if we are to salvage a relationship that has begun to sour.

Making the adjustment

Although the distinctions between being unmarried and married are not as great as they once were, marriage *feels* different even if, during it, a couple live and behave exactly as before. When you are married, you are expected to act

■**Wedding ceremonies**, *like the marriages they formalize, may be impulsive or intricately arranged, but inevitably they symbolize the traditions on* which the marriage is to be grounded. TOP LEFT *The sword of Sikh manhood. A Moscow couple and their wedding party* BOTTOM LEFT *brave the January* winds in Red Square to lay a wreath on Lenin's tomb. ABOVE LEFT *Flowers and orthodox wedding dress at a Jewish Orthodox ceremony.* ABOVE RIGHT *Streamlined informality in Nevada, where convenient marriage laws attract out-of-state couples, and weddings are an industry.*

in a certain, different way, and other people will treat you differently, too. For example, if you are going steady, you may be invited out on your own, but once you are married, your partner will be implicitly included in any invitation you receive.

Being married also means working out a routine for conducting a life together. By the time most couples get married, they know what they like to do together and the amount of time each needs to be on his or her own. Following the wedding, they will also have to decide how much time each must devote to sharing and carrying out household chores. These initial arrangements and routines may change as the marriage develops, but whatever arrangements a married couple have, it is important that they suit the attitudes and style of each partner.

Couples who share chores equally seem to be happiest. However, household routines usually develop in such a way that, after a certain amount of time, husbands take their leisure when they have finished their own chores and are not very likely to help their wives. There is some evidence that this state of affairs is changing, but even with nontraditional couples who attempt to share household work, equality is usually brought about by the woman reducing the amount of work she does rather than the man increasing his. It also appears that the birth of children propels the partners back to a more traditional way of dividing up chores.

Mothers who work outside the home may feel especially taxed by an unfair division of household labor. Working mothers with preschool-age children spend less time relaxing and sleeping than do either their husbands or full-time homemakers. In fact, recent statistics indicate that working mothers spend almost twice as many hours per day engaged in housekeeping and parenting than do their husbands. The latter tend to "help" more when their wives are working, but they do not take on the primary responsibility for any more tasks. In fact, the older children in the family are as likely as their fathers to assume extra responsibilities when their mothers work.

It seems likely that the discrepancy between husbands' and wives' involvement in domestic tasks contributes to the decline in marital satisfaction. Working women usually feel more satisfied with their marriages and pleased with their partners when they perceive equity in the execution of

LOVE BEFORE AND AFTER

■ *In the first year of marriage, couples do not make the same fuss over each other as they once did. There is an overall decline in all of the loving activities listed here. Several months before they married, couples were asked how often each activity occurred. Researchers asked them the same question one year later, and an average decline for each form of affection was compiled. Surprisingly, no significant difference was found between couples living together for the first time only after marriage and those who had practiced trial marriage. Both experienced about the same decline in affection after the formalities of a wedding. Perhaps living together as an unmarried couple has too much of an element of excitement to be a true test of the real thing.* **RG**

AFFECTIONATE BEHAVIOR

	Change in frequency in first year of marriage
Your partner	
– approved or complimented you.	30% less often
– did or said something to make you laugh.	34% less often
– said "I love you."	44% less often
– initiated sex.	39% less often
– did something nice for you.	28% less often
The two of you	
– had sexual intercourse.	38% less often
– shared physical affection (apart from sexual intercourse).	39% less often
– shared emotions, feelings or problems.	34% less often
– talked about day's events.	6% less often

HONEYMOON

In the traditional lore of the Teutons, the ancient people of northern Europe, several "moons" (or months) follow a wedding. The honeymoon, or sweetest month, is followed by the absinthmoon, or bitterest month (absinth is wormwood). Each passing month becomes alternately less sweet and less bitter. This obscure but penetrating piece of folk wisdom seems to have a good deal of truth in it. After the initial glitter and excitement wear off, couples begin to get down to married life in earnest. The peak for divorce comes during the first three years, when the greatest reorganization of life is required as the partners adjust to their new roles. **SD**

The prospect of becoming a family is usually an exciting and welcome challenge. However, a small but consistent decrease in marital satisfaction is recorded after the birth of the first child, including a loss of romance.

household chores Thus, even a small contribution by husbands around he home can make a big difference to their wives' satisfaction with their relationship. **SD**

The impact of children

The arrival of children often has a dramatic effect on marital satisfaction, especially if a couple have unrealistic expectations about what impact they will have on their marriage. The more realistic a couple is about the changes that accompany the early years of parenting, the higher their chances of maintaining a good relationship.

When a baby is wanted, both partners usually feel strongly committed to their marriage and more loving toward each other during the pregnancy, and the prospect of becoming a family is seen as an exciting challenge. Yet, despite this, a couple's satisfaction with their marriage almost invariably declines after the birth of the first child. This decrease is small, but it is consistent. Couples who were very happy during the pregnancy do not suddenly become very unhappy, but if difficulties existed in the marriage before the baby was born, or if the pregnancy is ill-timed, the birth may create sufficient strain on the marriage to put it at risk.

The most noticeable changes in the marital relationship occur soon after the baby's arrival. This can be a particularly difficult time for mothers. About 80 percent will suffer from the short-lived "baby blues," which takes the form of weepiness and a feeling of vulnerability, and some 20 percent of these may succumb to fully fledged *postnatal depression* (see *Ch 17*).

In addition to any depression she may be experiencing, a woman usually has to make far more of an adjustment to the effects of a baby's arrival than her husband. One reason for this may be that she is primarily responsible for caring for the new infant. Because the husband generally continues to work, a large part of his day remains unaffected. However, when a woman has always worked, this abrupt change in her schedule may leave her feeling bored and socially isolated. If she has also given up a valued career, she may feel unfulfilled by the routines of child care, and uncertain about the wisdom of her choice.

VITALITY, CONGENIALITY OR CONFLICT?

■ Researchers distinguish five styles of stable marriage. A small minority of partnerships are instances of the "total marriage." In these, husband and wife share large numbers of practical, work-related and leisure interests and feel a great deal of enthusiasm for doing these things together.

A rare category is the less-than-total but "vital marriage," in which the relationship is still the most important focus of the partner's lives. They enjoy doing things together and lack interest in activities they do not share.

The "devitalized marriage" is more common – a formerly vital marriage has become dull and uninteresting. However, the partners are still content. They feel no impulse to seek more exciting relationships with other people.

The "passive-congenial marriage" is one that has never been vital, but which the partners find convenient.

The "conflict-habituated marriage" tolerates constant arguing. **RC**

DEFICIT MARRIAGE

■ One of the earliest potential sources of stress in a marriage is tied to each partner's reasons for getting married in the first place. Any marriage that is the result of what is known as a "deficit position" is likely to suffer from early disappointments. A deficit position occurs when people get married not so much because they are attracted to their partner, but because of what marriage allows them to avoid.

Examples of deficit reasons for getting married include leaving the parental home, escaping loneliness, avoiding career decisions, and getting rid of financial pressures. A general characteristic of such marriages is that they are the result of unhappiness in one or both partners, and the marriage is burdened by the pressure to compensate for this essential unhappiness. **IHG CAC**

◄ **The arrival of the first child** accelerates the loss of romance in a marriage. Both husband and wife show less positive behavior and affection to each other. To observers, the couple appear less involved with each other than they did during the pregnancy. The mother tells less to her husband about her feelings. Men feel more disappointment at this decline in romance than women do. They have higher romantic expectations of marriage and fathering does less to give them a new, preoccupying role than mothering gives to their wives.

The loss of romance

After the birth of a child, both husband and wife may feel that their partner shows less positive behavior and affection toward them. Women also admit that they tell their husbands less about how they are feeling about the marriage and what they need emotionally. The woman's feelings of love for her partner decrease and her feelings of ambivalence increase.

For *both* partners there is a change in the nature of the relationship, which now feels less like a friendship or a romance and more like a partnership. The decline in romance is particularly noticeable to husbands, possibly because men have a more romantic view of marriage, while women tend to be more practical. When new parents are observed in their homes, they seem less involved with one another than they were during the pregnancy, and they show less affection.

Psychologists have concluded that it is the birth of the first child that particularly changes the focus of a marriage. If either partner is insecure in the relationship, this shift in emphasis can be very unsettling. Husbands may be especially vulnerable to feelings of insecurity as they cease to be the primary focus of their wives' attention. Simply being aware that this is a normal part of the childrearing experience may help reduce any negative feelings experienced by either partner.

The way that a couple cope with their new roles as parents can have a lasting impact. Some ways of doing this are more effective than others in reducing marital strain. Although, in general, it is unwise to let your negative feelings out through a confrontation or argument, the opposite is also true. Ignoring a problem or putting up with an uncomfortable situation tends to intensify stress. The most effective ways of dealing with both marital and parenting problems are to remain committed to resolving difficulties and to become actively engaged in the search for solutions to them.

Despite the negative effect that the arrival of children can have on a marriage, this relationship is also a vital source of support for the couple during the first year of parenting. For example, studies have shown that a new mother's happiness and satisfaction with life are primarily determined by her satisfaction with her marriage.

Luckily, the arrival of subsequent children does not have as dramatic an impact on the family as does the birth of the first child, but marital satisfaction does decline – particularly for women, who become increasingly responsible for child care and household chores. **IHG VEW**

Other stresses and strains

As a couple's lives develop together, the nature of their relationship changes and the demands on them alter. They either adapt – and this may have the effect of bringing them closer together – or they fail to adapt and, as a consequence, are pushed further apart.

Insufficient finances can have a devastating effect on a marriage. If trying to meet financial obligations is a constant battle, the self-esteem of both partners suffers and the number of disappointments soars. Even when there are adequate financial resources, there may be differences in a couple's expectations about the management of money. If one partner lives by the philosophy of saving for a rainy day, while the other believes that money should be spent to satisfy immediate desires, problems are inevitable.

▶ **Organizing a home** *and the care of children make a couple into practical partners. The emphasis of the marital relationship shifts away from intimate bonding between husband and wife toward fulfillment of their role expectations. Satisfaction is derived from feeling that we are fulfilling our roles as parents and providers, from receiving our children's love and affection and from sharing the continuing love and affection of our partner. The latter is enhanced by supporting each other in practical concerns.*

Couples who spend more time together in leisure activities have more marital satisfaction. Time to be together, however, can be difficult to find when children need attention and work responsibilities are demanding.

Finding enough time to spend together can also be a problem. When the husband works and the wife is a full-time homemaker, he must balance the time he spends at work with the time he devotes to his family. In marriages where both husband and wife are actively and independently pursuing careers, there is even greater pressure on the couple to juggle their family and career responsibilities. Yet concerns about work can leave both partners with less energy to devote to their marriage, and problems can be created that actually originate in the workplace. It is therefore important that couples make time for each other, and learn to identify the sources of their stress and anxiety and not take out frustrations at work on their partners.

Conflicts between work and marriage may also arise when a career introduces one partner to new ideas and social circles that are not shared by the other. Unless a couple make a concerted effort to keep in touch with each other's career developments and maintain common interests and goals, they are likely to grow apart. Research has shown that partners who spend more time together in leisure activities have higher levels of marital satisfaction.

A breakdown in communication is one of the most common problems cited by people whose marriages have begun to come apart. This may result in a wall of silence or, alternatively, a raging battle in which painful wounds are inflicted. Compared with couples in distress, happily married couples talk to each other more often, discuss a wider range of topics including personal problems and areas of disagreement, and display greater sensitivity to each other's unspoken messages.

Unhappy couples are much more likely to express themselves ambiguously, or to conceal emotions. Partners often say one thing and look as if they are saying another. For instance, they may appear to be happy but feel sad, or they may sound controlled but be almost overcome with anger. Unhappy couples are much more likely to reciprocate negative emotions and not "let things drop": if one partner says something negative to the other, the latter will try to score a few points by being equally negative, rather than produce a soft answer that will ease anger.

Communicating through touch is also very important. Whereas physical intimacy may start declining quite soon after the wedding, good marriages seem to thrive on simpler, more casual touches (see *Ch 10*). **IHG CAC**

The "empty nest"

The pattern of family life undergoes a marked change when the children leave home and the parents are left in the "empty nest." How they experience this important stage in

▲ **Shared leisure** *gives the marriage partners opportunities to be a couple and not simply co-workers in childcare, homemaking and providing. Being together for fun relieves the boredom of practical responsibilities and helps partners to avoid being identified by each other as objects of the boredom that everyday married life can cause. Rediscovering formerly shared pastimes can be very beneficial to couples as their children come to be more independent, and so can the joint exploration of new hobbies and interests.*

CONFLICTS BETWEEN LOVE AND FRIENDSHIP

■ *Both friendships and intimate partnerships are supportive, but in practice there may well be tension between the two. They often compete for precious free time, and the pressure can come from either side. We have all seen a group of colleagues or sports fans tease one of their number who is leaving to fulfill some marital or family obligation. Marriage partners and lovers in their turn may feel slighted, threatened or irritated by their partner's outside social commitments. Many couples deal with these conflicts by including each other's friends in their own social circle.*

This is often at least partially successful in defusing potential problems. But as many casual friendships are concerned with specific aspects of our lives, say, a particular spare-time obsession, it can be difficult for a partner who does not share in the activity to share in the friendship. Where an intimate and a more casual relationship are in direct conflict, the intimate one usually takes precedence. Even where direct conflicts do not exist, the exclusivity which is so much a part of a romantic relationship often leads lovers and recently married couples to see less of, or

even abandon, many of their friends. This level of exclusivity does not last indefinitely, and after the initial romance, friends become as necessary as they were before. Parents with friends tend to have children who are more socially skilled, well adjusted and happy. If a marriage or affair deteriorates or breaks down completely friends can provide badly needed emotional support. Research indicates that partners who share a network of friends are less likely to break up than those who have separate friends. **BM**

their lives – as a serious loss or a welcomed freedom – depends to some extent on how much of their lives they have invested in their children while they were still at home.

In the past, many gave credence to the belief that the last child's departure from the home leaves a void – especially in the life of the mother, who responds to this event with a depressive reaction known as the "empty nest syndrome." Since the role of loss in the development of depression is well known, it is not surprising that some psychologists predicted that the departure, or "loss," of the children from the home might cause depression.

These theories presented a rather pessimistic view of the empty nest stage of parenting. However, although some parents will experience it as a difficult phase, recent research has failed to support the notion that the empty nest syndrome is a common reaction to children leaving home. On the contrary, the departure of the youngest child is often anticipated by parents with a sense of relief, and for many couples, the middle years bring self-enrichment and a greater ability to cope with their lives.

Surveys of parents whose children have left home have found that, for a large majority, the "postparental" stage was as good as, or better than, the preceding stages of family life. In one survey, only 6 percent of the wives, and none of the husbands, considered the quality of their lives to be definitely worse. In general, a couple's marital satisfaction is at its peak in the first year of marriage, decreases gradually over the next 15 years, and then rises again to level off at a higher plateau as the children leave home to make a life of their own.

However, the quality of a couple's relationship may contribute to either or both partners developing some aspects of the empty nest syndrome. After years of living in a family-centered home, many adults find it difficult to adjust to a home that revolves only about themselves. The amount of work needed to maintain the household is reduced, leaving the couple more free time to spend together. For some, this may lead to marital problems, especially if they have previously avoided any upsets by spending time with the children. Alternatively, if the husband and wife have grown apart and developed separate interests during the childrearing years, they will have little in common once mutual interest in the children is no longer a concern.

The postparental period could be a time to *increase* shared activities and perhaps discover new aspects of your partner that have evolved during the period of childrearing. Many women now participate in activities outside the home, and for a great number, this is a time for cultivating interests and talents that they could not indulge while they devoted themselves to their families. In fact, recent statistics indicate that more than half of American women whose children have left home are now in the workforce. For many parents, the departure of the last child appears to have a positive effect on their happiness and enjoyment of life. Also,

▶ **After the children leave home**, *parents, especially mothers, may feel a sense of role loss. The majority, however, report that they find the postparental family stage as satisfying as, or more satisfying than, the childrearing stage. Husband and wife have more time to be a couple, increasing the time spent simply enjoying each other's company.*

The postparental period can be a time to enjoy an increase in shared activities and perhaps to discover new aspects of a partner's personality. This is a time for cultivating interests and talents that could not be indulged before.

it appears that this positive effect may well result from an increase in marital happiness. In the majority of cases, "empty nest" parents are not more depressed than parents who still have children at home, or those who have never had children – if anything, they are less depressed. This is as true for women who are "only" housewives as it is for women who are employed outside the home.

The empty nest does not appear to be a particularly stressful period in most parents' lives. In fact, the major threat to their well-being may be not in having children who leave home, but rather, in having children who do not leave home when they are expected to leave. **IHG VEW**

The "successful" marriage

We usually measure the success of a marriage by the length of time it lasts, equating permanence with happiness. Yet marriages often continue for quite different reasons. For example, the emotional and financial costs inherent in leaving a marriage are high, and religious and social sanctions also keep couples together even when they no longer enjoy the relationship.

Universal principles for the success of a marriage can be laid down only in a very general way. Studies indicate the value of open communication, of treating the partner as a friend, of sorting out daily routines, and of clear expression of emotions.

Telling your partner about your feelings and fears is usually a good thing, although couples will vary in how they achieve this. It is clear that loyalty to the partner is, for many people, a major issue in a successful marriage (although some marriages last for years in the face of affairs and misdemeanors). But what is meant by loyalty? Making criticisms of your partner to other people behind his or her back may be just as serious to some people as breaking the marriage vows through sexual infidelity.

Every relationship is different, and what works best for one couple depends to a great extent on the type of marriage they have and whether it satisfies their particular needs. Each partner in a marriage needs to be able to grow and develop during the life of it, just as the marriage itself grows and develops. Partners should therefore try to be clear about their own and the other person's needs, and negotiate a relationship that will take care of these in a mutually satisfying way. **SD**

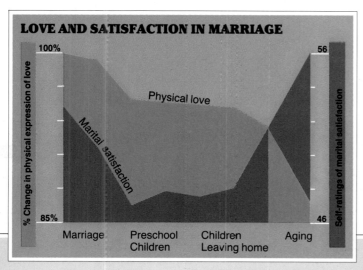

LOVE AND SATISFACTION IN MARRIAGE

% Change in physical expression of love — 100% ... 85%

Self-ratings of marital satisfaction — 56 ... 46

Physical love

Marital satisfaction

Marriage | Preschool Children | Children Leaving home | Aging

▲ **Physical love and marital satisfaction** *vary across the lifespan of a marriage. Each has its own pattern of change. Physical displays of affection become progressively less frequent, declining on average by about 15 percent by old age. Marital satisfaction fluctuates on average by fewer than 10 points (between 46 and 56) on the researcher's scale. It is lower when children are a main responsibility of the couple. It is highest in old age.*

■ **The greatest satisfaction** *with marriage is recorded by couples in old age. Partly, this statistic reflects the fact that most couples whose marriages survive into old age have liked each other enough all along to have stayed together through many trials. Partly, it reflects* *the fact that old age is a time when most of these trials, such as the demands of childrearing and pressures at work, are over.*

CULTURAL DIFFERENCES IN MARRIAGE

■ Within a culture, people know what is meant by the word "marriage," but for many years, researchers have been seeking a definition of the term that will cover the enormous variation in institutional arrangements found all over the world. The task has not been an easy one because the way in which one society defines the relationship can be quite different from that of another.

Such differences reflect the historical needs of each society – for example, inheritance of land and property, large families to work the land – as well as religious and other considerations. What does seem to be true is that the romantic aspects of marriage are by no means universal, and that, as societies change, so does the institution of marriage.

PURPOSES OF MARRIAGE

In Western society, if you have two spouses you are a bigamist and have committed a crime for which you may be sent to prison. Would this happen everywhere else in the world? Not in areas with polygamy. Polygyny is the most common form of this: in many societies, it is the norm for men to take more than one wife, and the number of wives a man has is often an indication of his status. This is far more common than polyandry – when a woman can marry more than one husband. Polyandry exists in an institutionalized form only in the Himalayan region, where a woman may go through a marriage ceremony with more than one man, and a further ceremony is required to recognize formally which is the father of each of her children. Group marriage, or the state of uncontrolled sexual promiscuity – a type of marriage much loved by historians who speculate on the evolution of social life – has never been recorded.

There is no simple explanation to account for the variable distribution of marriage practices. Having a number of wives may be to a man's economic and political advantage through the productivity of the women (and the children they bear) or the network of relationships that such marriages create. Throughout history, the creation and maintenance of dynasties have often depended on strategically arranged marriages. Almost everywhere, this institution is concerned with the transmission of rights and property, and marriage practices reflect this fact.

For example, marriage has to do with the identification of heirs, which for us usually means the legitimacy of our children. The Christian churches have always seen sexual intercourse and marriage as indissolubly linked, to the extent that it is wrong for the first to occur outside the second, and they have stated that the function of both is the production of children. Legitimate offspring are those conceived in wedlock, and the biological and social relationships together define the family.

In fact, much of the variation found in marriage practices can be traced to differing ideas and expectations about the relationship between social and biological fatherhood – known respectively as "pater" and "genitor." A great number of marital arrangements may exist once these two roles become separate and the legitimacy of offspring is defined by their relationship to the pater. For example, there is the widow inheritance practiced by the Hebrews in Old-Testament times, when a dead man's brother had the duty to have children by the widow, who were then regarded as the deceased's, not the genitor's. Or, perhaps more exotic, there is the so-called "ghost marriage" of the Chinese. If an unmarried man dies without issue, particularly without a son, a woman might go through a marriage ceremony with his "ghost" and the children she bears by a lover would be his.

These cases, and others like them, depend for their existence not only on the separation of the roles of pater and genitor, but also on certain social arrangements and religious ideas. Thus, in the Chinese case, not only is it important that a man should have sons in order to continue his line; a man without sons to worship him also has no existence as an ancestor.

THE LIMITS OF CHOICE

If the forms of marriage vary, so too do the practices associated with it – for example, how people choose a partner and where they live after marriage.

The form we give to the institution of marriage reflects the way we organize a whole society. Hence uncertainty about what marriage means goes together with social change, and cultural differences in marriage rules stand out.

We might think that those of us in industrialized countries are free to marry whom we like as long as we avoid committing incest, but in practice, this is not so. We have first to meet someone before we can marry them – and those we meet will be restricted by a whole range of factors including education, employment, and leisure interests.

Then there are the social pressures that intervene to make marriages between certain people that much more difficult. Commonly, this occurs when there is a great difference in the wealth, status, religion, ethnic background or age of the partners. Generally speaking, the higher the status, the more restricted the choice. This is clear in the case of the British Royal Family, but the Pharaohs of ancient Egypt were even more restricted – they were expected to marry their sisters.

Small-scale egalitarian societies, in which many of these factors do not apply, produce their own kinds of limitation. For example, young men may be highly dependent on the goodwill of their seniors in order to obtain the bridewealth that makes marriage possible. (A man's claim to his own children will not be socially recognized without this payment to his wife's family.) There are also societies in which marriages are arranged; the bride and groom have little or no say in the matter, and may not even meet each other face to face until after the ceremony has taken place.

In the latter case, it is clear that those involved are not marrying for love. In fact, for the majority of humanity, the reasons for marriage were and are much more down to earth and practical – often quite explicitly economic. In societies where the nature of the economy and the division of labor make the involvement of both men and women crucial to survival, there is little room for a romantic image of marriage.

Patterns of postmarital residence also vary greatly throughout the world. Ideally in our society, newly married couples go to live in their own home. Often, for financial reasons, this is not possible and in such cases it is usual for the couple to reside with the wife's parents. This pattern is adopted on the argument that it produces less tension for a mother and daughter to share the same kitchen than a woman and her daughter-in-law. In some societies, the bride lives with the groom's family, in others vice versa. Occasionally, both types of residence are found in the same society, although one – that where the bride joins her husband – is regarded as being of higher status, the other form suggesting the relative poverty of the groom (perhaps an inability to pay bridewealth).

MARRIAGE AND CHANGE

The form marriage takes in any given society is a reflection of the wider political, social, economic and religious setting. Just as these alter over time, so does marriage. Although it is often claimed that the institutions of family and marriage are threatened, they usually are merely becoming transformed along with other aspects of society.

Marriages in the Western world are constantly changing. The relative ease with which divorce can be obtained has increased the amount of serial polygamy – in which men and women have a number of marriages, but one after the other – and the number of step-relationships. (It is not generally realized that only in the past decade has the number of broken marriages reached the 19th-century rate – although then the cause was death, not divorce.)

Age at first marriage and at first child has oscillated over the years, and despite widely encouraged contraception, the illegitimate birth rate remains high and has even increased in recent years. Tax laws in the United Kingdom make cohabitation an attractive and advantageous alternative to marriage for some couples. In both the United States and United Kingdom, evidence is beginning to accumulate to show that a significant minority of intelligent women with good careers are not marrying, but this is not precluding them from having children. **PR**

◀ **Moslem wedding guests** in Marrakesh, Morocco, await the festivities. In the Moslem world a man may take up to four wives if he is able to support them. Divorce can be achieved by saying "I divorce thee" three times to a wife in the presence of a witness.

▲ **A man and his wives** pose for a family photograph in Zaire. In many parts of Africa transfers of money (bridewealth) to the family of the bride are needed to legitimize the union, and especially to legitimize the children that result.

Breaking Up

OUT OF ALL the people you will meet in your life, probably only a small number will attract you. Of these, a few will become your friends or romantic partners. Fewer still will remain close for a long time – in a study of couples "in love," about half had broken up within two years. Even close kin drift apart. Why do some of our relationships endure while others end?

The ritual of breakdown

When we think back on the breakdown of a relationship, we often think of a particular incident, such as a family dispute over a will that set brothers apart, or the sudden discovery that your partner has been seeing someone else for the last six months.

However, an unpleasant incident in itself is seldom enough to divide us. People who have reasons for getting along or for being close find ways of accommodating disagreements and even disputes. Relationships rarely end suddenly. Family break-ups have deep roots, and just as voluntary relationships become established in stages (see *Chs 21, 26*), they also only break down in stages. This process does not necessarily follow a strict pattern: some relationships miss certain steps: some do not decline irretrievably but move back and forth between different levels of intimacy and commitment; and others repeat some stages before moving on to their end. It is also important to realize that even relationships that do not eventually fail may go through some or many of these phases as part of their seesaw development.

Breakdown is not restricted to marriage and other love relationships. Friends drift apart. Neighbors can become enemies. Most research has tended to focus on the breakdown of close romantic relationships, but similar processes are at work elsewhere. Friends may have a less emotionally intense bond but the stages of breakdown are much the same as in the breakdown of a marriage, though

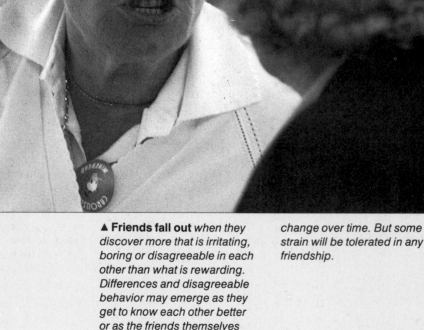

▲ **Friends fall out** *when they discover more that is irritating, boring or disagreeable in each other than what is rewarding. Differences and disagreeable behavior may emerge as they get to know each other better or as the friends themselves change over time. But some strain will be tolerated in any friendship.*

Relationships rarely end suddenly. Just as they become established in gradual stages, they break up in stages. Even those that do not eventually fail may repeatedly move toward break-up as part of their seesaw development.

usually less dramatic. Different researchers have proposed somewhat different models, but by combining these under the following headings we get a good picture of how relationships break down.

Differentiation

The more important a relationship is to us, the more we tend to think of ourselves as one. We focus on the "we" of the relationship and define ourselves less in terms of our own individuality. So we find the "family comes first" principle or the "two hearts beat as one" ideal. We give presents jointly, receive invitations jointly and arrive at parties carrying one bottle of wine. When stress occurs and the relationship seems to be putting heavy demands on us – as inevitably will happen – we are reminded of our own

identity as individuals. We may begin to correct the blurring of identity that we have allowed the relationship to bring about. As we try to emphasize our individuality, there is less attention to what is "ours" and more attention to what is "mine."

Differentiation exists to some degree in every relationship simply because we do have separate identities. It is crucial for neighbors whose relationship is largely preoccupied with showing friendly recognition of one another's territorial rights. Differentiation allows casual friends to limit the extent of their relationship. Although they have much in common in a limited context where they frequently see each other (such as their place of work or a leisure activity) they are aware of each other's separate interests and separate commitments to family and friends elsewhere. They can enjoy a stable and mutually supportive relationship without expecting too much from it (see *Ch 21*). Similarly, stable and long-lasting marriages reflect the partners successful negotiation of an equilibrium between their need to feel at one with each other and their need to be individuals.

An *increase* in differentiation is not always a very serious development, although it may be worrying if you are not prepared for it. Every romantic relationship undergoes it as the first excitement of romance wears off.

Much differentiation is unconscious. You simply feel more often like talking about the things that you identify with and want others to recognize as part of you – you find yourself feeling it important, for example, that your husband or wife should hear about precisely how things were done in

■ **Couples fall out** *for the same reasons as friends. In addition, their relationships often must face the burden of disappointed expectations. We usually hope for a degree of excitement and fulfillment in intimate relationships that we would not expect from a friend. And our hopes are often highly unrealistic.*

231

your family at Christmas. At parties you do not feel the same urge you once felt to be constantly near each other.

More extreme forms of differentiation can be a sign of trouble, but this depends on the kind of relationship. Adolescents, for example, go through a marked but healthy phase of differentiation from their parents. They may physically cut themselves off from other family members, retiring to their room or needing to stand at what seems to them like an unchildlike distance from parents in public places. They also like to dress differently from their parents. Underlying these superficial signals there is usually a continuing sense of emotional dependence, and by young adulthood a feeling of family identity causes many grown children to emphasize once again the points of similarity they find between parents and themselves.

Discovery

Everyone discovers things they do not like about people they are involved with. A second stage in breakdown occurs when difficulties and conflicts are recognized as significant. We become dissatisfied with the relationship, begin to brood about the other person's behavior and regard it as a cause of unhappiness. We may begin to make comparisons – wondering if we would not have been happier if we had someone else (often someone we can think of) as a lover,

marriage partner or friend. Nothing is actually said to the person we find wanting at this stage although we might discuss the situation with friends, relatives or even strangers to try to clarify our feelings.

Dissatisfaction may occur because we find that we are not so much alike as we thought we were. This is a hazard, in particular, of romantic relationships. In the excitement of falling in love, we do not take careful stock of a partner and may feel commitment without allowing time for an accurate impression to emerge of how similar – and therefore how well suited – we really are. When the excitement wears off and the differentiation stage sets in, we may find we have too many grounds for comfort on which to differentiate. Being as one will not be as rewarding as we expected because it will mean changing ourselves beyond recognition to conform with styles and standards we do not really see as ours. Differences in class, nationality, politics and personal values are all more common in divorced couples than in those whose marriages survive.

Differences also emerge as we change over time. People may also become dissatisfied as a result of changes – whether in the other person or in themselves. For example, husbands who rise socially after marriage by means of their jobs may sometimes begin to feel that their wives do not match them sufficiently in sophistication. Old friends who

If in the first stage we find too many grounds for differentiation we may enter the second stage – discovery of dissatisfaction. A growing sense of discontent may also emerge when we begin to feel bored or undervalued.

do not move in the same circles may in turn be alienated by these men's new interests and ambitions.

Two-career marriages often feel the stress of dual changes of interests. When both husband and wife take on exciting challenges and develop new talents through being committed to their own careers there is more difficulty in maintaining the sense of a shared life than when one partner is the chief provider for the family and the other is the chief homemaker. It is important for careerists to reserve time for joint leisure interests and homemaking activities.

Dissatisfaction may also emerge as a result of the boredom that we may discover after the first bloom of a romance wears off. Routine is rewarding – it gives us a sense of security. But we also need stimulation, and if we do not get this from each other, it will put a strain on our relationship. Couples especially need to inject variety into their joint experience. Holidays, new ways of sharing sex, exploring new sports, hobbies and studies together are all useful strategies. Change that involves them both can help a couple to avoid, on the one hand, the strain of growing apart through a growing dissimilarity, and, on the other, the boredom of knowing so much about each other that there are no stimulating surprises.

We discover a sense of dissatisfaction, as well, when we feel less valued. An important source of satisfaction comes from receiving expressions of positive emotions – from partners saying and showing that they love us, that they

233

◄ **The pressures of family life** can drive a young couple apart. For most, the drop in marital satisfaction that comes with the arrival of children does not lead to unhappiness. However, if the marriage has an unstable foundation, the extra strain of accom- modating children can bring to the surface all of the other stresses there are on the relationship.

▲ **When there is nothing left to say to each other** a relation- ship has reached a crossroads. Either new ways will be found of making it rewarding to be together, and communication will be restored, or the partners will make public to their friends and relatives that a breakdown is taking place. Each now turns to different friends for support.

want us, that they admire us, respect us. However, as time passes, partners typically reduce the amount of this positive input – "You no longer say you love me." In addition, they begin to pay more attention to each other's negative qualities, and they are more ready to express this.

Exposure – private and public

In the third phase of breakdown, people make their dissatisfaction known to each other. They do not always do this in a direct way – they may gradually reveal that problems exists, or avoid discussing the real cause of the problem and engage in recriminations by retreating, psychologically or physically, and become more distant from each other. Couples may spend less time together, friends may become involved with other people, children may spend much of their time away from home. But some people will directly confront the other person and express

their feelings and may then attempt to deal with the issues.

To some extent, open communication that allows us to air dissatisfactions can be beneficial to a relationship (see *Ch31*), but what is important is the relative proportion of positive and negative expression. If we feel we receive too much criticism and are valued too little, the rewards of the relationship decrease.

Many relationships have to get through patches of negative feeling. For example, adolescents may feel constantly criticized and hardly ever praised – and many parents of adolescent children feel the same. Negative things will come out in a marriage especially when a combination of stress factors – such as money problems, the demands of child care, job stress – are at work on the partners. If an imbalance of criticism over reward persists for too long, the relationship becomes vulnerable. Partners begin to restrict their conversation to a narrow band of safe

SEPARATING

■ *There are a number of ways of ending a spent relationship. A "swift" sudden-death ending occurs if the one who is leaving employs a very direct strategy to signal the desire to break-up – for example, explicitly stating that "this relationship is now over" and receiving immediate agreement.*

While such endings are un-complicated, they are also rare. A "prolonged" ending is more likely. It occurs when someone indirectly shows the desire to end the relationship, with hints or by withdrawing. The other is unlikely to understand the intentions behind such ambiguous behavior, and this creates the need for a series of "break-up messages," each becoming more direct and explicit until the other acquiesces.

Withdrawal messages may include keeping conversations brief, avoiding further dates, reducing disclosures, spending more time with others, curbing displays of affection, appearing distracted and restricting conversations to superficial topics. Partners who want to let their partners down gently may suggest that they "go back to being just friends," or stress that they both need their independence – "We're too young to be tied down." They may suggest a

trial separation to test the strength of the relationship, or recommend that both should see others before making a serious commitment to each other. Partners using this approach frequently report that they regret not having initiated a swift ending in the first place.

"Equivocal" endings can occur when a partner decides to test the strength of an intention to break-off the relationship by giving it "one more try." In the vast majority of cases the attempt is unsuccessful. **BMM**

TELLING THE STORY OF A BREAK-UP

■ *One way of putting a break-up into perspective is to give a personal "account" – a story about it, for both public and personal consumption. As with a literary story, an account has a cast of central characters, a plot, a climax and a resolution. Sometimes the teller is presented as a tragic hero, sometimes as the fool, but usually as a competent, respectable or likable person. This helps to bolster the teller's confidence*

about the prospect of future relationships. Just as important, the account helps the teller search the history of the relationship to identify potential pitfalls for the future. While the stories created by ex-partners usually do not agree, they are not necessarily intended as fiction. For each individual, his or her account is the most logical and acceptable explanation of what has happened. **BMM**

Revealing our dissatisfactions to each other can help. When an imbalance of criticism over reward sets in, however, we may make our disaffection public. If negotiation now fails, we may begin to avoid contact and then seek termination.

topics. Talk becomes more and more superficial and little new information is exchanged. Partners begin to communicate more in the way of strangers.

A very serious stage of breakdown – the "social stage" is reached when the problem is brought out into the open and admitted publicly to friends and family. In the social phase others are enlisted as allies. One consequence of this is that the breakdown of the relationship seems more real. As a result, the relationship begins to stagnate, to feel "hollow." Couples begin to think about what their life will be like after separation, and may include a different companion in their plans. Since this is a critical point there is likely to be a good deal of ambivalence and guilt, and an inclination to draw back and reconsider the decision to end the relationship.

A negotiation stage may occur, with efforts to reclaim the relationship, and friends and family may be called upon to help in a reconciliation. Unfortunately, without strong motivation from all sides, good communication and possibly expert assistance, these attempts are likely to fail.

Avoidance and termination

Avoidance comes next, an extreme form of differentiation. The affected parties spend most of their time away from each other, and may say "I need more space," "I need time to think things out." In most cases the relationship is now irretrievable. Finally, we reach the termination stage. This is usually not required in the case of a casual friendship that fizzles out. Nor is it required when brothers drift apart because they feel nothing – except perhaps a degree of rancor – in common. With intense friendships and

with couples, however, the relationship has to be acknowledged as over, and the partners have to focus energies on dealing with the consequences. They must now create a new life. This involves not only coming to terms with the social and emotional loss, but also putting the break-up into perspective (see box).

Relationships may end in several ways. Both or only one person may want to end it. The onset of the crisis may be sudden or gradual. Partners may speak bluntly or only hint at their intentions (see box). Deliberate attempts may be made to save the situation. The end result may be a complete break, or the relationship may continue in another form – for example, as an open marriage (in which both partners agree that either can have extramarital relationships) or as a friendship.

The strategy that people use to disengage themselves from a relationship depends to some extent on the degree of intimacy that formerly existed between them. When a relationship has not been very close, one partner is more likely to simply withdraw, physically and emotionally, from the other. If there has been a more intimate relationship, it is likely the terminating partner that will suggest that they should see less of each other, or try a separation. In a rather more intense relationship the person who initiates the break will make attempts to explain the reasons for leaving, and in doing so will take into account the feelings of the other. When the relationship has been very close, the person who initiates the end is likely to express a considerable amount of grief. The closer and more intimate the relationship has been, the more people feel the need to explain and justify their part in breaking it up. Closer relationships are the most difficult to end, and the end is more likely to cause loneliness, pain and fear. **RG**

THE AFTERMATH OF DIVORCE

■ *Losing a partner through divorce is, in many cases, more stressful than losing them by their death. Divorced men and women have a higher rate of mental and physical illness than those who are married, as well as higher rates of suicide. And the effects of a divorce are not confined to the couple. Their children, especially, also suffer. They are more likely to become seriously depressed or delinquent or to display aggressive or disobedient behavior. As adults, they are also more likely to end their own marriages in divorce.*

In the United States about 40 percent of marriages end in

divorce. Four-fifths of divorcees remarry. The second union is about 50 percent more likely to end in divorce than the first one.

Coping successfully with divorce depends most on being strongly supported by family and friends. In addition, people

who are more independent – have their own interests and can do the household repair jobs or meal preparations that are traditionally assigned to the opposite sex – are likely to cope better than those who are very dependent on a marriage part-

ner. If a couple can take time to organize their separation and divorce and are able to plan their future arrangements calmly, this will also help to reduce the ill-effects for them and for their children. **RG**

MINIMIZING THE EFFECT ON CHILDREN

■ *In many cases of divorce, children have to be considered. In the United States more than 20 percent of five-year-olds have experienced the break-up of their parents' marriage and many of them will experience yet another family break-up before they reach adulthood.*

To minimize the harm done to children by divorce, time must be taken to explain the situation to them – they should not be excluded. They should not be made to spectate at or become involved in bitter quarreling. It should be emphasized to them that what is happening is in no

way their fault – children can very easily feel that they are to blame for things that happen. Every effort should be made to ensure that the children maintain a relationship with both parents and spend time regularly with each of them. **RG**

Reclaiming Relationships

HOW CAN WE retrieve relationships that are at the point of breakdown, or revitalize those that have become less than rewarding? One essential step is to assess the way the rewards and the burdens of the relationship add up. Are you giving enough to the total to make the relationship satisfying for the other person? Are you receiving enough to make the relationship satisfying for you? It is also essential to communicate effectively. When you are communicative about what you like in another person, this in itself is rewarding for them, and it strengthens the relationship. And if there are rewards you lack and burdens you should not be carrying, it is often only by talking things through that you will be able to negotiate a solution.

The decision to continue

When a relationship is in difficulty, three obvious choices are available: to let it continue unchanged and invest more energy in other relationships, to end matters or to attempt to improve the relationship

Choosing the third option reflects commitment. The nature of this commitment should itself be considered, because it may or may not be appropriate. Generally speaking, the more positively based the commitment, and the more strongly it is felt on both sides, the more hopeful the prospect. A commitment that arises only from a desire to avoid social stigmas or other consequences of a break-up is less likely to lead the way to happiness.

In friendship there are fewer consequences of not continuing than there are with marriage and fewer social pressures to remain friends. You would probably not *feel* like letting an old friend down in a crisis, and neither would you want to face the social criticism you might receive on account of not paying the old emotional debts of your friendship by helping. However, there are few obstacles to drifting apart when you find yourselves diverging in your interests and your opinions.

Marriage, on the other hand, is a closely defined and highly valued social institution, and usually other people – especially children – are affected by a break-up. There is consequently a social stigma against being divorced or separated. Even in the case of an unmarried couple who are breaking up, the social factor is important. Being a couple is more conspicuous than being friends. Other people have to be told that the relationship is over, and avoiding the public humiliation of rejection may be a source of commitment for at least one of the partners.

The financial burdens of a divorce can sometimes be catastrophic. So can the emotional burdens (see *Chs 16, 30*). As sources of commitment, however, these disincentives to parting have to be weighed against the emotional costs of continuing with a marriage that produces only bitterness. The chief emotional burden of broken marriages even for their children is not the divorce itself but the unhappiness that produces it.

■ **Commitment** to a relationship gives us the motivation to keep it going through times of stress and to revitalize it when opportunities arise. Liking or loving someone in itself involves a commitment. We also draw commitment from outside the relationship – from our attitude in general toward the idea of friendship, for example, or marriage or a kinship tie. To contribute to a relationship's staying power, it is best if this attitude is a shared one and "internalized" – a personal value, not merely a feeling that there is social pressure to continue.

Reclaiming a relationship may mean putting back into it some of its old vitality, or this may mean, more seriously, pulling it back from the brink of break-up. Communication and renegotiation are keys to a successful outcome.

Positive commitment need not arise purely from liking your partner. Individuals have varying degrees of personal commitment to the ideal itself of stability in relationships. At one extreme are those who are, for example, determined to make their marriage last "forever," while at the other are those who are relatively casual about commitment – it lasts only as long as a relationship is satisfying: at the first sign of boredom or conflict, their "commitment" vanishes. The level of commitment of most people falls somewhere between these two extremes.

Family background and life experiences seem to play an important part in such attitudes toward relationships. Those who have grown up in families where the parents had positive and satisfying marriages generally hold strong beliefs about the viability of lasting relationships. And those who have a history of being satisfied with their choices in life are likely to be satisfied with their choice of friends and partner.

Because there is no such thing as a problem-free (and, therefore, stress-free) relationship, some commitment is necessary if a relationship is to last any time at all. However, although a person's overall ability to be committed can help them to make a relationship last, it is also true that problems left unresolved can give a relationship a weak foundation. Sometimes too firm a belief in our own loyalty can get between us and properly facing these problems. On the one hand, it is sensible to be stoically prepared for the typical stresses and strains in a relationship such as marriage (see *Ch 29*), but, on the other, it is as well to take positive steps to *help* your relationship endure these and to outgrow more fundamental problems.

Revitalization

A relationship that has begun to stagnate can often be made more rewarding for the other person – and for you – if you put some simple strategies into practice. First, try something that will enhance your attractiveness. For example, take part in activities that will make you a more interesting person – this could involve reading, developing new interests, or taking up a new activity. However, it is important to find a way to express this "new you" *within* your relationship. Avoid the familiar pitfall of becoming more expressive and dynamic with new acquaintances and friends than you are with your partner or with old friends. Use the same positive communication strategies with the latter as you would with new friends – smiling, attentive listening and so on. Effort can also be put into physical appearance and dress.

There are also a number of strategies that you and the other person can practice together. Ensure that your relationship continues to be a priority by scheduling time

► **Tending our relationships** *occupies our attentions on many fronts. When one relationship is strained – for example, that between a husband and wife – this may be a stress factor in their relations with their children, with their friends and with their kin, especially in-laws. The whole complex web of relationships we develop can be affected, and innocent bystanders may need special support in troubled times.*

237

together for matters of mutual interest, and make sure that this is "quality time." It is very easy to allow career and other aspects of your life to become substitutes for relationships. If you have children, it is essential that you and your partner remember that you are a couple as well as parents.

Partners can do a simple exercise that may help them to recognize the state of disrepair their relationship has reached, and which may also give them clues about how to restore some of its previous vitality. Both should separately list ten or more joint activities that have been important and enjoyable in the past. Next to each item note how much time has passed since the activity was last shared.

Most people will be genuinely surprised at how long it has been since they did favorite things together. Moreover, simply doing this exercise will often have an immediate

positive effect on a relationship, because it tends to produce many shared memories. Once the lists have been made, both partners should write specific dates and times into their diaries to schedule the listed activities. If they regularly set aside time to plan the next week's outings, the likelihood of backsliding or giving up is reduced.

Never take your relationship for granted and risk being lulled into a false sense of security. Keep in mind that there are many attractive and interesting people in the world who might replace you. **IHG CAC**

Toward the equitable marriage

A relationship may need to be revitalized. It may also need to be renegotiated. This means identifying the expectations that it is failing to fulfill – and it also means

▲ **Finding "quality time"** for the revitalization of a marriage means getting time to spend by yourselves, being a couple and not just parents. If it is possible to arrange, partners who have first spent several hours each on their own, without the stimulation of friends, colleagues or family, will find that an evening together is more exciting and refreshing than if they come together only after a busy and demanding day.

▶ **Rejuvenating yourself** can be a step toward rejuvenating a relationship. By enhancing your attractiveness – putting effort into your physical appearance through exercise and especially through dressing in a more positive way – you may excite your partner's renewed interest. An improved image will mean an improved self-image, as well. This boost to your self-esteem will almost certainly make you better company and it may make you feel less dependent.

We have difficulty expressing our hopes and fears, our fantasies and misgivings. Implicit marriage contracts evolve, and in our shared state of misinformation, neither party understands or agrees to the other's terms.

considering just how realistic these expectations are.

The actual terms of a typical marriage contract go well beyond the initial promises to love, honor and cherish. As a marriage grows and develops, so do the expectations each partner holds for the other. That is, they begin to evolve an *implicit* contract based partly on each partner's real experiences with the other, and partly on fantasies they have been carrying within themselves for many years. If the marriage is to last the couple must find ways of communicating to each other some of the terms of their respective implicit contracts However, such communication is often neither easy nor direct. Marriage partners can find it very difficult to talk together about their hopes and fears, their fantasies and their misgivings about each other. And so implicit contracts evolve that are based on misinformation, usually with neither partner understanding or agreeing to the other's terms.

Many of our everyday dealings with people center on the degree to which these relationships are seen as fair or unfair. An unfair (inequitable) relationship is one where the parties to it do not contribute equally, which results in one side feeling "underbenefited" and the other side feeling "overbenefited." Such relationships are highly unstable. Either the inequities will be resolved in some way – for example, by trading off certain items to strike a balance – or the relationship will end.

However, when deep emotions are involved, and particularly when two people are married, trading off is of limited use. Inequities tend to continue – few couples would sit down and rate, say, household chores against lavish displays of attention – and so stress is produced. To be trapped into "overbenefiting" can, of course, produce as much stress as the opposite.

To help in situations such as these, "equity theory" has been developed. Research into it has resulted in an inventory of the expectations that people usually have about their marriage – what they expect to contribute to and gain from it. All these expectations are then grouped in three categories – the personal, the emotional, and the day-to-day "dimensions."

Under the "personal" dimension are expectations about intelligence, physical attractiveness, social graces, personal hygiene, and fitness. These items are similar to those that play such an important part in attraction and courtship, characteristics that influence whether or not two people

▲ **Finding time for the family.** *Career pressures and the ambition for success can make a parent concentrate too exclusively on providing. The special rewards of the father-child relationship, however, are a benefit that should not be lost by either father or child. And a greater sense of shared parenting can help to keep a marriage vital.*

▶ **Doing things together** *is the hallmark of the "vital marriage." Rediscovering formerly shared interests and finding new joint activities are key strategies for reviving stultified relationships.*

who have just met will continue into a relationship. The "emotional" dimension brings in the expectations that are at the very heart of intimacy – matters of loving and expressing concern or appreciation, along with those to do with physical closeness and security. The "day-to-day" dimension covers those chores and duties necessary for a household to run smoothly – its finances and upkeep and related decisions. In addition, whether or not a partner is easy to live with is also important in day-to-day existence. However, "easy to live with" can mean many things, and this aspect of a marriage will often include quite diverse items.

As well as being less prone to discontent, partners in an equitable marriage – one where the benefit to both is about equal – tend to be happier with their relationship, more sexually compatible and generally more satisfied with their lives. Equitable marriages also last longer. By contrast, underbenefited and overbenefited partners consider divorce more frequently and are generally more pessimistic about the projected duration of their marriage.

On this page, you will find a shortened version of the equity inventory that researchers use. It will allow you to make an assessment of your own marriage. Note that you

IS YOUR RELATIONSHIP FAIR?

How equitable is your relationship? Compare your responses with those of your partner and discover your "equity index." For each item, score 2 points if you and your partner are about equal. Score 1 if the item applies more to you. Score 3 if it applies more to your partner.

PERSONAL DIMENSION
1 Intelligence
2 Physical attractiveness
3 Social graces
4 Taking care of health and appearance

EMOTIONAL DIMENSION
1 Liking
2 Loving
3 Understanding, concern for partner's well-being
4 Expressions of appreciation for partner's words, deeds
5 Showing physical affection, touching, hugging, kissing
6 Sexual pleasure: working toward a mutually satisfying sex life

7 Sexual fidelity
8 Commitment to a mutually fulfilling future together

DAY-TO-DAY DIMENSION
1 Maintenance of household: grocery shopping, cooking, cleaning, car maintenance
2 Finances: income to our "joint account"
3 Being easy to live with: having a sense of humor, not being too moody, being a good companion and good conversationalist, fitting in with family and friends
4 Decision-making: taking a fair share of the responsibility for things that matter.

Scoring. *Your relationship is equitable if your score is close to 32. You are underbenefited in the relationship (getting less than you deserve) if your total is substantially less than this. You are overbenefited (getting more than you deserve) if your total is substantially higher.*

You can evaluate the types of trade-off in your relationship by comparing dimension sub-totals and even individuals items. Equity in the personal dimension is reflected in a score near 8. In the emotional dimension an equity score is near 16. You may not mind being underbenefited in the

personal dimension if the emotional and day-to-day dimensions are equal. Or you may insist that one item – for example sexual fidelity – must be equitable, but will accept being underbenefited in other emotional areas of the relationship.

Ask your partner to complete the inventory and then show each other your scores. This will give both of you information about the expectations each has for the relationship. Comparing your equity inventories, should however, not be just an opportunity to score points against your partner. **JTP**

► **Sharing the domestic load**, a husband can find more points of shared experience with his wife than when they only share their leisure, for which there may not always be time. Husbands who can cook and iron clothes and wives who can fix things also have the advantage of being better able to cope with their needs than dependent partners in the event of bereavement or divorce.

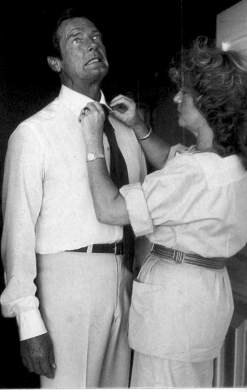

Partners in an equitable marriage are less prone to discontent. They tend to be happier with their relationship. They are more sexually compatible and more satisfied with their lives. They are not as likely to consider divorce.

are free to add items that are particularly relevant to you and/or your partner. For example, because research has focused on partners themselves, the compilers have not listed any items about childrearing, even though, in many marriages, children become the focus through which most interaction occurs. In addition, the division of labor between mother and father greatly influences the couple's feelings. You might therefore add items to do with each partner's expectations about childrearing responsibilities.

When fantasies surface

Equity theory can help make explicit the often unspoken assumptions of marriage. What it cannot clarify, however, are the fantasies that, while lying deep in the subconscious, move us to emotional extremes in our intimate relationships. At this level, an implicit contract can become extraordinarily ambitious. For example, women often believe that a man can transform them from timid, insecure beings into rising stars, or that a man can give them an identity they could not find on their own. Men also commonly hold unrealistic fantasies – how, through a woman's constant devotion, they will never have to be alone, that she will love them no matter what they do or say.

We are usually unaware of these deep expectations. However, when a marriage comes under stress for any of the many reasons that marriages typically do come under stress, such unfulfilled expectations are likely to surface. Partners find themselves locked in a never-ending argument about nothing, or so it seems; yet fighting stirs up a great deal of pain and resentment, and leads them further away from discovering their underlying disagreements.

If fantasies are allowed to dominate a relationship, this can lead to tragic consequences – perhaps to psychological or even physical abuse. It may be that a man, because of childhood experiences of rejection, gains inequitable control over his partner with verbal and physical abuse to prevent her from leaving. Or it could be that a woman, being neither valued nor protected from male aggressive behavior as a child, relates to men in a dependent, weak manner. If these two people were to get involved with each other, the resulting relationship could be very painful and unsatisfying for them both.

The ideas generated from equity research have been used in marital therapy with couples on the verge of break-up. It can be useful for both partners to verbalize the deep implicit expectations each holds for the other, no matter how utterly fantastic these may appear when expressed. Such open acknowledgment can be a first step toward a more balanced view of their own and of their partner's expectations. For example, a woman can begin to ask herself if her partner really can change the way she feels about herself, and start to see that change has to come from within her. A man may learn that he really wants his partner to stay with him not because she is afraid to leave but because she chooses to stay, and to achieve this, he must first learn to accentuate the rewards that he has to offer as a companion and partner.

To reclaim an intimate relationship such as marriage when it is in trouble, time must be taken to discuss both the explicit and implicit terms of the true contract that has developed between the partners. In addition, a couple have to untangle long overdue debts from the past that are caught

◀ **Small attentions** *and tokens of affection count for a lot. When we give and receive enough of them, this means not only do we achieve equity in the "emotional domain," it means together we invest enough in this category of joint experience to make our joint total a significant contribution to the relationship's vitality. The emotional domain can include expressions of liking, loving, commitment and also appreciation for the things your partner says and does. Under expressions of loving are also included shared sexual pleasure and shared expectations about sexual fidelity.*

▶ **The vision of a developing relationship** *that we each fix on may find its focus in separate fantasies. We implicitly expect our partners to make fantasies real, and yet these are the expectations we communicate least well. We often understand little about our own and our partner's deepest and most inarticulate hopes. When they are disappointed it is important to try to put these expectations into words, to assess how realistic or unrealistic they are, and to ask whether it is really our partner or us who should be making them come true.*

Partners in good relationships control their way of communicating rather than letting their way of communicating control them. Together, they work to build orderly discussions of how they can meet each other's needs.

up in current struggles. Each partner must learn to face up to their own expectations, unrealistic and quixotic though these may be, and to strive for fulfillment from within. **JTP**

Communicating grievances

If communication with a friend, family member, or partner is direct and open, the relationship will be more satisfying. This is probably the single most important activity in which two people can engage. Often the first sign that there are problems with a relationship is when people become uncommunicative. A stressful situation can be helped – the constant process of negotiation that every sound relationship needs will be more efficient – if there is good communication.

One important skill is "nondefensive listening" – when one person allows another to express their feelings and points of view. This means that the listener must put their own feelings on one side temporarily in order to understand what is meant, rather than replying or contradicting immediately, or trying to prevent the other from making the points that matter to them.

Partners in good relationships control the way they communicate rather than letting their communication control them. That is, they make clear and concise comments, they introduce topics smoothly and develop them appropriately, and they coordinate their nonverbal behavior. In short, they work together to built orderly conversations.

Good communication also means giving nondefensive feedback. Any reply that begins with the words "You do that, too!" is doomed to failure. Similarly, responses that are overly critical, angry or punitive will serve only to prolong the battle. The ability to stay on target can also enhance

communication. When people "cross-complain" – that is, throw in any grumble they have – this detracts from the issue at hand, and then disagreements often become too overwhelmingly complicated to resolve.

Expressing general concerns in a vague or abstract way can also make it difficult to find a method of changing them for the better. The more specific each person can be, the more optimistic the forecast for improvement in the relationship. Finally, some problems (such as irritating long-standing habits and differences in values or major life goals) will require time and repeated debating to resolve them. Those involved must not expect immediate results when their efforts center on such issues. **IHG CAC**

Standards of communication

There is not just one way of communicating. As the participants in a relationship decide what is important to them, they develop their own standard for good communication. The standard that emerges comes out of the process of communication itself. In day-to-day exchanges, two people make implicit claims and counterclaims about the way they think they should conduct their relationship. One person is unlikely to say to another, "Making fun of

242

◄ **Giving your partner the "silent treatment"** *is not a constructive style of communicating a grievance. It does not help you to define the possible solutions to the problem and it is an "ears closed" approach to the other person's needs and view of the situation.*

▲ **A touch of sardonic humor,** *depending on the style of communication that you have established previously, may help you to air negative feelings without seeming to pose a hostile threat to each other.*

each other is fun, and we should do it more often," but two friends might well arrive at that conclusion through the way they repeatedly joke with each other. Their behavior tailors their communication to their personal needs. It is important to build up this negotiating process and to take note of how it occurs.

Most Western societies emphasize three requirements for successful communication – positiveness, immediacy and control. Together, these amount to a powerful set of social traditions. People in close relationships are likely to combine their own standard for communicating with aspects of society's standards. A consequence of this is that they will share with others some ideas about what makes communication successful. However, what works for us may not work for other people. The things that contribute to one pair's happiness could conceivably add to others' unhappiness, depending on the standard they have negotiated in their relationship.

It is therefore impossible to specify what everyone should do to communicate successfully. But what can be said is that it is generally useful to talk with friends and partners openly and clearly *about* communication – a process that, in itself, encourages effective communication.

Affection and control

Sometimes talking will be difficult, inappropriate or inadequate. For example, consider a man who reaches for a woman's hand to convey his affection and caring. The man might, of course, choose to tell her how he feels, but it is unlikely that his message will ring right without a strong nonverbal component. By merely reaching out to her, he asserts his view of the kind of relationship they have. She also expresses her view – perhaps by slightly squeezing his hand if she agrees that they are to be highly affectionate, or pulling back and refusing to have her hand held if she views the relationship as less intimate than he does.

Depending on which action she chooses, two very different ways of going ahead with the relationship are being negotiated. One is clearly affectionate. The other is less clearly defined, and so additional negotiations about how to behave will probably ensue. The man may fall in with the woman's views by distancing himself from her in tone of voice or by a gesture. Or he may assert a less extreme level of affection by smiling at her, or simply engaging in light conversation. Whatever option the man chooses, the woman's response will signal whether she agrees or disagrees with the implied new assertion about the nature of

---

HOW TO HAVE A GOOD QUARREL

■ *A widespread belief exists that people in good relationships never argue and that our quarrels signal the end of relationships. Conflicting opinions, however, need not lead to a breakdown of a partnership. In fact, arguments, if used constructively, can help a relationship to grow, eventually even making it more harmonious. But it is important to avoid styles of arguing that are destructive and burden a relationship further.*

WHAT TO DO
Keep your fights away from innocent bystanders, especially children.
Each should define clearly what the fight is about, and make certain that you repeat the other's arguments in your own words, to be sure that you understand them.
Give full expression both to your positive and to your negative feelings.
Welcome the feedback in the other's evaluation of your behavior, even if you

eventually decide to reject it. Identify areas where you agree and those where you do not.
Define each other's areas of vulnerability and avoid touching on them.
Find out how deeply each of you feels about the issues. This enables you to decide how much to yield.
Offer positive suggestions for mutual improvement.
Ask questions that help the other to find the words to express what they feel.
Recognize spontaneous explosions that erupt for no apparent reason, and wait for them to subside – do not retaliate.
Try to score the fight by comparing how much you have learned and how much you have been injured. Winners are those who experience more learning than injury.
Declare a holiday, a period of truce in which no fights are to take place. This provides the conditions for exercising the fine art of making up and enjoying its benefits, such as

warm body contact, good sex and so on.
Be prepared for the next fight. Intimate conflict is more or less continuous. Paradoxically, to see it as a fact of life makes the quality of fights less vicious, the arguments shorter, the injury less and the learning greater.

WHAT NOT TO DO
Do not apologize prematurely.
Do not refuse to take the argument seriously.
Do not withdraw from confrontation by walking out on the other person or by giving them the "silent treatment."
Do not use your intimate knowledge of the other person to hit below the belt and humiliate them.
Do not bring in unrelated issues to bolster your attack.
Do not pretend to go along with the other's point of view for momentary peace, while hoarding doubts, secret contempt, resentments and/or private reservations to air

unexpectedly at a later time.
Do not attack indirectly by criticizing some person, idea, activity or object that the other person values.
Do not set up expectations while making no attempt to fulfill them, or give a rebuke when a reward is warranted.
Do not explain to the other how they are feeling.
Do not endlessly demand more from your partner, so that nothing they give is ever enough.
Do not threaten to withhold affection or other rewards of the relationship.
Do not undermine the other person by deliberately arousing or intensifying their emotional insecurities, anxieties or depression by keeping them on edge, or by threatening disaster.
Do not be a false friend, failing to defend your partner from the hostile opinions of outsiders, or by using such views to your advantage against your partner. **IHG CAC**

their relationship. But their relationship continues: nothing in the new assertion can be construed as ending it.

All relationships, of whatever kind, are continuously being negotiated, because all communication says something about how each partner views the association. This information revolves around two major themes. The first, dealt with above, is affection – the extent to which a relationship is based upon love or its opposite. The second is control – who is to be dominant and who is to be submissive, or are both partners to be more or less equal?

When you are with friends or other peers and you raise your voice, look directly at or touch another person, introduce a new topic of conversation, and/or interrupt, this suggests that you see yourself as in control. Conversely, you probably see the other person as the controller if you ask their opinion, avoid eye contact or touch, and/or speak softly. Equal or intimate partners negotiate the control issue with these types of exchanges just as they do affection. At times, this can go badly wrong, and for an important

Everyday communication, whether it is nonverbal or verbal, is full of implicit statements about how intimate we should be and who should control which decisions. In this way, every relationship is constantly being renegotiated.

reason. The following conversation shows how a couple may communicate dissatisfaction with each other yet leave unsaid what the real problem is.

> *He* – Don't you think you're driving a little too fast?
> *She* – Fast? I'm just keeping up with the rest of the traffic.
> *He* – Well, maybe they have a death wish, but I don't.
> *She (turning to him)* – Look, I'm driving this car, not you.
> *He* – No, but it looks like I should be!
> *She (looking back to the road)* – Well you're not. So I'll just drive the way I think best.
> *He* – You're obviously not thinking about our safety. Now slow down!
> *She* – I'll slow down! I'll stop the car! Now what do you think of that?

While this couple are clearly arguing about how to drive, they also have a deeper disagreement – who is in control? Each asserts a right to dominate the other, although these assertions are not explicitly put into words. Neither says, "I am dominant, and you must be submissive." Yet both convey that message by their commands and declarations, as well as by their body language. If exchanges such as this are typical and frequent, the couple may, in fact, be taking refuge in superficial issues to avoid the real problem – how to resolve the issue of control in their relationship. This can be particularly true of family disputes, which are seldom entirely candid. What must be noted is that masking or otherwise evading a major disagreement is no remedy. Problems must be acknowledged to be cured. **BMM**

244

■**Communicating basics**. *TOP Amazonian Indians negotiate nonverbally about the limits of the affection that will be displayed in their relationship – at least, when cameras are intruding. BOTTOM A California couple at the side of their pool try to put into words what they feel about which areas of their relationship each should control. Love and control are the two fundamental issues that have to be settled by every couple.*

▲ **Celebrating a relationship.** *Getting away together is important in order to be a couple. Symbolic gestures matter too.*

Anniversaries need to be remembered and enjoyed, to be made special in recognition of the importance the relation-

ship has in our lives – it need not be very romantic to matter and to be worthy of the effort we make to sustain it. It does

not have to be breaking up to be worth revitalizing.

WHEN we read nontechnical reports of the work of psychologists and other social scientists, it is often quite difficult to understand precisely what they did. Their conclusions might be quite straightforward – for example, eye contact between two people generally decreases as they move closer together. But how did researchers reach this conclusion? What methods were used to conduct the study which provided such a finding?

Some people still imagine that a psychologist spends the day "analyzing" people and their behavioral foibles, and the image of the analyst's couch still figures prominently in the popular stereotype. The tools of the trade of the psychologist, however, are varied, and there has been an increasing trend over the last 50 years towards precise, scientific methods of inquiry. The modern psychologist is now much closer to the biologist or physicist in the way he conducts his enquiries, leaving pure speculation about human behavior to astrologers and journalists.

Isolating the variables

At the heart of modern social psychology has been the development of experimental procedures. The aim has been to isolate particular features of human behavior and to examine them in the controlled conditions of the laboratory. Instead of trying to keep track of all of the various influences on behavior at the same time, the laboratory experiment allows the investigator to keep everything constant except for the particular variable that is the focus of the study.

This approach, of course, is something that social scientists have borrowed from their colleagues in the physical sciences. Investigations of human behavior are conducted under the same principles that a chemist would use, for example, when investigating the effectiveness of certain chemicals in preventing rust on sheet metals.

In this case, the experimenter would take two identical pieces of metal, coat one with the potential rustproofer while leaving the other untouched as a *control*. Both metals would be immersed in identical baths of water with all other factors such as temperature and so forth kept constant. After a suitable period, the metals would be removed and the amount of rust on them accurately measured. Such trials would be repeated several times and careful statistical analysis made of the data to demonstrate whether the chemical had significantly inhibited the formation of rust.

Here, we can see that there are two types of variable. First, there is what is known as the *independent variable*, which is manipu-lated by the experimenter. In our simple example, this is the presence or absence of the chemical thought to be a rustproofer. Second, there is a *dependent variable*. This is what is actually measured in the experiment – ie the amount of rust on the metals after they have been immersed in water. The other central characteristic of an experiment is also shown in the example – the testing of a clearly formulated hypothesis. It is hypothesized that the chemical will significantly reduce the amount of rust forming on the metal. The experimenter has to demonstrate that any differences in the amounts of rust on the treated and untreated metals could not be due to chance variation.

Measuring the "audience effect"

Many psychological studies have exactly these same characteristics. Consider an experiment on what is known as the "audience effect." Briefly, the presence of an audience can alter the performance of certain tasks.

If you are already skilled at a task, then having an audience around you should increase your level of performance through a process known as "social facilitation." On the other hand, if you are not very skilled at all, then "social inhibition" will tend to deflate your performance even further.

Psychologists testing the predictions of social-facilitation theory conducted an experiment in the poolroom of a university students' union building. They first observed the players unobtrusively to see who were the best players and who were the poorest.

In the second stage of the study, teams of four observers were positioned around the tables where good and bad pairs were playing. Data was collected in a systematic way to rule out the influence of such factors as the position of the table, or other individual variations.

The results they obtained were striking. The players originally classed as "above average" increased their shot accuracy from 71 percent with no audience to 80 percent when the group was standing by the table. In contrast, the accuracy of the "below average" players fell from 36 percent to 25 percent under the same conditions.

Although this study was not conducted in a laboratory, it has all the hallmarks of a well-designed and informative experiment that can test out a hypothesis stemming from a particular theoretical approach. Series of studies such as this, each focusing on different aspects of the effects of group presence, can enrich our knowledge and our understanding of human behavior in a way which pure observation could not.

Influence of the laboratory setting

The experimental method, however, has a number of drawbacks, particularly when conducted in a psychological laboratory. The social setting in which we are placed has a strong influence on our behavior (see *Ch1*). The laboratory in which behavior is studied, therefore, must also be seen as influencing that same behavior.

We know from the evidence that people will do things in an experimental laboratory that they will not do elsewhere. Consider the following situation: volunteers for a psychological experiment are given tables of numbers and asked to add up the rows and the columns; when each is finished, the experimenter takes the sheets, rips them up and gives each of the volunteers another to work on. Because this is an experiment, the volunteers meekly comply, thinking that there must be some point to the exercise. There is not, apart from demonstrating that you can get people to do almost anything if you call it an experiment.

This effect suggests that we should not rush to draw too many conclusions about real-life human behavior solely on the basis of experimental results. They could be due to characteristics and expectations generated by the laboratory conditions themselves. We should also note that while it is possible to generate quite aberrant behavior in the laboratory, it is often very difficult to simulate ordinary features of social interaction. Sexual behavior, for example, is difficult to examine in these conditions. The study of aggression is also not very amenable to this type of psychological method. We all know what people do in bed. We also know that people fight each other. But we cannot easily examine such behavior in the laboratory.

To overcome this problem, experimental psychologists take a less direct approach. If they cannot directly study such topics as aggressive behavior in children (because the children would hurt one another), then they *operationalize* the concept that is under investigation. A substitute behavior is found. In a famous set of experiments, children were shown aggressive films and then allowed to play with Bobo dolls – blow-up toys with a weight at the bottom. The experimenters took the frequency of hitting the doll as an indirect measure of the influence of films on aggression.

But some psychologists see this approach as problematic. Is hitting a Bobo doll really like aggression in the "natural" world? Can we base conclusions on such evidence? Usually, such results would be seen as informative but requiring further validation before being accepted completely.

Field experiments, such as the one in the

students' union poolroom, are less open to the kind of criticisms that are directed toward laboratory studies because they involve the measurement of "real-life" behavior. There are, however, still some problems with the method. Because the experiment is conducted in a particular kind of setting, the problem remains of extending the results to other situations. Only when sufficient experiments have been conducted in a range of social contexts can really valid conclusions be drawn.

Asking people what they think

While experimental social psychology is still the dominant approach in the United States, dissatisfaction with this approach and its underlying assumptions has been expressed in European psychological circles since the early 1970s. The philosopher and social scientist Rom Harré has argued that the experimental paradigm makes false assumptions about the nature of human beings. It is characteristic, they suggest, that psychologists refer not to the people but to the *subjects* who have taken part in their experiments. The individual is seen as essentially passive, merely responding to the stimuli to which he is exposed in the experimental design, rather than initiating action himself.

Harré has proposed an alternative to the traditional, experimental method. Principally, he argues that people must be involved far more in the explanations of their behavior. What they have to say, by way of justification and rationalization of their actions, should be given greater emphasis. He puts the matter very plainly when suggesting that if we want to know why people do the things they do, we should go and ask them.

The notion of "accounts" figures very prominently in this approach. Individuals, because they are active agents in social interaction, are able to give accounts of their actions. Contained within these accounts is the basis for an explanation of their behavior. By eliciting accounts in a systematic manner, and by devising ways of cross-checking and validating them, it is possible to develop a systematic research procedure which deals directly with real-life behavior in relevant and familiar terms.

Harré's approach, which has been rather grandly titled the "New Paradigm," has not led to major changes in the methods employed by social psychologists. But it has resulted in some questioning of the traditional scientific approaches. The account-collection method has been found to be problematic by those who have used it, because of the distortions present in our explanations of our own behavior. On

the other hand, the New Paradigm has reminded social scientists that the subjects of their inquiry are *persons*, just like themselves. After swinging toward what some psychologists perceived as a rather sterile pastiche of the physical sciences, social psychology has begun to return to the idea of a broader, human science.

This trend is evident not only in the progressive move away from the laboratory toward field research, but also in the way in which "softer" research methods are employed in parallel with experimental designs. Observation studies, for example, are increasingly common, often borrowing techniques from ethologists who for many years have patiently observed and analyzed the behavior patterns of animals. Even in questionnaires a concern for the relevance and salience of the questions asked is becoming more apparent.

Questionnaires are a simple and cost effective way of obtaining large amounts of data from a wide sample of people. The material collected is relatively easy to analyze. But the results and findings can only be reliable if appropriate questions were asked in the first place. The manner in which the questions are phrased, and the range of responses which is permitted, can make a significant difference to the results. Good studies of this kind, therefore, generally involve a pilot stage. To know what to ask, and how to ask it, the researcher must first spend time in discussion with respondents, getting to know the range of opinions and attitudes, and the language in which they are expressed. Only then can a truly appropriate research tool be designed.

Appropriate techniques

The particular research method that is employed must, of course, be determined partly by the nature of the topic that is being investigated. There would be little point, for example, in interviewing people about the nonverbal signals associated with deceit. This is because most people are not consciously aware of them. Nor would it be appropriate to ask them about the role of eye contact in sustaining conversations. These are aspects of behavior which need to be isolated and examined in detail in the laboratory. On the other hand, it would be very difficult to conduct a laboratory experiment to examine, in any meaningful way, aggressive behavior in crowds. For this, it is necessary to observe behavior at first hand.

Participant-observation methods come to the fore in social contexts such as these. While lacking the scientific rigor and precision of other psychological approaches, being involved in the action, as an observant social scientist, is perhaps the only way of

understanding and explaining the pattern of social behavior. Here, of course, the boundaries of social psychology overlap with those of sociology and even anthropology. But that, perhaps, is no bad thing.

To suggest that there is only one "right" way of examining the complexities of human social interaction is not only overly limiting, but also quite absurd. Social scientists, whatever their particular discipline, have the same goals in mind. They differ in terms of the conceptual frameworks which they employ and in the methods they habitually use, but they are all part of the same enterprise. In looking at the ways in which people interact with one another in their everyday encounters, *Eye to Eye* has drawn upon the largely experimental work of social psychologists. But we have also freely included findings from research conducted by animal behaviorists, anthropologists and sociologists where it has seemed appropriate – findings which can enrich our understanding of both commonplace and unusual aspects of our behavior.

Learning about ourselves

Whatever the methods used, and whatever conceptual and theoretical framework underlies the general approach, the real hallmarks of good social science remain the same. There must be a concern for the *validity* of the conclusions which are drawn from research in both scientific and real-life terms.

Results must not only pass the inspection of data-collection methods and statistical analysis, but they must also tell us something about ourselves. The subject matter of the human sciences is *us*. The conclusions which scientists reach are about *our* lives and patterns of interpersonal behavior. When we read their findings and examine their theories we have the right to ask "Is that really me?"

We should question whether we can be studied as if we were simply sheets of metal liable to become rusty. We should challenge the notion that we are only passive victims of our genes or of our environments. We should ask if studies of other animal species are really relevant to an understanding of our own complex encounters. But, like the human scientist, we should also keep a clear and open mind, and be prepared to entertain sensibly proposed ideas and explanations about our behavior that may at first strike us as surprising. **PM**

FURTHER READING
AND CONTRIBUTORS' SOURCES

READERS of *Eye to Eye* may want information about other aspects of a subject discussed, or detail on particular topics that have aroused their interest. With this in mind, some generally available books and periodicals suggested for further reading are listed below. The main published sources consulted by the contributors to this book come after these suggestions.

1 Adapting to the Occasion
Argyle, M, Furnham, A and Graham, J 1981 *Social Situations* Cambridge University Press, Cambridge; Goffman, E 1956 *The Presentation of Self in Everyday Life* Anchor Books, New York; Milgram, S 1974 *Obedience to Authority* Harper and Row, New York; Knapp, M 1984 *Interpersonal Communication and Human Relationships* Allyn and Bacon, Boston; Mackenzie, D D and McDonnell, P 1980 *How To Be Interviewed* Birn Foundation, London.

2 Marking Territory
Ashcraft, N and Scheflen, A E 1976 *People Space – The Making and Breaking of Human Boundaries* Anchor Books, New York; Becker, F D 1981 *Workspace – Creating Environments in Organizations* Praeger, New York; Deaux, K and Wrightsman, L S 1984 4th edn *Social Psychology in the 80s* Brooks/Cole, Monterey, CA.

3 Keeping a Distance
Hall, E T 1966 *The Hidden Dimension* Doubleday, New York.

4 Using Body Language
Forgas, J P 1985 *Interpersonal Behavior – The Psychology of Social Interaction* Pergamon Press, Rushcutters Bay, NSW, Australia; Knapp, M L 1978 2nd edn *Nonverbal Communication in Human Interaction* Holt, Rinehart and Winston, New York; Morris, D, Collett, P, Marsh, P and O'Shaughnessy, M 1979 *Gestures: Their Origin and Distribution* Cape, London.

5 Noticing Posture
Bull, P 1983 *Body Movement and Interpersonal Communication* Wiley, Chichester; Bull, P 1987 *Posture and Gesture* Pergamon Press, Oxford.

6 Assessing Appearances
Argyle, M 1975 *Bodily Communication* Methuen, London; Morris, D 1985 *Bodywatching*, and 1977 *Manwatching* Cape, London.

7 Reacting to Scent
Knapp, M L 1978 2nd edn *Nonverbal Communication in Human Interaction* Holt, Rinehart and Winston, New York; White, D 1981 "Pursuit of the Ultimate Aphrodisiac" *Psychology Today*, (September issue).

8 Making Eye Contact
Argyle, M and Cook, M 1976 *Gaze and Mutual Gaze* Cambridge University Press, Cambridge; Kendon, A 1967 "Some Functions of Gaze Direction in Social Interaction" in Argyle, M (ed) *Social Encounters* (1973) Penguin, Harmondsworth.

9 Reading Facial Expressions
Eibl-Eibesfeldt, I 1971 *Love and Hate* Methuen, London; Ekman, P (ed) 1972 2nd edn *Emotion in the Human Face* Cambridge University Press, New York.

10 The Language of Touch
Montagu, A 1978 3rd edn *Touching: The Human Significance of the Skin* Harper and Row, New York.

11 Greeting and Parting
Ferber, A and Kendon, A 1973 "Human Greetings"

Reprinted in: *Studies in the Behavior of Social Interaction* 1977 Indiana University Press, Bloomington, NY; Firth, R 1973 "Bodily Symbols of Greeting and Parting" *Symbols Public and Private*, 9, Allen and Unwin, London; Goffman, E 1971 "Supportive Interchanges" *Relations in Public*, 3, Harper and Row, New York.

12 Making Conversation
Argyle, M 1983 4th edn *The Psychology of Interpersonal Behavior* Penguin, Harmondsworth; Beattie, G 1988 *All Talk: How Language Keeps Us in Our Place* Weidenfeld and Nicolson, London; Duncan, S and Fiske, D W 1977 *Face-to-Face Interaction: Research, Methods and Theory* Lawrence Erlbaum, Hillsdale, NJ; Ellis, A and Beattie, G 1986 *The Psychology of Language and Communication* Lawrence Erlbaum, London.

13 Raising a Smile
Wilson, C P 1979 *Jokes: Form, Content, Use and Function* Academic Press, London.

14 Detecting Insincerity
Ekman, P and Friesen, W V 1975 *Unmasking the Face* Prentice-Hall, Englewood Cliffs, NJ; Knapp, M L 1978 2nd edn *Nonverbal Communication in Human Interaction* Holt, Rinehart and Winston, New York; Siegman, A W and Feldstein, S 1986 2nd edn *Nonverbal Behavior and Communication* Halstead Press, New York.

15 Polishing Social Skills
Argyle, M 1983 4th edn *The Psychology of Interpersonal Behavior* Penguin, Harmondsworth; Argyle, M and Henderson, M 1985 *The Anatomy of Relationships* Penguin, Harmondsworth; Argyle, M and Trower, P 1979 *Person to Person: Ways of Communicating* Harper and Row, London; Back, K and Back, K, 1982 *Assertiveness at Work: A Practical Guide to Handling Awkward Situations* McGraw Hill, London; Dickson, A 1987 *A Woman in Your Own Right* (revised and updated edition) Quartet Books, London; Duck, S W 1986 *Human Relationships* Sage, Beverly Hills, CA and London; Gambrill, E and Richey, C 1985 *Taking Charge of Your Social Life* Wadsworth, Belmont, CA; Hollin, C R and Trower, P 1986 *Handbook of Social Skills Training* (Vol 1: Applications Across the Lifespan, Vol 2: Clinical Applications and New Directions) Pergamon Press, Oxford; Jakubowski, P and Lange, A J 1978 *The Assertive Option* Research Press, Champaign, IL; Kleinke, C L 1975 *First Impressions: The Psychology of Encountering Others* Prentice-Hall, Englewood Cliffs, NJ; Trower, P, Bryant, B M and Argyle, M 1978 *Social Skills and Mental Health* Methuen, London.

16 Why Relationships Matter
Argyle, M and Henderson, M 1985 *The Anatomy of Relationships* Penguin, Harmondsworth; Broadhead, W E, Kaplan, B H, James, S A et al 1983 "The Epidemiologic Evidence for a Relationship between Social Support and Health" *American J of Epidemiology*, 117, pp521–37; Cohen, S and Smye, L (eds) 1985 *Social Support and Health* Academic Press, New York; Lynch, J J 1977 *The Broken Heart: The Medical Consequences of Loneliness* Basic Books, New York; Verbrugge, L M 1979 "Marital Status and Health" *J of Marriage and the Family*, 41, pp267–85.

17 Parents and Children
Richards, M and Dyson, M 1982 *Separation, Divorce and the Development of Children: A Review* DHSS Research Review, HMSO, London; Skynner, R and Cleese, J 1983 *Families and How*

To Survive Them Oxford University Press, New York; Yogman, M W and Brazelton, T B (eds) 1986 *In Support of Families* Harvard University Press, Cambridge, MA.

18 Brothers, Sisters and Only Children
Argyle, M and Henderson, M 1985 *The Anatomy of Relationships* Penguin, Harmondsworth.

19 Family Pets
Fogle, B 1986 *Games Pets Play (or How Not To Be Manipulated By Your Pet)* Viking, New York; Fogle, B 1985 *Pets and Their People* Viking Penguin, New York; Serpell, J 1986 *In the Company of Animals* Blackwell, Oxford.

20 Keeping in Touch with Kin
Mount, F 1982 *The Subversive Family* Allen and Unwin, London.

21 Friends and Acquaintances
Cooper, C L, Cooper, R D and Eaker, L 1988 *Living With Stress* Penguin, Harmondsworth; Derlega, V and Berg, J 1987 (eds) *Self-Disclosure: Theory, Research, and Therapy* Plenum, New York; Duck, S W 1983 *Friends, for Life* Harvester Press, Brighton; Hatfield, E and Walster, G W 1985 *A New Look At Love* University Press of America, Lanham, MD; Hendrick, C and Hendrick, S 1983 *Liking, Loving and Relating* Brooks/Cole, Monterey, CA; Hingley, P and Cooper, C L 1985 *The Changemakers* Harper and Row, London; Mangham, I C 1981 "Relationships at Work: A Matter of Tension and Tolerance" in Duck, S and Gilmour, R (eds): *Personal Relationships 1: Studying Personal Relationships* Academic Press, London; Reisman, D 1981 "Adult Friendship" in Duck, S and Gilmour R (eds): *Personal Relationships 2: Developing Personal Relationships*.

22 Child and Adolescent Friendship
Coleman, J C 1974 *Relationships in Adolescence* Routledge and Kegan Paul, London; Csikszentmihalyi, M and Larson, R 1984 *Being Adolescent: Conflict and Growth in the Teenage Years* Basic Books, New York; Douvan, E and Adelson, J 1966 *The Adolescent Experience* Wiley, New York; Duck, S W 1983 *Friends, for Life* Harvester Press, Brighton; Elkind, D 1984 *All Grown Up and No Place to Go: Teenagers in Crisis* Addison-Wesley, Reading MA; Rubin, Z 1980 *Children's Friendships* Fontana, New York.

23 Coping with Shyness
Dryden, W 1987 *Counselling Individuals: The Rational-Emotive Approach* Taylor and Francis, London; Ellis, A and Harper, R A 1975 *A New Guide to Rational Living* Wilshire, Hollywood, CA; Wolpe, J 1982 *The Practice of Behavior Therapy* Pergamon Press, New York.

24 Overcoming Loneliness
Burns, D D 1985 *Intimate Connections* Morrow, New York; Rubenstein, C and Shaver, P 1982 *In Search of Intimacy: Surprising Conclusions from a Nationwide Survey on Loneliness and What to Do About It* Delacorte Press, New York; Weiss, R S 1973 *Loneliness: The Experience of Emotional and Social Isolation* MIT Press, Cambridge, MA.

25 Finding a Partner
Duck, S W 1983 *Friends, for Life* Harvester Press, Brighton; Gottman, J, Notarius, C, Gonso, J and Markman, H 1976 *A Couple's Guide to Communication* Research Press, Champaign, IL; Knapp, M 1984 *Interpersonal Communication and Human Relationships* Allyn and Bacon, Boston; Murstein, B I 1987 *Paths to Marriage* Sage, Beverly Hills, CA.

FURTHER READING CONTINUED

26 Thinking about Love
Argyle, M and Henderson, M 1985 *The Anatomy of Relationships* Penguin, Harmondsworth; Hatfield, E and Walster, G W 1985 *A New Look At Love* University Press of America, Lanham, MD; Hendrick, C and Hendrick, S 1983 *Liking, Loving and Relating* Brooks/Cole, Monterey, CA; Wilson, G and Nias, D 1976 *Love's Mysteries: The Psychology of Sexual Attraction* Open Books, London.

27 Patterns of Jealousy
Buunk, A and Bringle, R "Jealousy in Love Relationships" in Duck, S W and Perlman, D (eds): *Personal Relationships, 2: Heterosexual Relations, Marriages and Divorce* Sage, Beverly Hills, CA; Clanton, G and Smith, L G 1977 *Jealousy* Prentice-Hall, Englewood Cliffs, NJ.

28 Enjoying a Sexual Relationship
Blumstein, P and Schwartz, P 1983 *American Couples: Money, Work, Sex* Morrow, New York; Brecher, E M 1984 *Love, Sex, and Aging* Consumers Union, New York; George, L K and Weiler, S J 1981 *Sexuality in Middle and Later Life: The Effects of Age Cohort and Gender* Archives of General Psychiatry; Hite, S 1976 *The Hite Report: A Nationwide Study of Female Sexuality* Dell Publishing, New York.

29 The Married Couple
Duck, S W 1986 *Human Relationships* Sage, Beverly Hills, CA and London; Fox, R 1983 *Kinship and Marriage: An Anthropological Perspective* Cambridge University Press; Kitzinger, S 1978 *Women As Mothers* Fontana, London; Murstein, B I 1987 *Paths to Marriage* Sage, Beverly Hills, CA; Mair, L 1971 *Marriage* Penguin, Harmondsworth.

30 Breaking Up
Argyle, M and Henderson, M 1985 *The Anatomy of Relationships* Penguin, Harmondsworth; Davis, M 1973 *Intimate Relations* The Free Press, New York; Knapp, M 1984 *Interpersonal Communication and Human Relationships* Allyn and Bacon, Boston; Rubin, L B 1983 *Intimate Strangers* Harper and Row, New York; Weiss, R S 1975 *Marital Separation* Basic Books, New York.

31 Reclaiming Relationships
Brehm, S S 1985 *Intimate Relationships* Random House, New York; Gotlib, I H and Colby, C A 1987 *Treatment of Depression: An Interpersonal Systems Approach* Pergamon Press, Oxford and New York; Ickes, W (ed) 1985 *Compatible and Incompatible Relationships* Springer, New York; Zerof, H G 1978 *Finding Intimacy: The Art of Happiness in Living Together* Random House, New York.

CONTRIBUTORS' SOURCES

1 Adapting to the Occasion Argyle, M, Furnham, A and Graham, J 1981 *Social Situations* Cambridge University Press, Cambridge; Brewer, M B and Kramer, R M 1985 "The Psychology of Intergroup Attitudes and Behavior" *Annual Review of Psychology*, 36, 219–43; Forbes, R J and Jackson, P R 1980 "Nonverbal Behavior and the Outcome of Selection Interviews" *J of Occupational Psych*, 53, pp65–72; Keenan, A and Wedderburn, A A I 1980 "Putting the Boot on The Other Foot: Candidates' Descriptions of Interviews" *J of Occupational Psych*, 53, pp81–9; Knapp, M L 1984 *Interpersonal Communication and Human Relationships* Allyn and Bacon, Boston; Miller, T and Turnbull, W 1986 "Expectancies and Interpersonal Processes" *Annual Review of Psychology*, 37, pp233–56; Webster, E C 1982 *The Employment Interview: A Social Judgment Process* SIP Publications, Schomberg, Ontario.

2 Marking Territory Becker, F D 1981 *Workspace – Creating Environments in Organizations* Praeger, New York; Deaux, K and Wrightsman, L S 1984 4th edn *Social Psychology in the 80s* Brooks/Cole, Monterey, CA; Malmberg, T 1980 *Human Territoriality* Mouton, The Hague; Mitchell, T R and Larson, J R, Jr 1987 3rd edn *People in Organizations – An Introduction to Organizational Behavior* McGraw-Hill, New York.

3 Keeping a Distance Argyle, M and Dean, J 1965 "Eye-contact, Distance, and Affiliation" *Sociometry*, 28, pp289–304; Ashcraft, N and Scheflen, A E 1976 *People Space – The Making and Breaking of Human Boundaries* Anchor Books, New York; Freedman, J L 1975 *Crowding and Behavior* W H Freeman, Oxford; Hall, E T 1966 *The Hidden Dimension* Doubleday, New York; Holahan, C J 1986 "Environmental Psychology" *Annual Review of Psychology*, 37, pp381–407; Kendon, A 1977 "Spatial Organization in Social Encounters: The F-formation System" in Kendon, A (ed): *Studies in the Behavior of Social Interaction* Peter de Ridder Press, Lisse, Holland; Marsh, P 1982 "Density and Crowding – Social Psychological Perspectives" *Man and Space* IATTS; Patterson, M L 1983 *Nonverbal Behavior: A Functional Perspective* Springer, New York.

4 Using Body Language Argyle, M 1983 *The Psychology of Interpersonal Behavior* Penguin, Harmondsworth; Bull, P E 1987 *Posture and Gesture* Pergamon Press, Oxford; Forgas, J P 1985 *Interpersonal Behavior – The Psychology of Social Interaction* Pergamon Press, Rushcutters Bay, NSW, Australia; Kendon, A 1981 *Nonverbal Communication, Interaction and Gesture* Mouton, The Hague; Knapp, M L 1978 2nd edn *Nonverbal Communication in Human Interaction* Holt, Rinehart and Winston, New York; Morris, D, Collett, P, Marsh, P and O'Shaughnessy, M 1979 *Gestures: Their Origin and Distribution* Cape, London; (1980) Stein and Day, New York.

5 Noticing Posture Bull, P E 1987 *Posture and Gesture* Pergamon Press, Oxford; Mehrabian, A 1967 "Orientation Behaviors and Nonverbal Attitude Communication" *J of Communication*, 17, pp324–32; Scheflen, A E 1964 "The Significance of Posture in Communication Systems" *Psychiatry*, 27, pp316–31; Spiegel, J and Machotka, P 1974 *Message of the Body* Free Press, New York; Ginsburg, H J 1977 "Altruism in Children: The Significance of Nonverbal Behavior" *J of Communication*, 27, pp82–8; Ginsburg, H J, Pollman, V A and Wauson, M S 1977 "An Ethological Analysis of Nonverbal Inhibitors of Aggressive Behaviors in Male Elementary School Children" *Developmental Psychology*, 13, pp417–418.

6 Assessing Appearances Argyle, M 1975 *Bodily Communication* Methuen, London; Marsh, P and Collett, P 1986 *Driving Passion* Cape, London; Morris, D 1985 *Bodywatching*, 1977 *Manwatching* Cape, London.

7 Reacting to Scent Baron, R A 1983 "'Sweet Smell of Success?' The Impact of Pleasant Artificial Scents on Evaluations of Job Applicants" *J of Applied Psych*, 68, pp709–13; Fillsinger, E E and Fabes, R A 1985 "Odor Communication, Pheromones and Human Families" *J of Marriage and the Family*, 47, pp349–59; Knapp, M L 1978 2nd edn *Nonverbal Communication in Human Interaction* Holt, Rinehart and Winston, New York; White, D 1981 "Pursuit of the Ultimate Aphrodisiac" *Psychology Today* (September issue).

8 Making Eye Contact Argyle, M and Cook, M 1976 *Gaze and Mutual Gaze* Cambridge University Press, Cambridge; Exline, R and Fehr, B 1978 "Applications of Semiosis to the Study of Visual Interaction" in Siegman, A and Feldstein, S (eds): *Nonverbal Behavior and Communication* (1st edn 1978) Halstead Press, New York; Kendon, A 1967 "Some Functions of Gaze Direction in Social Interaction" in Argyle, M: *Social Encounters* (1973) Penguin, Harmondsworth.

9 Reading Facial Expression Birdwhistell, R 1970 *Kinesics in Context* University of Pennsylvania Press, Philadelphia (1971 Allen Lane, London); Buck, R 1984 *The Communication of Emotion* Guilford, New York and London; Darwin, C (1872) 1972 *The Expression of the Emotions in Man and Animals* University of Chicago Press, Chicago and London; Ekman, P 1979 "About Brows: Emotional and Conversational Signals" in Von Cranach, M, et al (eds): *Human Ethology* Cambridge University Press, Cambridge and New York; Hall, J A 1984 *Nonverbal Sex Differences* Johns Hopkins University Press, Baltimore and London; Hinde, R A (ed) 1972 *Nonverbal Communication* Cambridge University Press, Cambridge and New York; Kendon, A 1976 "Some Functions of the Face in a Kissing Round" *Semiotica*, 15, pp299–334 (Reprinted in Kendon, A (ed): *Nonverbal Communication, Interaction and Gesture* (1981), Mouton, The Hague); Knapp, M L 1978 2nd edn *Nonverbal Communication in Human Interaction* Holt, Rinehart and Winston, New York; LaBarre, W 1947 "The Cultural Basis of Emotions and Gestures" *J of Personality*, 16, pp49–68; Rinn, W E 1984 "The Neurophysiology of Facial Expression: A Review of Neurological and Psychological Mechanisms for Producing Facial Expression" *Psychological Bulletin*, 95, pp52–77; Zuckerman, M, Klorman, R et al 1981 "Facial, Autonomic and Subjective Components of Emotion: The Facial Feedback Hypothesis versus the Externalizer-Internalizer Distinction" *J of Personality and Soc Psych*, 41, pp929–44.

10 The Language of Touch Frank, L K 1957 "Tactile Communication" *Genetic Psychology Monographs*, 56, pp209–25; Heslin, R and Alper, T 1982 "Touch: A Bonding Gesture" in Weimann, J M and Harrison, R P (eds): *Nonverbal Communication*, pp47–75, Sage, Beverly Hills, CA; Montagu, A 1986 3rd edn *Touching: The Human Significance of the Skin* Harper and Row, New York; Thayer, S 1986 "The Psychology of Touch" *J of Nonverbal Behavior*, 10, No 1; Thayer, S 1982 "Social Touch" in Schiff, W and Foulkes, E (eds): *Tactual Perception: A Sourcebook* Cambridge University Press, New York.

11 Greeting and Parting Davidoff, L 1973 *The Best Circles* Croom Helm, London; Donald, E B (ed) 1981 *Debrett's Etiquette and Modern Manners* Debrett's Peerage Ltd, London; Eibl-Eibesfeldt, I 1971 *Love and Hate* Methuen, London; Greenbaum, P E and Rosenfeld, H M 1980 "Varieties of Touching in Greetings: Sequential Structure and Sex-related Differences" *J of Nonverbal Behavior*, 5, pp13–25; Heslin, R and Boss, D 1980 "Nonverbal Intimacy in Airport Arrival and Departure" *Personality and Soc Psych Bulletin*, 6, 248–51; Morris, D 1971 *Intimate Behavior* Cape, London; Schiffrin, D 1974 "Handwork as Ceremony: The Case of the Handshake" *Semiotica*, 12, pp189–202 in A Kendon (ed): *Nonverbal Communication, Interaction, and Gesture* (1981) Mouton, The Hague; Schiffrin, D 1977 "Opening encounters" *American Sociol Rev*, 42, pp679–91; Wildeblood, J 1973 *The Polite World* Davis-Poynter, London.

12 Making Conversation Beattie, G W 1983 *Talk: An Analysis of Speech and Non-Verbal Behavior in Conversation* Open University Press, Milton Keynes; Beattie, G W, Cutler, A et al 1982 "Why is Mrs Thatcher Interrupted So Often?" *Nature*, 300, pp744–7; Bull, P E 1987 *Posture and Gesture* Pergamon Press, Oxford; Davis, J D 1976 "Self-Disclosure in An Acquaintance Exercise: Responsibility For Levels of Intimacy" *J of Personality and Soc Psych*, 33, pp787–92; Duncan, S 1972 "Some Signals and Rules for Taking Speaking Turns in Conversation" *J Personality and Soc Psych*, 23, pp283–92.

13 Raising a Smile Fine, G A and Linsk, F L "Perceptual and Evaluative Response to Humor: The Effects of Social Identification" *Sociology and Social Research*, 66; O'Quin, K and Aronoff, J 1981 "Humor as a Technique of Social Influence" *Social Psychology Quarterly*, 44, pp349–57; Rosenfeld, P, Giacalone, R A et al 1983 "Humor and Impression Management" *J of Soc Psych*, 121, pp59–63; Smith, S E and White, H L 1965 "Wit, Creativity and Sarcasm" *J of Applied Psych*, 49, pp131–4; Wilson, C P 1979 *Jokes: Form, Content, Use and Function* Academic Press, London; Witty, S 1983 "The Laughmakers" *Psychology Today* (August issue).

14 Detecting Insincerity Ekman, P and Friesen, W V 1969 "Nonverbal Leakage and Clues to Deception in Social Encounters" in Argyle, M: *Social Encounters*, (1973) Penguin, Harmondsworth; Knapp, M L 1978 2nd edn *Nonverbal Communication in Human Interaction*

Holt, Rinehart and Winston, New York; Siegman, A W and Feldstein, S 1986 2nd edn *Nonverbal Behavior and Communication* Halsted Press, New York; Zuckerman, M, DePaulo, B M et al 1981 "Verbal and Nonverbal Communication and Deception" in Berkowitz, L (ed): *Advances in Experimental Social Psychology* Academic Press, New York; Zuckerman, M, Koestner, R, et al 1984 "Anchoring in the Detection of Deception and Leakage" *J of Personality and Soc Psych*, 47, pp301–11.

15 Polishing Social Skills Argyle, M 1968 *Social Interaction* Methuen, London; Back, K and Back, K 1982 *Assertiveness at Work* McGraw Hill, London; Butler, P 1981 *Self-assertion for Women* Harper and Row, San Francisco; Dickson, A 1982 *A Woman in Your Own Right* Quartet Books, London; Jacubowski, P and Lange, A J 1978 *The Assertive Option: Your Rights and Responsibilities* Research Press, Champaign, IL; Leary, M R, Rogers, P A et al 1986 "Boredom in Interpersonal Encounters: Antecedents and Social Implications" *J of Personality and Soc Psych*, 5, pp968–75.

16 Why Relationships Matter Broadhead, W E, Kaplan, B H, James, S A et al 1983 "The Epidemiologic Evidence for a Relationship between Social Support and Health" *American J of Epidemiology*, 117, pp521–37; Cohen, S and Smye, L (eds) 1985 *Social Support and Health* Academic Press, New York; Lynch, J J 1977 *The Broken Heart: The Medical Consequences of Loneliness* Basic Books, New York; Verbrugge, L M 1979 "Marital Status and Health" *J of Marriage and the Family*, 41, pp267–85; Wright, P H 1983 "The Development and Selected Applications of a Conceptual and Measurement Model of Friendship" in Fischer, J L (ed): *Family and Close Relationships* Texas Tech UP, Lubbock, TX.

17 Parents and Children Ainsworth, M D S 1982 "Attachment, Retrospect and Prospect" in Parkes, C M and Stevenson-Hinde, J (eds): *The Place of Attachment in Human Behavior* Tavistock, London; Brown, J A C 1964 *Freud and the Postfreudians* Penguin, Harmondsworth; Elder, G H 1962 "Structural Variations in the Child Rearing Relationship" *Sociometry*, 25, pp241–62; Elder, G H 1963 "Parental Power Legitimation and its Effects on the Adolescent" *Sociometry* 26, pp50–65; Gorell Barnes, G 1984 *Working with Families* Macmillan, London, especially "Understanding Families," "Divorce and the Single Parent Family," "Step Families and Foster Families" ; Hoffman, L W and Manis, J D 1982 "The Value of Children in the United States" in Nye, F I (ed), *Family Relationships* Sage, Beverly Hills, CA; Jung, C G (issued posthumously 1968) *Analytical Psychology* Vintage Books, New York; Kolata, G 1987 "What Babies Know, and Noises Parents Make," *Science*, 237, p726; Lamb, M E et al 1981 *The Role of the Father in Child Development* Wiley, New York; Lomas, P 1973 *True and False Experience* Allen Lane, London; Parke, R D *Fathering* Fontana, London; Stern, D 1977 *The First Relationship* Fontana, London; Winnicott, D W 1971 *Playing and Reality* Tavistock, London.

18 Brothers, Sisters and Only Children Falbo, T and Polit, D F 1986 "Quantitative Review of The Only Child Literature: Research Evidence and Theory Development" *Psychological Bulletin*, 100, pp176–89; Ross, H G and Milgram, J L 1982 "Important Variables in Adult Sibling Relationships: A Quantitative Study" in Lamb, M E and Sutton-Smith, B (eds): *Sibling Relationships* Lawrence Erlbaum, Hillsdale, NJ.

19 Family Pets Anthrozoos: *A Journal on the Interactions of People, Animals and Environment* University Press of New England, Hanover, NH; Fogle, B (ed) 1981 *Interrelations Between People and Pets* Charles Thomas, Springfield, IL; Fogle, B 1985 *Pets and Their People* Viking Penguin, New York.

20 Keeping in Touch with Kin Adams, B N 1968 *Kinship in an Urban Setting* Markham, Chicago; Firth, R, Hubert, J, and Forge, A 1969 *Families and Their Relatives* Routledge and Kegan Paul, London; Hill, R et al 1970 *Family Development in Three Generations* Schenkman, Cambridge, MA; Mount, F 1982 *The Subversive Family* Allen and Unwin, London; Shanas, E, Townsend, P et al 1968 *Old People in Three Industrial Societies* Atherton, New York; Wellman, B 1979 "The Community Question: The Intimate Networks of East Yorkers" *American J of Sociology*, 84, pp1201–31.

21 Friends and Acquaintances Altman, I and Taylor, D 1973 *Social Penetration: The Development of Interpersonal Relationships* Holt, Rinehart and Winston, New York; Bateson, G 1979 *Mind and Nature* Dutton, New York; Berscheid, E 1985 "Interpersonal Attraction" in Lindzey, G and Aronson, E (eds): *Handbook of Social Psychology, Vol 2* Random House, New York; Cooper, C L 1981 *Executive Families Under Stress* Prentice-Hall, Englewood Cliffs, NJ; Cooper, C L 1980 *The Stress Check* Prentice-Hall, Englewood Cliffs, NJ; Dosser, D A, Balswick, J and Halverson, C F 1986 "Male Inexpressiveness: A Review" *J of Soc and Personal Rels*, 3, pp241–58; Hatfield, E and Sprecher, S 1986 *Mirror, Mirror . . . The Importance of Looks in Everyday Life* University of New York Press, Albany, NY; Knapp, M L 1984 *Interpersonal Communication and Human Relationships* Allyn and Bacon, Boston; Robertson, I T and Cooper, C L 1983 *Human Behavior in Organisations* Macdonald and Evans, London; Rosecrance, J 1986 "Racetrack Buddy Relations: Compartmentalized and Satisfying" *J of Soc and Personal Rels*, 3, pp441–56; Rosenbaum, M 1986 "The Repulsion Hypothesis: On The Nondevelopment of Relationships" *J of Personality and Soc Psych*, 51, pp1156–66.

22 Child and Adolescent Friendships Coleman, J C 1974 *Relationships in Adolescence* Routledge and Kegan Paul, London; Conger, J J 1973 *Adolescence and Youth* Harper and Row, New York; Csikszentmihalyi, M and Larson, R 1984 *Being Adolescent: Conflict and Growth in the Teenage Years* Basic Books, New York; Dickens W and Perlman, D 1981 "Friendship over the Life Cycle" in Duck, S W and Gilmour, R (eds): *Personal Relationships 2: Developing Personal Relationships* Academic Press, London; Douvan, E and Adelson, J 1966 *The Adolescent Experience* Wiley, New York; Elkind, D 1984 *All Grown Up and No Place to Go: Teenagers in Crisis* Addison-Wesley, Reading, MA; Furman, W 1984 "Enhancing Children's Peer Relations and Friendship" in Duck, S W (ed): *Personal Relationships 5: Repairing Personal Relationships* Academic Press, London; Kon, I S 1981 "Adolescent Friendship: Some Unanswered Questions for Future Research" in Duck, S and Gilmour, R (eds): *Personal Relationships 2*.

23 Coping with Shyness Jones, W H, Cheek, J M and Briggs, S R (eds) 1985 *Shyness: Perspectives on Research and Treatment* Plenum Press, New York; Stevenson-Hinde, J 1987 "Shyness in Young Children" *MRC News*, 36 (September issue) Medical Research Council, London; Zimbardo, P G 1977 *Shyness: What is it, what to do about it* Addison-Wesley, Reading, MA.

24 Overcoming Loneliness Peplau, L A and Perlman, D (eds) 1982 *Loneliness: A Sourcebook of Current Theory, Research and Therapy* Wiley, New York.

25 Finding a partner Athanasiou, R and Sarkin, R 1974 "Premarital Sexual Behavior and Postmarital Adjustment" *Archives of Sexual Behavior*, 3, pp207–25; Baxter, L A and Wilmot, W W 1984 "'Secret Tests': Social Strategies for Acquiring Information about the State of the Relationship" *Human Communication Research*, 11, pp171–2; Dillard, J P 1987 "Close Relationships at Work" *J of Soc and Personal Rels* pp179–94; Huston, T L, Surra, C A, Fitzgerald, N, and Kate, R M 1981 "From Courtship to Marriage: Mate Selection as an Interpersonal Process" in Duck, S W and Gilmour, R (eds): *Personal Relationships 2: Developing Personal Relationships* Academic Press, London; Lloyd, S A and Kate, R M 1985 "The Development Course of Conflict in Dissolution of Premarital Relationships" *J of Soc and Personal Rels*, 2, pp179–94; Newcomb, M D 1986 "Cohabitation, Marriage and Divorce among Adolescents and Young Adults" *J of Soc and Personal Rels*, 3, pp473–94; Quinn, R E 1977 "The Formation, Impact and Management of Romantic Relationships in Organizations" *Administrative Science Quarterly*, 22, pp30–45; Surra, C A, Arizzi, P, and Asmussen, L A 1988 "The Association between Reasons for Commitment and Development and Outcome of Marital Relationships" *J of Soc and Personal Rels*, 5, pp60–80; Yelsma, P 1986 "Marriage and Divorce in India" Paper presented to the Speech Communication Association, Chicago, November 1986.

26 Thinking about Love Berscheid, E and Walster, E 1974 "A Little Bit About Love" In Huston T (ed): *Foundations of Interpersonal Attraction* Academic Press, New York Berscheid, E and Walster, E 1978 2nd edn *Interpersonal Attraction* Addison-Wesley, Reading, MA; Hatfield, E and Walster, G 1985 *A New Look at Love* U P of America, Lanham, MD; Hendrick, C and Hendrick, S 1983 *Liking, Loving and Relating* Brooks/Cole, Monterey, CA; Lee, J A 1977 "A Typology of Styles of Loving" *Personality and Soc Psych Bulletin*, 3, pp173–82; Rubin, Z 1973 *Liking and Loving: An Invitation to Social Psychology* Holt, Rinehart and Winston, New York; Sternberg, R J 1987 "Liking versus Loving" *Psychological Bulletin*, 102, pp331–45; Sternberg, R J 1986 "A Triangular Theory of Love" *Psychological Review*, 93, pp119–35.

27 Patterns of Jealousy Buunk, B 1984 "Jealousy As Related to Attributions for the Partner's Behavior" *Soc Psych Quarterly*, 47, pp107–12; Buunk, A and Bringle, R 1986 "Jealousy in Love Relationships" in Duck S W and Perlman, D (eds): *Personal Relationships 2 Heterosexual Relations, Marriages, and Divorce* Sage, Beverly Hills, CA; Clanton, G and Smith L G 1977 *Jealousy* Prentice-Hall, Englewood Cliffs, NJ; Ellis, C and Weinstein, E 1986 "Jealousy and the Social Psychology of Emotional Experience" *J of Soc and Personal Rels*, 3, pp337–57; Hansen, G 1982 "Reactions to Hypothetical Jealousy Producing Events" *Family Relations*, 31, pp513–18; Pines, A and Aronson, E 1983 "Antecedents, Correlates and Consequences of Sexual Jealousy" *J of Personality*, 51, pp108–36; Salovey, P and Rodin, J 1986 "The Differentiation of Social-Comparison and Romantic Jealousy" *J of Personality and Soc Psych*, 50, pp1100–12; Shettel-Neuber, J, Bryson, J B et al, L E 1978 "Physical Attractiveness of the 'Other Person' and Jealousy" *Personality and Soc Psych Bulletin*, 4, pp612–15; White, G 1981 "Jealousy and Partner's Perceived Motives for Attraction to a Rival" *Soc Psych Quarterly* 44, pp24–30.

28 Enjoying a Sexual Relationship Blumstein, P and Schwartz, P 1983 *American Couples: Money, Work, Sex* Morrow, New York; Wilson, G and Nias, D 1976 *Love's Mysteries* Open Books, London.

29 The Married Couple Belsky, J, Spanier, G B and Ronine, M 1983 "Stability and Change in Marriage Across the Transition to Parenthood" *J of Marriage and the Family*, 45, pp567–77; Newcomb, M D 1981 "Heterosexual Cohabitation Relationships" in Duck, S W and Gilmour, R (eds): *Personal Relationships 1: Studying Personal Relationships* Academic Press, London; Newcomb, M D 1986 "Cohabitation, Marriage and Divorce among Adolescents and Young Adults" *J of Soc and Personal Rels*, 3, pp473–94; Waldron, H and Routh, D K 1981 "The Effect of the First Child on the Marital Relationship" *J of Marriage and the Family*, 43, pp785–98.

30 Breaking Up Baxter, L A 1984 "Trajectories of Relationship Disengagement" *J of Soc and Personal Rels*, 1, pp29–48; Byrne, D and Murnen, S 1987 "Maintaining Loving Relationships" in Sternberg, R J and Barnes, M L (eds): *The Anatomy of Love* Yale University Press, New Haven; Hill, C T, Rubin, Z and Peplau, L A 1976 "Breakups before Marriage" *J of Soc Issues*, 32, pp147–68.

31 Reclaiming Relationships Forward, S and Torres, J 1986 *Men Who Hate Women and the Women Who Love Them* Bantam Books, New York; Hatfield, E and Sprecher, S 1986 *Mirror, Mirror . . . The Importance of Looks in Everyday Life* University of New York Press, Albany, NY; Jacobson, N S and Margolin, L 1979 *Marital Therapy: Strategies based on Social Learning and Behavior Exchange Principles* Brunner-Mazel, New York; Miller, J B 1976 *Toward a New Psychology of Women* Beacon Press, Boston; Montgomery, B 1988 "Quality Communication in Personal Relationships" in Duck, S (ed): *Handbook of Personal Relationships*, pp342–59 Wiley, London; Traupmann, J, Hatfield, E and Wexler, P 1983 "Equity and Sexual Satisfaction in Dating Couples," *British J of Soc Psych*, 22, pp33–40 Reprinted in Olson, D H (ed) 1984: *Inventory of Marriage and Family Literature, Vol 10* Sage, Beverly Hills, CA; Traupmann, J, Peterson, R, Utne, M and Hatfield, E 1981 "Measuring Equity in Intimate Relations" *Applied Psychological Measurement*, 5, pp467–80 Reprinted in Olson, D H (ed) 1983 *Inventory of Marriage and Family Literature, Vol 9* Sage, Beverly Hills, CA; Watzlawick, P Beavin, J and Jackson, D 1967 *Pragmatics of Human Communication* Norton, New York; Wilmot, W 1987 *Dyadic Communication* Random House, New York; Wolman, B B and Stricker, G 1983 *Handbook of Family and Marital Therapy* Plenum, New York.

ACKNOWLEDGMENTS

PICTURE AGENCIES/SOURCES

AP The Associated Press Ltd, London.
APA Ace Photo Agency, London.
BBC HPL BBC Hulton Picture Library, London.
BC Bruce Coleman Ltd, Uxbridge, Middx.
BPCC/AA BPCC/Aldus Archive.
C Colorific Photo Library Ltd, London, New York.
DAA Daniel Angeli Agency.
F Format Photographers, London.
FSP Frank Spooner Pictures, London.
H The Hutchison Library, London.
HS Homer Sykes, London.
I Impact Photos, London.
MG Magnum Photos Ltd, London, Paris.
N Network Photographers, London.
R Rex Features Ltd, London.
RHPL Robert Harding Picture Library Ltd, London.
RG Roberto Granata, Rome.
SGA Susan Griggs Agency, London.
SI Syndication International.
SRG Sally and Richard Greenhill, London.
TCL The Telegraph Colour Library, London.
V Viewfinder Colour Photo Library.
VI Vision International, London.
WC Woodfin Camp, New York.
Z Zefa, London.

PICTURE LIST

Page number in **bold** type. Photographer's intitials in parentheses.

Frontmatter

2–3 Title Page (AW) SGA. **6** R. **7** (CF) H. **8** (AW) SGA. **9** (LP) C. **10** (HM) SGA. **11** (LP) C. **12** Z. **14** Little girls (ST) Andromeda. Young lovers (CP). **15** Two sisters (NDMcK) H. Old friends in pub (MA) N.

Part title How People Interact **16** Family priest (AC) I.

1 Adapting to the Occasion

18 Reception (PP) FSP. **19** Tea on lawn (NR) R. **20** Swimming baths, Japan (FH) TCL. Chess, bath house, Hungary (AR) C. **21** Japanese wedding (PJG) MG. **22** Professional couple (AE) Z. Graduation, Columbia University (GZ) C. **23** Midshipmen at football match (JH) C. Police at clown convention (JN) I. **24** Strikers, San Francisco (MN) MG. Thanksgiving dinner (JP) C. **25** Wall St, NY (KL) C. **26** Wine bar (AW) SGA. **27** Fight on rugby pitch (HS) HS. New York subway (BD) MG. **28** Interview (JP) C.

2 Marking Territory

30 Treehouse (SRG) SRG. **31** Cottages, Ireland (MH) V. Chelsea, London (AW) SGA. Rooftops, Bulgaria (DB) C. **32** Writer at home (GG). **33** Open-plan office (CH) Z. Woman behind files (JM) C. **34** Women arm-wrestling, Finland (L) C.

35 Men in office (JH) C. Woman and employer (JH) C. **36** Montreal Airport, security (JMe/Picture Group) C. **37** Study room (IJ) APA. Argument over water rights, Yunnan, China (SRG) SRG.

3 Keeping a Distance

38 Business people (SS) SGA. Bench R. **39** Ice-cream parlor, Prague (LT) H. Labor Day on beach (JV) SGA. **40** Doctor and patient (JOB) F. Open-air café (FS) MG. **41** Tokyo Stock Exchange (SF) MG. **43** Women, Rome (RK) MG. Men at business lunch (MM) F. Crowd, Amsterdam (AW) SGA. **44** Man and woman, London Underground (JOB) F. Subway, Tokyo (BB) MG. Three men, London Underground (MM) F. **45** Liverpool football supporters (HS) HS. Pop concert Z.

4 Using Body Language

46 Handstand (BT) R/SIPA. Couple in discussion (SEP) H. **47** Lawyers (JH) C. Alain Delon at Lido FSP/Gamma. **48** Jack Lang and Jean Poperen (AD) FSP/Gamma. Women, France (CSP) MG. **49** Desmond Tutu (GM) MG. **50** (1) Couple in street (PB) R. (2) George Bush (DH) FSP/Gamma. (3) Italian women in street (GB) SGA. (4) Men in French café (RB) MG. (5) Men in dinner jackets, Britain (JS) N. (6) Edward Kennedy (SL) FSP/Gamma. **52** Couple (AW) SGA. **53** Woman in telephone booth (JOB) F. Pregnant woman on telephone (GN) R. Man in telephone booth (JOB) F. **54** Tennis FSP/Gamma. Skiers at lunch, France (AH) SGA. **55** Hindus in Banga river (RR) MG. Child on tricycle, Las Vegas (HG) MG.

5 Noticing Posture

56 Postures of agreement and disagreement Andromeda. **57** Audience boredom (SRG) SRG. Postures of interest and boredom Andromeda. **58** Lunch in open-air café (EY) RHPL. Three men (SRG) SRG. **59** Chinese couple H.

6 Assessing Appearances

60 Two women on beach (RL) SGA. Three women, St Tropez R/Kosmos. **61** Indonesian girl FSP. Woman tanning face (RLa) SGA. **62** Man with taxi (IR) Z. **63** Regatta, England 1987 (MF) F. Crowd, Tokyo (BB) MG. Sisters of Perpetual Indulgence, San Francisco (MN) MG. Kamuzu Academy (CC) I. **64** Barristers (SRG) SRG. **65** Schumi curlers (PBr) R. Girl straightening hair (BL) N. **66** Yanomani woman, face-painting (HT) RHPL. **67** Newsstand operator, Los Angeles (MN) MG. Tattoo (PW) N.

7 Reacting to Scent

68 Monroe look-alike (FR) FSP/Gamma. **69** Couple (LP) C. **70** Breath test, USA (LP) C. Testing deodorant, USA (LP) C. **71** Sampling perfume, Grasse, France RHPL.

8 Making Eye Contact

72 Eyes and moods, top detail from Clive James portrait (Sn), 2nd Andromeda, 3rd Andromeda, bottom detail from Rik Mayall portrait (Sn). Chimpanzee BC. **73** Mother and baby (SRG) SRG. Nastassja Kinski with husband and newborn daughter RG. Face, by kind permission of copyright holder. **74** Farrah Fawcett-Majors (YK) R. Margaret Thatcher (PA) I. **75** Liv Ullman and John Gielgud (RGa). Cher (RGa). Carlo Ponti and Sophia Loren (RGa). Marlon Brando (JPD) DAA. **76** Lord Olivier in role of Lear (Sn). Soldier and

252

KEY TO PHOTOGRAPHERS

AC Anita Corbin. **AD** Alain Denize. **AE** A Edgeworth. **AF** Albert Fenn. **AH** Anthony Howarth. **AHe** Andreas Heumann. **AN** Albane Navizet. **AR** Alon Reininger. **AS** Anthea Sieveking. **ASe** Art Seitz. **ASt** Audrey Stirling. **AW** Adam Woolfitt. **BB** Bruno Barbey. **BD** Bruce Davidson. **BG** Bernard Gérard. **BL** Barry Lewis. **BP** Brenda Prince. **BR** Bernard Régent. **BT** Barth/Thevenin. **BW** Bill Weems. **CB** Catherine Blackie. **CC** Christopher Cormack. **CCa** C Capton. **CF** Carlos Freire. **CH** C Hammell. **CP** Caroline Penn. **CSP** Chris Steele-Perkins. **DB** David Burnett. **DD** Donald Dietz. **DH** Dirk Halstead. **DHu** Don Hunstein. **DM** D Maiani. **DMe** Dilip Mehta. **DR** Dick Rowan. **EC** Eric Crichton. **EF** Enrico Ferorelli. **EY** Earl Young. **FA** Francis Apesteguy. **FH** F Hughier. **FR** F Reglain. **FS** F Scianna. **GB** Gert von Bassewitz. **GG** Guglielmo Galvin. **GK** G de Keerles. **GKa** G Kalt. **GM** Gideon Mendel. **GN** G Neri. **GP** G Palmer. **GPe** G Peress. **GR** G Rettinghaus. **GW** George Wright. **GZ** George Zimbel. **HG** Harry Gruyaert. **HH** Henri Huet. **HM** Horst Munzig. **HS** Homer Sykes. **HT** Hanbury/Tenison. **HWa** Howard Walker. **IJ** Ingrid Johnson. **IL** Ian Lloyd. **IR** I Robertson. **IY** Ian Yeomans. **JB** John Bulmer. **JC** Joe Clarke. **JD** Julio Donoso. **JH** Jim Howard. **JM** John Moss. **JMa** Jenny Matthews. **JMc** Joe McNally. **JMe** Jim Merrithew. **JN** Jeremy Nicholl. **JNa** James Nachtwey. **JNi** Julian

Nieman. **JOB** Joanne O'Brien. **JP** Jim Pickerell. **JPa** John Panton. **JPD** Jean-Paul Dousset. **JPf** J Pfaff. **JS** John Sturrock. **JV** Joseph F Viesti. **JVP** J V Puttkamer. **KA** Katalin Arkell. **KB** K Benser. **KL** Katherine Lambert. **L** Lehtikuva . **LLR** L L T Rhodes. **LP** Louie Psihoyos. **LR** Lincoln Russell. **LS** Laurie Sparham. **LT** Liba Taylor. **MA** Mike Abrahams. **MB** Martha Bates. **MBA** Micha Bar Am. **MBu** Mike Busselle. **MC** Mark Cator. **MF** Melanie Friend. **MGr** Marianne Grøndahl. **MH** Martin Haswell. **MM** Maggie Murray. **MMI** Michael MacIntyre. **MN** Michael Nichols. **MP** M Pitner. **NDMcK** Nancy Durrell McKenna. **NR** Nick Rogers. **PA** Philippe Achache. **PB** Paul Brown. **PBr** Peter Brooker. **PJG** Philip Jones Griffiths. **PP** Pierre Perrin. **PT** Pennie Tweedie. **PW** Patrick Ward. **R** Rothstein. **RB** Rene Burri. **RBl** Ron Blakeley. **RGa** Ron Galella. **RJ** Rob Judges. **RK** Richard Kalvar. **RKn** Robert Knight. **RL** Robin Laurance. **RLa** Richard Laird. **RM** Robert McFarlane. **RN** Richard Nicholas. **RR** Raghu Rai. **RS** Rick Smolan. **S** Suriani. **SEP** Sarah Errington Porlock. **SF** Stuart Franklin. **SL** Steve Liss. **SLo** Sandra Lousada. **SM** Steve Mayes. **SMe** Susan Meiselas. **Sn** Snowdon. **SRG** Sally & Richard Greenhill. **SS** Sepp Seitz. **ST** Susan Turvey. **SV** Sal Veder. **TG** Tom Grill. **VW** Val Wilmer. **WB** Wil Blanche. **WS** W Schmidt. **YK** Yoram Kahana. **Zi** Zihnioglu.

girlfriend (HS) I. Baseball dispute (BW) WC
77 Eyes (EC). Iris Z.

9   Facial Expressions
78 Stare (RS) C. Ronald Reagan FSP/Gamma.
Football fans, England (HS) HS. **79** Italian street
vendor (JC) RHPL. Mother soothing baby (DR)
SGA. **80** Six basic emotions, Andromeda. **81**
Duchess of York at Wimbledon R. **82** Woman
smiling (RJ) Andromeda Girl simulating ferocity
(IY) SGA. Princess Diana (GK) FSP/Gamma.
83 President Kim, South Korea (JNa) MG.
84 Nancy Reagan and security men FSP/Gamma.
Old man, Los Angeles (BL) N. **85** W H Auden BBC
HPL. **86** Women with sunglasses, Dallas (BL) N.
87 Shakira Caine FSP/Gamma. Alberto Moravia's
wedding to Carmen Llera (DM) R/SIPA.

10   The Language of Touch
88 Nuns and parents (HS) HS. Through fence
R/SIPA. **90** Congratulatory handshake (Zi) F/SIPA.
Men touching (HS) HS. **91** Women touching (SRG)
SRG. **92** Feeding twins (NDMcK) H. Mother and
baby in shower (LR) C. Boy crying (KA) N. Girl
with toy rabbit (HS) I. **94** Couples: top left (DHu) C, bottom left
(MN) MG, top right (SRG), bottom right (AW) SGA.
95 Touching feet (RKn) C. **96** Girl (SRG) SRG.
97 Covent Garden, England (HS) I.

11   Greeting and Parting
98 Vietnam POW's return (SV) AP. **99** Falklands
War Departure (BL) N. **100** Mitterand and Queen
Beatrix R/SIPA. Richard Nixon with Belgian crowd
AP. Café meeting (BB) MG. **102** Air kiss (HS) HS.
Baby kissing mother (EF) C.

12   Making Conversation
104 Teenagers on beach (AW) SGA. Tennis
players (JP) C. **105** Open-air café (JH) C.
106 Doctor and patient (JMa) F. **107** Meeting (JH)
C. **108** Witness (JH) C. **109** Meeting (JH) C.
110 Stockholders' meeting (AF) C.

13   Raising a Smile
112 Royal Family laughing (HWa) SI. **113** Nurses
joke (BL) N. **114** Cowboy (SRG) SRG. Child with
monkey (NDMcK) H. **115** Girl guides (JD) C. Nuns
(BL) N.

14   Detecting Insincerity
117 Hands and feet (DD) C. Man and woman (BR)
H. Three women (MP) Z. **118** Policeman in Dallas
(BL) N. Japanese girls (SF) MG. **119** Richard Nixon
(DH) C. Doctor and family (LS) N.

15   Polishing Social Skills
121 Tourist asking for information (SRG) SRG.
122 Mother, baby and kitten (SRG) SRG. **123** Girl
admiring biceps (LLR) TCL. Dressing up R.
124 Couple in pub (MA) N. Couple in street (SRG)
SRG. Trio at table (SRG) SRG. **126/7** Sale at
Harrods, London (KA) N. **127** Meeting (JH) C.

Part title How Relationships Work **128** Crowd,
Amsterdam (AW) SGA

16   Why Relationships Matter
130 Cheese stall in Bordeaux (AW) SGA. **131** Man
with parrot (BG) H. Crowd in Amsterdam (AW)
SGA. **132** Baking (CB) R. Priest with parishioners
H/Camerapix. Two women, N Ireland (GPe) MG.

134 Mother and child on beach (DB) C. **135** At
home (SRG) SRG. **136** After car bombing, West
Beirut R/SIPA. **137** Old woman with cat, Italy Z.

17   Parents and Children
138 Birth (SRG) SRG. Baby at breast (SRG) SRG.
139 Mother kissing baby (SLo) SGA. **140** Mother
with baby (SLo) SGA. Father and son (NDMcK) H.
141 Clutching mother's skirt (SLo) SGA. Climbing
stairs (SLo) SGA. **142** Reaching for dessert (SLo)
SGA. Mother with shopping (AS) VI. Mother with
children at table (AS) VI. **143** Israeli couple and
baby H. **144** Family outing (TG) SGA. **145** Mother
comforting daughter (SLo) SGA. Father feeding
baby (GR) Z. **146** Mother working (SRG) SRG.
Male au pair (NDMcK) H. **147** Family at home
(JNi) SGA. McEnroe Jnr and Snr (ASe) FSP/
Gamma. Father teaching cricket (LT) H.
148 Father and daughter (SRG) SRG. **149** Teenage
girls (AW) SGA.

18   Brothers, Sisters and Only Children
150 Boy bathing baby (KA) N. Children pitching
tent (AS) VI. **151** Children with computer (SRG)
SRG. **152** Family with twins (SLo) SGA. **153** Twins
(MB) C.

19   Family Pets
154 Woman with cat (AHe) SGA. **155** Man with
Irish Setter (DR) SGA. **156** Man with orangutan
(WS) Z. Woman with turtle (JV) SGA. **157** Woman
feeding pigeons (JNi) SGA.

20   Keeping in Touch with Kin
158 Wedding, Dorset, England (JPa) APA.
160 Three generations (SRG) SRG. Christening of
Louis of Luxemburg R/SIPA. Jean-Paul Belmondo
and family (FA) FSP/Gamma. **162** Grandmother
and baby (NDMcK) H. **163** Grandmother and
granddaughter (SRG) SRG. Grandfather and
granddaughter (LT) H.

21   Friends and Acquaintances
164 Women (SRG) SRG. Snowball fight (SRG)
SRG. **165** Neighbors (MA) N. **166** Meeting (SRG)
SRG. **167** Venice Regatta (MC) I. Students, USA
(DB) C. Woman comforting friend (SRG) SRG.
168 Men at races, Ascot, England (HS) HS. Women
in gymnasium (JOB) F. **169** Sharing joke (BL) N.
Girls in cafeteria, Germany (AW) SGA.
170 Women chatting (SRG) SRG. Three men
(GW) C. **171** Girls in fountain, England R. French
girls on country walk (BR) H. **172** Wounded
Vietnam medic and wounded man (HH) AP. Girl
fighters (CP) C. **173** Three women at table (NDMcK)
H. Chess players Z. Harvard girl rugby players
(MBA) MG. Arab officers holding hands H.
174 Police officers (SRG) SRG. Executive meeting
(VW) F. **175** Factory workers (BP) F.

22   Child and Adolescent Friendships
176 Babies (GP) Z. **177** Boys in tree (JB) SGA.
Boys comparing penknives RHPL. **178** Girls playing (SRG) SRG. **179** Girls in kindergarten (AS) VI.
180 Girls hugging, England (SRG) SRG. Teenagers,
Tokyo (BB) MG. **181** Teenagers at party, England
(SF) MG. Students in café, Austria (AW) SGA.

23   Coping with Shyness
182 Shy schoolgirls (SRG) SRG. **183** Women
hiding faces, Morocco (HG) MG. **184** Out-patients,

Spain (CP). **185** Coy girl (SRG) SRG. Children in
park (ASt) TCL. **186** College ball (HS) HS.
187 Schoolgirl (CCa) Z.

24   Overcoming Loneliness
188 Girl in bed (SRG) SRG. Lt Col Tevar Saco's
widow R. **189** Man in woods (WB) R. **190** Woman
in car (JH) C. **191** Homeless men on bench (MA)
N. **192** Boy in café (SRG) SRG. Mother and child on
bus (SRG) SRG. **193** Capsule hotel, Tokyo (MMI)
H. **194** Debutantes' ball (LS) N Iona Abbey Z.

25   Finding a Partner
196 Couple at swimming pool (RBl) C.
197 Couple walking (GW). **198** Couple at café,
Paris (BL) N. Couple at nightclub (RBl) C.
199 Couple (HS) HS. **201** Pop music fans R.
Couple in Beirut (PT) C. **202** Couple in snow
(SRG) SRG. Couple on lawn SGA/Comstock.
Embracing (SRG) SRG. **204** Philippine bride (SMe)
MG. Bridal store, Los Angeles (MN) MG.

26   Thinking about Love
207 Couple drinking wine (KBa) Z. Couple
embracing Z. **208** Couple (RN) Z.

27   Patterns of Jealousy
210 Fight (AH) SGA. **211** Couple R. **212** Refugee
family, Eritrea (CP). **213** Couple arguing (HS) HS.

28   Enjoying a Sexual Relationship
214 Couple in bed (MBu) BPCC/AA. **215** Couple
embracing R. Couple with infant (AS) VI.
216 Couple talking R/Photoreport. **217** Woman in
shower (SLo) SGA.

29   The Married Couple
218 Couple kissing (DMe) C. **219** Paul Newman
and Joanne Woodward (S) FSP. **220** Sikh wedding
H. Wedding in Moscow (PJ). **221** Jewish
wedding (EF)/Dot C. Wedding in Nevada (CP).
222 Family by lake (JPf) Z. **224** Couple and
daughter (TG) SGA. **225** Couple on yacht kissing
(AW) SGA. **226** Frank Bough and wife (GG).
227 Couple, N Honshu, Japan (CL) H. Elderly
couple walking (GKa) Z. **228** Moroccan wedding
(BB) MG. **229** Man and two wives, Zaire H.

30   Breaking Up
230 Elderly women arguing (SM). Couple arguing
(MBu) BPCC/AA. **231** Man shouting at pregnant
woman R. **232** Woman and child (MGr) FSP.
233 Couple at open-air café (BL) N. **234** Couple R.

31   Reclaiming Relationships
236 Retired couple walking (JMc) C. Couple at
home (SLo) SGA. **237** Mother and daughter
chatting SGA/Photofile. **238** Couple at restaurant
(BL) N. Woman at keep-fit class (SRG) SRG. Father
and children in sea RHPL. **239** Couple hand-in-
hand (HS) I. **240** Paul Newman in kitchen (R)
FSP/Gamma. Roger Moore and wife (AN)
FSP/Gamma. **241** Loving couple (RM) SGA.
242 Couple in garden (WB) R. Couple at home
(JNi) SGA. **244** Amazonian couple (JVP) H. Couple
at poolside (SRG) SRG. **245** Couple on beach
(RBl) C.

Backmatter Andromeda.

INDEX